Allegory, Myth, and Symbol

HARVARD ENGLISH STUDIES 9

Allegory, Myth, and Symbol

Edited by
Morton W. Bloomfield

Harvard University Press
Cambridge, Massachusetts
London, England
1981

Library of Congress Cataloging in Publication Data

Main entry under title:

Allegory, myth, and symbol.

   (Harvard English studies;   9)
   1. Allegory—Addresses, essays, lectures. 2. Myth
in literature—Addresses, essays, lectures. 3. Symbolism in literature—Addresses, essays, lectures.
4. English literature—History and criticism—Addresses,
essays, lectures. I. Bloomfield, Morton Wilfred,
1913–   . II. Series.
PN56.A5A4   809′.915   81-6655
ISBN 0-674-01640-8   AACR2
ISBN 0-674-01641-6 (pbk.)

Preface

After a lapse of three years *Harvard English Studies* is bringing out a new volume devoted to allegory, myth, and symbol. The next volume is scheduled for the fall of 1982 and will be devoted to Ralph Waldo Emerson. It is conceived as a commemoration of the hundredth anniversary of his death.

The subject this volume is concerned with is large and at the same time central to much present-day literary concern. After a long period of neglect and disdain, allegory and myth in the broadest sense of those words have again come into their own. These two subjects are now seen as central to the understanding of the literary art. Although the Romantic attack on allegory was originally basically an attack on what may be called personification allegory, in fact the late eighteenth, nineteenth, and early twentieth centuries made few distinctions in allegory and condemned any method of composition to which that term could be applied. We now realize how germane the notion of allegory is to the problem of interpretation, which is the primary activity in approaching the literary work on almost every level.

Myth has been expanded in our times to include the recurrent patterns of action and meaning in literature. It no longer refers only to Greek and Latin beliefs about the heroes and gods; thanks to writers like Hyman and Frye it now comprises the basic narrative patterns of much literature, both great and mediocre.

Symbol has not undergone the fate of allegory, but it has been a cliché of literary criticism for a long time. It was considered by Romantic thinkers as the answer to their objections to allegory, providing at the same time something sufficiently like the latter to handle its metaphoric role. Symbolism to Coleridge was the only legitimate allegorical mode and rested upon the primary as opposed to the secondary imagination.

(There is evidence that Coleridge grew doubtful of these distinctions later in life.) Imagination had given poets and philosophers many difficulties long before Coleridge. Coleridge enthroned it, following his German influences, to a position of preeminence in the psyche.

Allegory, myth, and *symbol* are terms used to describe the polysemous meaning of the literature emphasizing either the type of meaning or the meaning itself. They all have various meanings, although allegory is the most complex and elusive, a condition I think accounting for the fact that most of the articles in this volume concentrate upon that subject. The literary text usually has a literal meaning. To get at its underlying meaning or significance we interpret it allegorically, mythically, and symbolically, often employing more than one of these modes depending on the nature of the text. Myth and symbol themselves can even, if we define allegory broadly enough, be seen as aspects of allegory.

In recent years we have become aware that an endless multiplicity of interpretations is often possible, and even allowing a certain priority to the historical circumstances of the work of art's creation we still are faced with a variety of possible meanings for literary works. In fact this very multiplicity is what gives a great literary work its power to appeal over the centuries. This variety has recently given rise to an attempt to "deconstruct" the literary text. Deconstruction in practice certainly, however, does not solve the problem of polysemy but seems to add to it.

Deconstruction as a method is a kind of answer to the Oxford school of philosophy in its narrower sense, which attempts to analyze the language used in propositions to arrive at the truth. Its ideal is exact meaning. The deconstructionists, however, aim at as many meanings as possible. New Criticism admired a multiplicity of meanings provided they cohered organically. Deconstruction questions, on the other hand, any specific meaning at all in the text and emphasizes the creative, often unconscious, powers of the creator and his rhetorical stance.

This volume is largely composed of articles on particular texts or authors although it also contains essays on theory, literary comparisons, intellectual and cultural history, and some essays which combine several of these approaches. The subjects are not confined to English literature and history, but most do deal with that general topic.

It would be extremely naive to expect that this volume will put to rest the disputes over the meaning and role of allegory, but I do hope that, besides making their contributions to the understanding of particular literary works and authors, these essays will make a worthy contribution to understanding the major role allegory plays in literature and indeed in life.

M.W.B.

Contents

MURRAY KRIEGER

"A Waking Dream":
The Symbolic Alternative to Allegory

The war between the poets and the philosophers, out of which Western literary theory began, is with us still. Though it has taken many forms it is there now, stimulating yet new varieties of dispute. As a war it continues to partake of the oppositional force of the Platonic dialectic, forcing us to choose which of the two ways we will accept as a path to knowledge, or which of the two we shall reject for having no valid claim to lead us there.

In recent times we have become increasingly aware of that other enemy of the poet since antiquity—the historian. Plato himself saw the poet as substituting his illusions for empirical reality as well as for philosophic truth; indeed, if the phenomenal world of experience was an inadequate imitation of universal truth, still its small particularities required, as a first step toward truth, a fidelity which the distortions of the artist invariably thwarted. Thus, at the level of worldly experience, the poet had to overcome the empirical reality of the historian even before he came up against the rational purity of the philosopher. We know that Plato had good reason to distrust the influence of the poet, whose readers would allow his authority to spill over into history and philosophy. What role could there

1

be for those devoted to describing the experiential world around us or speculating reasonably about the ontological world beyond, if the mythologies of Homer were to serve also as both source of fact and guide to metaphysics and morality? For Aristotle, who had a greater commitment to worldly phenomena, the crucial line of distinction was that drawn between history and poetry, between the world of what is and the world of what (aesthetically) may be in accordance with the laws of probability and necessity.

In these distinctions and antagonisms we find the intense effort, arising out of a growing awareness of science and philosophy, of fact and metaphysic, to come to terms with and to limit the untamed realm of myth. The presumptuous attempt by the mythmaker to be our historian and philosopher can succeed only by precluding those rigorous disciplines which the de-mythifier among us must take to be history and philosophy. So demythification must proceed, in the name of discursive and rational progress, to reduce the leaps of the poetic imagination —no longer seen as a divinely sanctioned irrationality—to the rejected nostalgia of a romantic primitivism. Myth, like poetry (or *as* poetry), is to be accepted only as a projection of the human imagination—the shape which the imagination imposes on the flow of experience to make it conform to itself. From the perspective of its enemies, myth, in spite of its high-flying pretensions, is seen only as an untruth, a wishful projection out of accord with how things really are. One consequence of this attack on myth is the charge that its imposition of a human shape upon our experience is a deceptive spatialization of elements that are ineluctably temporal. It is charged that spatial form, as an anthropomorphic delusion, characterizes the way our minds work rather than the way the world does. Thus the denial of its authenticity shifts all interest away from the anthropological concern with how we envision our realities to the epistemological concern with what our existential destiny— controlled by the clock and beyond mythifying—really is.

As, through the history of Western thought, our philosophic interest becomes more riveted to our earthly existence, with methods that, accordingly, become more empirical, the emphasis falls more heavily upon the clash between myth and history (than upon that between myth and philosophy), at the expense of myth. At stake is the concept of time which will govern our sense of experience: will our imagination confront and yield to the stark disappearances of all the moments of our time, or will it transform them into the comforting metaphors of space which allow us to hold onto them? As man seeks—as seek he must—to dominate the history of sensory events, to what extent should he distrust the forms he invents to order the repetitions, the internal relations, which he finds (or creates) among them? If he comes to cherish those fictions which he cannot help but create to order his world, can he not set out, willfully and self-consciously, to create special free-standing fictions which are unfettered celebrations of the fiction-making power itself? He would thus be brought around to a new affirmation of myth, of poetry, of the spatializing power of humanly created forms: the romantic reassertion of his (momentary) power to overwhelm his temporal destiny.

I have put the matter in this melodramatic manner in order to set the scene for the emergence of the romantic doctrine of *symbol,* as it claimed ascendancy over *allegory,* and to do so in a way that set it *up* for the post-Structuralist critique, which would once more invert our comparative estimates of the two. And I continue my narrative still emphasizing the spatial and temporal languages, the examination of which will concern me later. The dream which myth had early inspired of subduing— by rereading—the recalcitrance of our historical experiences, of unifying time and the forms of the mind, was threatened with extinction first by rationalist and then by empiricist forces in the seventeenth and the eighteenth centuries. Psychological doctrines that related "sensations" to "ideas" and to one another reminded us of the inevitably sequential nature of human experience and the equally inevitable "belatedness" between our experiencing and our thinking. Language, seen as the words that represented our ideas, was similarly belated— which is to say secondary—in its relation to the mental recollections of sensory presence. As an idea was only the ghostly memory of a sensation—in effect the remnant of a sensation with the object removed—so the way was open for the notion of language as essentially empty, pointing to the past and representing an absence. Language, then, was in a tertiary position with respect to the immediacies of sensation.

Here was an exaggeration of the dualistic character of the signifier looking helplessly across the chasm of time at an unreachable signified. Any attempt at a poetic representation that would accord with this notion of language clearly had to stop at allegory, the modest device that permitted no pretension on the part of the signifier to exceed its self-abnegating function of pointing to an earlier and fuller reality outside itself. It is this cursed principle of anteriority that governs the chain that links events to one another, that links events to the language that seeks to represent them, and that links the elements of that language to one another. It is this principle that humanistic and romantic thinkers of the late eighteenth and the nineteenth centuries saw as beating the human mind into mere passivity, enslaving it into resignation to unelevated temporality. In reaction the new metaphysic, with its consequent psychology and poetic, insisted from the outset on the unifying power of mind, a form-making power that could break through the temporal separateness among entities, concepts, and words to convert the parade of absences into miracles of copresence. The spatializing magic of human metaphor was again granted privileged status, and myth and poetry were returned to their place of visionary eminence. Where the incapacity of normal language to reach beyond belatedness was recognized, poetry could be given special powers to leap across the breach between word and meaning, achieving an identity between them and thereby establishing a presence and a fullness in the word.

It is no wonder that allegory, as dualistic and thus subservient to the normal incapacities of language, was relegated to an inferior place as a less than poetic device, and that the symbol was newly defined as a monistic alternative that became identical with the poetry-making power. From Goethe's early groping toward a definition of the distinction between symbol and allegory to Coleridge's firmer formulation (by way of Schelling), and to the systematic exposition in the Idealism of Croce and the practical analyses of the New Critics, the dichotomy holds fast between the dualistic as the character of all our fallen language (including nonpoetry and allegory) and the monistic magic that poetry as symbol can accomplish.[1] The union in the symbol between subject and object, man and nature, of which Goethe spoke, is extended by Coleridge into the statement that becomes characteristic of claims made for the symbol: that it "always partakes of the reality which it renders intelligible; and while it enunciates the whole, abides itself as a living part in that unity, of which it is the representative."[2] It is, of course, the participatory power of the symbol, partaking fully rather than pointing emptily, that allows it to overcome otherness, thereby distinguishing it from allegory. And "an allegory is but a translation of abstract notions into a picture-language which is itself nothing but an abstraction from objects of the senses; the principal being more worthless even than its phantom proxy, both alike unsubstantial, and the former shapeless to boot" (p. 30).

In the many attempts to enunciate this distinction in a way that valorized the symbol (and poetry associated with it), we consistently find allegory allied to the unexceptional way language functions as a dualistic instrument, while that something special beyond the normal incapacities of language—a power to participate in and thus fuse with its meaning—is reserved for the symbol. Obviously, what is being sought in the symbol is an alternative to the fate of words to be empty, belated counters (Coleridge's phantom proxies) testifying to an absence, whose immediate presence would be beyond language, the instrument of mediation. If the language of these theoretical monists dissatisfies us, as we see it in Goethe or Schelling or Coleridge or Croce, we must acknowledge that there may be no discursive problem more difficult than the attempt to use our dualistic language to describe a monistic way of language-functioning—in other words, than the attempt to use a lan-

1. Thirty years ago, in my first published essay, I began my own career by treating the symbol-allegory distinction and affirming my affiliation with those arguing for the power of the symbol (among whom I then placed Croce and the New Critics). See "Creative Criticism: A Broader View of Symbolism," *Sewanee Review*, 58 (1950), 36–51.

2. *The Statesman's Manual, The Collected Works of Coleridge, Lay Sermons*, ed. R. J. White (London: Routledge and Kegan Paul, 1972), p. 30.

guage that accepts its differential nature to define a language
that functions in the breakthrough realm of identity. It is this
difficult attempt which habitually seems to lead theorists into
evasive mystifications[3] or led Coleridge, for example, to resort
to desperate terms like "esemplastic" or "coadunative" as he
sought to find a way of making discursively credible the subversive verbal process of fusing many into one.

The difficulty of finding a formula for the unmediated in the
language of mediation did not inhibit the continuing efforts of
these theorists and their followers. One way or another, since
the original attempt to achieve a special definition of symbol
within a symbol-allegory dichotomy, this need to describe a
manipulation of language that explodes its usual limits has extended this dichotomy to a number of others. The New Critics,
concerned with a poetics demanding figurative unity, translate
the opposition between symbol and allegory into a more ob-
servable opposition between functional metaphor and ornamental analogy. Further, members of this symbolist tradition,[4]
confronted by the challenge of Structuralism, recognize elements of their pet project on the opposite side of the Structuralist's principle of verbal difference (their own commitment to
identity) and on the opposite side of the Structuralist's interest
in metonymy (their own interest in metaphor). So when the
post-Structuralist attacks the assumptions of verbal presence
in Western logocentrism, the symbolists' theoretical need to
find an alternative to the absence that haunts the usual process
of signification leads them to embrace that very notion of presence.

As I have framed the problem here in its historical and problematic dimensions, underlying these several sets of opposi-

3. As in Goethe's finding "true symbolism . . . where the particular represents the more general, not as a dream or a shadow, but as a living momentary
revelation of the Inscrutable." This is from his Maxim no. 314. The translation
is René Wellek's.
4. In this essay I am using the word *symbolist* to designate the theoretical
tradition (or a member of it) that seeks a separate definition of *symbol* and proceeds to claim it to be the defining characteristic of poetry. I mean to use the
word here in this broad way, for purposes of shorthand, without intending to
relate the word or this group of theorists in any precise way to French symbolists or their doctrine.

tions are the alternatives of difference and identity. The dualistic conception of language, the language of rationalist or empiricist, of philosopher or historian, assumes its signifiers to be arbitrary in their relations to their signifieds, and hence utterly distinct from them and from all other signifiers with which they are joined in a system. In poetics the proponents of such a conception find allegory to be an acceptable device, one that does not violate this conception of language. On the other side, the symbolists, who seek in poetry the power of monistic breakthrough beyond the powers of differential discourse, try —however hedged in by their own discursive limits—to define a poetic symbol as a signifier that generates and fills itself with its own signified. The magic of poetry, for them, must begin only where prose leaves off, restoring man to the world around him (or rather making the world around him once again *his*) as if the effects of the Fall had been momentarily undone.

It is not surprising that theoretical movements of recent years have seen this symbolist aesthetic as being no more than an extravagant romantic mystification. With it the New Critics' theory of poetry as a unity of meaning within the functional metaphor has been similarly dismissed. For more than a century and a half, our most exciting theorists urged one or another variety of the claim that the poet could force his word to become privileged. Borrowed from our fallen language, that word was to be forced by the poet to become participatory, creating a union that filled gaps in the distances of time and otherness through the healing touch of human form. The plea for the poet to settle for nothing less required such a theorist to reject as unpoetic the practice of allegory in which, as in ornamental analogy, words settled for the arbitrary, differential role they normally had to accept. Through metaphoric union words (and meanings) were to be manipulated into overrunning their bounds of property and propriety, overlapping—if not appearing to turn into—one another.

It is not difficult to view the monistic conception of metaphor as a romantic reversion to the sacramental union put forth in Christian theology. In Renaissance typology and in the Renaissance habit of verbal play borrowed from it, we can find a model for the way in which metaphor was supposed to work

for the secular poet capable of creating symbols. The dissolution of distinctness into identity—in effect the destruction of
the logic of number—is the very basis of the divine-human
paradox of Christ and leads to the miraculous figure behind
such breakthroughs as the Trinity and the transubstantiation in
the Eucharist.[5] Further, through the typological *figura*, the
unredeemed sequence of chronological time can be redeemed
after all into the divine pattern, that eternal, spatial order
which exchanges history for eschatology. With every moment
existing doubly—both in the temporal order and in the timeless structure—history remains history even while it is rewritten as a divinely authored myth. Every act or person seems
random, arbitrary; yet each is a necessary signifier that partakes of the single Transcendental Signified. In borrowed form
this paradoxical relation between what is in time and what is
out of time is also turned into a model for poetic form. As in
the special sequence of events which transforms history into
teleology in metaphysics or transforms history into poetry in
the proper Aristotelian tragedy, as in the manipulation of
words into fully embodied metaphors by the symbol-making
poet, so the rules of earthly time, which put the separateness
of distance between isolated subjects, are suspended and
transgressed by the divine Author as by the human author in
imitation of Him. In this context we perhaps better understand
Coleridge's definition of the primary imagination as ''a repetition in the finite mind of the eternal act of creation in the infinite I AM.''[6]

Since the latter half of the nineteenth century we have been
increasingly concerned about the extent to which these formulations in the realm of poetics require a metaphysic or even a
theology to authenticate them. Whatever the sources of metaphor in the substantive miracles of theology, does the poetic
production of a verbal identity between distinct terms and concepts or does the poem's overcoming of the disappearing se-

5. See my *A Window to Criticism: Shakespeare's Sonnets and Modern Poetics* (Princeton: Princeton University Press, 1964), especially parts 2 and 3,
for a study of this Renaissance habit of modeling its poetic metaphors on elements borrowed from typology and Christian sacrament.
   6. *Biographia literaria*, chap. 13.

quence among verbal entities rest upon a substantive mystery that can be justified only by a literalizing faith? Or can verbal devices earn the aesthetic illusion of such identities and spatial forms—if only in the realm of appearance—in the secular precincts of a poetry without faith? The quarrel is essentially the one which was carried on against Matthew Arnold by his antagonistic follower T. S. Eliot. In "The Study of Poetry" Arnold defined the need for poetry to serve as a substitute for religion, producing a psychological satisfaction that was the more secure and effective because it no longer rested on the "supposed fact" which had failed religion and undermined its capacity any longer to function psychologically in the way that poetry, in its absence, now could. Here was the call for a poetic ungrounded in any metaphysic—indeed, one that depended on our keeping it free of untenable truth claims. If myth was to challenge the dull factuality of history with its own manmade transformations of time into human pattern, it was to remain true to its own domain of psychology and emotion and was not to pursue its challenge into the verifiable realm of "what is." One might say that the verbal power of metaphor depended upon its resistance to "existential projection," upon the shrewdness with which it avoided becoming "a literalist of the imagination."

Eliot, who was not afraid of being literally devout, rejected making poetry a substitute for religion but rather—in Christian fashion that recalled Renaissance typology with its literalizing of metaphor—saw the secular and sacred elements of metaphysics as one. His search in *Four Quartets* for "the still point of the turning world" was also a search through language for the still point of the moving words, which would transform them into the moving Word, projection of the Unmoved Mover. The passages about human experience and the passages about the poet's struggle with words become increasingly reflective of one another, so that the poem's theological quest and its poetic quest to subsume human temporality within the divine should become for the reader a single, simultaneous quest. The poem's meaning is its method is its medium. Yet, of course, if we come to the poem with the cool, skeptical eye of an Arnoldian modernist, we can find its apparent religious doctrine utterly subsumed within its verbal metaphors, so that the resolution of movement in a stillness which is still moving is but a brilliant aesthetic effect whose theological extensions seem momentarily persuasive only because of the power of its dramatic resolution in words. The aesthetic effect may be a breakthrough within the realm of myth and may thus affect our vision, but it need not break through as a literal alteration of our external world and our beliefs about what can or cannot transpire in it.

Eliot is perhaps our ultimate modernist poet, and his powers of dissolving time into his spatial forms, of pressing his language toward a filled presence, and of fusing his thematic problems with technical ones, are powers we look for in modernism generally. The work of these writers (think, among the poets, of Yeats and Stevens also, for example) seems continuous with the hopes for poetry of those who, distinguishing symbol from allegory, asked for the creation of symbols. Indeed, that work turned out to be the furthest realization of those hopes, shortly to be followed by poets writing to a different prescription. In addition they seem to have sponsored their own criticism as a fulfillment of those critical notions which we earlier traced back to those writing in the wake of Kant, and here the furthest realization was the New Criticism.

Early in the heyday of the New Criticism, Joseph Frank provided, with his doctrine of "spatial form," a major notion to characterize its practices, as well as the practice of the modernist literary works which helped inspire it and which provided an endless field on which it could sharpen its instruments. It is in Frank that the "still movement" of Eliot is pressed into a candid insistence on simultaneity, a formal play that "dissolves sequence" by undermining "the inherent consecutiveness of language."[7] In *The Waste Land* "word groups must be juxtaposed with one another and perceived simulta-

<hr>

7. *The Widening Gyre: Crisis and Mastery in Modern Literature* (Bloomington: Indiana University Press, 1963), pp. 15, 10. The essays on "Spatial Form in Modern Literature" originally appeared in 1945. Frank does not himself refer to *Four Quartets* but confines himself to Eliot's earlier works. For more recent discussions by Frank and others of the claims made in the original essays, see *Critical Inquiry,* 4 (1977).

neously" (p. 12). But Frank sees such formal devices as also altering our philosophic attitudes toward time and space, history and myth. It is as if, in modernist works, words can annihilate time thematically by destroying their own serial nature technically. The return of the supremacy of myth over history is the thematic consequence of the poet's overcoming verbal sequence by the forms of his spatial imagination. So the aesthetic devices reshape our sense of reality by reasserting the primary role of the mythic imagination over mere facticity.

The skeptical reader may worry about how easily Frank slips from formal to thematic matters, thereby literalizing his metaphoric insight. Thus, in joining together the *Cantos, The Waste Land,* and *Ulysses* as works which "maintain a continual juxtaposition between aspects of the past and the present," Frank draws large conclusions about their effect on how we now apprehend time:

By this juxtaposition of past and present . . . history becomes ahistorical. Time is no longer felt as an objective, causal progression with clearly marked-out differences between periods; now it has become a continuum in which distinctions between past and present are wiped out . . . Past and present are apprehended spatially, locked in a timeless unity that, while it may accentuate surface differences, eliminates any feeling of sequence by the very act of juxtaposition . . .

What has occurred, at least so far as literature is concerned, may be described as the transformation of the historical imagination into myth —an imagination for which historical time does not exist, and which sees the actions and events of a particular time only as the bodying forth of eternal prototypes.   (pp. 59–60)

Now this is an extreme statement and smacks of a literalistic extension of the metaphor of spatial form. One of Frank's central terms, "juxtaposition," is seriously suspect. Having borrowed the term from Lessing (who reserved it for the spatial arts) in order to move the time art of poetry toward space, he seems to be begging the question in his use of it: as if the word itself could generate enough figurative force to persuade us of its literal applicability to modernist literature. After all, it does not seem that we can speak literally of juxtaposing passages of words that are widely separated—not unless we naively believe that the spatial copresence of books literally represents the copresence of discourse and our experiencing of it. So the word *juxtaposition* itself claims a reality that verbal sequence belies, as verbal sequence similarly belies any literal sense of simultaneity.

If we are talking about our response to a work and, in that response, about an illusionary impression of something for which we use the metaphoric notion of simultaneity, sponsored by something in the work that feels like juxtaposition, then we still are acknowledging the primary constitutive role of temporality in language and in experience, however strongly we entertain a momentary illusion of verbal stasis. But Frank, coming toward the end of the symbolist tradition and fixing its claims in their most uncritical and extravagant manifestation, would lose temporality altogether in the instantaneity of spatial form.[8] This version of the symbolist aesthetic, so easily adapted to the objectives of the New Criticism, seems most exposed to the skeptic's charge of evasive mystification. It is similar to the nostalgic celebration of sacramental presence in the work of the historian of religion Mircea Eliade (mentioned favorably by Frank), who defines sacred time as time again and again redeemed, as the continuing recurrences of cutoff entities that take on the characteristics of objects in space.

Once we take the matter of juxtaposition less literally, we can accept repetition as the temporal analogue to juxtaposition and can see literary form—found in the many kinds of repetitious arrangements invented by the poet or his tradition—as that which returns time on itself, shaping temporality out of its nature as pure, unelevated sequence. In this sense we may define form (as I have elsewhere) as the imposition of spatial elements on a temporal ground without denying the figurative character of the word *spatial* and the merely illusionary escape from a temporal awareness which is never overcome.

Granting that repetition of one sort or another constitutes the basis for our finding form in the temporal arts, once we begin to question the extent to which repetition can be seen in

8. Frank's discussion takes off from Pound's definition of an image as "that which presents an intellectual and emotional complex in an instant of time." The quote appears in *The Widening Gyre*, page 9.

such works as equivalent to juxtaposition in the spatial arts, then the radically temporal character of moment-by-moment succession can no longer be altogether transcended, so that the entire transformation of history to myth is threatened. Paul de Man, profound enemy of the symbolist aesthetic as I have outlined it, hits precisely at this sense in which repetition is never a total return, as he attacks the spatial basis of the symbol and its claim to an achieved simultaneity. "Repetition is a temporal process that assumes difference as well as resemblance. It functions as a regulative principle of rigor but asserts the impossibility of rigorous identity, etc."[9] In an earlier defense of allegory at the expense of symbol, de Man used *his* sense of repetition (which he says is Kierkegaard's) to justify the temporality of the allegorical process and to deny the feasibility of the symbolic process: "It remains necessary, if there is to be allegory, that the allegorical sign refer to another sign that precedes it. The meaning constituted by the allegorical sign can then consist only in the *repetition* (in the Kierkegaardian sense of the term) of a previous sign with which it can never coincide, since it is of the essence of this previous sign to be pure anteriority."[10]

De Man's stalwart attack upon symbol in the name of allegory is a climactic moment in the theoretical turnaround against the long and impressive development of organic poetics from the late eighteenth century through the New Criticism. After so long a period during which allegory was shunted aside as an unpoetic impostor while the symbol was held aloft in unchallenged glory, allegory began to have its good name reestablished as critics arose, beginning in the late 1950s, to push the New Criticism, and almost two centuries of organic

9. *Blindness and Insight: Essays in the Rhetoric of Contemporary Criticism* (New York: Oxford University Press, 1971), p. 108.

10. "The Rhetoric of Temporality," in *Interpretation: Theory and Practice,* ed. Charles S. Singleton (Baltimore: Johns Hopkins University Press, 1969), pp. 173–209. This quotation appears on page 190. I should acknowledge at the outset that, in de Man's more recent work, there are refinements and even changes in these claims which would have to be discussed if this were a study of his career. But in the study of the career of the relations between symbol and allegory it is de Man's work of the late sixties and early seventies that is central.

theorizing behind it, from its position of dominance. After
early signs of the reversal in Edwin Honig's *Dark Conceit: The
Making of Allegory*[11] and the development of it in Angus
Fletcher's monumental volume, *Allegory: The Theory of a
Symbolic Mode*,[12] it was in de Man's "The Rhetoric of Temporality" that the theoretical consequences of the resurrection
of allegory and the casting out of the symbol marked out and
grounded the theoretical revolution that had taken place. It is
de Man's formulation which my presentation here of the case
that has been made for the symbol, as well as of the excesses
and naiveté in the making of that case, has been intended to
anticipate. For, however unsympathetic his response to the
symbol, his is a most important response with which one must
deal before being able to salvage any part of the symbolist tradition—as I wish to do.

We have seen that, in his concept of repetition, de Man insisted on retaining a residue of temporality and of difference,
so that he could prevent the term from serving a sense of simil-
taneity, that which could achieve an identity of several moments that together would sacrifice the unique before-ness and
after-ness of their relations to one another within a succession
of unrepeatable moments. With that other, simpler notion of
repetition from which—as in juxtaposition—time and its differences were purged, the infinite variety of time's movements
could be fused into a unity into which all would converge: an
instantaneous emblem, the very essence of the romantic symbol and of spatial form. De Man is too faithful to the need for
existential authenticity, to the need for a demystified confrontation of the temporal conditions of the human predicament, to
allow to literature the privilege of evading these through the romantic delusions of the symbol; so he denies the simpler sort
of repetition. In the linguistic world of difference the dream of
identity is just such a delusion; in the fading-away world of
time the dream of true simultaneity ("which, in truth, is spatial
in kind") is, again, such a delusion: "Whereas the symbol pos-
tulates the possibility of an identity or identification, allegory

11. Evanston: Northwestern University Press, 1959.
12. Ithaca: Cornell University Press, 1964.

designates primarily a distance in relation to its own origin, and, renouncing the nostalgia and the desire to coincide, it establishes its language in the void of this temporal difference" ("The Rhetoric of Temporality," p. 191).

In this quotation and elsewhere de Man seems also to create spatial metaphors of his own ("distance," "void") for time: we might claim "distance" to be his spatial equivalent of "temporal difference," much as symbolists treat juxtaposition as a spatial equivalent of repetition. But the antisymbolist would be quick to point out that, unlike "juxtaposition," which—with its sense of simultaneity—adds elements that repetition, as a temporal concept, cannot warrant, the de Man equivalent ("distance" for "temporal difference") is not misleading since it emphasizes those very attributes (void, hiatus) which characterize the temporal. So "distance" does not transfer to time for time's benefit any privileged attributes of space (such as simultaneous form) but only suggests those attributes which space, as broken up, shares with time. To put it another way, we might say that de Man is giving us only an analogy or allegory, not a metaphor or symbol, in his use of spatial language for temporal claims.

It is the monistic pretense, the claim that in poetry sign and meaning can be made to coincide, that constantly bothers de Man about the symbolist aesthetic. And it bothers his existential sense as well as his aesthetic sense: indeed, for de Man, literature, as temporal, seems to enjoy a special mimetic advantage over the spatial arts in its relation to experience. Consequently, in the temporal extremity of language, whose signs seem to march in imitation of the temporal extremity of existence, there can be neither total repetition nor coincidence, these being other terms for simultaneity or identity, spatial concepts all. For sign and meaning to coincide, then, is for literature to evade "the fallen world of our facticity" (*Blindness and Insight,* p. 13). In effect, literature would be seeking to abrogate the terms upon which language serves as mediation; and "unmediated expression is a philosophical impossibility" (p. 9). Instead, in obeying the dualistic conditions upon which mediation rests, literature can claim no privilege and must abandon the deluded hope of coincidence: "The discrepancy between sign and meaning (*signifiant* and *signifié*) prevails in literature as in everyday language" (p. 12). Thus literature should accept allegory as being as much of a device as it can hope for, if, as discourse (*any* discourse), it is to claim authenticity in its relation to existence. The rest—any notion of a separate definition and destiny for poetry based on a dream of unity that transcends time and difference—is at worst "an act of ontological bad faith" ("The Rhetoric of Temporality," p. 194) and at best nothing but a delusion born of wanhope. It is tantamount to a denial of death and "the fallen world of our facticity"—and about as vain. In life and discourse, time is unredeemable, and any dream of redemption requires a mystification probably as inflated as the Christian myth, with its paradoxical extensions into metaphor, to which I referred earlier.

But it is quite evident that de Man does some privileging of his own—not of literature surely, but rather of the world of unredeemed time which all of us, all events, and all our writings serve as part of an egalitarian doom. The modestly dualistic role he assigns literature is to stand on bedrock existential reality, calling back the more flighty among us from our heady imaginings, reminding us that the one truth is below and inescapable and that our metaphors are mere dreams from which reality must awaken us. In "The Rhetoric of Temporality" de Man freely uses terms or phrases like "in truth," "authentically temporal," "actual," to describe our "truly temporal predicament." But is not this metaphysical confidence in time's objective truth—the one reality from which delusions can be gauged—an extralinguistic dependence which stacks the deck in matters both philosophic and literary? Does it not also predispose us to valorize those literary works which, thematically, oppose facticity to dream, oppose the reality of death to our attempt at escaping it by means of mystification? Are we not being encouraged to valorize such works or, even worse, to interpret all works we wish to valorize as having this theme? We may ask, in other words, whether the defense of allegory on these grounds is an aesthetic claim or a thematic one, whether it is grounded in a semiotic or in an existentialist ontology of temporality.

After the long reign of a symbolist aesthetic grown too self-confident, de Man has performed an indispensable service in reminding us of the mystifications which that aesthetic too long assumed to be theoretical truths. He has helpfully warned against our reification of the literary object through taking the spatial metaphor of poetic form literally in a way that belies the serial nature of the medium and of our experiencing of it. This freezing of verbal sequences, he also reminds us, creates sacred objects whose spatial presence permits us to think we have found a way to transcend time through the unifying power of imagination; in this way we exaggerate unrealistically the human power to transform ineluctable fact. So, for de Man, this aesthetic has unfortunate, because delusive, existential or thematic consequences as well.

In warning us effectively against such mystification, however, does not de Man too strongly urge the other extreme? If the uncritical projection of spatial categories vitiates the authority of myth, does not the acceptance of the reality of temporal categories enslave us to history as facticity? My way of putting this question presupposes my answer, since in referring to time as no less categorical than space, I am not viewing spatiality exclusively as an empty metaphor constructed to evade a temporality that is viewed as unquestionably real. In recent linguistic theory, after all, the diachronic, no less than the synchronic, relates to, and can function only within, the arbitrary conventions of human creation; the temporal model is as much the linguist's construction as is the spatial model. If, as we conceive it, the temporal shares with the spatial the state of being a constructed reality, then we cannot easily find a point of privilege to justify a claim about which serves as a metaphor for which. It can go either way, depending upon the purposes of the discourse—whatever we may claim to know about the facts of clock time and the inevitability of death. It may be that de Man implicitly concedes as much when he himself is forced to resort to spatial language to portray man's "truly temporal predicament." Terms like "distance," "void," or even "space" itself in the phrase "blank space," remind us that even the metonymic consecutiveness of existence and of discourse (of existence *as* discourse?) may re-

quire borrowings from the spatial realm to express our metaphoric understanding of it. Indeed, the myth of temporality
may be the more insidious, may woo us the more seductively
from our sense that it *is* but discursive, because of our lifelong
obsession with the reality of death.

I want us to earn a chance to retain some of the symbolist's
ambitious hopes for what man, as fiction-making creature, can
accomplish in language, without falling prey to the ontologiz-
ing impulse which symbolist theory has previously encouraged. To do so we must balance a wariness about
projecting our myths onto reality with an acknowledgment that
we can entertain the dream of symbolic union, provided it does
not come trailing clouds of metaphysical glory. Within the aesthetic frame of a fictional verbal play the poem can present us
with a form which creates the illusion of simultaneity, though
even as we attend it we remain aware of its illusionary nature.
What else except such spatial relations have literary critics
since Aristotle been celebrating in their celebrations of structural unity? Only when an excess of enthusiasm leads some of
them to reify these illusions must we draw back to a more modest claim. On the other side, under the auspices of the same
aesthetic occasion, the poem may well remind us of those temporal and decentering metaphors which threaten each moment
to undo (or at least to "unmetaphor")[13] those spatial configurations which we conspire with the poem to create.

So I suggest that we can meet de Man's concerns while still
conceding—if only provisionally—the special unifying force
that the symbolists have attributed to poems. If we are conscious of the provisional nature of the aesthetic dream which
the poem nurtures, we also look for the poem's own self-consciousness about its tentative spatializing powers. Its fiction,
and our awareness of it, contain the twin elements of symbol
and antisymbol, of words that fuse together even while, like
words generally, they must fall apart in differentiation. Even
further, the poem, together with our apprehension of it, com-

13. I borrow the term from Rosalie L. Colie, who invented it to describe the
act of literalizing the image. It functions significantly throughout her book,
"My Ecchoing Song": Andrew Marvell's Poetry of Criticism (Princeton:
Princeton University Press, 1970).

bines its transformation of time into myth with its resignation to the countermetaphor of time as mere historicity.

The poem and its fully attending reader are in the ambiguous position of the speaker in Keats's "Ode to a Nightingale." What is the nature of his illusion, or delusion? of the lasting or evanescent metaphoric force of the bird or its song? of the residue of these after the vision or dream passes? Are we, observing and listening, to consider the bird as a true metaphor or as the speaker's mistaken metonymy: are we, that is, to consider the bird as one with its voice and thus with all nightingales that have lived, or are we to consider the voice as only a sign of the bird and to be distinguished from it as it is distinguished from other nightingales? Or are we, somehow, to consider the bird both ways? and, if so, at different times or simultaneously?

Indeed, the bird seems to function for the enraptured speaker as a metonymic metaphor. The magic of the speaker's momentary indulgence leads him to identify the single, mortal bird with its voice and song and to make the voice and song identical with those of the distant past. All nightingales become one bird because the songs are one song, heard but unseen.[14] On the strength of this transfer Keats treats the bird itself as immortal, in contrast to his own mortality and that of the historical or mythological personages who earlier heard the same bird (voice, song). Humanity's individual lives are tied together by the bird once it has been turned into the all-unifying metonymic metaphor, so that history across the ages has been turned into the instantaneous vision of myth. Thanks to a repetition so complete that it achieves the identity of eternal recurrence (de Man's objections notwithstanding), time is redeemed.

---

14. I have shown elsewhere how romantic poets make use of their hearing rather than seeing the bird to allow them to move from identity of song to identity of occasion (and of bird), as they use their auditory (and blindly visionary) experience to collapse time. See *The Classic Vision: The Retreat from Extremity in Modern Literature* (Baltimore: Johns Hopkins University Press, 1971), pp. 161–164. It is this swift—indeed immediate—movement ("on the viewless wings of poesy") which causes the speaker's reason ("the dull brain"), trapped in the empirical world, which requires sight, to slow him down in confusion ("perplexes and retards"). As we shall see, the struggle between poetic vision and the brain never altogether lets up.

This strange conversion of history reminds me of Keats's ascribing to the Grecian urn the role of "sylvan historian" in the companion great ode. It is a historian which does not respond to the series of factual questions put to it by the speaker. As "sylvan," the "silent form" is a historian of another than historical kind—like the nightingale. The urn brings history together as myth within its own emblematic being. Cleanth Brooks thus chose just the right title for his essay on the "Ode on a Grecian Urn": "Keats's Sylvan Historian: History without Footnotes."[15] But, like others I have noted in the symbolist tradition, Brooks is too unqualified in his commitment to myth: "Moreover, mere accumulations of facts—a point our own generation is only beginning to realize—are meaningless. The sylvan historian does better than that: it takes a few details and so orders them that we have not only beauty but insight into essential truth. Its 'history,' in short, is a history without footnotes. It has the validity of myth—not myth as a pretty but irrelevant make-believe, an idle fancy, but myth as a valid perception into reality" (p. 151). Associated with the urn as symbol here is an excess of romantic ontological fervor, to which (thanks to critics like de Man) we have, in recent years, had ample correction—and overcorrection.

It is the more balanced view of myth and history, one which can contain our skepticism without foreclosing our capacity for vision, that I mean to point out in my observations about the "Ode to a Nightingale." In that poem the speaker's illusion or delusion is sustained only while he is simultaneously aware of his continued existence in the death-ridden world of the individual life that concludes by becoming "a sod." And when, in the final stanza, he returns from his all-unifying fancy to his "sole self," he looks back upon his momentary trance as mere deception ("cheat," "deceiving elf") as he bids it farewell with the bird. The metaphor *was* a mistake. From his perspective as "forlorn" individual, isolated in time and space, there can no longer be any entertaining of his fancy's visionary reality. Yet the final words of the poem ("Do I wake or sleep?")

15. *The Well Wrought Urn: Studies in the Structure of Poetry* (New York: Reynal and Hitchcock, 1947), pp. 139–152.

suggest that the final moment of demystification is not necessarily privileged as the only authentic reality.

As the bird's song leaves the speaker's consciousness, it "fades" away, a very different fading—apparently—from what occurred early in the poem when the speaker sought to fade away into the world of the nightingale's song. As before, seeking an act of self-dissolution, he tried to fade out of the world of human time, collapsing the distance between himself and the bird, so at the end the bird's song fades away from the speaker back into the differentiated world of time and distance. Now "buried deep" in the next valley, it is—separated by time and distance—an absent part of the speaker's dead past. Yet repeating the word *fade* suggests a similar activity in fading out of or fading back into the realm of worldly experience. The repetition functions at once to move us toward the identity of opposites (as in the symbolic aesthetic of spatial form) and to remind us of the unbridgeable differences between apparently repeated elements (as in de Man's definition of "repetition").

Consequently, the perspective which sees the fancy as cheating is itself not a final reality, and the magic of the fancy is not altogether dispelled. Even more, the experience itself is still cherished, even in the aftermath of loss. The struggle in the speaker between the poet's willed visionary blindness that has permitted the fancy and the mortal's dull, perplexed brain that has resisted it has not relaxed: once again—or rather still —the struggle between myth and history. The music has fled, we learn in the opening of the final line, though its continuing effects lead to the uncertainty about the present reflected in the question that concludes the poem ("Do I wake or sleep?").

Before he asks about his present state, the question in the preceding line suggests the double nature of his judgment of his magical episode now concluded: "Was it a vision, or a waking dream?" The second of these alternatives is not wholly a denial of the first: if the vision becomes a dream, it is yet the product of a waking consciousness. I have borrowed the phrase "a waking dream" for my title because I find in the oxymoron the two sides of the dialectic I have been tracing. As in dream, the symbol creates for us a surrogate reality, claiming the completeness of an irreducible domain within its eccentric terms, although it also stimulates a wakefulness that undercuts its metaphoric extravagances and threatens to reduce symbol to allegory. Whatever the incompleteness of the vision, later seen as such even by the speaker, the poem that contains it contains also the vision of that incompleteness. The poem unifies itself aesthetically around its metaphoric and its counter-metaphoric tendencies, even as its oppositions remain thematically unresolved. It is, then, self-demystifying, but as such it does not fall outside the symbolist aesthetic so much as it fulfills what that aesthetic, at its most critically aware, its most self-conscious, is able to demand: nothing less than a waking dream.

SAMUEL R. LEVIN

Allegorical Language

"In the simplest terms," writes Angus Fletcher, "allegory says one thing and means another." Some such observation about the disjunctive or dualistic nature of allegory is made by just about everyone who writes on the topic (so Quintilian: "*Allegory* . . . presents one thing in words and another in meaning"). According to Northrop Frye, "We have allegory when the events of a narrative obviously and continuously refer to another simultaneous structure of events or ideas, whether historical events, moral or philosophical ideas, or natural phenomena." As the authors of these characterizations are well aware, such definitions ("in the simplest terms") are useful primarily as "starting" points. Caveats against reading adequacy or conclusiveness into them are voiced by various authors. Thus Honig writes, "The insistence on a disjunction between the 'inside' and the 'outside' [interpretations] succeeds only in isolating a rather barefaced kind of personification allegory." Even more strongly, Quilligan claims that "the vertical conceptualization of allegory and its emphasis upon disjunct 'levels' is absolutely wrong as a matter of practical fact."[1]

All of these authors have gone on from the description of allegory's bipartite design to discussion of its larger significance —raising questions of typology, classical backgrounds, biblical exegesis, "levels" of interpretation, iconography, and so on. In this essay, however, I will confine my attention to allegory's fundamental structure, to the linguistic mechanism that functions as its basis. I will concentrate on the language and try to show how the build of our language both enables allegory and at the same time imposes a limit such that the possibility of "pure" allegory, a mode that is logically conceivable, is left unexplored.

The staple of allegory is personification. By definition personification is a metaphoric, hence mixed, mode—something nonhuman is endowed with human characteristics. This "endowment" results from the transfer of semantic features from a predicate normally associated with humans to a noun (typically functioning as subject) that designates something nonhuman.[2] If we read "The rock was merry" or "The rock spoke to the grass," the rock will be personified if we transfer the feature of humanness which is normally associated with the respective predicates to the ordinary meaning of "rock." If an entire narrative about rocks is built up in this way we have an allegory. To be sure this would be a primitive, rudimentary type of allegory, a "rock fable," if you will; still, this rudimentary type exhibits all the characteristics of allegory with which I am here concerned.

It may be observed of the disjunction customarily attributed

1. Angus Fletcher, *Allegory: The Theory of a Symbolic Mode* (Ithaca: Cornell University Press, 1964), p. 2; Quintilian, *Institutio oratoria* 8. 6. 44, Loeb edition (Cambridge, Mass.: Harvard University Press, 1953); Northrop Frye, "Allegory," in *Encyclopedia of Poetry and Poetics,* ed. Alex Preminger (Princeton: Princeton University Press, 1965) pp. 12–15; Edwin Honig, *Dark Conceit: The Making of Allegory* (Evanston: Northwestern University Press, 1959), p. 5; Maureen Quilligan, *The Language of Allegory: Defining the Genre* (Ithaca: Cornell University Press, 1979), p. 28.

2. For a thorough discussion of personification from the grammatical standpoint see Morton W. Bloomfield, "A Grammatical Approach to Personification Allegory," *Modern Philology,* 40 (1963), 161–171.

to allegory that the literal level is conveyed by the predicates, the allegorical or metaphoric level by the personified nouns. Thus when it is claimed that allegory says one thing and means another, it is the predicates that "say" the one and the (personified) nouns that "mean" the other. This formulation, while oversimplified, is correct in its essentials. We have to bear in mind in this connection that our interest here is not in the question of metaphor generally but in that specific variety known as personification. On its face a sentence like "The rock was merry" is open to a number of metaphoric interpretations. For one thing we could construe "merry" to mean "glistening," "variegated in color," or something similar. On such a construal it would be the item "rock" that retained its literal meaning, not the predicate. Since, however, we are considering such sentences in the context of allegory and thus assuming that their construal is that of personification, the formulation above can be said to hold.

Let us now look at the language that the author has available when he undertakes to write an allegory. In a critical, if not a statistical, sense, the language contains more nouns than predicates. This may seem counterintuitive inasmuch as predicates comprise both verbs and adjectives. In the sense relevant to my concerns, however, the claim is correct. Whereas for a few areas of physical activity we have species-specific predicates —thus we can say of a horse that it ramps or whinnies, of a bird that it molts or is fledged, of a tree that it transpires and photosynthesizes—for the entire range of volitional, affective, emotional, moral, and ethical states, dispositions, and activities, the predicates that the language makes available are specific to humans. It is this fact which in a very real sense explains the ascendancy of personification as a metaphoric device—that other semantic modifications, say, equinization, petrification, dendrification of human objects are not readily effected metaphorically, even though such modifications would appear to be just as possible *a priori*. One explanation sometimes given for this state of affairs is that man sees the universe through his own eyes and this leads to an anthropomorphic view of that universe. This answer no doubt contains a large element of truth; but we must remember that in coining and construing metaphoric expressions man is theoretically free to create entities of whatever shape and nature he desires. Thus, in principle there would appear to be no reason why metaphoric transfer should not produce semantic entities of all descriptions. The real reason that personification tends to predominate, it seems to me, is that even in his creative freedom man is constrained to anthropomorphism, constrained not necessarily by his seeing the universe in his own image but by having a limited and skewed number of predicates at his disposal (this condition, of course, derives from the fact that it was man who developed language, not animals or plants). Suppose one wished to equinize a man. What predicates specific to horses could one use? What specifically equine activities or states of mind could one attribute to the man? One might say that the man cantered, that he whinnied, that he grazed, that his mate dropped a foal, and a few other things. It is not even clear that all the preceding predicates are specific to horses. The great bulk of the description, however, would have to be carried on by means of predicates like *sad, envious, admire, tell, rejoice,* which are specific to humans and which carry that specificness with them in their extended application. The same limitation applies for the processes of petrification, dendrification, and so on. On the other hand, for personification—of any object—the wealth of predicates specific to man's every mood, impulse, and action is available.[3]

We should bear in mind, however, that this same latent pre-

---

3. There is of course a literary tradition of long standing in which humans are transformed into nonhuman objects. I believe, however, that examination of the work written in this tradition would serve to corroborate my contention. If we take Ovid's *Metamorphoses* as an exemplar we find that in many cases the transformations take place at the end of a narrative—that the personages are treated in their own right, as humans, until the metamorphoses are accomplished, at which point the poem immediately shifts to another narrative. Dendrification, petrification, and other types of nonhuman metamorphoses differ in this respect from personification, which typically is effected at the outset and is then sustained through the entire narrative. Moreover, on those occasions when Ovid continues the same narrative past the transformation, the metamorphosed object is commonly treated as inherently human, so that in the consequent narration the object—be it a stone, a stream, a tree, a bird, or an animal—is in fact personified.

disposition in the language that makes personification so viable essentially forecloses the possibility of our gaining any insight into the life and nature of nonhuman entities. We say of a horse that it is frightened, or contented, or would like some sugar. But what does a horse feel when it is frightened? Whatever it feels, "frightened" is not the predicate that *specifically* describes that feeling. It is a makeshift that we use because of a deficiency in our lexicon. There is some irony in the fact that this very deficiency, in its full extension, is what makes allegory possible.

The problem of predicate-skewedness is of course intensified when what is personified is not something natural like a rock or a horse, but something abstract. Here it is not clear that we have any specific predicates. Let us examine in this connection and in light of the considerations raised in the preceding discussion a passage from Spenser's *Faerie Queene*. In book 1, canto 4, Lucifera (Pride) enters her coach, which is drawn by six beasts, on each of which rides one of her "sage Counsellors,"

> Of which the first, that all the rest did guyde,
> Was sluggish *Idlenesse*, the nourse of sin;
> Upon a slouthfull Asse he chose to ryde,
> Arayd in habit blacke, and amis thin,
> Like to an holy Monck, the service to begin.
>
> And in his hand his Portesse still he bare,
>   That much was worne, but therein little red,
>   For of devotion he had little care,
>   Still drowned in sleepe, and most of his dayes ded;
>   Scarse could he once uphold his heavie hed,
>   To looken, whether it were night or day;
>   May seeme the wayne was very evill led,
>   When such an one had guiding of the way,
> That knew not, whether right he went, or else astray.

We notice that if we were to substitute for "Idlenesse" a noun that signified a man, say "Theodore" or "Tom the cook," the entire passage would be deallegorized—we would have a straightforward narrative. This follows from my observation about the respective roles played in allegory by nouns and predicates. The same result would be achieved in the succeeding stanzas also if such substitution were effected for the names of the other vices introduced (Gluttony, Lechery, Avarice, and so on).[4]

Allegory, as based on personification, is a mixed mode. It can be "unmixed" by replacing the allegorizing nouns with others that conform with the predicates. This move reduces allegory to literal narrative—a narrative by humans about humans. Conformity could be achieved in another way if we were to add to the lexicon species-specific predicates for all those contingencies where in default of specific terms we employ human predicates. Thus "The rock was merry" might be rendered as "The rock was oobis," where "oobis" is defined as "merry, *sp*. of rocks." If such a procedure were feasible its utilization would also reduce allegory to literal narrative. This would be a literal narrative by humans about rocks. Such an

---

4. Another pertinent fact traceable to the build of the language is noted in Richard Whately, *Elements of Rhetoric* (Boston: James Munroe, 1841), pp. 194–197. Whately commented on the status of personal pronouns in different languages and suggested that English is advantageously designed for personification in having a natural gender system. In languages like Greek, Latin, or German, where gender is grammatical, it is not possible arbitrarily to personify (as masculine or feminine) abstract or natural nouns, inasmuch as pronouns must agree in gender with their antecedents. Thus in Greek the word for idleness (sloth) is *argia,* which is feminine; in Latin of the two words for idleness, *cessatio* is feminine, *otium* is neuter; in German *Faulheit* and *Trägheit* are both feminine. Spenser, on the other hand, is free to make Idleness masculine ("Upon a slouthfull Asse he chose to ryde"). In the same way Pride is (earlier) cast as feminine ("So forth she rode").

It is not clear that the effect of this structural fact is as one-sided as Whately makes out, however. Certainly, agreement requirements do not seem to have hampered Ovid in achieving his multifarious mutations. We must remember that in Latin poetry personal pronouns are (except for purposes of emphasis) omitted altogether, their function being absorbed by and manifested in verbal endings. Subsequent to metamorphoses, this grammatical characteristic has the gainful effect of neutralizing—thus holding in suspension—any opposition that might exist between the gender of the human and that of the object into which it may have been transformed. In the great majority of cases, on the other hand, Ovid contrives that there be no such opposition; in this he is aided by the variation in gender (masculine or feminine) permitted nouns in poetry, particularly those designating animals.

account would differ from an account that might be given by a petrologist, which would also be literal, but which would use predicates that referred to a rock's physical and dispositional characteristics, and would not attribute affective or mental states to rocks.

The suggestion of introducing species-specific predicates like "oobis" points to another way in which allegory can be reduced. Suppose that in reading "The rock was merry" we ask ourselves what it would be like for a rock to be merry—we try, that is, to project ourselves into rock life. Unlike the usual move made in interpreting allegory, where the focus of construal is on the nouns, we here focus the construal on the predicates. Where in the former case the semantic incompatibility is so resolved that the result is personification of the noun, the incompatibility here is resolved to modify the predicate; "rock" retains its normal meaning but "merry" is construed so as to mean a state in rocks that is analogous to merriment in humans. In other words we read "merry" as though it meant what "oobis" means.

It is of course clear that the word "oobis," as we have introduced it, is only a counter; it has no semantic redeemability. Thus to suggest that "merry" be read as meaning what "oobis" means is so far to build on a void. The same void obtains when we suggest that "merry" be read so as to mean what merriment consists in for rocks, although in this case the void might better be said to be conceptual. Is there any point then in suggesting a reading for which there is no semantic or conceptual backing? We will return to this question.

To this point we have described, in addition to that mode of construal focused on the noun and resulting in personification, two modes focusing on the predicates: in one the result is a reading that resolves the semantic incompatibility by bringing the predicate into conformity with the *meaning* of the noun— "The rock was merry" → "The rock was glistening;" in the other the predicate is modified to represent a state or condition that would be congruous with the *object* named by the noun— we try to conceive of merriment as something that might be experienced by a rock. The former type of construal is semantic, in that it resolves a semantic incompatibility; the latter is conceptual, in that it resolves a conceptual incongruity.[5] I will refer to the former mode of construal as *dispersonification,* to the latter as *radical dispersonification.*[6]

In asking what it would be like for a rock to be merry we try to project ourselves into rock life. I will not offer any ontological or epistemological arguments that might ground this possibility; it is not clear that any such arguments can be given. I will, instead, present some collateral considerations which I think indicate that such an attempt is not altogether misguided. Consider Wordsworth when, in one of his intensest moments, he spoke of "that blessed mood, in which the burthen of the mystery is lightened," when "we see into the life of things." It seems to me that the mood Wordsworth had in mind can be most approximately attained if we adopt the approach that I am advocating. Rocks, trees, streams, and mountains, perhaps also goodness, beauty, and mercy, are among the "things" that have a life into which we may try to see. And insight into that life can only be achieved, as I see it, if we manage somehow to unshackle ourselves from the semantic and conceptual constraints that our language imposes on us. Above all, poets struggle against these constraints. But except for the relatively rare occasions of borrowing or neologism they must use the words that the language makes available. Evidence of their struggle appears, however, in their combining of nouns and

5. The respective allocations of these two construal routes to meaning and conception may appear to be tendentious or equivocal. Naturally, behind the meaning of "rock" is our knowledge of rocks—so that to say that the move to "glistening" is semantic may strike one as arbitrary, if not indeed as begging the question. The claim that the first move is semantic is based, however, on the assumed existence of a grammar or linguistic description of the language. In the context of such a description our knowledge of the world's contents is distilled into semantic features, and a construal can then proceed in terms of those features. Thus the semantic features of "rock" being incompatible with those of "merry" as specified in the grammar, we may try to construe "merry" (on this direction of transfer) so as to bring its meaning into accord with the semantic features of "rock." For the conceptual construal, on the other hand, no such distillation has been effected—there being no "grammar" of these relations—hence there are no explicit features, semantic or otherwise, that we might use in the attempt to arrive at a construal.

6. The construal leading to *dispersonification* is described in my *The Semantics of Metaphor* (Baltimore: Johns Hopkins University Press, 1977), pp. 50–54; *radical dispersonification* is a notion that I introduce here.

"incompatible" predicates. In turn such "mismatching" imposes on the reader the obligation to effect a construal. Where allegory is concerned, tradition has codified one of the *a priori* available modes of construal—that issuing in personification. Among the *a priori* modes dispersonification (focused on the predicate) is also available. What I am arguing for here, however, is the radical type of dispersonification. In the standard case dispersonification leads to an interpretation in which the predicate is understood to mean a state, attribute, or activity that is compatible with the meaning of the noun or noun phrase with which it is paired; this interpretation, therefore, will be accordant with our mundane conceptions of the objects named by those nouns. Since for rocks to glisten or be multicolored is part of our everyday experience, we will interpret "The rock was merry" (on the dispersonification mode) in some such fashion. Under radical dispersonification, on the other hand, we try to construe the predicate such that its *normal* meaning, "full of gaiety or high spirits," is attributed to the rock. Although we speak in this case also of construal, the construal is not semantic. Rather, the words of the sentence are taken literally; so taken, however, they instigate a construal, or transformation, of our conceptual habits. We try to conceive what it would be like for a rock to be merry.

I believe that Keats's notion of negative capability, at least in one of its aspects, also supports this reading of allegory. The notion has received an extended treatment in Bate's *John Keats,* to which subsequent citations refer.[7] The phrase occurs in a letter written by Keats to his brothers George and Tom: "It struck me, what quality went to form a Man of Achievement especially in Literature and which Shakespeare possessed so enormously—I mean *Negative Capability,* that is when a man is capable of being in uncertainties, Mysteries, doubts, without any irritable reaching after fact and reason— Coleridge, for instance, would let go by a fine isolated verisimilitude caught from the Penetralium of mystery, from being incapable of remaining content with half knowledge" (p. 249). Bate paraphrases this passage as follows: "In our life of uncertainties, where no one system or formula can explain every-

---

7. Walter Jackson Bate, *John Keats* (Cambridge, Mass.: Belknap Press, Harvard University Press, 1964.)

thing—where even a word is at best, in Bacon's phrase, a 'wager of thought'—what is needed is an imaginative openness of mind and heightened receptivity to reality in its full and diverse concreteness. This, however, involves negating one's own ego.'' As I see it the condition that Keats is describing implies not the negating of the ego but rather the curbing of its reflexivity. So we do not abandon contemplation of what we cannot thoroughly and completely understand—as if the contemplation of such ''Mysteries'' were an embarrassment and derogation of the ego—but are content to understand certain things partially, are satisfied—since in the nature of the case that is all that is possible—with half knowledge. Negative capability is thus not an *arbitrary* limitation imposed by the ego on itself; it is instead the recognition of a *necessary* limitation, a limitation imposed by our congenital inability to see totally into the nature and life of certain phenomena. This is the negative aspect. The positive aspect lies in proving the capacity to overcome this limitation.

In his letters Keats makes clear that some of the uncertainties that a poet must recognize and attempt to fix are attributes of human beings and their natures (as in the frequent invocation of *King Lear* in the context of his explanations). At the same time, however, it is clear that his views on the subject of negative capability extend to nonhuman ''ethereal'' things. Richard Woodhouse (a friend of Keats's, ''who by now had acquired a close knowledge of Keats'') describes in a letter the impression he has of Keats's poetical character, an impression he has gained from Keats's own description of himself: ''The highest order of Poet will not only possess all of the above powers but will have [so] high an imagination that he will be able to throw his own soul into any object he sees or imagines, so as to see feel be sensible of and express, all that the object itself would see feel be sensible of or express—and he will speak out of that object—so that his own self will with the Exception of the Mechanical part be 'annihilated'.'' (p. 261). Bate adds another comment made by Woodhouse in the same letter: ''He [Keats] has affirmed that he can conceive of a billiard ball that it may have a sense of delight from its own roundness, smoothness volubility and the rapidity of its motion.'' Earlier

(p. 34) Bate has characterized this remark of Keats's as "puckish." I prefer to think that it was meant in all seriousness. Consider in this connection what Bate presents in a footnote on page 254: "In a letter to Bailey . . . is [Keats's] often-quoted remark, 'If a Sparrow come before my Window I take part in its existence and pick about the Gravel'—later echoed in the little poem, "Where's the Poet?'":

> "Tis the man who with a bird,
> Wren or eagle, finds his way to
> All its instincts; he hath heard
> The lion's roaring, and can tell
> What his horny throat expresseth."

Given the impulse to "see into the life of things," and given that the impulse must be realized in language ill-disposed to serve that purpose, the poet proceeds by makeshifts—conjoining nouns with ill-matched predicates. For the reader such conjunctions pose a challenge. To interpret them as semantic metaphors, I am arguing, is to mistake the nature of the challenge. They are to be taken, rather, as metaphors of conception. Now in view of the close, almost necessary, correspondence that obtains between meaning and conception, it might appear that a distinction is being drawn where there is no difference. But such is not the case. Meaning and conception coincide only when the language is used prosaically, for everyday purposes, when the range of conceptions expressed is defined by and limited to our ordinary experience of the world about us. For the expression of such conceptions, inasmuch as they arise from and hence are consistent with mundane experience, our language provides adequate—in the sense of correspondent—means. This homology between meaning and conception is disrupted, however, when we encounter in poetry a "deviant" expression—a conjunction of a noun with an incompatible predicate. In the face of this incompatibility two basic interpretive moves have customarily been implemented: the predicate can be made conform with the noun ("The rock was glistening"), or the noun can be personified. These two construal routes have radically different implications for the meaning-conception homology. In the former the homology is restored—rocks can and do glisten. The personification construal, on the other hand, offers us an opportunity to extend our conceptual range. To regard a rock as animate is to conceive of a possibility for which our ordinary experience provides no warrant. If approached in this way, therefore, personification would represent a conceptual move beyond the bounds of our experience.

The opportunity personification offers for expanding our conceptual horizons is, however, not taken up by the approach which sees allegory as a poetic mode that says one thing and means another. On this approach, although two levels of interpretation are recognized, neither level comprehends entities or states of affairs that exceed what our worldly experience has prepared us for. An abstraction, as personified, is reduced to the status of a human object through which the narrative, conducted by the predicates, is projected and, in its own right (as an abstraction) is used as a basis for reading allegorical meanings into that narrative. (It is interesting to note in this connection that the allegory is in what is said, not what is meant.) In this procedure the personified noun is not seen as designating a compacted entity, an interpretation which, if made, would involve an extension of our conceptual capacities; rather, it is seen alternately as one of two different things, both conceptually conventional. The semantic compaction that the language motivates is not exploited for its conceptual novelty; instead, it is disintegrated to accommodate our ontological preconceptions. Thus, in the passage from Spenser, for purposes of narrative development "Idlenesse" is read as designating a man, for the allegory as representing a sin. On this approach to allegory what we are not invited to do is to conceive of idleness, that very thing, as embodying (counterparts of) the mental or physical states associated with humans.[8]

8. This description of the manner in which allegory is articulated may seem excessively reductive (although it merely reformulates accepted views). It must be borne in mind, however, that I am abstracting from all "higher" levels of interpretation to which allegory gives rise. Moreover, in treating personification as analyzable into discrete semantic components I am not unaware of approaches to metaphor which see in it an ultimate synthesizing of semantic characters. Claims like the latter, however, are usually made for the *theory* of metaphor being advanced; in the application of those theories to actual examples the synthesis claimed to result from the semantic interaction disintegrates

Even if we took personification seriously, entertained the notion of a rock as jointly mineral and human or idleness as jointly abstract and human, personification would still be a hybrid form, comprising in its juncture elements from disparate generic domains. This disparity is forced upon us, determined by the gaps in our lexicon, these gaps engendering a concomitant underdevelopment of our conceptual capacities. About the gaps there is little that we—along with the poet—can do. A remedy can be provided, however, by exercising our conceptual capacities. We can try to redress the poverty of our language by augmenting our powers of thought. Along these lines we can approach a pure allegorical reading—pure in being univocal, not hybridized. In this reading predicates are construed so as radically to dispersonify their meanings. When a noun referring to a nonhuman object or an abstraction is paired with a predicate denoting a human attribute, we take the noun in its attested meaning but try to construe a meaning for the predicate that is compatible with the object named by the noun. We do this, however, not from our standpoint but from the standpoint of that object. Thus to construe "The rock was merry" to mean "The rock was glistening" is to dispersonify the predicate. The dispersonification "glistening" is, however, a meaning that brings "merry" into conformity with the world as *we* know it. Under radical dispersonification "merry" is to be construed to mean what merriment would mean in a world as experienced by rocks. In other words we try to think of a "literal" sense in which a rock can be merry (or idleness ride on an ass).

As an indication of how a reading such as this would function I will use the last stanza of Keats's "Ode on Melancholy":

She [Melancholy] dwells with Beauty–Beauty that must die;
And Joy, whose hand is ever at his lips
Bidding adieu; and aching Pleasure nigh,

---

into paraphrases which are conceptually straightforward. Quilligan's approach to the problem should also be noted; she sees allegory as deriving its metaphoric force from the polysemy inherent in certain words strategically located in the actual text—so that the allegorical level is not one ("vertically") superimposed by the reader but is developed "horizontally," from serial cross-textual references activated by the layers of meaning that reside in key words.

> Turning to poison while the bee-mouth sips:
> Ay, in the very temple of Delight
> Veiled Melancholy has her sovereign shrine,
> Though seen of none save him whose strenuous tongue
> Can burst Joy's grape against his palate fine;
> His soul shall taste the sadness of her might,
> And be among her cloudy trophies hung,

Five abstractions are mentioned in this stanza. We think of them as abstract qualities and try to conceptualize all the predications made of them in terms of states, activities, and characteristics that such qualities might enjoy, perform, or exhibit. Melancholy dwells with Beauty—Beauty must die; Joy's hand is at his lips bidding adieu. With the abstractions taken at face value we focus on the predications; we try to conceive of two abstractions dwelling together, of an abstraction dying, of a "hand" belonging to an abstraction and how it would bid adieu. I believe that such conceptions (perhaps in a degenerate form) are achievable. They may have about them an evanescent or dissolving quality; we may not be able to fix them in our minds (our inability in this regard following, of course, from there being no words at our disposal to serve as designations). But they can be endowed with some substance; the mind in its effort to conceive of these possibilities will achieve some degree of success. In fact, this effort, if not actually envisaged by is at least a logical extension of Keats's "greeting of the Spirit."⁹

9. In a letter to Bailey (cited by Bate, p. 241) Keats writes, "As Tradesmen say everything is worth what it will fetch, so probably every mental pursuit takes its reality and worth from the ardor of the pursuer—being in itself a nothing—Ethereal thing[s] may at least be thus real, divided under three heads—Things real—things semireal—and no things—Things real—such as existences of Sun Moon and Stars and passages of Shakespeare—Things semireal such as Love, the Clouds etc. which require a greeting of the Spirit to make them wholly exist—and Nothings which are made Great and dignified by an ardent pursuit—which by the by stamps the burgundy mark on the bottles of our Minds, insomuch as they are able to *'consec[r]ate whate'er they look upon.'*" This passage, like many of Keats's "philosophical" musings, is more suggestive than explicit, and it may be that in enlisting it as support for my own position I am misreading or distorting its import. At the same time, however, I feel that when seen in light of my position Keats's various pronouncements achieve a definition and consistency which is otherwise hard to find in them.

The "Ode on Melancholy" is, of course, no allegory, and some of the arguments I have been advancing here may have more bearing on metaphor generally than on allegory in particular. However, I think that allegory too may be read in the way that I am proposing. It is interesting, and suggestive of implications which I cannot here go into, that my proposal on how allegory should be read corresponds with the views of Vico concerning how the first poets approached the task of composition. For Vico the first poets were theological poets, appearing after the Flood and producing as their initial work a divine fable, wherein Jove is portrayed as hurling a lightning bolt (§ 379). The language of these poets was "a fantastic speech making use of physical substances endowed with life and most of them imagined to be divine" (§ 401). In his next paragraph Vico explains that the sky, the earth, and the sea were apprehended as gods: Jove, Cybele, and Neptune. Similarly, all flowers were subsumed under the goddess Flora, all fruits under Pomona. Vico then goes on: "We nowadays reverse this practice in respect of spiritual things, such as the faculties of the human mind, the passions, virtues, vices, sciences, and arts; for the most part the ideas we form of them are so many feminine personifications, to which we refer all the causes, properties, and effects that severally appertain to them. For when we wish to give utterance to our understanding of spiritual things, we must seek aid from our imagination to explain them and, like painters, form human images of them. But these theological poets, unable to make use of the understanding, did the opposite and more sublime thing: they attributed senses and passions, . . . to bodies, and to bodies as vast as sky, sea, and earth."[10]

The line I have taken in this essay opens onto fundamental questions of romantic sensibility, aesthetics, and criticism. The arguments (mostly urgings) that I have presented for the role and significance of conception in various types of construal could be recast in the context of the romantic imagination with little change in import. The following statement by Bate indicates, I think, that such a conversion would be feasi-

10. Thomas Goddard Bergin and Max Harold Fisch, trans., *The New Science of Giambattista Vico* (Ithaca and London: Cornell University Press, 1968).

ble: "It is one of the common tenets of English romantic criticism that the imagination is capable, through an effort of sympathetic intuition, of identifying itself with its object; and, by means of this identification, the sympathetic intuition grasps, through a kind of direct experience and feeling, the distinctive nature, identity, or 'truth' of the object of its contemplation."[11]

11. Walter Jackson Bate, *From Classic to Romantic: Premises of Taste in Eighteenth-Century England* (1946; rpt. New York: Harper Torchbooks, Harper and Row, 1961), p. 132. The two books by Bate that I have cited have assisted me greatly to see the implications of the essentially linguistic analysis of allegory presented in this essay for larger questions connected with the romantic temper and practice.

MARTIN IRVINE

Cynewulf's Use of Psychomachia Allegory: The Latin Sources of Some "Interpolated" Passages

Recent scholarship has shown that *boclar,* Latin learning, is evident in nearly all surviving Old English poetry, especially in the poems associated with Cynewulf and his followers. The interest in Latin influences on Old English poetic composition has resulted in a revision of the formulaic theory in light of the education of Anglo-Saxon lettered poets and their self-conscious artistic methods influenced by Latin *ars grammatica* and *rhetorica*.[1] Clearly two different rhetorical traditions, the

1. Many scholars have contributed to our knowledge of the Latin influences on Old English poetry. Only some of the pertinent studies can be mentioned here. Larry D. Benson's pioneering study, "The Literary Character of Anglo-Saxon Formulaic Poetry," *PMLA,* 81 (1966), 334–341, demonstrates that the poems of the lettered tradition are as formulaic as earlier, presumably oral, Old English poetry. The full implications of Benson's argument have yet to be appreciated. In the case of Cynewulf Robert E. Diamond has shown that a learned poet wrote in traditional formulas; see his "The Diction of the Signed Poems of Cynewulf," *Philological Quarterly,* 38 (1959), 228–241 and "The Diction of the Old English *Christ,*" in *Anglo-Saxon Poetry: Essays in Appreciation,* ed. Lewis E. Nicholson, and Dolores Warwick Frese (Notre Dame: University of Notre Dame Press, 1975), pp. 301–311. On Cynewulf and his sources see: M.-M. Dubois, *Les Éléments latins dans la poésie religieuse de Cynewulf* (Paris: E. Droz, 1943) and Claes Schaar, *Critical Studies in the*

native Germanic and the Latin, contribute to Old English poetic style and subject matter. We are only beginning to understand the extent to which Anglo-Saxon poets were influenced by Latin poetry as well as the theology and exegesis of Latin Christian tradition. All the signed poems of Cynewulf are from Latin sources, and the whole corpus of Cynewulfian poetry shows influences from Latin poetic theory and Latin Christian poetry in addition to the previously documented sources from liturgy, exegesis, and hagiography. Another stylistic feature distinctive of Cynewulfian poetry is the use of psychomachia allegory drawn from Prudentius and Gregory the Great.

In *Christ II* (756–782a), *Juliana* (382–409a), and *The Phoenix* (447–473), a poem in the Cynewulfian tradition, the poet employs a consistent pattern of psychomachia allegory to amplify and enhance his theme. In Latin poetic theory *allegoria,* a species of metaphor or *translatio,* is a primary figure or trope for amplification or poetic expansion. Cynewulf's amplified passages provide valuable test cases for applying our knowledge of Latin influences on Old English composition. In each of these examples the poet departs from his immediate source and amplifies his theme by drawing from the conventions of the spiritual warfare *topos* as established in Latin poetry by Prudentius in the *Hamartigenia* (Birth of Sin) and the *Psychomachia* and in homily and exegesis by Pope Gregory I in the *Moralia in Job.*[2]

Cynewulf Group (Lund: C. W. K. Gleerup, 1949). Jackson J. Campbell believes that the Anglo-Saxons knew Latin poetry and rhetorical figures; see his "Learned Rhetoric in Old English Poetry," *Modern Philology,* 63 (1966), 189–201, and "Knowledge of Rhetorical Figures in Anglo-Saxon England," *Journal of English and Germanic Philology,* 66 (1967), 1–20. For a survey of present problems see Philip B. Rollinson, "The Influence of Christian Doctrine and Exegesis on Old English Poetry: An Estimate of the Current State of Scholarship," *Anglo-Saxon England,* 2 (1973), 271–284.

2. By *topos* I mean a poetic "commonplace," *locus communis,* available to poets in a common tradition and employed whenever useful for thematic enhancement. The origins of *topoi* have been studied by E. R. Curtius, *European Literature and the Latin Middle Ages,* trans. Willard R. Trask (New York: Pantheon Books, 1953; Harper and Row, 1963), pp. 70, 79–105. The psychomachia *topos* has a long history in literary tradition from Prudentius to Spenser.

The first step toward an understanding of the poetic principles operative in the lettered tradition of Old English poetry is a thorough study of the literary education available to the Anglo-Saxons. Although a complete study remains to be written, evidence from the main sources of Anglo-Latin culture allows us to recognize *ars grammatica,* the art of letters, as the foundation of literary education in Anglo-Saxon England and in the early Middle Ages in general. To have a Latin education in Anglo-Saxon England meant to have studied *grammatica* in its Christian form as a preparation for daily activities in the monastery or church (liturgy, office, reading), as well as for advanced study in exegesis and Christian literature. The centrality of *grammatica* is responsible for the literary and scholarly activity of Aldhelm, Bede, Alcuin, and Ælfric, and for the use of Latin sources in Old English poetry.

The art of grammar, as handed down from Alexandria into the schools of Rome and the early Middle Ages, had two branches (the reading and explication of the poets and other writers, and the rules for correct speaking and writing) and four main parts (oral reading, interpretation, textual correction, criticism). Diomedes, a fourth-century Roman grammarian, states that "the whole of grammar consists primarily in the understanding of the poets, prose writers, and historians by ready exposition, and in the rules for correct speaking and writing."[3] Some version of this definition appears often in grammatical texts, and the works of Donatus, Servius, Priscian, Isidore, Cassiodorus, Bede, and Alcuin exemplify, if not always define, the scope and domain of grammatical studies. What distinguishes *grammatica* from *rhetorica* is its concern for the literary text in all of its aspects. In short, anything

3. "Tota autem grammatica consistit praecipue intellectu poetarum et scriptorum et historiarum prompte expositione et in recte loquendi scribendique ratio." Diomedes' complete definition, of which this quotation is a part, can be found in *Grammatica Latini,* ed. H. Keil, 7 vols. (Leipzig: Teubner, 1857–1880), I, 426–427. See also Quintilian, *Institutio oratoria* 1. 4. 2, in the Loeb edition by E. H. Butler (Cambridge, Mass.: Harvard University Press, and London: William Heinemann, 1920–1922), I, 62–63. The standard definition is repeated by Rabanus Maurus, the student of Alcuin, in *De clericorum institutione, Patrologia Latina* (hereafter *PL*) 107:395.

written down and valued highly enough to be studied as an example of good Latin, preserved by correct orthography, explained by commentary and exegesis, or esteemed by poets for imitation was considered to be in the domain of grammar.[4]

That Latin literature was read at all in Anglo-Saxon England bears witness to the existence of a grammar curriculum. The need to open the Latin scriptures, liturgy, and Christian literature to non-Latin speakers motivated many Anglo-Saxon teachers and missionaries like Aldhelm, Boniface, Tatwine, Bede, and Alcuin to compose their own grammatical texts. The number of late classical grammatical texts preserved by Irish and Anglo-Saxon scribes is quite extensive.[5]

St. Augustine, once a *grammaticus* himself, showed how the methodology of classical grammar could be transformed for Christian purposes in the *De doctrina christiana*, 1–3. In monastic schools the classical program which upheld rhetoric as its goal was replaced by a new program which emphasized

4. The relationship between medieval *ars grammatica* and literary theory has been neglected because of scholarly preoccupation with rhetoric. On the literary aspects of late classical and medieval *grammatica* see Curtius, *European Literature*, pp. 36–53; M. Roger, *L'Enseignement des lettres classiques d'Ausone à Alcuin* (Paris: Alphonse Picard, 1905); H.-I. Marrou, *A History of Education in Antiquity*, trans. G. Lamb (London: Sheed and Ward, 1956); Pierre Riché, *Education and Culture in the Barbarian West from the Sixth to the Eighth Century*, trans. John Contreni (Columbia: University of South Carolina Press, 1976). The studies by J. W. H. Atkins, *English Literary Criticism: The Medieval Phase* (Cambridge: Cambridge University Press, 1943), and C. S. Baldwin, *Medieval Rhetoric and Poetic* (New York: Macmillan, 1928), are inadequate and incomplete. The grammatical tradition of medieval literary theory is the subject of my Harvard dissertation.

5. See the chapter on "Learning and Scholarship" in Wilhelm Levison, *England and the Continent in the Eighth Century* (Oxford: Clarendon Press, 1946), pp. 132–173. See also the introduction by Charles W. Jones to *Bedae venerabilis opera, Pars I, Opera didascalica*, ed. C. W. Jones, and C. B. Kendall, *Corpus Christianorum series Latina* (hereafter *CCSL*), 123A, (Turnhout: Brepols, 1975), and T. J. Brown, "An Historical Introduction to the Use of Classical Latin Authors in the British Isles from the Fifth to the Eleventh Century," *Settimane di studio del centro italiano di studi sull'alto medioevo*, 22 (1975), 237–293. On Bede's learning see M. L. W. Laistner, "Bede as a Classical and a Patristic Scholar" and "The Library of the Venerable Bede," in *The Intellectual Heritage of the Early Middle Ages* (Ithaca: Cornell University Press, 1957), pp. 93–116, 117–149.

reading and exegesis.[6] The figurative language studied by
grammarians was made to serve the purposes of biblical exegesis.[7] As Alcuin makes clear in the preface to his treatise on
grammar, *grammatica christiana* is a preparation for *sapientia*
by training the mind to search out the meaning in Holy Scripture.[8]

Within the program devoted mainly to reading and exegesis,
ars grammatica also included precepts for composition—
grammar in its prescriptive or preceptive function.[9] Donatus'
Ars maior, well known in insular schools, is a central text in
this tradition and the account of the figures of speech in book 3
is the source of much of the preoccupation with *schemata* and
tropoi in medieval poetics. The figures could be studied both in
their exegetical and composing functions. Implicit in the grammar curriculum in the Anglo-Saxon period is a theory of com-

6. On monastic education and literary culture see especially Jean Leclercq,
The Love of Learning and the Desire for God, trans. Catharine Misrahi (New
York: Fordham University Press, 1961). On Anglo-Saxon monastic grammati-
cal studies see Margot H. King, "*Grammatica mystica,* A Study of Bede's
Grammatical Curriculum," in *Saints, Scholars, and Heroes: Studies in Medieval Culture in Honor of Charles W. Jones,* ed. Margot H. King, and Wesley M.
Stevens (Collegeville, Minn.: Saint John's Abbey, 1979), I, 145–159; Hugh
Farmer, "The Studies of Anglo-Saxon Monks (A.D. 600–800)," in *Los monjos
y los estudios, IV semana de estudios monasticos* (Poblet: n.p., 1963), pp. 87–
103; Henry Mayr-Harting, *The Coming of Christianity to Anglo-Saxon England* (London: B. T. Batsford, 1972), pp. 191–219.

7. Figures of speech were studied by grammarians as well as rhetoricians,
although the exegetical study of figures was considered to be in the domain of
grammar alone. See book 3 of Donatus' *Ars maior,* in Keil, *Grammatici Latini,*
IV, 397–404, and Isidore of Seville, *Etymologiarum sive originum,* ed. W. M.
Lindsay, 2 vols. (Oxford: Clarendon Press, 1911), in book 1, *De grammatica,*
36–37.

8. Alcuin, *Grammatica, PL* 101:850–854. See also Alcuin's definition of
grammar, cols. 857–858. The need for grammatical study as an introduction to
understanding the spiritual sense of Scripture is emphasized in Charlemagne's
mandate on the revival of grammatical studies, *De litteris colendis,* composed
mainly by Alcuin. See the text and study by Luitpold Wallach, *Alcuin and
Charlemagne: Studies in Carolingian History and Literature* (Ithaca: Cornell
University Press, 1959), p. 290.

9. On preceptive grammar see James J. Murphy, *Rhetoric in the Middle
Ages* (Berkeley and Los Angeles: University of California Press, 1974), pp.
135–193.

position based on the study of poetics and figures of speech.[10] Aldhelm's *De metris* or *Epistola ad Acircum*[11] and Bede's *De arte metrica* and *De schematibus et tropis*[12] reveal that the understanding of Latin poetry and, consequently, the acquisition of principles for poetic composition were a major part of Anglo-Saxon literary education.

In the grammatical tradition allegory does not necessarily involve what we recognize as "personification" but is a more general figure classified under metaphor. *Allegoria* is a major trope which, according to Donatus and others, embraces seven subspecies. The definition of allegory in Donatus and other grammarians involves a distinction between sound or letter or the signifier (something sensory) and meaning or what is signified (something intelligible).[13] Bede follows Donatus in his *De schematibus et tropis* but uses biblical examples to show that the Scriptures contain the same poetical figures found in classical literature. Bede also departs from Donatus by including an extensive treatment of exegetical allegory or the four levels of biblical exegesis after discussing the grammatical forms of allegory, thus making allegory the most extensively treated trope

10. I doubt very strongly that the Anglo-Saxons learned any rhetoric in the traditional sense described by Campbell in "Learned Rhetoric in Old English Poetry" and "Knowledge of Rhetorical Figures in Anglo-Saxon England." Although some "rhetorical" texts were known, the main source of poetic theory and knowledge of poetic figures came from grammar in the Anglo-Saxon period.

11. Aldhelm's works have been edited by R. Ehwald, *Monumenta Germaniae historica, auctores antiquissimi* (hereafter *MGH*), 15 (Berlin: Weidman, 1961), pp. 452–465.

12. Bede's grammatical works have been edited by C. W. Jones and C. B. Kendall, *Bedae venerabilis opera, Pars I, Opera didascalica, CCSL,* 123A (Turnhout: Brepols, 1975).

13. Donatus states that "allegory is a trope in which something other than what is said is meant." ("Allegoria est tropus, quo aliud significatur quam dicitur,") text in Keil, *Grammatici Latini,* IV, 401. Isidore defines allegory as "other-speaking," the sound is one thing and the understanding another. ("Allegoria est alieniloquium. Aliud enim sonat, et aliud intellegitur,") from the text edited by W. M. Lindsay, *Isidori hispalensis episcopi etymologiarum sive originum* (Oxford: Clarendon Press, 1911), I, sec. 22.

in Bede's treatise.[14] Cynewulf, then, would have learned from Donatus, Isidore, and Bede that poetical figures like allegory were an essential element of composition, perhaps even the main distinguishing feature of poetry.

The evidence available to us confirms that classical and Latin Christian poets were studied in Anglo-Saxon England.[15] Favorite authors were Vergil, Statius, Boethius, Sedulius, Arator, Prosper, Lactanius, Fulgentius, Fortunatus, Ambrose, and, most important, Prudentius. Aldhelm imitated Prudentius in his account of the struggle between the virtues and vices in his verse version of *De laudibus virginitatibus* (2246–2762).[16] Bede knew the works of Prudentius and other Christian poets and illustrated metrical principles from their poetry in *De arte metrica*. Bede evidently held Prudentius in high esteem. With reference to the *Psychomachia*, he illustrates the iambic hexameter, a meter "in which the most noble and learned Aurelius Prudens Clemens of Spain wrote the preface to the *Psychomachia*, that is, in a book about the battle of virtues and vices in heroic style."[17] The works of Prudentius were probably found in many monastic libraries. Alcuin mentions Prudentius in his inventory of books in the York library.[18]

Manuscript evidence also suggests that the major centers of learning in Anglo-Saxon England had access to Prudentius'

14. See Bede, *De schematibus et tropis*, in *Bedae opera*, ed. Jones and Kendall, pp. 161–171.

15. See the evidence compiled by J. D. A. Ogilvy, *Books Known to the English, 597–1066* (Cambridge, Mass.: Medieval Academy, 1967). Paleographical and textual evidence has been surveyed by Brown, "An Historical Introduction to the Use of Classical Latin Authors in the British Isles."

16. See the text edited by R. Ehwald, *MGH, Auct. Ant.*, 15 (Berlin: Weidman, 1961).

17. "Quo nobilissimus Hispaniarum scolasticus, Aurelius Prudens Clemens, scripsit proemium Psychomachiae, id est, libri quem de uirtutum uitiorumque pugna heroico carmine conposuit." From *De arte metrica* 1. 21, ed. Kendall, *CCSL*, 123A, 135.

18. In the list of Christian poets appears the name *Clemens*, in *Versus de sanctis Euboricensis ecclesiae*, line 1551; the relevant section of the poem is printed in Gustav Becker, *Catalogi bibliothecarum antiqui* (Bonn: Max Cohen, 1885; rpt. Hildesheim: Georg Olms, 1973), p. 3.

works. Some surviving manuscripts of Anglo-Saxon provenance are illuminated and several have Old English glosses.
The number of surviving manuscripts of Prudentius' works of
Anglo-Saxon provenance, a total of at least ten from my own
preliminary survey, is quite remarkable.[19]

Bishop Leofric's donation to Exeter Cathedral (c. 1072) contains many classical and Christian works in addition to *The Exeter Book* of Old English poetry. The catalogue of books is

19. The first systematic study of the mss of Prudentius was undertaken by
Joannes Bergman, *De codicum Prudentianorum generibus et uirtute*, in *Sit-
zungsberichte der Kais. Akademie der Wissenschaften in Wien*, Philo-
sophisch-historische Klasse, vol. 157, no. 5 (Vienna, 1908). The results of his
survey, though incomplete, form the basis for his edition of the works of Prudentius, *Corpus scriptorum ecclesiaticorum Latinorum*, 61 (Vienna: Hoelder-
Pichler-Tempsky, 1926). Bergman's ms classification has been revised by
M. P. Cunningham, *Aurelii Prudentii Clementis Carmina, CCSL*, 126 (Turnhout: Brepols, 1966). MSS of Prudentius of Anglo-Saxon provenence are the
following (catalogue numbers from N. R. Ker, *Catalogue of Manuscripts Containing Anglo-Saxon* [Oxford: Clarendon Press, 1957], follow library shelf
marks and date of ms.): Cambridge, Corpus Christi College 223 (MS. in conti-
nental minuscule of s. ix med. with Old English glosses of s. x-xi. Ker, 52);
Durham Cathedral Library B.4.9 (MS. in Anglo-Saxon minuscule of s. x med.
with glosses of s. xi. Ker, 108); Oxford, Oriel College 3 (MS. in English caroline minuscule of s. x. ex. with glosses of s. xi. Ker, 358); Boulogne-sur-mer,
B.M. 189 (MS. in caroline minuscule of s. xi with 900 glosses of s. xi. Ker, 7);
Oxford, Bodleian Library Auct. F.3.6. (MS. in caroline minuscule of s. x–xi
with glosses of s. xi. Ker, 296); Munich, Bayerische Staatsbibliothek, CLM
29031b (MS. in English caroline minuscule of s. xi with glosses on only surviving leaf of the *Psychomachia* of s. xi. Ker, 286); Cambridge, University Library Gg 5.35 (florilegia of classical and medieval poetry, Prudentius included,
with glosses of s. xi. Ker, 16); London, British Library Cotton Cleopatra C.8
(MS. in English caroline minuscule of s. x–xi with glosses of s. xi. Ker, 145);
Cambridge, Corpus Christi College 23 (MS. in caroline minuscule of s. x, originally from Malmesbury, with glosses of s. x–xi and xi–xii. Ker, 31b); Oxford,
Trinity College 12 (MS. of s. xii). On the illustrated mss of Prudentius see
Helen Woodruff, *The Illustrated Manuscripts of Prudentius* (Cambridge,
Mass.: Harvard University Press, 1930). Some of the glosses of two manu-
scripts have been edited by Julius Zupitza, "Englisches aus Prudentiu-
shandschriften," *Zeitschrift für Deutsches Altertum*, 20 (1876), 36–45. Other
glosses have been edited by Herbert D. Meritt, *The Old English Prudentius
Glosses at Boulogne-sur-Mer* (Stanford: Stanford University Press, 1959), and
A. S. Napier, *Old English Glosses* (Oxford: Clarendon Press, 1900). Campbell
discusses the glosses to Bodleian Auct. F.3.6 in "Knowledge of Rhetorical
Figures in Anglo-Saxon England."

probably representative of a late Anglo-Saxon library. Sixty-six manuscripts are included, five volumes of which contain Latin Christian poetry—the *Carmen Paschale* of Sedulius, Arator's epic *De actibus apostolorum*, and the complete works of Prudentius. This manuscript of Prudentius with Old English glosses survives and is now MS. Oxford, Bodleian Library, Auct. F.3.6. The record of Leofric's bequest contains this item:

> liber Prudentii sichomachie ⁊ Prudentii ymnorum ⁊ Prudentii de martyribus on anre bec.[20]

The influence of Gregory the Great was felt everywhere in Anglo-Saxon England. The *Moralia* was a favorite text and a list of citations and references by Anglo-Saxon authors would be quite extensive. The *Moralia*, originally addressed to a monastic community requesting spiritual understanding of the difficult book of Job, was naturally a favorite of Anglo-Saxon monks trained in an intellectual environment largely indebted to Gregory.[21]

Evidence from contemporary citations, surviving manuscripts, and other records like library catalogues, donations, and glosses permits us to conclude that while Cynewulf could have found models for psychomachia allegory in a variety of patristic and Christian literary sources, Prudentius and Gregory would have been more readily available and more clearly within the mainstream of Anglo-Latin culture. Furthermore, Prudentius would have supplied the requisite poetic model for an Old English rendering of what is essentially a Latin poetic *topos*.

What did Prudentius and Gregory contribute to the tradition of psychomachia allegory? First of all, Prudentius, writing

20. Cited in Max Förster's introduction to the facsimile edition of *The Exeter Book of Old English Poetry*, ed. R. W. Chambers et al. (London: Percy Lund, Humphries, 1933), pp. 28–29.

21. On Gregory's stature in England see especially Paul Meyvaert's Jarrow Lecture, *Bede and Gregory the Great* (Jarrow: St. Paul's Church, 1964). On the influence of the Gregorian mission see Mayr-Harting, *The Coming of Christianity to Anglo-Saxon England*. See also the evidence for knowledge of Gregory's works in Ogilvy, *Books Known to the English, 597–1066*, pp. 148–153.

around A.D. 400, found a way to represent the various aspects
of inner spiritual struggle (the battle between the inner forces
of paganism and Christianity, the psychology of conversion
and temptation, and the awareness of moral adversaries) in a
literary form adapted from the diction, meter, style, and imagery of Vergil's *Aeneid*. This adaptation or conversion of a
pagan poetical vehicle for Christian uses may have greatly interested Anglo-Saxon poets whose literary environment was
remarkably parallel to that of Prudentius: they were engaged in
a similar conversion of their own native Old English poetic diction, style, and imagery, transforming pagan heroic conventions into Christian ones. What would Cynewulf have found in
Prudentius that could have supplied models for the psychomachia allegory in *Juliana, Christ II,* and *The Phoenix?*

The literary motif of spiritual combat represented by satanic
machinations against the soul and the battle of the personified
virtues and vices is first expressed in Latin poetry in Prudentius' *Hamartigenia*. In this work, written in dactylic hexame-
ters, Prudentius addresses the heresy of Marcion's dualism
and defends the orthodox view of God, sin, and moral awareness. Theological and moral oppositions are elevated to epic
proportions. Satan is the *inventor vitii* (159), a cruel hunter
who continually stalks careless souls to work his deadly triumphs (136–148). The diabolical devices against the soul are
also described in terms of the animated vices:

> his aegras animas morborum pestibus urget
> praedo potens, tacitis quem viribus interfusum
> corda bibunt hominum; serit ille medullitus omnes
> nequitias spargitque suos per membra ministros.
> namque illic numerosa cohors sub principe tali
> militat horrendisque animas circumsidet armis,
> Ira, Superstitio, Maeror, Discordia, Luctus,
> Sanguinis atra Sitis, Vini Sitis et Sitis Auri,
> Livor, Adulterium, Dolus, Obtrectatio, Furtum.
> informes horrent facies habituque minaces.
> Ambitio ventosa tumet, Doctrina superbit,
> personat Eloquium, nodos Fraus abdita nectit.

(389–400)[22]

22. The text and translation of Prudentius' works are from the Loeb edition
by H. J. Thomson, *Prudentius,* 2 vols. (Cambridge, Mass.: Harvard Univer-

With these plagues of sin the powerful robber besets our sickened souls. With his stealthy forces he infiltrates into men's hearts and they draw him in. He sows all manner of wickedness in their inmost parts, and scatters his agents through their frames. For there a large force serves under this wicked commander and invests men's souls with dreadful weapons—Anger, Superstition, Sickness-of-Heart, Strife, Affliction, foul Thirst-for-Blood, Thirst-for-Wine, Thirst-for-Gold, Malice, Adultery, Craft, Slander, Theft. Hideous and frightful are their shapes, threatening their carriage. Vaunting Ambition is puffed up, Learning is proud, Eloquence thunders, Deceit contrives snares in secret.

Here the inner conflict becomes represented not only in metaphors of aggression and battle, but also in the animated or personified abstractions which signify various aspects of diabolical influence in the human soul. These abstractions follow established literary convention. Roman religion tended to deify and personify abstract qualities (for example, Victory), and Latin literature contains many examples of allegorical abstractions.[23] Prudentius utilizes the tradition which supplied a poetic shorthand to allow the representation of the forces perceived to be struggling within and against the soul of man.

Prudentius comments on the Pauline doctrine of spiritual warfare and continues the portrayal of diabolical treachery with the motif of the siege with spears and arrows:

> Parthica non aeque ventos transcurrit harundo,
> cuius iter nullus potis est conprendere visus;
> praepes enim volucres dum pennis transvolat auras,
> inprovisa venit, nec stridor nuntiat ante
> adventum leti quam pectoris abdita rumpat,
> securam penetrans medicato vulnere vitam;
> sed magis aligera est magis et medicata sagitta,

sity Press, and London: William Heinemann, 1949). See also the edition of the *Hamartigenia* by Jan Stam (Amsterdam: H. J. Paris, 1940). On the *Psychomachia* see the recent study by Macklin Smith, *Prudentius' Psychomachia: A Reexamination* (Princeton: Princeton University Press, 1976).

23. For example, the abstractions in Vergil's underworld, *Aeneid* 6. 268–281. On late Roman allegory see C. S. Lewis, *The Allegory of Love* (Oxford: Oxford University Press, 1936), pp. 44–111.

quam iacit umbrosi dominatio lubrica mundi,
eludens excussa oculos calamique volantis
praepete transcursu cordis penetralia figens.

$$(533-542)^{24}$$

Not so quickly through the breezes flies the Parthian arrow,
whose path no eye can perceive; for flitting swiftly with its feathers
through the winged airs it comes unforeseen, and no hissing pro-
claims the approach of death before it bursts its way into the re-
cesses of the breast, piercing the unconcerned life with a poisoned
wound; but it is a swifter arrow with a deadlier poison that the de-
ceitful lord of the darksome world shoots, one that baffles the eye
when it is launched, and with the quick passage of its flying shaft
pierces the inmost heart.

In the *Psychomachia* Prudentius expands the struggle between the fortified soul and the agents of Satan into an allegorical drama: the stages or facets of spiritual warfare are individualized in an allegorical combat. In the preface to the poem
Prudentius interprets the story of Abraham's rescue of Lot in
battle as a *figura* of the Christian psychomachia (*Praef.* 50–
55). *Fides* enters the battle first against the vices of paganism
struggling in and for the soul of man.

We must not forget the historical context of the *Psychomachia*. The poem is not simply an allegory of the battle between
the virtues (Christian excellences, gifts of the Holy Spirit) and
the vices (the deadly sins in all of their manifestations com-
manded by Satan, the *inventor vitii*), but is a representation of
the struggle between paganism and Christianity for the allegiance of man.[25] The theme of *militia Christi* against pagan persecution appears throughout Prudentius' martyrology, the
Peristephanon.[26] Although the psychomachia *topos* acquired a

24. For additional examples of the use of diabolical spears in the *topos* see
Hamartigenia, lines 409–431, 498.
25. This point is discussed by Smith, *Prudentius' Psychomachia*, pp. 29–
108.
26. For example, *milites quos . . . Christus vocat*, *Peristephanon* 1. 32; *ar-
mata pugnavit fides, spes certat et crudelitas*, *Peristephanon* 5. 214, in *Prudentius*, ed. Thomson, vol. 2. The passions of the martyrs, especially that of
St. Vincent, are often portrayed as miniature epics by Prudentius.

more general meaning in later tradition, the fourth-century context of Prudentius' innovation cannot be neglected if its original meaning is to be appreciated. (That the Anglo-Saxons inherited an element of the original meaning of the psychomachia can be seen in the analysis of *Juliana* below.)

The primary encounter is between *Fides* and *Veterum cultura deorum* (Worship-of-the-Old-Gods):

> ecce lacessentem conlatis viribus audet
> prima ferire Fidem Veterum Cultura Deorum.
> illa hostile caput phaleratque tempora vittis
> altior insurgens labefactat, et ora cruore
> de pecudum satiata solo adplicat et pede calcat
> elisos in morte oculos, animamque malignam
> fracta intercepti commercia gutteris artant,
> difficilemque obitum suspiria longa fatigant.
>
> (28–35)

Lo, first Worship-of-the-Old-Gods ventures to match her strength against Faith's challenge and strike at her. But she, rising higher, smites her foe's head down, with its fillet-decked brows, lays in dust that mouth that was sated with the blood of beasts, and tramples the eyes under foot, squeezing them out in death. The throat is choked and the scant breath confined by the stopping of its passage, and long gasps make a hard and agonizing death.

The allegorical combat is represented in the diction and style of the *Aeneid,* complete with all the heroic conventions of battle. The virtues and vices engage in battle in appropriate pairs with a variety of weapons—burning torches (43), swords (50, 137), javelins (111, 130–136), spears (115), pine shafts (121), and other missiles (151). At the conclusion of the battle *Concordia* leads the victorious army of virtues back to the camp in which they build a temple for *Sapientia,* or Christ, following the example of Solomon (804–808). The camp is a "holy city" (750–754) in which the temple is the ultimate fortress against the siege of anti-Christian forces (809–915).

We enter a different world in the pages of Gregory's *Moralia.* Gregory uses psychomachia allegory in his exposition of Job to illustrate how Job became the intermediate subject of the struggle between God and the devil.[27] Gregory describes "all the engines of Satan's warfare constructed against Job." Temptations are satanic *machinae* raised against the fortified city of Job's mind:

> Ecce ad feriendum invictissimum robur inimicus saevens, quot tentationum jacula invenit; ecce quot obsidionum machinamenta circumposuit; ecce quot percussionum tela transmisit: sed in his omnibus mansit mens imperterrita, stetit civitas inconcussa.[28]

> Behold the enemy raging to strike down his unconquerable strength, how many spears of temptation he devised; behold how many beleaguering engines of war he set around him; behold how many weapons of attack he let fly; but in all of these his mind remained undaunted, the city stood unshaken.

Job reveals how the Christian stands in a field of battle daily: the warfare rages with spiritual darts, but the soul fortified by God sends his own darts against the adversary by responding with humility.[29] The church is beset on every side with the lances of temptation hurled by the enemy.[30] The warfare is also portrayed as a battle between the vices and the *miles dei:*

> Tentatia quippe vitia, quae invisibili contra nos praelio regnanti super se superbia militant, alia more ducum praeeunt, alia more exercitus subsequuntur . . . Ipse namque vitiorum regina superbia cum devictum plene cor ceperit, mox illud septem principalibus vitiis, quasi quibusdam suis ducibus devastandum tradit . . . Sed habent contra nos haec singula exercitum suum . . . Sed miles Dei, quia solerter praevidere vitiorum certamina nititur, bellum procul odoratur.[31]

> For the tempting vices, which fight against us in invisible combat in behalf of the pride which reigns over them, some of them go first,

---

27. *Moralia, Praef., PL* 75:520. The *Moralia* has been translated in the edition by Charles Marriott et al., *Morals on the Book of Job,* 3 vols. (Oxford: John Henry Parker, 1844–1850).

28. *PL* 75:522. For the motif of the siege on the fortress of the mind see also *PL* 76:118–119, 354–355.

29. Ibid., 75:571.

30. Ibid., 75:1026.

31. Ibid., 76:620, 621, 623.

like captains, others follow like an army . . . For when pride the queen of sins has fully taken a conquered heart, she surrenders it immediately to seven principle sins, as if to her generals, to lay it waste . . . But these individual sins each have their army against us . . . But the soldier of God, since he endeavors to pursue skillfully the struggle with vices, smells the battle afar off.

The main struggle in the *Moralia* is against the vices in the army of pride. In this context the psychomachia motif is used as an illustration of a moral rather than an essentially theological or religious struggle like that in Prudentius' works.

There are actually two closely related motifs in the psychomachia *topos*. The first is the representation of diabolical aggression against the soul in metaphors of battle, hunting, or robbery (flaming arrows, spears, snares, and so on), and the second is the expansion of this metaphor into a full-scale allegory with the personified virtues and vices as individualized representations of the primary spiritual struggle. The main elements of the *topos* in either form usually include: the machinations of the devil and his agents against the soul, the weapons of the diabolical forces, the wounds of sin inflicted by the enemy, God's ability to defend the faithful, the fortress of the soul, the use of heroic conventions and the diction of epic poetry.[32]

With the models provided by Prudentius or Gregory Cynewulf found several ways to amplify a theme by using psychomachia allegory. In *Christ II*, which is based on Gregory's homily on the Ascension,[33] Cynewulf adds another dimension to the significance of the Ascension by showing how the

---

32. The elements of the psychomachia *topos* are, of course, expanded from biblical metaphors and became part of the Latin hagiographic and exegetical tradition. On the biblical origins of the allegory see Smith, *Prudentius' Psychomachia*, pp. 126–141. On the exegetical sources known to the Anglo-Saxons see the comments by Frederick Klaeber on the arrows of sin motif in Hrothgar's sermon on pride in *Beowulf* in "Die christliche Elemente im Beowulf," *Anglia*, 35 (1911), 112, 127–136. On the doctrine of sin in Gregory's *Moralia* in relation to *Juliana* see James F. Doubleday, "The Allegory of the Soul as Fortress in Old English Poetry," *Anglia*, 88 (1970), 503–509.

33. *In Evangelia* 29, *PL* 76:1213–1219.

church is protected from the diabolical siege by a gift of God's
grace:

> Forþon we a sculon   idle lustas
> synwunde forseon,   ond þæs sellran gefeon.
> Habbað we us to frofre   fæder on roderum
> ælmeahtigne.   He his aras þonan,
> halig of heahðu,   hider onsendeð,
> þa us gescildaþ   wið sceþþendra
> eglum earhfarum,   þi læs unholdan
> wunde gewyrcen,   þonne wrohtbora
> in folc godes   forð onsendeð
> of his brægdbogan   biterne stræl.
> Forþon we fæste sculon   wið þam færscyte
> symle wærlice   wearde healdan,
> þy læs se attres ord   in gebuge,
> biter bordgelac,   under banlocan,
> feonda færsearo.   þæt bið frecne wund,
> blatast benna.   Utan us beorgan þa,
> þenden we on eorðan   eard weardien;
> utan us to fæder   freoþa wilnian,
> biddan bearn godes   ond þone bliðan gæst
> þæt he us gescilde   wið sceaþan wæpnum,
> laþra lygesearwum,   se us lif forgeaf,
> leomu, lic ond gæst.   Si him lof symle
> þurh woruld worulda,   wuldor on heofnum.
> Ne þearf him ondrædan   deofle strælas
> ænig on eorðan   ælda cynnes,
> gromra garfare,   gif hine god scildeþ,
> duguða dryhten.
>
> (756–782a)[34]

> Therefore we shall ever   despise empty desires,
> Wounds of sin,   and rejoice in the better.
> We have the Father Almighty   in the heavens
> As a comfort.   He, in his holiness,
> Sends his heralds   hither from on high,
> Who shield us   against the deadly

34. All quotations from Old English poetry are from the edition of G. P.
Krapp and E. V. K. Dobbie, *The Anglo-Saxon Poetic Records,* vol. 3, *The
Exeter Book* (New York: Columbia University Press, 1936). Translations
throughout are my own.

Arrow-flights of foes,   lest the fiends
Should work wounds,   when the blame-bearer
Sends forth   a bitter shaft
From his bent bow   into the folk of God.
Wherefore, we must   ever firmly and warily
Keep watch   against a sudden shot
Lest the poisoned point   pierce into
The bone lock—   the bitter dart,
Sudden guile of fiends.   That is a perilous wound
Most livid of gashes.   Let us then defend ourselves
While we dwell   on earth.
Let us beseech   the Father for peace,
Pray the Son of God,   and the merciful Spirit,
That he shield us   against the enemies' weapons,
Lie-crafts of foes;   He gave us life,
Limbs, body, spirit.   Give him praise forever,
Glory in heaven,   world without end.
   There is no need   for any of the race of men
On earth to dread   the devil's arrow-onslaughts,
Spear-flight of fiends,   if God shields him,
The Lord of hosts.

Earlier scholars noted that this passage is an interpolation with no counterpart in Gregory's homily.[35] The addition of this passage is best explained as a poetic amplification on the theme at hand. It appears between a section of the poem which calls the reader to follow Christ's example by "leaping" with him to the things above and a section concerned with the Last Judgment. The psychomachia *topos* used by Cynewulf expands on the theme of the benefits of the Ascension for the church. In 659–691a the poet utilizes the familiar "gifts of men" theme to describe how Christ's ascension benefits all mankind. Lines 691b–711 tell us how the Ascension strengthened the church, "godes tempel," in the midst of persecution "under hæþenra hyrda gewealdum." In 756–782a the theme takes another turn by the introduction of the satanic machinations against the "folc godes." Divine protection against the poisoned darts of

---

35. For example, see A. S. Cook's analysis of sources in his edition, *The Christ of Cynewulf* (Boston: Ginn, 1900), pp. 115–116, and Schaar, *Critical Studies in the Cynewulf Group* p. 32.

the adversary is yet another gift of Christ's ascension. Through
the application of the spiritual warfare *topos* Cynewulf makes
the doctrine of faith more explicit: the church's defense against
the adversary comes by prayer and divine intervention, not by
human fortitude.

In *Juliana* Cynewulf greatly expands on the episode of Juliana's confrontation with the devil. The deeper interest in the
psychology of sin and temptation distinguishes Cynewulf's
version from his Latin source, now believed to be nearly identical to the *Acta S. Julianae* preserved in the Bollandist *Acta
sanctorum* under the date of February 16. When the devil appears in Juliana's cell *in figura angeli* ("engles hiw") to begin
his temptation Juliana seizes him and compels him to confess
his methods of spiritual subversion.[36] At this point in the narrative Cynewulf departs from the Latin *Vita* and amplifies on the
theme of temptation by having the devil describe his devices
against the soul in a psychomachia allegory. The Latin *Vita*
which corresponds to *Juliana* 362b–417 simply relates the
devil's confession without the use of allegory:

When I find a prudent one standing firm in prayer, I make him hun-
gry for many desirable things, turning his soul to the things we set
before him; and making his thoughts wander I do not permit him to
persevere in prayer or any good work whatsoever. And again, if I
see any people flocking together in church, afflicting themselves because of their sins, and desiring to hear the Holy Scriptures that
they may keep a portion with them, immediately I enter their house
and do not permit them to do anything good, and I send many
thoughts into their hearts. But if he is able to overcome some of
them and withdraw from his own empty thoughts and go to pray and
hear the Holy Scriptures and to receive the divine sacrament, then I
flee from him rushing headlong. For when Christians receive the divine sacrament, that hour we withdraw from them. I conduct none
of my affairs unless only to subvert those living well. If indeed I see
them doing something good, I introduce bitter thoughts so that they
follow my will.[37]

36. See the account of the devil's confession by Doubleday, "The Allegory
of the Soul as Fortress."
37. "Et ubi invenerimus prudentem ad opus Dei consistere, facimus eum
desideria multa appetere, convertentes animum ejus ad ea quae apponimus ei;
facientes errorem in cogitationibus ejus, et non permittimus illum vel in quo-

Cynewulf incorporates this straightforward account of the methods of temptation in his version of the story (362b–381) and then continues the speech by adding the following amplification:

> Gif ic ænigne   ellenrofne
> gemete modigne   metodes cempan
> wið flanþærce,   nele feor þonan
> bugan from beaduwe,   ac he bord ongean
> hefeð hygesnottor,   haligne scyld,
> gæstlic guðreaf,   nele gode swican,
> ac he beald in gebede   bidsteal gifeð
> fæste on feðan,   ic sceal feor þonan
> heanmod hweorfan,   hroþra bidæled,
> in gleda gripe,   gehðu mænan,
> þæt ic ne meahte   mægnes cræfte
> guðe wiðgongan,   ac ic geomor sceal
> secan oþerne   ellenleasran,
> under cumbolhagan,   cempan sænran,
> þe ic onbryrdan mæge   beorman mine,
> agælan æt guþe.   þeah he godes hwæt
> onginne gæstlice,   ic beo gearo sona,
> þæt ic ingehygd   eal geondwlite,
> hu gefæstnad sy   ferð innanweard,
> wiðsteall geworht.   Ic þæs wealles geat
> ontyne þurh teonan;   bið se torr þyrel,
> ingong geopenad,   þonne ic ærest him
> þurh eargfare   in onsende
> in breostsefan   bitre geþoncas

---

cumque opere bono perseverare. Et iterum si viderimus aliquos concurre ad ecclesiam et pro peccatis suis se affligentes, et scripturas divinas cupientes audire, ut aliquam partem ex ipsis custodiant, statim ingredimur domos ipsorum et non permittimus illos boni aliquid agere, et multas cogitationes immittimus in corda eorum. Nam si quis ipsorum superare potuerit et recesserit a cogitationibus suis vanis et ierit orare et sanctas scripturas audire et communicare divinum mysterium, ab illo praecipites effugamur. Quando enim Christiani communicant divinum mysterium, recedentes nos sumus illa hora ab eis. Nos enim nullius rei curam gerimus, nisi solum subvertere homines bene viventes. Si vero viderimus eos aliquid boni tractare, amaras cogitationes inferimus illis ut nostras voluntates sequantur." The text of the *Acta sanctorum* is printed in the edition of *Juliana* by William Strunk (Boston: Heath, 1904), pp. 40–41. My translation.

þurh mislice   modes willan,
þæt him sylfum   selle þynceð
leahtras to fremman   ofer lof godes,
lices lustas.

(382–409a)

If I meet   any courageous
And bold   champion of the Lord
Opposing my arrow-attack,   will not far from thence
Bend in battle,   he raises up
His board, wise in mind,   the holy shield,
Spiritual war-armor,   will not abandon God,
But bold in prayer   gives resistance,
Fast among fellows,   I must turn
Far from thence, abashed,   bereft of joys,
In the embers' grip,   bewail my grief,
That I may not   through craft of might
Withstand at battle;   but I, saddened, must
Seek out another,   one lacking courage,
Beneath the war-banner,   a more lazy warrior,
Whom I may oppose   with my enticements,
Hinder at battle.   Although he, partly good,
Begins in spirit,   I am sooner ready
To look through all   his inner thoughts,
How fast the soul   may be from within,
A wrought rampart.   I rend the wall's gate
Through onslaughts;   the tower is pierced,
An entrance opened,   then I first
Through arrow-siege   send him
Bitter thoughts   into bosom,
Through various   desires of the heart,
That he thinks   it better
To continue his sins   over the love of God,
Desires of the body.

Although there are a few echoes of the *Vita* in this passage,[38]
on the whole it is an amplification on the devil's "confession"
which develops the devil's *modus operandi* in greater detail.

38. *Consistere:* "bidsteal gifeð" (388b); *praecipites effugamur:* "ic sceal feor þonan/heanmod hweorfan" (389b–390a); *amaras cogitationes inferimus:* "ic . . . in onsende/in bresotsefan bitre geþoncas" (403b–405b).

The continuation of this dialogue between Juliana and the devil gives the story both a dramatic quality and a sharper focus on the agency behind the pagan antagonists of the saint.[39] In Cynewulf's version the devil's account of his engines of spiritual warfare allegorizes what the devil hoped would occur with Juliana who faces torture at the hands of pagans.

Juliana, in effect, reenacts the combat between *Fides* and *Veterum cultura deorum* in the *Psychomachia* and embodies the steadfast opposition of the *milites Christi* in the *Peristephanon*. The devil admits that he motivates the persecution of saints and he aligns himself with Eleusius and the pagan persecutors of Juliana. As in the *Psychomachia* much of the spiritual conflict receives its meaning and vitality from the pagan-Christian antithesis. The devil is both the adversary who sends his arrow assault against the fortress of the soul and the author of evil who motivates the persecution of the faithful. The exact source of this passage may be difficult to pin down, but the resemblances between the elements of the psychomachia *topos* in Prudentius and Cynewulf's amplification are too obvious to discount.[40]

The portrayal of the saint as Christ's soldier is a common motif in hagiographic literature and often occasions brief allegorical representations of combat with devils. The devil in *Juliana* directs his attack against "metodes cempan," the maker's warrior, and phrases like "Christes cempa" and "eadig oretta" appear frequently in the Old English *Guthlac A* and *B*.[41] The eighth-century *Vita Guthlaci* by Felix of Crowland is modeled on Evagrius' Latin translation of Athanasius' *Life of St. Anthony*, in which combat with devils in the desert is explicitly described. The poets of the Old English versions

39. On the intensified dramatic quality of the poem see Rosemary Woolf's comments in her edition of *Juliana* (New York: Appleton-Century-Crofts, 1966), pp. 15–16.

40. Claes Schaar offers another, and I think less plausible, source for this passage in St. Jerome's Commentary on the Epistle to the Ephesians. See *Critical Studies in the Cynewulf Group*, pp. 30–31.

41. See G. H. Gerould, "The Old English Poems on St. Guthlac and Their Latin Source," *Modern Language Notes*, 32 (1917), 79–80, and Rosemary Woolf, "Saint's Lives," in *Continuations and Beginnings*, ed. E. G. Stanley (London: Nelson, 1966), p. 55.

of Guthlac's life, usually identified as part of a Cynewulfian school, continually heighten the episodes of spiritual warfare and employ the diction of heroic poetry to describe the encounters between the saint and the devils. These poets seem to have a deep interest in Christian psychology. This intensification of the psychological dimensions of temptation with recourse to psychomachia allegory is consistent with the portrayal of the spiritual conflict in *Juliana* and appears to be characteristic of the poems associated with Cynewulf.

A further example of amplification which follows the pattern in *Christ II* and *Juliana* appears in *The Phoenix*. The poem is based on the Latin *De ave phoenice* attributed to Lactanius.[42] The author of the Old English version adds a greater dimension of tropological and anagogical allegory to the legend. After narrating the legend and meaning of the phoenix the poet recounts that when the bird grows old it forsakes its homeland and fashions a new abode in a high tree in a forest. Then a passage is added which has no parallel in the original:

```
Dæt is se hea beam      in þam halge nu
wic weardiað,      þær him wihte ne mæg
ealdfeonda nan      atre sceþþan,
facnes tacne,      on þas frecnan tid.
þær him nest wyrceð      wið niþa gehwam
dædum domlicum      dryhtnes cempa,
þonne he ælmessan      earmum dæleð,
dugeþa leasum,      ond him dryhten gecygð,
fæder on fultum,      forð onetteð,
lænan lifes      leahtras dwæsceþ,
mirce mandæde,      healdeð meotudes æ
beald in breostum,      ond gebedu seceð
clænum gehygdum,      ond his cneo bigeð
æþele to eorþan,      flyhð yfla gehwylc,
grimme gieltas,      for godes egsan,
glædmod gyrneð      þæt he godra mæst
dæda gefremme;      þam biþ dryhten scyld
in siþa gehwane,      sigora waldend,
```

42. See N. F. Blake, ed., *The Phoenix* (Manchester: Manchester University Press, 1964), pp. 88–92, for the text of *Carmen de ave phoenice*, and pp. 17–24 on the problem of sources.

weoruda wilgiefa.   þis þa wyrta sind,
wæstma blede,   þa se wilda fugel
somnað under swegle   side ond wide
to his wicstowe,   þær he wundrum fæst
wið niþa gehwam   nest gewyrceð.
Swa nu in þam wicum   willan fremmað
mode ond mægne   meotudes cempan,
mærða tilgað.

(447–472a)

That is the high tree   in which the holy
Have their dwelling,   there the old enemies
May not harm them   at all with their poison,
Token of malice,   in this perilous time.
There God's champion   fashions himself a nest
With glorious deeds   against every attack,
When he gives alms   to the poor,
Those without weal,   and calls the Lord,
The Father as helper;   he hastens forth
From this loaned life,   quenches sin,
Black evil deeds,   holds the Maker's law
Bold in his breast,   and seeks prayer
With pure thoughts,   and bends his knee
Nobly to earth,   shuns every evil,
Grim guilt,   in fear of God,
Glad at heart   he yearns to achieve
The greatest amount of good deeds;   the Lord is his shield,
In every time,   Ruler of Victories,
Gracious giver of hosts.   These are the herbs,
The fruits of plants,   which the wild bird
Gathers far and wide   under the sky
For his dwelling place,   when it fashions its nest,
Wondrous firm,   against every attack.
So now in their dwellings   the Maker's champions
Work his will   with heart and might,
Attempt glorious deeds;   the eternal Almighty
Will grant them   blessed reward for that.

The poet expands his account of the significance of the phoenix by relating the tropological dimension of meaning to the spiritual warfare of the church. The nest in the high tree is the fortress of the faithful against the diabolical attack. God's warrior will fashion a secure stronghold and repel any attack with the weapons of glorious deeds, fidelity to God's law, and prayer.

These examples illustrate that poetic amplification through psychomachia allegory is a characteristically Cynewulfian stylistic convention. The central position assigned to *grammatica* in Anglo-Saxon monastic education provided an environment in which Latin Christian literature could be read and imitated and Latin poetics adapted for Old English poetry. Because the study of poetical figures like *allegoria* were a major part of preceptive and exegetical grammar Cynewulf was able to use the psychomachia *topos* as an aid to composition. The heightening of the psychomachia theme is consistent with what we know about the monastic environment in which Cynewulf wrote. The monk was aided in his own spiritual conflicts by meditating on the Scriptures and Christian literature, which provided wisdom for the religious life. That *Christ, Juliana, Guthlac,* and *The Phoenix* are all found in *The Exeter Book* provides further evidence for the monastic origin of the collection of poems found in this volume.

The occurrence of psychomachia allegory in the poems of Cynewulf parallels the popularity of the works of Prudentius and Gregory in Anglo-Saxon England. Although we may not be able to identify an exact source for Cynewulf's amplified passages, we may conclude that Cynewulf and his contemporaries were familiar with the poetical and exegetical versions of psychomachia allegory found in the works of Prudentius and Gregory.

JON WHITMAN

From the *Cosmographia*
to the *Divine Comedy:*
An Allegorical Dilemma

Allegory, like the Middle Ages during which it matured, has its darker and brighter sides. In one sense it disturbs our standards of clarity and order. Deliberately elusive, it "says one thing," in the traditional formula, "and means another." The very attempt to name the procedure, even by those who have sanctioned it in various degrees, exposes its obliquity. An "other-speaking" (*allegoria,* from *allos* plus *agoreuein*), the Hellenistic world named it; *inversio,* Quintilian called it in the first century; the *alieniloquium,* said Isidore in the early Middle Ages; more ominously, in the Renaissance Puttenham called it "the figure of false semblant." In a modified form something of this sense of disjunction has dominated views about allegory since the Romantics. It seems to be a peculiarly subversive technique.

In another sense, its defenders have argued, allegory tends to reconstitute the very order it seems to disrupt. By openly proclaiming the deflections of language, it directs the mind away from deception toward the truth. Historically, the defense takes various forms: allegorical language preserves the

truth for those worthy of it, or increases the pleasure of those
who penetrate its secrets, or refracts and magnifies the direct
light of truth. Indeed after a long period of decline allegory has
recently become almost what it once was: the vogue. Claiming
to correlate disparate things, it seems to be a uniquely conciliatory technique.

These conflicting tendencies reflect the dilemma of a procedure caught between the demands of division and consolidation. Allegory seeks to approach the truth by diverging from it,
to explain one thing by pointing to what it is not, as if the
darker the allegory, the brighter the illumination. The claim for
such an inverse relationship recurs throughout the history of
allegorical interpretation and composition. In the exegetical
tradition, Porphyry, interpreting Homer in the third century,
argues that the very contradictions of enigmatic language
oblige us (*anankazonta*) to seek the plain truth beyond it. In
the early Middle Ages Gregory declares that the more vile the
literal reference of Scripture, the more useful its spiritual
meaning ("quo viliora per litterae sensum, eo per spiritalem
significationem utiliora"). Even those not given to *in malo* / *in
bono* exegesis endorse such inversions in the case of divine
truth; as Aquinas maintains in the later Middle Ages, the more
remote the similitude, the better.[1] In the rhetorical tradition,
already during the first century, Quintilian sanctions contrary
relationships (*contrarium*) between apparent and actual mean-

---

1. For Porphyry's argument and similar late antique claims see J. Pépin, "A
propos de l'histoire de l'exégèse allégorique: l'absurdité, signe de l'allégorie,"
in *Studia patristica* I, ed. Kurt Aland and F. L. Cross, Texte und Untersu-
chungen, 63 (Berlin: Akademie-Verlag, 1957), 395–413. Gregory's statement
is quoted by Henri de Lubac, *Exégèse médiévale: Les quatre sens de l'Écri-
ture,* pt. I, vol. II (Paris: Aubier, 1959), p. 461; compare the severe assessment
of this strategy by A. C. Charity, *Events and Their Afterlife: The Dialectics of
Christian Typology in the Bible and Dante* (Cambridge: Cambridge University
Press, 1966), p. 109, n. 1. Aquinas, *Summa Theologiae* I, q. 1, art. 9, ad 3, is
invoking pseudo-Dionysius; see Peter Dronke, *Fabula: Explorations into the
Uses of Myth in Medieval Platonism* (Leiden: E. J. Brill, 1974), p. 44, on
pseudo-Dionysius' preference for "incongruous" images, rather than "appropriate" ones. This strategy has much in common with the theology of the *via
negativa.* Here and elsewhere I limit my references to selected examples of
widespread tendencies. In an extended study of medieval allegory to appear
soon, I explore in detail these and other issues discussed below.

ings, though he does not use the term systematically. In a larger sense the radical disposition toward reversal in allegory accounts for the long association between *allegoria* and *ironia,* from the classical period to the Renaissance. In fact, the practice of signifying by contraries continues to distinguish allegorical writing in later centuries.[2] Antithesis of this kind, however, is a fragile technique, liable to slip into contradiction or mannerism. Not endorsed by every commentator on allegory, contrariety is rather the extreme case of allegory's dilemma, the dilemma of defining one thing by reference to what it is not.

In the late Middle Ages allegory addressed the philosophic counterpart to this dilemma, and in the process it became self-conscious of its own technique. The view that things are defined by contraries, after all, is one of the oldest traditions in philosophy. As the first historian of philosophy put it, all his predecessors made their first principles contraries, "constrained as it were by the truth itself."[3] At the same time, Aristotle continued, the issue is not a simple one. In the twelfth and thirteenth centuries allegory made the broad philosophic issue a literary problem and sought to resolve both dilemmas together.

Three different but related versions of the philosophic tradition distinguish, respectively, three seminal allegories of the Middle Ages. It should be emphasized that the traditions themselves overlap; furthermore, none of them defines the "philos-

2. For Quintilian see *Institutio Oratoria* 8. 6. 44–47. On *allegoria* and *ironia* in the classical and early medieval rhetorical tradition see Reinhart Hahn, *Die Allegorie in der antiken Rhetorik,* Diss. Tübingen 1967 (Tübingen, 1967), pp. 16–17, 25, 28, and 60–77. For the practical connection between the two techniques in late medieval and Renaissance works, see Rosemond Tuve, *Allegorical Imagery: Some Mediaeval Books and Their Posterity* (Princeton: Princeton University Press, 1966). On the centrality of the "about-turn" in baroque allegory see Walter Benjamin, *The Origin of German Tragic Drama* (first pub. as *Ursprung des deutschen Trauerspiels;* Frankfurt: Suhrkamp Verlag, 1963), trans. John Osborne (London: New Left Books, 1977), pp. 175 and 232–233. For "irony" and "dialectic transfer" in more recent allegorical work see Edwin Honig, *Dark Conceit: The Making of Allegory* (Providence: Brown University Press, 1959), pp. 129–145.

3. Aristotle, *Physics* 188b27–30, trans. R. P. Hardie and R. K. Gaye, in *The Basic Works of Aristotle,* ed. Richard McKeon (New York: Random House, 1941).

ophy'' of any particular allegory, much less of any medieval period. Rather, each approach, brought into the foreground by broad changes in medieval intellectual life, illuminates a different allegorical work. The first approach might be called the absolute, or metaphysical, correlation of opposites. It divides the very universe into contraries, arguing that one side implies the other. In the first truly philosophic allegory of the Middle Ages, the *Cosmographia,* Bernard Silvestris seeks to resolve this division. The limits of such grand, mid-twelfth-century strategies, along with the increasing influence of Aristotelian and Arabic scientific treatises, encourage closer investigations of the natural world itself. The natural world, however, has oppositions of its own; the effort to define them might be called the relative, or generative, correlation of opposites. It argues that everything in the sublunary world develops by reference to its contrary, and it preoccupies Alain de Lille's more troubled vision in the *De planctu naturae,* written somewhat later in the century. The relation between nature and the human mind receives new attention in the late twelfth and thirteenth centuries. In what might be called the perceptual, or epistemological, correlation of opposites, the mind itself becomes the center of action. This approach stresses that an individual can *know* something only by knowing its contrary. A century after the *De planctu,* in the era of Aquinas and Bonaventure, Jean de Meun's *Roman de la Rose* dramatizes the strategy. Two generations later, Dante, drawing upon other sources, consolidates and transforms these three approaches in the *Divine Comedy.* Here there is space for only a brief sketch of such developments in allegory, broadly suggesting some shifts in orientation during the late Middle Ages.

The first of these approaches, the absolute correlation of contraries, makes the universe itself the framework for the conflicting tendencies of division and consolidation. Its extreme expression is dualism, in which absolute principles of light and darkness, good and evil, struggle against each other. It acquires a more conciliatory and systematic form in Plato. Here the perfect world of Being—uniform, indissoluble, and unchangeable—is reflected, rather than antagonized, by the imperfect world of Becoming—multiform, dissoluble, and changeable. Though the precise terms and analyses vary, the effort to mediate between these two realms preoccupies ancient and early medieval philosophy, from the Pythagorean and Academic controversies over the relation between the One and the dyad, or material principle; to the Neoplatonists' cosmic dialectic between the One and all other things, which emanate from the One and return to it; to Boethius' distinction between simple being, on the one hand, and composite beings, on the other, which participate in being, but which differ in *esse* and *id quod est*. The realm of the other is thus divided from the One not only externally, as it were, but internally, by its own disparities and limitations. The natural philosophers of the twelfth century adapt the terminology and the cosmology to a creationist perspective. "It is well said that Oneness creates matter," writes Thierry of Chartres. "For from Oneness [*unitas*] descends otherness [*alteritas*]," and "the other is called 'other' by reference to the One." Eerily prescient of our modern talk about "alterity," such efforts to reconcile the two sides of the universe help to make the world itself an image, the *imago mundi,* as if to prepare it for exploitation in allegory.[4]

4. For Plato's distinction between Being and Becoming see, for example, *Timaeus* 27D–29D, with *Phaedo* 80B, in *Plato,* vol. I, ed. and trans. Harold North Fowler (Cambridge, Mass.: Harvard University Press, and London: William Heinemann, 1914). For variations and controversies among the Pythagoreans, the Academy, and Aristotle, see Harold Cherniss, *Aristotle's Criticism of Plato and the Academy,* I (Baltimore: Johns Hopkins University Press, 1944), pp. 83–173 and 479–487, and Philip Merlan, *From Platonism to Neoplatonism,* 2nd ed. (The Hague: Martinus Nijhoff, 1960). On the Neoplatonic One and the problem of multiplicity see *The Cambridge History of Later Greek and Early Medieval Philosophy,* ed. A. H. Armstrong (Cambridge: Cambridge University Press, 1967; rpt. with corrections, 1970), especially pts. 1, 3, and 4. For Boethius' distinction see *The Theological Tractates. The Consolation of Philosophy,* ed. and trans. H. F. Stewart and E. K. Rand, rev. trans. S. J. Tester (Cambridge, Mass.: Harvard University Press, 1973), *Quomodo substantiae,* ll. 28–48, and *De Consolatione* III, pr. 11 and pr. 12. On the development of this distinction from Boethius to the twelfth-century natural philosophers see Tullio Gregory, *Anima mundi: La filosofia di Guglielmo di Conches e la Scuola di Chartres* (Florence: G. C. Sansoni, 1955), pp. 59–67 and 81–97. For the statement by Thierry (or one of his "school") see the *Commentum super Boethii librum de Trinitate,* in *Commentaries on Boethius by Thierry of*

That allegory is the *Cosmographia*.[5] In telling his story of
creation Bernard Silvestris adapts the philosophic distinction
between Oneness and the diverse ("unitas et diversum," *Mic.*
13. 1) to the allegorical distinction between truth and obliquity.
He divides the literal action of the one God into the personified
transactions of diverse characters. Matter (Hyle or Silva), of
course, is the paradigm for this diversity. A mass discordant
with itself ("sibi dissona massa"), abounding in darkness
("noctis habundat"), able to frighten its own Creator ("Auc-
torem terrere," *Meg.* 1. 19–31), it seems to pose an almost
Manichaean threat to unity.[6] In Bernard's poem, though, as in
the more systematic philosophic tradition, all forces beside
God himself display in some measure that diversity on the
other side of the One. They are but partial images of his undivided truth. Even Noys, the "mind of God," is but the "image
of unfailing life" ("Vite viventis ymago," *Meg.* 1. 4), or, as
Bernard later revealingly puts it, as if to check himself, "the
image, or perhaps I should call it a face inscribed with the
image, of the Father" ("imago nescio dicam an vultus, patris
imagine consignatus," *Meg.* 4. 5. 2). Such personifications can
divide the narrative foreground only when God himself re-
cedes into the background. The One's division into the many is

---

Chartres and His School, ed. Nikolaus M. Häring (Toronto: Pontifical Institute of Mediaeval Studies, 1971), p. 81, ll. 86–89: "Bene autem ex eo quod
unitas est materiam creare dicitur. Ab unitate namque descendit alteritas . . .
Alterum etenim ab uno alterum dicitur." On the twelfth-century development
of the *imago mundi* tradition see M.-Th. d'Alverny, "Le cosmos symbolique
du XIIe siècle," *Archives d'histoire doctrinale et littéraire du moyen âge*
(hereafter *AHDL*), 28 (1953), 31–81. For an overview of the ancient and medieval tradition of the One see Etienne Gilson, *Being and Some Philosophers,*
2nd ed. (Toronto: Pontifical Institute of Mediaeval Studies, 1952), chap. 1,
"On Being and the One."

5. Quotations refer to the *Cosmographia,* ed. Peter Dronke (Leiden: E. J.
Brill, 1978), cited by section and line number in the case of verse passages, by
section, paragraph, and line number in the case of prose passages. Translations are based on *The "Cosmographia" of Bernardus Silvestris,* trans.
Winthrop Wetherbee (New York: Columbia University Press, 1973).

6. Gregory, *Anima mundi,* p. 199, says that Bernard's Matter is "character-
ized by adjectives of a frankly Manichaean cast." Strictly speaking, however,
Bernard's position is not dualistic; see Theodore Silverstein, "The Fabulous
Cosmogony of Bernardus Silvestris," *Modern Philology,* 46 (1948), 98–104.

no longer a philosophic issue alone. It is inseparable from the literary dilemma of truth's refraction into the images of allegory.

The effort to resolve this dilemma is thus a test not only of the claims of this world, but of the technique of allegory. The opening scene of the poem best dramatizes Bernard's strategy. It describes the primal moment when rudimentary matter pleads for refinement:

> Silva, intractable, a formless chaos, a hostile coalescence, the motley appearance of being, a mass discordant with itself, longs in her turbulence for a tempering power; in her crudity for form; in her rankness for cultivation. Yearning to emerge from her ancient tumult, she requires the shaping influence of number and the bonds of harmony.

> > Silva rigens, informe chaos, concretio pugnax,
> > Discolor Usie vultus, sibi dissona massa,
> > Turbida temperiem, formam rudis, hispida cultum
> > Optat, et a veteri cupiens exire tumultu,
> > Artifices numeros et musica vincla requirit.
> > > (*Meg.* 1. 18–22)

In this daring scene the very universe seems split in two, with Silva near the far end, as it were, and Noys near the other. To bring these two extremes closer to each other Bernard here plays on the double-edged concept of *want,* referring on the one hand to the recipient's passive need, on the other hand to the petitioner's active desire. The attributes of longing (*Optat*), yearning (*cupiens*), and requiring (*requirit*) hint just enough about desire to give matter fictional effects, without deviating too much from matter's actual deficiency to vitiate the text philosophically. Severely constricted in fact, Silva begins to expand in the fiction. What she actually requires she seems to request; what she actually lacks she seems to seek. In a sense her literal liabilities are her allegorical assets, impelling her toward Noys.[7]

---

7. On the philosophic foundation for matter's "desire" in Aristotelian, Hermetic, and Calcidian texts see Brian Stock, *Myth and Science in the Twelfth*

Noys, for her part, responds in kind. Like Matter, the figurative "mind of God" can also face in two directions. Serenely provident in fact, it is deeply concerned in the fiction. Noys seems "old and sad" ("vetus et gravis," *Meg.* 1. 57); she herself admits that she is "indeed troubled" ("Pertesum michi," *Meg.* 2. 2. 14; editor's line numbering corrected) by the deprivation in the universe. As Silva obliquely aspires to her, she obliquely inclines to it. The other side of a Matter that speaks is a Mind that listens.

As a result an extraordinary convergence between the most divergent principles begins to develop. Silva, a "mass discordant with itself," continually troubled in her own nature, is somehow bursting with vitality, yearning for the formative power of Noys. Noys, on the other hand, who is by definition supremely vital and filled with form, is troubled and concerned. It is the division of personality in these characters that allows them to be reconciled with each other—the very division that signifies their distinction from the One. Overlapping in part, they tend to reconstitute the divine order as a whole. By seeing each opposite from the point of view of its counterpart, Bernard dramatizes in literature what the philosophic reconcilers of dualism had long been yearning to show. Seen from both sides, God's condescension to matter *is* matter's ascension to God.

In the process the austere antitheses of early medieval allegory begin to acquire a more fluid narrative motion. The flexibility remains limited; it does not achieve the cool sophistication of later allegory, when by leaving Una one meets Duessa. Still, encounters in the *Cosmographia* have a subtle sense of anticipation about them, as if each character knew the other's mind and fulfilled its needs. Thus Nature divines from the start that her appeal to Noys will be granted (*Meg.* 1. 11–17); indeed, during the very act of appeal Noys is already consenting to it (*Meg.* 2. 1. 19–21). Urania responds in advance to Na-

---

Century: A Study of Bernard Silvester (Princeton: Princeton University Press, 1972), pp. 97–125. On the Neoplatonic longing of matter, adapted by John the Scot, see Wetherbee's introduction in *The "Cosmographia,"* pp. 37–38 and 54. While the anticipations of Bernard's conception are sometimes striking, he first deploys the philosophic principle in a coherent literary framework.

ture's potential question (*Mic.* 3. 13. 3–5, and 4. 1–2). Physis is already following nature ("naturam . . . sequebatur"), when Nature and Urania arrive, who help to fulfill in act nature's potentiality to construct man, about which Physis dreams ("Plasmaturam quoque hominis—de nature possibilitate coniciens—quadam velud sub ymagine sompniabat," *Mic.* 9. 6. 7–8, and 9. 8. 1–2). It is not until Dante that allegory fully invokes the relation between potentiality and act to reconcile different degrees of the truth. Already in the *Cosmographia,* though, diverse characters are fulfilling each other, fitting together like component parts of a whole.

The most striking expression of this insight occurs in the great vision at the midpoint of the poem's action, when the greater universe is complete, and the smaller universe is about to begin: the final chapter of *Megacosmos.* The chapter recapitulates all that has gone before, but also anticipates all that is to come, the eternal transformation of diversity into coherence. At this intense, central moment, in fact, the poem's diverse characters seem to coalesce:

> Thus, from the life of Mind, from the spirit of Silva, from the World Soul, from the very quick of created life, the eternity of things grows together . . . For the universe is a continuum, a chain in which nothing may be dispersed or broken off. Thus, roundness, the perfect form, determines its shape.

> Ex Mentis igitur vita, Silve spiritu, Anima mundi, mundialium vegetatione, rerum eternitas coalescit . . . Mundus enim quiddam continuum, et in ea cathena nichil dis/sipabile vel abruptum. Unde illum rotunditas, forma perfectior, circumscribit.
>
> (*Meg.* 4. 8. 10–12, and 4. 9. 5–8)

In this circularity it is difficult to tell just what is the source of life: Mind, Silva, the World Soul—or all of them at once. It is a cosmos bursting on all sides with vitality, where ultimately there is no up or down, where the circumference defines the center. The eternity of things, says Bernard in that astonishing verb, does not merely preside over all: it "grows together," it "coalesces" (*coalescit*). Even eternity, after all, is divided, divided into time, and yet this very division recoils upon itself and returns to eternity. "From oneness it separates into number, from the unmoving into movement" ("De unitate ad numerum, de stabilitate digreditur ad momentum"), only to be "resolved into the bosom of eternity" ("in eternitatis resolvitur gremium," *Meg.* 4. 11. 4–7). The sentiment is not new; its function here is striking. The display of time returning upon itself, of temporal division flowing into eternal vision, is the goal of Bernard's whole allegory, which exploits factions to show the integrity underlying them, which deploys the others to generate the One.

Accordingly, at the end of his poem, when Bernard glimpses the end of time, even his language whirls dizzyingly about itself:

> The nature of the universe flows back into itself, and so survives itself; it abides, nourished by its very flowing away. For that which is cast outward runs back into the sum of things, and dies not once that it may die often.

> > Influit ipsa sibi mundi natura, superstes,
> > Permanet et fluxu pascitur usque suo:
> > Scilicet ad summam rerum iactura recurrit,
> > Nec semel ut possit sepe perire perit.
> > (*Mic.* 14. 171–174; editor's punctuation omitted in last line)

The universe's centrifugal tendencies (*iactura*) are but the other side of its centripetal ones (*recurrit*). It expands and contracts at once. "Not once, that it may often" ("Nec semel ut possit"), the last phrase begins, as if to suggest continuing activity, like the cycle just described. But then the last two words of the phrase come crashing in on this activity—"it dies to die" ("perire perit")—only to cancel themselves out in turn, by doubling up upon themselves. Like the universe as a whole, the text contradicts the act of death in the very process of asserting it. Death is made permanent because even it continues to die, so that life may continue to live.

There is a darker side to this luminous vision. In the eternal flux all composite things, including man himself, must dissolve (*Mic.* 14. 175–178). For all their glories, the divisions of this world and the dualities of allegory remain images, the *imago*

melioris mundi (*Mic.* 10. 9). Bernard never denies the disparity
between all things and God. Instead, he exploits the disparity
until such dualities recoil upon themselves and proclaim the
One. In his vision man approaches Heaven not by renouncing
earth, but by probing it in all its plenitude, knowing that in the
end this plenitude declares the plenitude of God (*Meg.* 4. 11.
2–3). Like Silva in the opening scene of the poem, we truly
receive the light from above only as we obliquely aspire from
below. Alienation from the One is our dilemma; the *alieniloquium* is our consolation.

The *Cosmographia* is an inspiring work. Already in Bernard's time, though, newly translated scientific treatises are
complicating this view of the world as *imago melioris mundi*.
Images are not enough; substantive forces need to be scrutinized. Indeed, the poem itself exposes the limits of its mirror
vision, where reflections reflect upon each other. The world
turns in cycles; man exhausts his life. Perhaps this side of the
universe, in its very otherness, does reflect the One. In itself,
though, it remains in limbo.

This is the dilemma of Alain de Lille in his *De planctu naturae*. Here, in the case of man, division has turned into dissi-
pation. To overcome it Alain seeks to distinguish a principle of
integrity within the natural realm itself. His allegory thus
brings into the foreground a tradition in which the natural
world in its own right is defined by contraries.

Though this tradition overlaps with the absolute division between the world as a whole and God, it has its own emphasis.
It makes the concrete object itself the focus for the confrontation of opposites and argues that the object's shift from one extreme toward the other constitutes change. As Plato puts it,
absolute opposites themselves cannot interact with their
counterparts, but concrete objects develop only by participat-
ing in the contraries. "The weaker is generated from the
stronger," writes Plato, "and the slower from the quicker; the
worse from the better, and the more just from the more un-
just." It is Aristotle who clearly distinguishes matter itself as
susceptible to either extreme, but identical with neither. This
distinction gives new point to the natural world; matter becomes potentiality, the potential for form, as well as formless-

ness, and substance itself is distinguished by its ability to admit
contrary qualities. In Stoic and Neoplatonic writing the shift
from privation to fulfillment acquires a new moral design, in
which the different degrees of perfection contribute to the harmony of the whole. Augustine, drawing upon this tradition, explains the movement of historical events themselves as the
shift between contraries of good and evil, and he associates
this movement with the literary technique of antithesis. God,
he claims, enriches the course of "world history by the kind of
antithesis which gives beauty to a poem." The stress on moral
regeneration through contraries converges, in Augustine, Isidore, and others, with the ancient medical tradition of healing
by antidotes. As Isidore puts it, cures may be wrought "by
contraries, as cold by warm or dry by moist, just as in man
pride cannot be cured unless it is cured by humility." Later in
the Middle Ages Anselm brings a new precision to the sense in
which the human will arbitrates between these extremes, despite the fact that human language may obliquely attribute this
movement to abstract privations themselves. "When justice
withdraws from where it was, we say that injustice approaches," he points out, although it is the individual himself
who deserts justice. The framing of the natural world by contraries is a broad, varied tradition with different foundations.
As a whole, though, this tradition stresses the generative element in antithesis, the shift in the object's own nature as it
moves from one contrary to another.[8]

8. For Plato's argument see *Phaedo* 102D–103C and 70E–71B. For Aristotle see *Physics* 188b21–26; 190b29–35; 192a3–34 (quoted by Calcidius);
Metaphysics 1051a4–17; and *Categories* 4b17–19. On moral antithesis in Stoicism see E. Zeller, *The Stoics, Epicureans, and Sceptics,* rev. ed., trans. Os-
wald J. Reichel (London: Longmans, Green, and Co., 1892), pp. 187 and 190;
on this perspective in Neoplatonism see Arthur O. Lovejoy, *The Great Chain
of Being: A Study of the History of an Idea* (Cambridge, Mass.: Harvard University Press, 1936), pp. 64–66. For Augustine see *The City of God,* trans.
Henry Bettenson (Harmondsworth: Penguin, 1972), XI, 18. For Isidore see *Isidori Hispalensis Episcopi: Etymologiarvm sive Originvm Libri XX,* ed. W. M.
Lindsay, 2 vols. (Oxford: Clarendon Press, 1911), 4. 9. 5, a passage to which
Wilfrid Bonser refers in *The Medical Background of Anglo-Saxon England*
(London: The Wellcome Historical Medical Library, 1963), p. 40. For Augustine's use of this tradition see *De doctrina christiana* I, 14. Both authors also
invoke the countertradition of cures by likenesses. For Anselm see *S. Anselmi
opera omnia,* ed. F. S. Schmitt, I (1938; rpt. ed., Edinburgh: Thomas Nelson

Such internal transformations preoccupy Alain de Lille's *De planctu naturae*.[9] In the perverse world of this poem, though, the prevailing movement between contraries is inverted, leading not to generation, but to degeneration. It is as if man had no sooner emerged in the Garden—emerging, with the *Cosmographia*, into sophisticated allegory—than he and his language had fatally fallen. The poem opens with the narrator's own reversal, as he changes "laughter to tears, joy to sorrow" ("In lacrimas risus, in luctus gaudia uerto"), upon seeing the decrees of Nature fall silent ("silere," 1. 1–3). Human nature as a whole is divided—not only from the One, but against itself,

> When Venus, fighting with Venus, makes men women;
> When with her bewitching art she unmans men.
>
> Cum Venus in Venerem pugnans illos facit illas
> Cumque sui magica deuirat arte uiros.

> (1. 5–6)

The objects, like the words, undermine their own foundation. They no longer subtly reflect each other, as in the *Cosmographia*, but undertake reflexive actions. By feeding off themselves they turn away from the One toward its opposite, the void.

The failure to reflect a counterpart vitiates figurative language itself. Man

> is both predicate and subject; the same ending is made twofold.
> He spreads the laws of grammar too far.
> He denies that he is a man of Nature, fashioned in art—
> The barbaric alien. Art does not please him, but rather trope.
> And yet such trope could not be called metaphor;
> Rather, the figure sinks into vice.

---

and Sons, 1946), 275: "Quando iustitia inde recedit ubi erat, dicimus accedere iniustitiam." On the oblique approach to abstract privations see Desmond Paul Henry, *The Logic of Saint Anselm* (Oxford: Oxford University Press, 1967).

9. Quotations refer to the edition of Nikolaus M. Häring, "Alan of Lille, 'De Planctu naturae,'" *Studi medievali*, 3rd Ser., 19 (1978), 797–879. Translations are based on *The Complaint of Nature*, trans. Douglas M. Moffat (New York: Henry Holt and Company, 1908), and *The Plaint of Nature*, trans. James J. Sheridan (Toronto: Pontifical Institute of Mediaeval Studies, 1980).

Predicat et subicit, fit duplex terminus idem.
Gramatice leges ampliat ille nimis.
Se negat esse uirum Nature, factus in arte
Barbarus. Ars illi non placet, immo tropus.
Non tamen ista tropus poterit translatio dici.
In uicium melius ista figura cadit.

(1. 19–24)

Moral depravity is inseparable from rhetorical excess; the alienation of man barbarizes the *alieniloquium*. In the twistings and coilings of this fallen world men try to de-nature the very nature of nature ("nature naturalia denaturare," 8. 20). Flourishing in vice they deflower the flower of form ("forme florem in uicia efflorendo deflorant," 8. 66–67). Such reversals dominate the poem: the famous meter on love's oxymorons (9); Venus' adultery with Antigenius (some mss, "Antigamus," antimarriage); their bastard son, called "Iocus" *per antifrasim* (10. 131–154). Here, at least, the baroque, schematic imagination that Alain displays throughout his works has special point. With its images of grammar, its figures of division, its obsession with *integumenta*, the whole allegory is constantly talking about itself, preoccupied with its own introversions.[10]

The *De planctu naturae* thus explores a defective side to the realm of otherness that the *Cosmographia* relegated somewhat to the background. The world is not only poised as a counter to God, whom it reflects. It is also suspended above the abyss, into which it can slip. For Alain the problem here is not so much how to reach the One, as how to escape the void. This shift in perspective has its literary consequences. The more objects tend toward privation, the more their doubling up, so promising in the *Cosmographia*, simply deepens the crisis. When Alain writes that "fraud deceives itself by fraud," and "deception presses upon deception" ("fraus quoque fraudem / Fallit fraude, dolo sic dolus instat," 11. 15–16), it is plain that the recoiling technique of Bernard Silvestris has

10. Among a multitude of examples see the grammar of love (10. 30–114); the divisions of clothing, narrative, and communion (8. 161–172, 249, and 16. 212); and the *integumenta*-cloaks of Nature, Genius, Truth, and Falsehood (2. 138–292, and 18. 64–110).

turned against itself. In a larger sense this reflexive, self-destructive tendency seems to undermine the very position of
Nature, who, before telling a tale filled with the figures of poetic fancy, herself criticizes the fancies of the poets, as if to
give her own story the lie.[11] In the *De planctu* natural objects
keep slipping into privations, as fictions keep slipping into
falsehoods.

In this respect Nature's self-conscious literary defense as
she begins her tale becomes a decisive turning point in the
poem. After her initial indictment of human vice and her critique of poetic integuments, she plans to speak "in a loftier and
nobler style" ("Ab altiori . . . excellentiorique stilo"). She
will not "profane profanities with new profanities of speech"
("profanis uerborum nouitatibus prophanare prophana"). It is
necessary to distinguish oneself from such evil,

> to gild with the golden ornaments of modest words matters for
> modesty, and to clothe them with the variegated colors of beau-
> tiful expression.

> pudenda aureis pudicorum uerborum faleris inaurare uariisque
> uenustorum dictorum coloribus inuestire.

Sometimes, continues Nature, the deformity of things should
be expressed with deformity of speech. In the discourse to follow, however, she will bestow upon these monstrous vices "a
cloak of well-sounding language" ("uiciorum monstris eu-
phonia orationis uolo pallium elargiri," 8. 182–195).

In this critical passage, so troubling to the modern taste for
frankness, the speaker and the story seek, as it were, to rise to
the occasion, and the poetic *integumentum* itself acquires a
subtle new defense. Traditionally, as we have noted, oblique
language had many functions: to preserve the truth, to enhance
the pleasure of discovering the truth, to magnify the truth, and

11. On this turning-inward of the fiction upon itself, which Richard Hamilton Green, "Alan of Lille's *De Planctu Naturae*," *Speculum,* 31 (1956), 670,
calls "the fable-within-a-fable," see Winthrop Wetherbee's acute remarks in
*Platonism and Poetry in the Twelfth Century: The Literary Influence of the
School of Chartres* (Princeton: Princeton University Press, 1972), pp. 193–
197: Nature "compounds the dilemma by coining myths of her own."

the like. In all these cases, though, the *integumentum* existed
for the sake of the good that it covered. This traditional view
appears prominently in the *De planctu naturae,* most famously
in Nature's declaration that she veils herself to preserve the
naked truth from defilement (6. 121–127).[12] Still, as Nature's
own comments about the integuments of the poets suggest,
such coverings, however splendid, bring "the shadow of fal-
sity" ("falsitatis umbra," 8. 141) to the truth; they are defective when compared with the good itself. By contrast, as she
begins her own poetic discourse, Nature has the opposite extreme in mind. She embraces *integumenta* here not so much to
protect the plain truth as to escape from bare falsehood. When
compared with falsehood, allegory is no longer defective; it
has a positive, if limited, value of its own. The real lie is not
allegory, but the fraud that confesses its own deception, the
nakedness that bares itself shamelessly. The real truth in a
fallen world is the recognition that we have left the Garden and
must cover our nakedness. In this darkened world allegory is
more chastened than in the *Cosmographia;* it does not so easily reflect the divine truth. At the same time, however, by de-
flecting duplicity, it is finally acquiring a certain integrity in its
own right. Like Nature herself, it is defined by reference to opposites, poised between formlessness and form, a potentiality
capable of either, but distinguished from both.

Such poise, however fragile, salvages Nature's own position
in the *De planctu* as a whole. Both her long discourse and the
excommunication scene have their parodic sides, of course. If
Nature becomes newly self-conscious, she also keeps betraying her own deficiencies; she is the ancestor of the prolix Nature of the *Roman de la Rose*. If the excommunication imitates
the trump of doom, it does not actually bring Grace down from
Heaven. On the other hand Nature is finally finding her own

12. On the history of the terms *involucrum* and *integumentum* see M.-D.
Chenu, "*Involucrum*: le mythe selon les théologiens médiévaux," *AHDL,* 30
(1955), 75–79; Édouard Jeauneau, "L'usage de la notion d'*integumentum* à
travers les gloses de Guillaume de Conches," *AHDL,* 32 (1957), 35–100; Stock,
Myth and Science, pp. 49–62; and Dronke, *Fabula,* p. 25, nn. 2 and 3; pp.
48–49, n. 2; p. 52, n. 1; and pp. 56–57, n. 2. In chap. 1 Dronke suggests some
subtle shifts in emphasis in William of Conches and Abelard.

voice, reversing her "silence" at the beginning of the poem (1. 3). The excommunication confirms the potential of this world to reflect the divine, by distinguishing natural integrity from unnatural deprivation.[13] Instead of vicious men "denaturing the nature of nature," now they are "degraded from the *grace* of Nature" ("a Nature gracia degradetur," 18. 144–145). This celebrated scene is not exactly parody or heresy. Nature here possesses Grace not actually, but obliquely—in the language developing in Alain's time, potentially. She is acquiring not new force, but new clarity, as a middle term capable of moving from one opposite toward the other.

For all its promise this middle position between extremes never fully develops in the *De planctu naturae*. "Nature" is still too comprehensive a figure, like her counterpart in the *Cosmographia*, to be at the same time a clear center of consciousness, shifting from one side of herself to the other. It is rather a particular nature, human nature, that must change, and despite the perceiving narrator the allegory only vaguely suggests how this transition can occur. Further, despite her self-conscious claims, Nature's (and Alain's) style never truly shifts into a higher register when she creates her own *integumenta*. Alain seeks a more distinguished style in the *Anticlaudianus*, but there even the Almighty cannot quite disentangle himself from rhetorical involutions, as he promises that the world, "though now deflowered, may spring up anew in a single flower" ("Iam defloratus in flore resurgeret uno"). Allegory needs a more precise center of consciousness and a clearer statement of its principles.[14]

At great cost it achieves these goals in Jean de Meun's *Roman de la Rose*. With its alert narrator, poised to strike, shifting between strategies quite plainly exposed, Jean's poem brings not only Alain's work, but that of Guillaume de Lorris, to a logical conclusion. In the process Jean organizes his alle-

13. On obliquely reflecting the divine by refraining from evil compare Alain's *Regulae,* 97; *PL* 210: 673A.
14. On *Natura* and *humana natura* see Stock, *Myth and Science,* p. 224. For the *Anticlaudianus* passage see the edition of R. Bossuat (Paris: J. Vrin, 1955), 6. 396.

gory around a third tradition of opposites, in which the individual personality *perceives* by contraries.

In its various forms this tradition shifts the emphasis from the dualities of the world to the discriminations of the human mind. As a method of scientific definition, dividing an object into its opposite components plays a central role in the early Academy. Carefully qualified by Aristotle, diaeresis becomes a way to define a genus, since the specific differences of a genus are contrary to each other. At the same time the need for the human mind to know contraries develops a more practical, experiential side. Aristotle argues that the mind recognizes evil by good, and black by white. Two centuries later the Skeptic Carneades carries the general strategy to its extreme. Since pleasure can be known only in contrast to pain, continence in contrast to incontinence, he claims, no virtue can be ascribed to God. If this double edge to experience challenges God, it consoles man. Honey, says Boethius' Philosophy, is sweeter if a bitter taste precedes it. Abelard applies the argument to human reasoning itself. It is necessary to know deceptive sophistry as well as legitimate dialectic, he writes, since "no one would attentively know the virtues who was ignorant of the vices." The challenge to God, incidentally, does not go unanswered. As Aquinas puts this controversial issue, God does know evil, since he "would not know good things perfectly unless he also knew evil things." Indeed, it is a general principle that "one opposite is known through the other." As a whole this general tradition gives an epistemological, even a psychological, emphasis to the correlation of contraries. In effect it divides the mind itself between good and evil.[15]

15. For Aristotle on diaeresis and contraries see especially *Posterior Analytics* 96b25–97a6 and *Metaphysics* 1037b27–1038a35; on Aristotle's relation to the Academy see Cherniss, *Aristotle's Criticism,* chap. 1, especially pp. 41–42, 48, and 61–62. On the recognition of evil and black, see Aristotle's *De anima* 430b21–23. On Carneades see Zeller, *Stoics,* p. 547. For Boethius see *De Consolatione* III, metr. 1. For Abelard's statement, "Nemo enim virtutes diligenter noverit, qui vitia ignoret," see *Petri Abaelardi opera,* ed. Victor Cousin, I (Paris: Aug. Durand, 1849), 697, to which Jean Jolivet refers in *Arts du langage et théologie chez Abélard* (Paris: J. Vrin, 1969), p. 270. For Aquinas' arguments see *Summa Theologiae* I, q. 14, art. 10, and I, q. 48, art. 1, trans. based on Anton C. Pegis, *Basic Writings of Saint Thomas Aquinas*

The strategy is made to order for Jean de Meun.[16] Jean is not the first to organize allegorical action around the shifting perspectives of an individual mind. This procedure had acquired increasing sophistication in the late twelfth and early thirteenth centuries, culminating in Guillaume's *Roman de la Rose*.[17] Jean, however, gives the technique an acute, dialectical edge, using the major characters to expose—sometimes excessively —the logical implications of diverse points of view.[18] Unlike Guillaume, who dramatizes the interaction between two people, Jean stresses the alternative orientations of a single intelligence.

This dialectical spirit tends to transform allegorical activity into the literal analysis of intellectual and emotional dispositions. Significantly, Jean opens his story with the approach of Reason, who transforms the question of love into the technique of *sic et non:*

> Quenois le tu point? — Oïl, dame.
> — Non fez. — Si faz. — De quoi, par t'ame?
> — De tant qu'il. . . .

(ll. 4223–4225)

(New York: Random House, 1945), I; compare *Supplementum tertiae partis Summae Theologiae*, q. 94, art. 1. Not every Christian theologian took this position on God's knowledge; see, for example, Peter Damian, *Lettre sur la toute-puissance divine*, ed. and trans. André Cantin (Paris: Les Éditions du Cerf, 1972), pp. 390 and 396. A countertradition, that similars are perceived by similars, may originate with the Pythagoreans; it has a quite different foundation.

16. Quotations refer to *Le Roman de la Rose*, ed. Félix Lecoy, 3 vols. (Paris: Champion, 1965–1970). Translations are based on *The Romance of the Rose*, trans. Charles Dahlberg (Princeton: Princeton University Press, 1971).

17. See Charles Muscatine, "The Emergence of Psychological Allegory in Old French Romance," *PMLA*, 68 (1953), 1160–82; Hans Robert Jauss, "Form und Auffassung der Allegorie in der Tradition der *Psychomachia* (von Prudentius zum ersten *Romanz de la Rose*)," *Medium aevum vivum: Festschrift für Walther Bulst*, ed. Hans Robert Jauss and Dieter Schaller (Heidelberg: Carl Winter, 1960), especially pp. 191 and 196–202; and Marc-René Jung, *Études sur le poème allégorique en France au moyen âge*, Romanica Helvetica, 82 (Bern: Editions Francke, 1971), especially pp. 241–310.

18. See, for example, Alan M. F. Gunn, *The Mirror of Love: A Reinterpretation of "The Romance of the Rose"* (Lubbock, Tex.: Texas Tech Press, 1951), and Patricia J. Eberle, "The Lovers' Glass: Nature's Discourse on Optics and the Optical Design of the *Romance of the Rose*," *University of Toronto Quarterly*, 46 (1977), 241–262.

It seems that Jean's contemporaries have taught the debaters a trick or two: *Utrum. —Videtur quod. —Sed contra. —Respondeo*. This analytic impulse ruthlessly undermines the delicate figures of Guillaume, to say nothing of the bolder flourishes of Alain de Lille. When Reason seeks to expose the lover's lack of knowledge ("sanz sciance"), he invokes Alain's oxymorons: love is drunken thirst, thirsty drunkenness, and so on (ll. 4249–4304). "Lady," says the lover at the end of this list of cancellations, "there are so many contraries [*contraire*] in this lesson that I can learn nothing [*neant*] from it" (ll. 4334–4335). Perhaps he is speaking for the reader as well. A proper *disputatio* requires the clear distinction of alternatives, not their conflation. Setting sensual love to one side, Reason proceeds to explain a reasoned love not contrary ("n'est pas contraire," l. 4734) to her purpose. She clarifies the contraries; the lover must choose between them.

Unfortunately this austere distinction between alternatives deepens the allegorical dilemma. In the *De planctu naturae* it was possible at least to make sensual love reflect divine love, by distinguishing natural affection from unnatural defection. By contrast Jean no sooner marshals the host of natural impulses—Friend, the Old Woman, Love—into the grand design of Nature, than he subverts any such oblique strategy. First, Nature herself relegates the kind of dreamworld in which the lover moves to the level of lies (*mançonge*, ll. 18331–18334; compare also ll. 18359–18364), thereby reversing Guillaume's celebrated claim in the first lines of his poem ("ne sont mie mençongier," ll. 1–5). Then, in the great excommunication scene, modeled on the *De planctu*, Genius not only excommunicates those who do not follow Nature; he irrepressibly undercuts those who do. Urging the forces of Love toward their natural consummation, he devastatingly cuts the ground out from under them, by insisting with each exhortation that the natural framework in which they operate pales in comparison with the heavenly park. It is as a fable (*fable*) to the truth (*voir*), he says; and lest we draw any hasty allegorical conclusions he stresses that it is "nothing" in comparison with the heavenly enclosure ("neanz / au regart de ceste closture," ll. 20249–20263). The forces of Love are, so to speak, damned if they don't, and damned if they do. The whole allegorical enterprise seems on the verge of collapse before the strict demands of divine propriety (l. 20543). For all its passion Jean's world is more difficult to translate into divine terms than Alain's, and as for the glorious vision of Bernard Silvestris, that dream is irrevocably fading away.

Faced with a world that resists the old metaphors, Jean turns inward at the close of his poem to explore the possibilities of human perception. He grants the last word to the lover, who invokes the dialectic of perception to elevate his quest. As if to give Hugh of St. Victor's famous exhortation to "learn everything" an experiential twist, the lover argues that "it is good to *try* everything" ("qu'il fet bon de tout essaier," l. 21521). After all,

> he who has not tried evil will scarcely know anything of the good.

> qui mal essaié n'avra
> ja du bien guieres ne savra.
>
> (ll. 21533–21534)

It is as if the correlation of opposites vindicated the realm of experience, no matter how roguish the behavior. Yet the same dialectic of perception exposes the deficiencies of such behavior:

> Thus things go by contraries; the one is the gloss of the other. And if anyone wants to define the one, he must remember the other, or he will never, by any intention, give it a definition.

> Ainsinc va des contreres choses,
> les unes sunt des autres gloses;
> et qui l'une an veust defenir,
> de l'autre li doit souvenir,
> ou ja, par nule antancion,
> n'i metra diffinicion.
>
> (ll. 21543–21548)

By encompassing both extremes the mind can shift from one object to its gloss. Instead of contrasting the two contraries in his mind, however, the lover enacts one of them in fact. While he thus distorts his own rule, his principle suggests that process by which the turning of the mind can transform the realm of experience itself.

In an allegory that constantly digresses into the external world, then, the internal world is acquiring a new importance. These two tendencies, in fact, complement each other. For Jean's generation the outside world is increasingly becoming a hard body of data, losing some of its allegorical resonances, demanding literal exposition. This process remains incomplete, of course, even in our own century. Still, the consummation scene, with its outrageous imagery of pilgrimage and worship, dramatizes the disjunction between the hard facts and the old nuances. Its extended metaphors exhibit not a paradise on earth, but the fantasies and distortions of the human imagination. To refine the allegory of human perception it will be necessary to coordinate more closely this perceptual shift between opposites with the actual movement between one object and another. This promise is fulfilled by Dante, in whose work the drama of the mind coincides with the panorama of the world.

The *Divine Comedy* itself is beyond the scope of this paper. Drawing upon a vast range of philosophic and literary traditions, Dante's achievement has an intensity and a coherence of its own, and its precise debt to Bernard, Alain, or Jean is uncertain. Still, Dante shares with these earlier allegorists the dilemma of a two-sided technique, and in resolving that duality he consolidates and transforms the three philosophic traditions which distinguish their work.

The epistemological tradition of knowing one thing by its contrary, enriched by Dante with the religious demand for humility before aspiration, now shapes the entire education of the narrator. To attain the illuminated summit (*Inf*. 1. 13–18), the wayfarer must take another path ("tenere altro vïaggio," 1. 91), descend in order to ascend. To know paradise he must understand the inferno.[19] In this conversion the wayfarer mas-

---

19. See Charles S. Singleton, "In Exitu Israel de Aegypto," *Seventy-Eighth Annual Report of the Dante Society* (Boston: Dante Society of America, 1960), pp. 1–24.

ters the challenge of Jean de Meun's lover, by plunging through the depths of human experience only to displace those deficiencies on the other side.

At the same time, because the earth is upside-down not only in Dante's moral outlook, but in his cosmological design, to go down *is*, physically, to go up. This extraordinary perspective transforms the generative tradition of opposites exploited by Alain de Lille, in which an object's internal nature changes as it moves from one contrary to the other. The wayfarer's downward spiral turns into a purgatorial ascent, where men reverse their old reversals; the *Complaint*'s shift from unnatural defection to natural integrity thus acquires a structural foundation. Indeed, this regenerative movement illuminates man's harmony with the celestial spheres themselves (*Purg.* 13. 13–21), which in their spiral motion resolve the opposition between retrograde and rotary movement.[20]

Even the harmonious circling of the spheres, however, remains distinct from its centering point, God himself; as in the absolute tradition of the *Cosmographia,* all creation is divided from the One. To resolve this duality Dante elaborates and deepens the mirror relationships of Bernard Silvestris with the inverse relation of potentiality and act (*Par.* 2. 127–148), where matter and spirit complement each other. This relationship underlies the celebrated scene at the edge of the created universe (*Par.* 28. 1–78), in which the cosmos itself turns inside out; God, at the circumference, as it were, of the material universe, is at the center of the spiritual universe.

In a larger sense Dante exploits the principle of potentiality and act to reconcile the basic duality of allegorical language itself, the distinction between vision and truth. The figures Dante meets are potentialities of his own soul, possibilities which he briefly activates in his personal vision. Yet these figures are also fulfillments in their own right, who continue to exist—eternally—when Dante leaves them behind. Everything in the *Comedy* has a visionary status, yet everything has an actual existence as well. In this sense Dante's allegorical vi-

20. On these points see John Freccero, "Dante's Pilgrim in a Gyre," *PMLA,* 76 (1961), 168–181, and "The Final Image: *Paradiso* XXXIII, 144," *Modern Language Notes,* 79 (1964), 14–27.

sion converges with that divine poem, the world, which, as Augustine had said a millennium earlier, God himself organizes by contraries. All this, however, requires an analysis—or a millennium—of its own.

In the history of medieval allegory the force of division acts like some primal impulse in the history of the world, disrupting one order to create a new one. No sooner is one breach closed than a new division opens up inside it. However limited and broad the overview, perhaps there is something of the shift in late medieval orientation in this movement from an absolute distinction between the supernatural and natural worlds in the *Cosmographia*, to the relative antinomies of the natural world itself in the *De planctu naturae*, to the perceptual dialectic of human nature in the *Roman de la Rose*. Even in this general form, of course, the movement is not orderly. In some measure each of these complex works explores all these questions, along with a host of other issues. Again, the works themselves are only parts of a complicated literary and philosophic history. Finally, the history is not only sequential, but simultaneous. None of these dualities, after all, is ever truly resolved and superseded. As in the *Divine Comedy*, where the last stage in this process, man, returns to its starting point in God, the same basic questions—or question—are posed continuously, at new levels of intensity. It is a question of our own dilemma, the disparity between what we say and what we mean, between our abilities and our aspirations. If, with its double edge, allegory openly exposes those deficiencies, by the same token it displays the other side, as well, the yearning for fulfillment. Allegory's divisions and consolidations, its weaknesses and strengths, are inseparable. In the end its darker and brighter tendencies are two sides of the same truth.

STEPHEN A. BARNEY

Visible Allegory:
The *Distinctiones Abel* of
Peter the Chanter

For over a generation now, at least since the publication of
Robertson and Huppé's *Piers Plowman and Scriptural Tradition* (1951), students of medieval and Renaissance literature
have scoured the *Patrologia Latina* and kindred sources of
medieval lore for help in unfolding specific allegories and in
discovering the right literary context of medieval art in general. Although the search has often gone astray—the minimal
requirements of baby Latin and a quick thumb for indexes
have encouraged a higher illiteracy—it has often enough borne
fruit. We have unriddled some passages in literary works, and
we have restored in part the mental set of some poets. Perhaps
most interesting, we have sometimes been distracted from that
search for the meanings of particular images which can be trivial (why is Hrothgar's hall *horned?* why does Redcrosse wake
in the *morning?*), into a larger exploration of the technique and
social context of the most abundant form of pre-Enlightenment
letters, biblical exegesis.

We have even been drawn into an exploration of what the

exegetes say: the new interest in biblical symbolism, and the newer interest in the theory of interpretation, have encouraged students of language departments to enter the terrain once exclusively held by historians and theologians, who remain its masters, the terrain of Spicq, d'Alverny, Wilmart, Hunt, Daniélou, Smalley, de Lubac, Baldwin, Rouse, the scholars of patristics and Scholasticism. Any student of Dante now is aware of, if not deeply learned in, the *Glossa ordinaria*. Inchoate discriminations among the vast array of exegetical sources have been undertaken, and new texts are being edited.

I am now editing one of these new texts, the *Distinctiones Abel* of Peter the Chanter, a work available in print only in excerpts published by Pitra over a century ago. Peter was a master at the University of Paris in the late twelfth century. His *Distinctiones* is extant in some seventy manuscripts scattered over Europe, a manuscript witness about four times as abundant as that of Chaucer's *Troilus*. The text it most resembles is the nearly contemporary distinctiones of Alain de Lille, conveniently available in the *Patrologia*. Most of the other works in the genre have never been printed.

The era in which the *Distinctiones Abel* was compiled, its initial purpose, and perhaps most of all its form, make it an especially useful entrée into the methods and ideals of medieval allegoresis. Unless the sister work of Alain predates it, the *Abel* (named for its first word) is the earliest work of its kind, a kind that increased mightily in the thirteenth century. (André Wilmart made a preliminary survey of major works in the genre in *Mémorial Lagrange,* 1940.) The genre is called *distinctiones* from its distinguishing the various allegorical senses of a given word, according to more or less systematic principles. Peter the Chanter's *Distinctiones* arranges the words whose meanings are to be distinguished in alphabetical order—a technological innovation in exegetical works of this sort—and displays the various senses of the word with special clarity. He puts the words to be "distinguished" in the left margin of his text, and from this title draws strings which radiate to the brief explanations of each sense in the block of text. The first article, for instance, appears thus in MS. Reims 508:

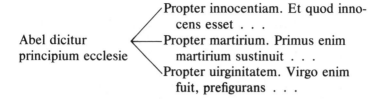

Abel dicitur
principium ecclesie

Propter innocentiam. Et quod inno-
cens esset . . .

Propter martirium. Primus enim
martirium sustinuit . . .

Propter uirginitatem. Virgo enim
fuit, prefigurans . . .

Here three significations of "Abel" explain his general significance as "the beginning of the Church." It is obvious that the
form of display, with title and clearly marked sections, and the
easy access of alphabetical order make the *Distinctiones Abel*
unusually handy—to either a medieval or a modern reader.
Peter usually supports or exemplifies each of the various
senses with a biblical citation, here Matthew 25:35, Revelation
13:8, and (loosely) Genesis 4:25. The *Distinctiones Abel*
makes no claim to give original interpretations of the words it
expounds, but its originality of format made it a useful, desirable, popular, and influential text.

Peter's chief purpose in compiling the *Distinctiones Abel*
was to give order, to organize. In the context of the nascent
University of Paris, where Peter as cantor—precentor, head
of the choir—of Notre Dame was a master, the need for such a
work must have been obvious. At a center of learning and libraries like Paris the sheer quantity of books, the biblical commentaries and treatises of the Fathers and their successors,
had clearly outstripped the capacity of a student to digest for
himself. The twelfth century schools, among their many innovations, emphasized orderliness and the development of new
techniques in curricula and tools of study, their focus remaining as always on mastery of the Sacred Page, and their new impulse to assimilate and arrange in convenient form the bulky
store of past wisdom. Four of the most important texts of the
century are those to which, outside of the Bible and the major
Fathers, Peter the Chanter most often refers: Gratian's *Decre-
tum,* the *Glossa ordinaria,* Peter the Lombard's *Sentences,*
and Peter Comestor's *Historia scholastica.* The Chanter himself wrote commentaries on all the books of the Bible—he is
said to have been the first to do so—and a comprehensive

Summa of moral and sacramental theology. All these texts were much used in the schools; all were technological innovations in the storage and articulation of large quantities of authoritative information. Richard Rouse speaks of the rise in this period of *homo tabulator*.

As an alphabetical dictionary of the "spiritual" or "mystical" senses, as they were called, of biblical words, Peter's *Distinctiones Abel* first aimed to educate the students in the schools of Paris, especially, as local references and an emphasis on liturgy and the actions of the choir indicate, those in his own school at Notre Dame. A student would refer to the *Abel* to find out what the various uses of a biblical word might be (the full concordances to the Vulgate appeared in the early thirteenth century), or why certain liturgical hours were observed, or what were the five sheddings of Christ's blood. Many of the articles, in fact, have no allegorical content and make no distinctions but give facts like an encyclopedia; in later decades these functions would be more carefully split. A special use of the *Distinctiones Abel* was as an aid to the composition of a sermon: a new type of sermon of the period amounted to an elaborate distinguishing of the senses of that day's Scriptural text. Peter himself, in the course of explicating a term, will often be distracted into a small homily, even assuming the homilist's *oratio recta,* on some vice or Christian duty. Teaching and preaching are not always distinct. This homiletic use of the genre distinctiones became dominant in the thirteenth century, when the friars especially produced a number of huge distinctiones compiled for preachers, which are more efficient and duller than the *Abel.*

The context of the distinctiones is the schools. Peter's work aims at clerical students—often it observes that a vice is dangerous "maxime clericis"—and its allegories emphasize priestly functions, especially preaching. Medieval exegesis generally addresses laymen at second hand, and interpretations (the ox is a prelate) will seem to us self-centered (the interpreter is a prelate) unless we remember the prime audience. Likewise a literary critic can go astray (*King Arthur* means *sacerdos*) if he forgets this clerical orientation. Students of secular literature will be disappointed if they look for allegories re-

mote from ecclesiastical concerns. *Abel* means church, not
poet or scapegoat. The heavy emphasis on the Psalms also
points to the schools: as poems, they abound in bold and difficult images which call for allegorical interpretation, but they
are also the texts most deeply memorized by clerics, as their
early Latin primers and their daily companions in the divine
office. Peter will seldom trouble to say "in psalmo" when he
quotes from a psalm, and if the best copies are reliable guides
he seldom troubles to give a complete quotation of a psalm
verse—often he omits the key word and assumes the reader
will supply it from memory. Many of the articles present materials so terse and metaleptic, like allegory itself, that only a
reader well versed in exegesis could grasp their point. Although the *Distinctiones Abel* offers much information that
would insult the intelligence of a university student, who
would know for instance the seven petitions of the Paternos-
ter, packaged information of this kind would still be useful for
the cleric as he advanced from student to minister of the laity.
The style of the text is simply the most utilitarian, plainest
style possible for maximum clarity. Aureate and baroque biblical tropes are rendered in the flattest Latin. Any difficult expression is repeated in another form; words even slightly unfamiliar are glossed forthwith (which makes text-critical
principles of *difficilior lectio* and *brevior melior* hard to apply).

But in the *Abel* we can discern another purpose at work, a
by-product of its new form, especially of its effort to exhaust
the plurality of traditional allegorical meanings attached to a
word in biblical use. I cannot describe this except to speak of it
as an intellectual play, a devout delight in the discovery and
highly articulate presentation of multiple senses. To find, for
example, that the apostles are like mountains because they
first caught the glory of Christ as mountains first catch the rays
of the sun is only partly to explicate the "holy mountains" of
Psalm 86:1; it is also to leap with the mind in a way that gives
pleasure in itself. Like a lively metaphor it issues from a stroke
of the imagination; it seems to glow with the possibility of further analogies (how else is Christ like the sun? how else are the
apostles massive and high?), and it freshens and deifies the natural world. In his article "Littera est obscura" Peter lists three

reasons for Scriptural allegory: it exercises us, it is beautiful, it
results from original sin. I would emphasize the second as a
prime motive for writing or reading the *Distinctiones Abel*.

Peter relies on and summarizes a millennium of allegorical
interpretation of the Bible, and his method of presentation requires him to have a special consciousness of the methods of
interpretation themselves, the possible modes of explicating a
biblical word. The *Abel* is perforce an exegesis of exegesis—
but only, it should be observed, implicitly so: when he comes
to explain the method of biblical interpretation in his article
"Scriptura sacra habet quatuor partes," he rehashes the usual
four senses (historical, allegorical, tropological, anagogic) in
the usual way. Only once, among the many hundreds of articles in the *Abel*, is the fourfold scheme actually used as the
framework of a distinction, and that case (Jerusalem) occurs
doubtless because the array of the four senses of Jerusalem
(the city, the Church Militant, the soul, the Church Triumphant) was already the traditional example of the fourfold
method of interpretation. Medieval men did not examine very
deeply their own methods of interpretation. I do not know why
this is so, but I would suggest three possible reasons. The
methods were old and had taken on such status of authority
that they did not need to be scrutinized. The methods were
lively, open-ended, and working, and no more seemed in need
of questioning than I need to question my methods in this
essay—since the subject was not dead, the anatomist held off.
Finally, the methods seemed secondary and tangential to the
primary burden of understanding Writ—metacriticism of
God's Word may not have been comfortable to the faithful.

In any case in the *Distinctiones Abel* we have an abundant
and highly schematized body of interpretation, which displays
for us the machinery of allegoresis in tantalizing clarity.
Peter's formal innovations so compress his exegetical matter
as to make the *Abel* different in kind, not just in degree, from a
typical phrase-by-phrase glossing commentary. A selective
survey of the disposition of the articles can show us the making
of allegory in process.

The unit of composition of the *Distinctiones Abel* is a particular interpretation of a word or phrase (when the difference be-

tween a word and the thing the word signifies is important
Peter will often signal it: "Hoc nomen 'Spiritus' signifi-
cat . . ."). We can imagine Peter gathering his materials—
usually, I would guess, in his mind, rather than in writing—by
drawing on his memory of Scripture and his own and others'
interpretations of Scripture. In effect for each word he makes a
partial concordance of biblical texts containing the word. For-
tunately, because the concordances to the Bible were not yet
available, he makes no effort to exhaust the biblical uses of a
word, and furthermore he will bring to bear related but different words, beyond the capacity of a mechanical concordance,
as he writes his article. Then Peter performs the work that
makes the *Distinctiones Abel* special: he organizes the words
and senses into parallel sets.

The principle of parallelism is crucial. In a large majority of
the articles the sections containing individual senses of the key
words are parallel in form. Each of the sections of the article
"Abel" quoted above, for example, begins with "Propter"
and a noun in the accusative. The three nouns also form a
parallel set: Innocents, Martyrs, and Virgins, one has to know,
are standard types (often with Confessors replacing Innocents)
of the early Church Militant who are promoted to high places
in the Church Triumphant—hence *Abel* signifies the beginning
of the Church. A small minority of articles, especially those on
important, usually moral topics like Caritas, Crux, Elemosina,
Jejunium, Penitentia, Oratio, are long and not completely broken down into parallel sets of distinctions. In these cases the
articles ramble, citing authorities and making comments,
sometimes glossing Scriptural passages in detail, somewhere
between commentaries and essays on the topics. These jum-
bled articles look like the inchoate raw material of the distinctiones, their usefulness is limited as particular materials are
hard to find, and they seem pointless to the same degree that
the fully formed distinctions seem pointed. If Peter had not
often constructed his parallel sets from such heaps of information the *Distinctiones Abel* would not have succeeded; the wit
of it, the discovery of parallelism in apparent disorder, would
have been lost.

A well-formed article in the *Distinctiones* may be compared

with a rewrite rule in modern linguistics: a token on the left
(the title) is "rewritten" on the right in an expanded "realization" of the token, often with optional, arbitrary choices included in the expansion. A sentence "may be rewritten as" a
subject and a predicate, the latter with a verb optionally copu-
lative, transitive, or intransitive; so Abel is the beginning of the
Church, as Innocent, Martyr, and Virgin. Even the layout of
the articles in the *Abel* in the better manuscripts resembles a
linguist's table of rewrite rules. The right-hand, expanded material does not replace, but rather explicates, unfolds, divides
the left-hand token. Two processes are at work. The first, invisible, is addition, the accumulation of explications from various sources (as, in the 1950s, we may be sure Chomsky gathered his materials from the traditional textbooks of grammar).
The second, visible, and innovative process is the inverting of
this addition into division: the accumulated materials are so ordered that the left-hand tokens are divided, apparently inevitably, into the right-hand unfoldings. The exegetical materials
are condensed as they are subsumed under a title, admitting of
that metalepsis (that Innocents are types of the Church, and so
on) which causes the enigmatic quality of allegory. Then the
materials are expanded, still in compressed form, into the
array of sections naming the particular senses.

The power of the work, again, resides in the discovery of
how to make the divisions (texts like those of Peter Comestor
and the *Glossa* had already made the additions), and this discovery amounts to the discovering of parallel orders. If we
were told that a sentence may be realized as a subject and a
preposition we would feel uncomfortable, as if apples and mus-
culature were reduced to the same order. A similar discomfort
would follow if *Abel* were explicated as Martyrs, Virgins, and
Hope. The trick is to discover terms, at least two, of the same
order among the materials, and to array these in parallel.

To see how Peter manages this trick we should look more
closely at the form of a typical, fully articulated article (keeping in mind that a large number of the articles do not conform
to this ideal). The article can be divided into four parts: first, a
word or phrase placed in the margin, the notion (vocable,
term, word, concept, thing) to be distinguished, the *Title;* sec-

ond, a word or phrase, or a derivational or inflectional ending, that introduces a sense of the Title and suggests the grammatical or logical order of the sense, the *Articulator;* third, a word or phrase, often a sentence or more, that denotes the allegorical signification of the Title, according to the logic or grammar established by the Articulator, the *Sense;* fourth, the *Citation,* introduced by a term such as *whence,* quoting the Bible or another authoritative source, or referring to an argument or liturgical usage, that supports or exemplifies the Sense. In the example we have used the Title is "Abel dicitur principium ecclesie" (the Title does not usually express so much of the allegorical relationship, but often it does); the Articulator is "Propter"; the Senses are Innocence, Martyrdom, and Virginity (related to the Title by the logical category of cause, signaled by the Articulator "Propter"); the Citations are those biblical references noted above.

The Articulator establishes the form of the allegorical relationship posed. Writers will know from their own experience that setting up a parallelism induces the discovery of enough parallel terms to fill out the scheme, to make it presentable—sometimes we stretch a point to make it presentable. So Peter would have pressed his memory, and sometimes he would have invented a happy invention, urged by form to complete form. More of the articles have three sections than any other number, I suspect because three is the minimum representation of completion: with three terms we have a beginning, a middle, and an end, a set which suggests numerousness and continuity—so, perhaps, things are done thrice in fairy tales and other literary forms. Although the fact is rarely displayed as obviously as in the *Abel,* all allegories employ Articulators, even when they are not expressed, because they are the necessary connectors between the items being explicated and the *aliud,* the "Other," to which the items are referred.

The choice of an Articulator will force the Senses to be parallel, and the Citations will follow these parallel Senses, with more or less strain of meaning. Among the Articulators, potentially infinite in number, several types stand out. The most frequent is *Quandoque,* "Sometimes"—a Title will "sometimes" means this, that, or the other—but this Articulator generally requires a further articulation to insure the parallel forms of the Senses. Others of this kind are *quia,* "because"; *primus / secundus /* and so on, *de quo dicitur,* "of which it is said"; *quando,* "when": these and others introduce various forms. We have seen already the most common Articulator which insures parallel Senses: *propter,* "because," which requiring an accusative noun strictly limits the form of the Sense. Many other prepositions similarly demand parallelism: A Title takes its allegorical meaning *per* something, *contra* something, *ab* something, *quantum ad* something, *ex* something, *in* something, *de* something, *pro* something, *cum* something. Establishing a looser parallelism are Articulators which will require a clause with a verb: *qui, quidam, alii,* or *ut.*

Instead of Articulators of these kinds Peter often makes his Senses parallel by means of Articulators bonded into the Senses. As the first words of the sections, immediately after the Title, come nouns all in the same case (*stulti / infirmi / sancti; labore / timore / dolore*), or verbs of the same form (*confitendo / sustinendo / viuendo / prestando; dicens / lugens / moriens; currunt / sedent / iacent*), or various adjectives (of which *malus / bonus / beatus* is a recurring sequence), or degrees of an adjective (*sancte / sanctiores / sanctissime*). Ideally, then, the Senses take parallel grammatical form whether or not a preposition or pronoun introduces them. Furthermore, Peter usually, but not always, reinforces these parallels of inflection by choice of words in the same declension or conjugation. A tendency to go further, and to find words with the same derivational endings as well (*incensionem / consumptionem / illuminationem; congruitatis / necessitatis / vtilitatis*), brings the process to its logico-grammatical fruition: rhyming Senses.

The desire to make parallels as strong as possible rises from logic to grammar to the phonology of the distinctions: the ideal is to find a minimum difference among tokens as like as possible. We find this tendency everywhere in medieval exegesis and in allegoresis of other kinds (mythography, iconography) as well. The discovery of rhyming or grammatically agreeing distinctions of meaning must have seemed to authenticate the array of Senses, as if language itself concurred in the significations. Martyrs, Virgins, and Innocents (or Confessors) might not have formed a standard triad had one of their number escaped from the third declension; we might not have a classic essay "Nature and Grace in *The Faerie Queene*" if *Natura* and *Gratia* were not a familiar first-declension opposition; that most common allegorical differentiation of all—*In bono / In malo*—would have lost its power if it were *In bono / In male*. By repeating the principle hundreds of times with striking clarity the *Distinctiones Abel* helps us see what I take to be true of medieval allegoresis generally, that before the logical operations of discovering various meanings in biblical terms comes a selection of traditional meanings made on essentially poetic grounds, namely repetition of grammatical or phonological forms. The hunt for meaning can go in any direction, but the hunter succeeds and ceases when his language identifies his prey. The science of allegory starts with poetry—the texts in which it finds meaning—and, so regularly that we may consider it the ideal medieval allegoresis, it ends in poetry.

The Articulators are the bottlenecks through which the flow of meanings must pass, taking their form; they direct the aesthetics of the distinctiones. The Titles are freely chosen, practically all from the vocabulary of the Bible. The Citations, please rest assured, although they are the vehicles of the Titles, are last in the chain rationally as well as spatially, for the sense of the Bible had been stretched, the context of biblical passages ignored, the focus of biblical language and events had been fixed on the present concerns of the church, long before Peter the Chanter was born, and he made no effort to alter the tradition. Medieval allegoresis springs from the Bible and finally settles back on it for authority, but its chief business is the acrobatics it performs while in the air.

We might think the array of Senses would be freely chosen, the result of a ransacking of the world of things and ideas. But although they are not as limited as the Articulators, surprisingly few sets of Senses are not traditional. I will call the array of Senses in an article a Scheme (like Innocent / Martyr / Virgin): here are exemplary Schemes from among some 120 clearly organized sets I noted. Perhaps the most common Schemes designate moral qualities (*mala / peior / pessima;* the

Deadly Sins; *detestanda / laudanda / adoranda*), moral agents (*corpus / anima;* the very common *corde / ore / opere*), or moral results (*fructus tricesimus / sexagesimus / centesimus; infernum / gloriam*). Some refer to states of life (*virginalem / coniugalem / vidualem; incipientium / proficientium / perfectorum / pervenientium; scolarium / claustralium; rex / officiales / plebs*); some to the soul's passions (*timor / spes / gaudium / dolor*), conditions (*necessaria / symulatoria / voluntaria*), faculties (*corporalis / imaginaria / intellectualis; vi / virtute / virore;* the five senses), or powers (*unctio / oblatio / intercessio*). Some Schemes coordinate the sacraments (*contritio / confessio / satisfactio; aqua / verbum / remissio; benedixit / fregit / dedit discipulis*) and liturgical matters (*festis / profestis;* the seven orders of priesthood; the seven hours). Some are temporal (*naturalia / mosayca / evangelica; temporalis / spiritualis / eternalis; persecutores / heretici / falsos fratres / antichristus; nox / mane / meridies / vespera*), and some are spatial (*dexter / sinister; inferior / superior / anterior / posterior; sublimitas / profunditas / latitudo / longitudo*). Some refer to groups of people (*iudei / heretici / catholici; pueri / adulti*), the deeds of men (*rapiunt / mercantur / furantur; aratur / seminatur / irrigatur / metitur*), or the parts of the body (*in fronte / in occipite / a dextris / a sinistris; in uertice / inter scapula / in pectore*).

A common type of Scheme draws immediately on some set of things in the Bible: the gifts of the Magi, the horses of the Apocalypse, the fearful things of Psalm 90:5–6, Old Testament types of evil women, the World / Flesh / Devil triad, the Theological Virtues, various objects in the Song of Songs (eyes, hair, neck, tower, dish, dove, cedar), the proverbial things that drive a man from home (smoke, a leaky roof, a fractious wife), the three just men of Ezekiel 14:14, the table / chair / bed / candlestick of IV Kings 4, the acts of Christ (conception, nativity, preaching, working miracles, passion, descent, resurrection, ascension). Even more frequently the Chanter distinguishes the Sense according to the qualities of some thing. The fact that oil illuminates, feeds, heals, rises above other liquids, and signifies peace, makes it like Mercy.

The fact that dogs are born blind, will not acknowledge their masters, have corrosive teeth, lick blood, and return to their own vomit, makes them like bad prelates. Similar Schemes, based on various lore of the kind found in bestiaries or treatises on the nature of things, allegorize the hen, sheep, dove, ox, fish, serpent; sand, wine, water, bread, dew, salt; the sun, wind, stars, land; the tuba, hair, fleece, mountains. These two types may be called the distinctiones "Dicitur in scripturis" and the distinctiones "Dicitur de natura rerum"; they represent two large and well-known classes of medieval allegory.

Another common type of Scheme more abstractly distinguishes Senses according to logical or rational or grammatical categories: *falsa / vera, bona / melior / optima, intrinseca / extrinseca, specialis / generalis, diminutus / perfectus / superhabundans, econtrario / utrumque / in neutrum, positiuum / comparitiuum / superlatiuum, qualitas / quantitas / locus / tempus, levis / grauis, causalis / effectualis / figuralis, similitudinis / dissimilitudinis, enigmatica / comprehensiva, obscura / plana, equalitatem / minoritatem / maioritatem.* To these Schemes we should add some dozen Schemes of distinction based on assertion and negation, or on the permutated assertion and negation of sets of things. One article, for example, distinguishes four types: those who are cast down but do not cast down, who cast down but are not cast down, who cast down and are cast down, who neither cast down nor are cast down—that is, the permutations of the verb (*abiciunt*) in positive / negative and active / passive combination. Another distinguishes those who want to hear, know, and do; those who hear and know, but do not do; those who hear, but neither know nor do; those who neither hear, know, nor do—that is, some of the permutations of negation.

These Schemes begin our task of rationalizing the underlying methods of distinguishing, but before attempting that I should mention the numerous articles that list sets of things without any allegorical distinguishing, but simply for the reader's information, like an encyclopedia. So listed are the clauses of the Creed, the hours of the day, the Decalogue, the grades of obedience, the sheddings of christ's blood, the Beatitudes, the sins of Galatians 5:19–21, a set of various sevens and threes, the nine gates of Jerusalem, the seven columns, the orders of angels, the ten Prefaces, the three principal processions, the fears, the vestments of a priest, the ages of the world and a man's life, the signs of judgment, and so forth. These sets reveal an intention which the Schemes of distinctions also realize, to hand down classes and divisions of things which the church found useful to know.

In exemplifying the various Schemes of Senses I have presented a neater book than the *Distinctiones Abel* actually is. Many of the articles look like failed distinctions, which begin to establish a recognizable Scheme and then leave it incomplete or turn in another direction. Often a distinction will omit one of the four parts of the hypothetical ideal article: the Citations will be dropped, or a Sense will be used in place of the Title. The work shows signs, in fact, of being the first of its kind, its potential form—if I have understood it right—only partly realized, as Peter groped toward a sense of what he was about. I wish I had some knowledge of his working notes, which could ground this speculation. I think the distinctiones on the Psalms by Prepositinus and Peter of Poitiers, probably composed earlier than Peter the Chanter's distinctiones, represent a less-accomplished form of what the *Abel* more nearly perfected. These earlier compilations arrange their material according to the sequence of the Psalms rather than the alphabet —a fact that points to the nature of their intended audience— and are even rougher suppliers of various kinds of information, only occasionally adducing a full-fledged distinction. Even the appearance of the manuscript pages of these Psalm distinctiones (I have seen Paris, Bibliothèque Nationale MS. Lat. 417, 425, 454) is confused and disorderly compared with that of the *Abel*. The history of this development remains to be written.

One could probably characterize the Schemes of distinctions in the *Abel* in as many ways as it contains articles: I will mention three. First, the Senses, merely by their form of display, invite us to discover patterns of relationship among them. They fall into Schemes of equal order, like the sins or the traits of oil; or of graded order, usually ascending, like the states of life or the various temporal Schemes; or of permutative and combinative order, like the assertions and negations. The various Senses, ideally, are locked into place with a satisfying look of completion and inevitability. Second, the parallel format drags into fellowship types of order which would not usually sort well together. On the face of it a distinction based on things, like Virgin / Married / Widowed, would operate in a different sphere from a distinction based on logical categories like Causal / Efficient / Figural, yet the various orders of Senses are comparably displayed and seem to allegorize in comparable fashion. The form of the *Distinctiones Abel,* then, tends to bring order out of the vast, unwieldy chaos of a millennium of biblical interpretation with all its variety of method. Third, the Schemes of Senses may be either ad hoc—Peter's inventions of the moment as he wrestled an article into shape —or traditional, but I think it obvious that traditional Schemes numerically dominate, and they certainly dominate in form. Those Schemes which are new model themselves on traditional Schemes, the ultimate authority being the Schemes found in the Bible, a number of which as we have noted are included in the *Abel* without any pretense of allegorical distinguishing, as if to fulfill a desire to present Scheme in general.

That the *Distinctiones Abel* finds traditional Schemes of traditional meanings reminds us of the generally conservative nature of medieval allegoresis. The appeal is strictly to insiders: anyone not already familiar with most of the Schemes could not understand much of the book. Allegory relies on prior learning and demands an appreciation of some large frame of reference, like medieval biblical commentary, even when it criticizes it. The quantities of information which the church considered useful embedded in the *Abel* and later distinctiones helped guarantee their support by the largest audience and the principal patron of medieval literature: the church and its schools. While this conservatism may seem stultifying to us it must have seemed to medieval students as liberating as New Criticism seemed to us a generation ago, to discover how freely and widely interpretation could ramble in deducing meaning from the Page. The powerful principles of etymology or typology or, we see now, of distinguishing, were as stimulating as the notions of ambiguity and rhetoric and Structuralism have been to us.

But the *Distinctiones Abel* added a new thing to its conservative matter, which we might call allegory as visible metaphor. The text may be called a "medieval symbol dictionary" or an "allegorical dictionary," but its essential figurative operation, much repeated, is metaphor. Who knows what a metaphor is? Try this: a metaphor is the transformation of one token (item, counter, locution—we need a colorless term) into another according to certain rules. The analogy with the rewrite rules of linguistics can help us again: "Abel" may be rewritten as "the beginning of the Church," according to certain procedures, governed by the Articulators (*propter*) and enumerated in the Senses (Innocence / Martyrdom / Virginity). The physical format of the *Distinctiones Abel,* just as it suggests the analogy of the rewrite rules, likewise suggests this notion of metaphor. A rewrite rule, as it is read from left to right, suggests an unfolding of the left-hand tokens in time, and a kind of intellectual priority: the upper rules and the left-hand tokens seem more inclusive, more general, more important. But this is misleading: we are to take the right-hand statements (subject plus predicate) as equivalent to the left-hand statements (sentence). The double arrows ($\rightleftharpoons$) of a chemical formula of equilibrium are a better image. So in the metaphors of the *Distinctiones Abel* the flow of meaning from Title to Sense is an alternating current. Peter sometimes proves this equivalence by transposing Title and Sense: under the title "Apostles" we find that, among other things, they are "Hair"; under "Hair" we find the Sense "Apostles."

Two plans merge in the *Distinctiones Abel.* In one, ideally, an ultimately abstract Title (God) would be rewritten, distinguished, in multiple, less-abstract Senses, which in turn would be distinguished, down the Chain of Being, until we would arrive at the concrete things of this world. The other would reverse the process, putting concrete things as the first Titles and mounting toward God. The *Distinctiones Abel* shows us the general relationship that obtains between the processes of allegorization and metaphor making and the idea of an orderly

world. Roland Barthes and the other moderns teach us to distrust metaphor in literature because they see the implication in
any metaphor of an ultimate, privileged world accessible to
reason and sustained by divinity, a world they consider false.

Our habit is to read metaphors as it were from left to right,
from concrete and specific to abstract and general, from Hair
to Apostles. We have little use for the alternative, because
when we find an abstract term in a poem we customarily rest
content with its "literal" meaning. But an allegorical narrative
will sometimes read in the other direction. A personification
will be labeled with an abstract name (Forced Abstinence) or
an object or person of abstract force will emerge (a Jeweled
City, a Bad Priest). In these cases we may wish to know the
proper concrete attributes of the abstractions. Many of the articles in the *Abel* have Titles that are more abstract than the
Senses, whereas a modern dictionary of symbols would display as its Titles all concrete terms. Peter's purpose differs
from ours: he wishes to provide materials for teaching and
preaching, as for a sermon on the apostles—materials as it
were for future allegories as well as an index to biblical meanings.

In the line of literary tradition of which the *Distinctiones
Abel* is a part we can construct a sequence of narration and interpretation of this form: the Bible is allegorically interpreted,
piecemeal; the interpretations, taking on a separate life, are organized; new allegorical narratives are composed; we criticize
them (narrative to interpretation to organization to narrative to
interpretation). The *Abel* is the central term in this sequence. I
would argue that the Chanter's handling of the flow of meaning
in the articles, from concrete to abstract and the reverse, displays visibly the kind of thinking that an allegorist, a Jean de
Meun or a Dante or a Langland, undertakes as he constructs
his narrative. The allegorist and his audience would need to be
familiar with the ways meaning will flow through metaphoric
channels, and they would need some sense of the usual types
of things which mean (the biblical tokens) and the ways in
which they mean (the set of Articulators). These conditions
seem special, but in fact we meet no more common conditions
of literacy for some twelve hundred years of our history.

Our metaphor, that meaning "flows," draws attention to another visual image which the format of the *Abel* calls to mind: the sets of strings from the Titles to the various sections radiate (in the best manuscripts) like a river debouching across a delta into an ocean. It is an image of abundance divided. The meaning flows across numerous channels: the idea of division involves the idea of a plurality contained within a unity.

The prophet says, "And knowledge shall be manifold" ("Et multiplex erit scientia", Daniel 12:4). Involved in the idea of distinguishing, marking off in sets, pointing—the article on "Distinctiones" in the *Distinctiones Abel* concerns the placing of pauses, points, in sentences—discriminating, is the notion of multiplicity, of what we may call "numerousness" to distinguish it from the special science of numerology. Russell and Whitehead, in the *Principia*, define numbers as classes of classes; the definition would suit the *Distinctiones Abel* well because, as we have seen, it consists of an order (visual, alphabetical) of orders (the Schemes of Senses). It is a numerous work, in what Alexander Murray has argued (*Reason and Society in the Middle Ages*, 1978) is an age when an arithmetic consciousness spread rapidly in Europe. The division of the Vulgate into chapter and verse was developing in Peter's time, a development as significant as pagination in printed books, and Peter was the first Latin scholar regularly to cite biblical chapter numbers in his commentaries (only rarely in the *Abel*). Several articles in the *Abel* dwell on numbers themselves, for instance on the two senses of a perfect number (Peter, borrowing ultimately from Philo, says one kind of perfect number is the sum of its factors: $6 = 3 + 2 + 1$). The presence of number will often draw the attention of Peter and his exegetical precursors to a passage in the Bible. The dimensions of ark and temple, the dates of New Testament events, justified the teaching of the quadrivium. Whenever a biblical locution is repeated (Holy, Holy, Holy; Return, return in Canticle of Canticles 6:2; Spare . . . spare in Joel 2:13), the exegete finds as many meanings as there are repetitions. Isaiah says, "For Sion's sake I will not hold my peace, and for the sake of Jerusalem I will not rest" (62:1); the Chanter finds in the redundancy an occasion for distinction of meaning, just as my high school English teacher taught me that the repeated "And miles to go before I sleep" in Frost's poem suggested further meaning. Peter's interest in repetition led him to compose an article on it: Writ repeats itself for confirmation, commendation, memory, explanation, correction, continuity, and retribution. If a triad is the minimum sign of a complete series, a repetition is the sign of numerousness. The principle "number is a sign of allegory" in biblical exegesis rivals in importance the principle "absurdity is a sign of allegory," which Jean Pépin has described (*Studia patristica,* 1957). The pure recognition of things countable leads to allegory.

When Peter applies a scheme of Senses to a Title he enumerates its metaphoric possibilities, often with numbers heading its sections: *primo, secundo,* and so on. When he arranges the Titles in a list he enumerates the topics which he distinguishes (later distinctiones will actually supply article numbers, keyed to a table for quick reference). I once heard Borges in a lecture on metaphor tell of the Chinese saying that there are a thousand things in the world; if so, said Borges, the number of possible metaphors could be computed. We have spoken of an "ideal form" of the *Distinctiones Abel,* in which each article would present, in four elegantly articulated parts, all the distinctions of meaning of biblical words, using a complete concordance of biblical texts as the set of citations. The numerous form of the *Abel* implicitly aims to exhaust the senses of the Bible and the world, to produce a complete concordance of allegorical meaning.

This aim I think is especially medieval. The evidence suggests that a medieval writer preferred (perhaps because fundamentals needed repeating in an era when books were not as accessible as they are now) ordering things, enumerating the divisions of things, to stating first principles. An encyclopedist typically would give an etymology or translation of a term ("angel" is *nuncius*) and hasten to enumerate its divisions (the nine orders) where we might expect a more Socratic effort at definition. Definition, the bounding of a thing, more often meant exhausting a thing's number of manifestations, taxonomizing, than isolating those distinctive features which make it one of a class, rationalizing. In some manuscripts Peter's work is titled *Summa Abel;* the notion of summarizing, adding a total, rivals the notion of distinguishing, dividing features. This mode of knowing has lost favor, especially since the Enlightenment blasts against taxonomy, the subject of Foucault's attention. We distrust a speaker who tells us the five causes of an event—why not six?—and we prefer to hear about the rational, logical possibilities of cause for the event (all events are caused by oil). But the *Distinctiones Abel,* child of its age, seems satisfied to coordinate one set with another, the ages of man with the ages of the world, without exploring such categories as age.

Against the impulse toward exhaustiveness and encyclopedism runs a contrary impulse toward reduction and compendiousness. The activity of coordinating numerousness itself stimulates the rational movement toward a minimum number of categories. Number parallels this movement: the notion *three* more elegantly reduces a class of things than the notion *one and another and another,* as the counting up presupposes that some parallel things, a single class of things, are reckoned. The enumeration of things implies the scheme (these are all apples, all apostles) according to which they may be numbered. A summa aims to *reduce all* the information in previous texts, as it reconciles "reduce" and "all" in a more or less conciously produced system. Multiplication and division, increase and reduction, reciprocate; fullness and brevity go hand in hand.

Order requires number. If Scripture said the woman's breasts were better than wine, we would rest content, in mildly baffled surmise, in the presence of a strong metaphor. But when we hear in one short book that her breasts are furthermore roes, clusters of grapes, towers, we are tempted to become scholastics, we concord the metaphors and look for the order in them, we distinguish. The liturgy, with its cycles of hours and days, even outnumbers the Bible. The numerousness of the phenomenon makes possible the discovery of abstract order, and encourages allegorical interpretation. The scholar's ability to remember such parallel texts preceded an almost inevitable desire to add them and then to divide them. The collation and coordination of things is their interpretation.

Anyone asked which is "more allegorical," *Joseph Andrews* or *Ulysses,* would answer the latter, because while both works allude to ancient epic, *Ulysses* is more numerous. The *Distinctiones Abel* especially reveals the essence of medieval allegoresis because its form makes visible the enumeration which causes allegory and which results from allegory.

Readers will use the *Distinctiones Abel* to find ready, authentic, and conventional meanings of images that interest them, or they may turn to articles like Circumcisio and Stercus out of mere curiosity. I have emphasized here the formal, ordering qualities of the *Abel*—its paralleling, rhyming, coordinating, abstracting, schematizing, enumerating—in an effort to uncover some essential qualities of medieval allegorization in an especially articulate text. A modern sensibility may judge the *Abel* and its kindred texts as so much intelligence wasted on improper objects, so much delight in the technology of interpretation at the expense of the spirit of the Bible. Yet the methods of interpretation made especially visible in the *Distinctiones Abel* represent the main line of medieval literary criticism—there can be no question of that. Nor should we consider the rage for anatomy, with its methods and results so delighting in number, an obsolete mode of criticism: the examples of Frye and Bloom prove its currency. A study of the *Abel* and its precursors and successors may even help us along our way to understanding allegory.

MARGUERITTE S. MURPHY

The Allegory of "Joie" in
Chrétien's *Erec et Enide*

Gaston Paris, in his review of Wendlin Foerster's *Erec und Enide* in *Romania,* 1891, censures the episode of "la Joie de la Cort" as foreign to the rest of the tale, absurd, incoherent, uninteresting, in short, a remnant of "un vieux conte mal transmis" ("an old story, poorly transmitted").[1] This dismissal has spurred subsequent critics to justify its inclusion, to interpret the episode as coherent in itself and necessarily linked to the rest of the narrative. Chrétien's own claim to

---

1. "Il est assurément impossible d'imaginer quelque chose de plus absurde, de plus incohérent et en même temps de moins intéressant que ce récit, allongé d'ailleurs par le poète à grand renfort de détails inutiles et raconté avec une fatigante prolixité. Il est clair qu'on se trouve en présence d'un vieux conte mal transmis, que le poète français ne comprenait plus et qu'il a rendu encore plus inintelligible en essayant de l'expliquer" ("It is assuredly impossible to imagine anything more absurd, more incoherent and at the same time less interesting than this narrative, drawn out, moreover, by the poet by the addition of useless details and retold with a tiring prolixity. It is clear that we are in the presence of an old story, poorly transmitted, that the French poet no longer understood and which he made even more unintelligible by trying to explain it" [my translation]). Gaston Paris, "Compte rendu de l'édition de W. Foerster," *Romania,* 20 (1891), 154.

109

fashion "une molt bele conjointure"[2] from a "conte d'avan-
ture" lends credence to those who discern here a consciously
ordered structure. One possible role for this seemingly super-
fluous adventure is interpretative: in the heightened terms of
medieval allegory the "Joie de la Cort" retells the "san," the
moral, of Érec's quest. Certainly much of what is unique to the
adventure of the "Joie" attests to another plane of meaning:
the predominance of the "merveilleux" over the mimetic, the
mystery which envelopes "la Joie," the mere assignation of a
name to the adventure within the fiction. If Northrop Frye is
correct when he states that "actual allegory" exists "when a
poet explicitly indicates the relationship of his images to examples and precepts, and so tries to indicate how a commentary

2. All verse quotations are taken from *Les Romans de Chrétien de Troyes:
I. Erec et Enide,* ed. Mario Roques (Paris: Librairie Honoré Champion, 1973).
   The translation of *conjointure* is still a matter of controversy. William Albert
Nitze, in "The Romance of Erec, Son of Lac," *Modern Philology,* 11 (April
1914), finds that Chrétien seems to be using the word in a rhetorical sense to
mean the "combination of features or motifs" taken from his source, equivalent to his later use of the word *roman.* In a footnote to another article, "Sans
et matière dans les oeuvres de Chrétien de Troyes," *Romania,* 44 (1914–
1917), 16, he cites Horace's use of the word *junctura* in *Ars poetica* as a classical authority for the meaning, "combination." D. W. Robertson, Jr. seems to accept Nitze's use of Horace, while finding an additional example in Alain de
Lille's *De planctu naturae.* He explains: "When Chrétien says that his poem is
'une molt bele conjointure,' he implies (1) that it is a fable as opposed to an
actual sequence of events, a *conjunctura* of events not joined in nature; (2) that
this *conjunctura* is 'bele,' that is, that it is made 'cum decore aliquo,'; and (3)
that this pleasing *cortex* covers a *nucleus* of truth." ("Some Medieval Literary
Terminology, with Special Reference to Chrétien de Troyes," *Studies in Philology,* 48 [1951], 685). Douglas Kelly devotes an entire article to the exploration of the precise meaning of this word: "The Source and Meaning of Conjointure in Chrétien's Erec 14," *Viator,* 1, (1970), 179–200. He criticizes Nitze
for an ambiguity left between *conjointure* in *Erec'*s source and *conjointure* as
"the disposition given to that work by Chrétien himself" (p. 180). After citing
numerous authorities Kelly concludes that the "meaning of 'iunctura' in the
Latin period, the arrangement of material in Horace's *Ars poetica* and in medieval romance, indicate that the 'conjointure' is specifically the result of the interlacing of different elements derived from the source or sources (or, for that
matter, from the author's imagination)" (p. 200). For my purposes the assumption of a conscious interlacing or ordering suffices for the further argument of
the inclusion of allegory in the text.

on him should proceed,"[3] then this assumption of allegory is probably sound. Although "la Joie de la Cort" does not take the form of a personification, the word *joie* accrues a special significance as it appears in contexts beyond its normal compass of meaning. Indeed, as Jacques Ribard suggests for *Le Chevalier de la charrette* and *Le Conte du graal,* narrative allegory as opposed to personification allegory is finally "plus large et plus fondamentale."[4] For *Erec et Enide* the allegory grounds itself in the relationship of the "récit" of the final adventure to the rest of the "roman."

To substantiate an allegorical intent we must consider both the nature of Chrétien's message and the patent guideposts to this meaning. For the former, recent interpretations have ranged from Tom Artin's argument that Érec's defeat of Maboagrain, the knight of "la Joie," reflects "the victory of heaven over sensual love, of reason over passion" to Douglas Kelly's suggestion that the goal of Érec's quest is his reconciliation with Énide, to Maria Luisa Meneghetti's concentration on the societal situation, Érec's initiation into the courtly milieu.[5] On the whole the emphases waver between the problem of the love relationship and the opening of Érec to the collectivity. Would not an interpretation that unites these two cruces be most valid? Of course, to lead to such an inclusive and intermediate interpretation we must address the second consideration: the symptoms of allegory in Chrétien's romance.

In the light of allegory the nature of the garden, the "vergier," colors the adventure that unfolds there. Scholars have declared it emblematic of "the garden of delights," of the state of the soul dominated by passion instead of reason, of courtly society, and of life itself. Reto R. Bezzola remarks in his book, *Le Sens de l'adventure et de l'amour,* that "le vergier rappelle

3. Northrop Frye, *Anatomy of Criticism: Four Essays* (Princeton: Princeton University Press, 1957), p. 90.

4. Jacques Ribard, "Les romans de Chrétien sont-ils allégoriques?" *Cahiers de l'association internationale des études françaises,* 28 (May 1976), 8.

5. See Tom Artin, *The Allegory of Adventure: Reading Chrétien's Erec and Yvain* (Lewisburg: Bucknell University Press, 1974), p. 125; Douglas Kelly, "La forme et le sens de la quête," *Romania,* 92 (1971), 341; and Maria Luisa Meneghetti, "Joie de la Cort," *Cahiers de civilisation médiévale,* 4 (October–December 1976), 371–379.

les jardins enchantés des innombrables contes orientaux et
européens'' (''the vergier recalls the enchanted gardens of innumerable oriental and European tales'').[6] Meneghetti notes
the similarity between the court of love in Andreas Capellanus'
The Art of Courtly Love and this earlier garden of ''la Joie''
and finds further affinities between the celebration in the garden of the *Roman de la rose* of Guillaume de Lorris and the
''Joie'' which results from the liberation of the ''vergier'' by
Érec. An essential difference between the garden of Maboagrain and the other two gardens of love lies in the absence of
joy in the former until Érec opens it to the community that it
had excluded. Maboagrain calls it a ''prison.'' In it resides
only the couple; rather than a microcosm of courtly life the
garden is an island of isolation, a most exclusive court of love.

Certainly the various features of the garden hold symbolic
value. An impenetrable wall of air, like iron, surrounds the garden; a single entrance breaks it. Iron and sorcery suggest unnatural imprisonment. Yet it resembles a paradise as well with
flowers and fruit year-round, ''tot esté et tot yver'' (''all summer and all winter''); the fruit, however, must be eaten within
the garden, another detail of its exclusiveness. Whoever attempts to carry a fruit beyond the wall can never leave until the
fruit is returned to its original bough:

> Et li fruiz avoit tel eür
> que leanz se lessoit mangier,
> mes au porter hors fet dongier;
> car qui point an volsist porter
> ne s'an seüst ja mes raler,
> car a l'issue ne venist
> tant qu'an son leu le remeïst.

(ll. 5698–5704)

> And the fruit had a property such
> that it could be eaten there within,
> but to carry it outside was dangerous;
> for whoever wished to carry some outside

---

6. Reto R. Bezzola, *Le Sens de l'aventure et de l'amour* (Paris: La Jeune
Parque, 1947), p. 213; my translation.

> would never know how to return,
> for he would not come to the exit
> until he had put the fruit back in its place.

Does not such guarded fruit suggest the fidelity and exclusiveness of the marital state, a condition fulfilled too well by Érec in his state of "recreantise," a fidelity proven on the part of Énide through the trials of their adventures? The rhyme "mangier" / "dongier" brings the Garden of Eden to mind: initial paradise, man's fall, the presence of evil. Both the newly married Érec and the present chivalrous captive of the garden, Maboagrain, were guilty of uxoriousness. The songs of the birds charm men, a sign of the delights and intoxication of the garden. All sorts of spices and medicinal plants grow there, offering exotic luxuries and sustained bodily health to the dwellers.

Érec, upon entering the garden, is further incited to seek the "Joie" by the seductive foretaste of bird song:

> Erec aloit, lance sor fautre,
> par mi le vergier chevauchant,
> qui molt se delitoit el chant
> des oisiax qui leanz chantoient,
> que la Joie li presantoient,
> la chose a coi il plus baoit.
>
> (ll. 5718–5723)

> Érec went riding, his lance in its rest,
> into the middle of the garden,
> taking much delight in the song
> of the birds singing there,
> which gave him a foretaste of the Joy,
> the thing after which he most aspired.

This anticipation suggests that the "Joie" is both present and pleasant. But he then espies "une grant mervoille," a row of heads on stakes. The helms are "luisanz et clers" as if to dazzle the beholder and divert his attention from their pernicious significance. He sees the horn without understanding its meaning:

Il ne set que ce senefie,
ne de neant ne s'an esfrie,
einz demanda que ce puet estre
au roi, qui lez lui ert a destre.

(ll. 5737–5740)

He did not know what this meant,
but was not at all disturbed by it,
instead he asked the king, who was beside him
on his right, what this could be.

At this point Érec, like us, knows that this adventure with its special name has a larger significance than previous exploits, but this significance is not yet clear. King Evrain answers Érec with only a warning against "la Joie" and discloses the expectation of a hero, predestined someday to blow the horn. Chrétien's audience may surmise that Érec is this hero. This predetermined character to the adventure, this probable connection to Érec, implies that the "Joie" is a prepared obstacle for Érec, a landmark of sorts, fated, significant for him and his previous quest. Meanwhile, the enchanting songs, marvelous, though horrifying sights, and their mysterious character dull the senses of the interloper. Later, in combat, both knights begin with sparkling eyes, "li oel lor estancelent," but are soon blinded by sweat and blood so badly that their blows often miss. Likewise, we, Chrétien's readers, in the midst of narrative, temporarily share this blindness to the inner level of meaning, to the larger significance that the "Joie" as allegory might trace. Often the purpose of allegory is to veil arcane truth from the uninitiated. In such a vein this "Joie" will be Érec's initiation into knowledge of his kingly role of liberator: he liberates a vassal from isolation into the community and protection of the court as he liberates him from an uxorious passion.

The sense of mythical mystery grows with the sight of a "dameisele" on a silver bed covered with a cloth of gold brocade in the shade of a sycamore. She is the fairy, the queen of the "Autre Monde" of Breton fairy tales. She is the seductress, her bed a possible recess for luxurious lovemaking. Moreover, the presence of a prominent tree in the garden clearly alludes to the Garden of Eden and the Tree of Knowledge of Good and Evil. Just as Adam and Eve hid in the tree after they sinned, the damsel sits in its shade. According to D. W. Robertson, Jr., in his article, "The Doctrine of Charity in Mediaeval Literary Gardens," "to hide within the tree is to hide within oneself in self-love or cupidity."[7] The *Distinctiones dictionum theologicarum* of Alain de Lille, reprinted by Migne, exemplifies the sycamore's biblical reputation:

> *Sycomorus* est arbor similis ficui, unde sycomorus quasi ficus fatua, quia similis est ficui non in fructibus sed in follis, unde legitur de Zachaeo quod *ascendit arborem sycomorum.* Dicitur etiam fragilis, unde Isaias: *Sycomoros succiderunt, sed cedros immutabimus.*[8]

> The sycamore is a tree like the fig tree, whence the sycamore is, as it were, a foolish fig tree, since it is like a fig tree not in its fruit but in its leaves, whence it is said of Zacchaeus that he climbed up a sycamore tree. It is also said to be fragile, whence Isaias: they felled the sycamores, but we will leave the cedars unchanged.

With foliage like figs the sycamore evinces illusory fertility. The contrast with the immutable cedars adds impermanence to illusion. Hence, according to this tradition, the sycamore's presence signifies that the garden holds false fruits, transient and unsatisfying pleasures. The great size of Maboagrain may well cast him in the fairy-world role of protector-giant, but in the human world it possibly represents a lack of proportion in the life that he was leading. By extension, his size magnifies the obstacle which Érec must overcome, the image of Érec's immoderate ardor in early wedlock.

The splendors of the "vergier" vie with those of Brandigan, the other dominant place in the "Joie" sequence. Chrétien describes it as:

7. D. W. Robertson, Jr., "The Doctrine of Charity in Mediaeval Literary Gardens," *Speculum*, 26 (1951), 26.
8. J.-P. Migne, *PL* 210, 964.

> Un chastel fort et riche et bel,
> clos tot an tor de mur novel;
> et par desoz a la reonde
> coroit une eve si parfonde,
> roide et bruianz come tanpeste.
>
>   (ll. 5323–5327)

> a fortified town, rich and beautiful,
> enclosed entirely by a new wall;
> and below in a circle
> ran a very deep stream,
> rapid and roaring like a storm.

Both Brandigan and the garden are enclosed by a wall and fortified in some sense. The magic wall of air secures the garden; Brandigan, however, is so well fortified otherwise that its wall is sheer embellishment. Moreover, Brandigan is an island, encircled by a rapid, noisy, deep course of water; this commotion may presage the spirited town life within. Robertson mentions that gardens often have wells or streams which water the trees and flowers, with the religious association of the Water of Life.[9] This displacement of the stream from the magical garden to a town circuit both heightens the significance of Brandigan and lessens the allure of the garden. Brandigan, the court deserted by Maboagrain, becomes an example for all courts through such consequential detail. The deceptive garden "hors del chastel" is its antithesis, its opponent; it lacks the true and proper life that exists in the château. Both places are self-sufficient, yet the walls of Brandigan exert no restraining force on its populace. Leaving the château to go seek the "Joie," Érec is strongly and repeatedly warned against entry into the enchanted place. After Érec has liberated Maboagrain from the garden's spell, all joyfully return to the town since they have already stayed too long in the garden of "Joie." The irony is clear: the place of the "Joie" is joyless and dangerous, while the "chastel fort" is joyful and safe. The parallel has an obvious consequence: Brandigan has community and a court life; the "vergier" is a place of isolation and imprisonment orna-

---

9. Robertson, "The Doctrine of Charity," pp. 30–31.

mented with false delights. Although the duty and devotion implicit in the love of Maboagrain and his mistress is not wrong, their sequestration and secrecy pervert their love, as we see symbolically in the features of their surrounding garden of love.

As the garden is the inverted image of Brandigan and, by extension, of all courts, so the couple reflects the problematic relationship of Érec and Énide. Indeed the "dameisele" is a cousin to Énide just as the chevalier is nearly Érec's equal in prowess. Érec's major string of adventures begins in reaction to the accusation of "recreantise." He then refuses an accompanying train of knights; of necessity, Énide is to be his sole companion. He must prove his valiance and test Énide's love. This aloneness stresses the building of Érec's personal character and this single relationship. Significantly, he enters the place of the "Joie" alone, battles Maboagrain alone. Here is a representation of the crux of Érec's quest. Is not Maboagrain simply a second self, his situation a heightened replica of Érec's former overwhelming devotion to Énide? As Érec liberates the garden he liberates himself symbolically from the preoccupation of the bridal bed. But Érec is already reunited with Énide in an even more fervent and loyal love after their numerous trials. Chrétien depicts the garden of "la Joie" as the epitome of closed love, but teaches that too-exclusive love, not marital love, is wrong. Such love alienates the couple from that society in which their marriage is properly based and to which it is a base. Érec's attachment to Énide solves the white stag dilemma of Arthur's court, raises Énide's parents to deserved social stature, and is expected to provide for the continuance of King Lac's race. Érec necessarily learns the seemly behavior of a king alone. Likewise, he liberates "la Joie" alone, an allegorical reproduction of the purpose of his quest, a relating of "images" in narrative form to a "precept." The garden, like the marriage, has the promise of paradise, but when totally insular it is deadly.

This reading of the garden as a special representation of connubial love, Edenic only when open before the collectivity and founded in fidelity, does not completely answer the puzzle of the garden's name. The joy which reigns in Evrain's court after

Maboagrain's return seems a too-facile solution, one which disregards the larger significance of the "Joie" for Érec and Énide. Furthermore, why call the adventure "la Joie de la Cort" while the garden is still dolorous and closed? Chrétien's use of the word *joie* throughout the romance, however, both readies his audience to deduce its special significance and signals the presence of allegory, this measuring of exploits to a dictum.

One of its earliest instances is in the description of the town of Énide and her parents where Érec first meets her. The people of the town are in the midst of preparation for a festival. In it Érec will win the sparrow hawk for Énide and thereby honor her as the greatest beauty present. When Érec first approaches the town he sees:

> El chastel molt grant joie avoit
> de chevaliers et de puceles,
> car molt en i avoit de beles.
>
> (ll. 348–350)

> In the town there was great joy
> among the knights and maidens,
> for many beautiful ones were there.

Érec will find and win the most beautiful "pucele." As beauty here is associated with "molt grant joie," this early search for "joie" and its winning might adumbrate Érec's winning of "la Joie de la Cort." His finding an appropriate wife is the first step to the eventual embellishment of his own court with a queen. Moreover, the "joie" expressed in this passage is a communal joy shared by the whole town, a precedent for the "Joie" in Brandigan after Maboagrain's release.[10] Of course, the description of the marriage of Érec and Énide at Arthur's court at Caradigan, the celebration of Érec's consummate winning of

---

10. Godefroy includes "divertissement populaire" among the definitions of *joie* in medieval French. This connotation of public festivity enhances the sense of *joie* as a communal event and makes Chrétien's punning even more resonant than might be apparent to the modern reader. See Frédéric Godefroy, *Dictionnaire de l'ancienne langue française* (1885).

Énide, employs "joie" repeatedly for both the festivity in the
palace and the enjoyment in the nuptial chamber:

> Molt fu granz la joie el palés,
> mes tot le sorplus vos an les,
> s'orroiz la joie et le delit
> qui fu an la chanbre et el lit,
> la nuit, quant asanbler se durent;
> evesque, et arcevesque i furent.
>
> (ll. 2015–2020)

> Great was the joy in the palace,
> but all the rest I will leave aside,
> you will hear of the joy and pleasure
> in the bedchamber and the bed,
> that night, when they retired together;
> bishops, and archbishops were there.

Even in the nuptial chamber the bishop and archbishop are
present to bless the joyful marriage, celebrated openly before
the community and with the community, unlike the illicit relationship between Maboagrain and the demoiselle of the silver
bed. The "joie" of the bridal chamber degenerates to mere
"delit" (l. 2472) when Érec becomes "recreant."

Érec plays the role of bearer of "joie" on other occasions.
"Joie" is found frequently at moments of recognition and welcoming. When Érec returns to Arthur's court with Énide,
Queen Guinevere and all the court rejoice at his arrival, as
does the court of Evrain when Maboagrain finally returns:

> La reïne grant joie an mainne,
> de joie est tote la corz plainne
> ancontre son avenemant,
> car tuit l'ainment comunemant.
>
> (ll. 1515–1518)

> The queen had great joy in it,
> all the court was full of joy
> at his arrival,
> for all without exception loved him.

"Comunemant" emphasizes once again the unity of the court.
Érec's father, King Lac, gives the parents of Énide a similarly
joyous reception and several châteaus with property and chevaliers as gifts:

> Grant joie et grant enor lor fist,
> por Erec son fil les ama.
>
> (ll. 1850–1851)

> He gave them a joyous welcome and paid them
> great honor,
> for the sake of Érec, his son, he loved them.

Even here Érec is an agent of joy, although he is not present;
he enhances the court of his father with the presence of
Énide's parents.

In the advent of the marriage of Érec and Énide, King
Arthur assembles all his barons. When he sees them together
he becomes joyous in his heart:

> Li rois Artus a la parsome,
> quant asanblé vit son barnage,
> molt an fu liez an son corage.
> Aprés, por la joie angraignier,
> comanda .c.vaslez baignier,
> que toz les vialt chevaliers faire.
>
> (ll. 1960–1965)

> Finally King Arthur,
> when he saw all his barons assembled,
> was very happy for it in his heart.
> Afterwards, to augment the joy,
> he commanded one hundred pages to be bathed,
> for he wanted to make them all knights.

This gathering of the complete court acts as a vivifying source
of joy for its king and gives us a distinct image of the joy of
political communality.

King Lac, of course, experiences great joy at his son's return to his court. To welcome Érec,

> li rois fist maintenant monter
> qu'il ot oïes les noveles
> clers, et chevaliers, et puceles,
> et comande les corz soner
> et les rues ancortiner
> de tapiz et de dras de soie
> por son fil reçoivre a grant joie.
>
> (ll. 2276–2282)

> when he heard the news,
> the king had clerks, knights, and maidens mount,
> and ordered the horns sounded
> and the streets decorated
> with hanging tapestries and draped silks
> so that his son would be received with great joy.

This welcome includes the sounding of horns, just as the welcome of Maboagrain to the court is initiated when Érec blows the horn. "Joie" at Érec's return proliferates in the town and in the text. Hyperbole extends the joy to young and old alike:

> Einz nus ne vit joie greignor
> que feisoient juesne et chenu.
>
> (ll. 2316–2317)

> No one has ever seen greater joy
> shown by young and old.

"Joie" colors the welcome for Érec, his father's greeting, his reception by the townspeople, and finally the festivities of celebration, the ritual welcoming of Érec with his bride. These examples emphasize the joy at moments of reunion and community, the joy denied Maboagrain when he fails to return to his uncle's court and inspire such joy in that community. Érec's return is a climax of right joy for he combines the chivalric life and the duties to homeland with love for his bride.

Once Érec isolates himself from court life and courtly activities to spend all of his time with Énide, the word *joie* conspicuously disappears. Words such as *duel* (grief), *angoisse,* and *triste* become more frequent. In the interim of the quest before "la Joie de la Cort," *joie* only appears in instances of recogni-

tion of Érec by nobility along his journey who either know him
or recognize his high rank by his name. Such recognitions are
microcosms of a courtly reception and recognition, since they
appreciate his part in courtly society. After defeating Guivret
le Petit, for instance, Érec reveals his name, his father's name,
and what lands his father holds. Guivret responds in joy to
learn that at least he has been defeated by a knight of high
birth:

> Quant Guivrez l'ot, molt s'an mervoille,
> et dist: "Sire, grant mervoille oi;
> onques de rien tel joie n'oi
> con j'ai de vostre conuissance.
>
> (ll. 3868–3871)

> When Guivret heard this, he showed great surprise,
> and said: "Sire, this is astonishing news I hear;
> never have I had such joy in anything
> as to make your acquaintance.

Later, the defeated Maboagrain finds the same solace when in-
formed of Érec's noble stature and renown. "Joie" pervades
Érec's reunions with Gauvain in the forest, with Arthur and
Guinevere at their tent. Their joy changes to grief at the sight
of Érec's wounds, bitter marks of the quest trials he underwent
to maintain his place in courtly society:

> Et quant ses plaies ont veües,
> si retorne lor joie en ire
> et le roi et tot son enpire.
>
> (ll. 4190–4192)

> And when they saw his wounds,
> joy turned to grief
> for the king and all his train.

Chrétien here reminds us of the dual consequences of chivalric
activity: the return of the knight is often bought at a high price,
the ensuing "joie" in the court a sigh of relief at his survival.
Once "la Joie de la Cort" has been designated as the name

of an adventure, hence removing *joie* from its normal context
of meaning, the use of the word in the text is seldom straightforward. Chrétien puns on the word and so creates ambiguities
and ironies that add to the enigma of the adventure, but this
perversion of its sense does not aid us in identifying what
Chrétien actually meant by the phrase. Such an instance
occurs in Evrain's permission to seek the "Joie" combined
with his usual warning against it:

> —Bien le savoie, fet li rois:
> vos l'avroiz ancontre mon pois,
> la Joie que vos requerez,
> mes molt an sui desesperez,
> et molt dot vostre mescheance.
> Mes des or estes an france
> d'avoir quanque vos covoitiez:
> se vos a joie an esploitiez,
> conquise avroiz si grant enor
> onques hom ne conquist graignor;
> et Dex, si con je le desir,
> vos an doint a joie partir.

(ll. 5609–5620)

> —I know it well, said the king:
> you will have the joy you seek
> in spite of me,
> but I greatly despair of it,
> and fear your downfall.
> But now be assured
> that you will have what you desire:
> if you succeed with joy,
> you will have won such great honor
> that never has man won greater;
> and may God, as I desire,
> give you joy in the outcome of it.

Evrain's wishes that Érec finish the adventure "with joy" employ a double entendre which merely amuses rather than suggests further nuances for the ultimate significance of "Joie" in
Chrétien's narrative. Only in situations such as the entertain-

ment of Érec and Énide in Evrain's court does a context for
"joie" like previous contexts arise:

> An la chanbre antrent main a main,
> si con li rois les i mena,
> qui d'ax grant joie demena.
>
> (ll. 5520–5522)

> They entered the room hand in hand,
> and as the king led them there,
> he took great joy in them.

This "joie" again is the delights afforded by "courtoisie" and
participation in courtly society.

The crowd's cry to Érec as he passes spearheads the riddle
of the "Joie":

> "Haï! Haï!
> chevaliers, Joie t'a traï,
> ceste que tu cuides conquerre,
> mes ta mort et ton duel vas querre."
> Ne n'i a un seul qui ne die:
> "Ceste Joie, Dex la maudie,
> que tant preudome i sont ocis."
>
> (ll. 5655–5661)

> "Alas! Alas!
> knight, the Joy has tricked you
> that you expect to win,
> but you will win your death and your grief."
> And there is not one who does not say:
> "This Joy, God curse it,
> for so many men of valor have been killed by it."

The paradox of an evil "Joie" seems to falsify Érec's early
supposition that "an joie n'a se bien non," in joy there is necessarily only good. To resolve this enigma Chrétien's audience
can only suppose that this joy is either a sham or that it is a sort
of joy that leads to the ruin of noble chevaliers. As Érec approaches the garden, the birds' songs lend him a foretaste of
the "Joie." Again, this detail would imply that this joy already

exists in the garden or that this impression of joy is illusory. Repeatedly we are told that Érec stalwartly, obstinately desires "la Joie" although cautioned so strongly against it. A joy that is treacherous, that lures knights and leads them to their undoing and death, falls into the tradition of Sirens' songs and the charms of Circe. Érec's indolence in the first blush of marriage sprang from such luxurious "joie," no matter how guileless Énide's attractions were. This remiss behavior would lessen his prowess eventually and finally damage the court to which he would succeed as king. Such "joie" enticed Maboagrain into captivity. Érec has deepened his love for Énide while acting the part of a valiant chevalier. He has conquered sensual subjugation and may now win the greater "Joie de la Cort." The adventure lures him especially for it is a heightened, fantastic reformulation of the true end of Érec's quest. This final "Joie" promises both marital bliss and courtly esteem. Chrétien warns us of the follies of even conjugal love when the knight's infatuation with his beloved overwhelms his sense of chivalric duty. The medieval political structure could not risk such "recreantise" even for the most virtuous beauty.

After Érec's liberation of Maboagrain and the garden the word *joie* reappears repeatedly, both as the name of the adventure and as the spirit which pervades, the result of liberation and reunion. Only Maboagrain's mistress has no pleasure in the "Joie" until she learns of her close relationship to Énide, who is also an example for her of the mixture of love and duty in marriage. The demoiselle can then, too, partake of the communality, rooted in blood ties. Overhearing the cousins' exchange, one of the ladies leaves the group to narrate this further detail to the barons "por la Joie croistre et monter" (l. 6278). This succession of retellings and reunions only emphasizes that true "Joie de la Cort" resides in the fusion of personal love and community; the unliberated "Joie," the previous "Joie" of the garden, is solely the former. As a "lai de la Joie" is sung, joy grows and we remember Chrétien's own role of joy-maker through storytelling. The "Joie" and simple joy coalesce. Chrétien's detail, however, that the "Joie" culminated after three days with the departure of Érec and Énide insists once more on the meaning of the adventure for Érec and of the sense of communal strength which is naturally lessened by a valiant knight's egress.

Érec, as hero of the romance, is the bearer of "joie" and savior of the court. None of the kings is able to accomplish this without him. In fact an earlier episode prefigures this role for Érec. Early in the romance King Arthur proposes the hunt of the white stag. Whoever kills the stag must kiss the most beautiful maiden in the court. Gauvain objects to the hunt, for he fears that each knight will defend his lady as most beautiful and that disorder and violence within the court circle will result. Nevertheless, Arthur commands the hunt and takes the white stag himself. Since Érec is absent from the court at the moment, Guinevere urges the king to wait until his return to decide who will receive the kiss. Arthur acquiesces. Érec returns eventually with Énide; Arthur and all the court agree that she is the most beautiful, she receives the honor, and no disorder does result. Érec has unknowingly saved the court from chaos by bringing Énide with him to Caradigan. Likewise, in the adventure of "la Joie de la Cort," he unknowingly saves Evrain's court from the continued absence of the king's nephew. Acting as rescuer of the courtly community Érec is assuming a king's role as ultimate protector of his vassals, and through the climactic "Joie de la Cort" trial he has rightfully earned the crown of his father.

The ultimate consequence of Érec's victory over his trials, over Maboagrain, and over himself, arises soon after his return to Arthur. His father dies; he succeeds to the throne. Érec has survived the test; his character is prepared for kingship. Chrétien repeatedly apologizes for the inadequacy of his art to describe the wonders of this zenith in Érec's career. Superlatives proliferate in the description of the coronation, as do Chrétien's intrusions to explain his purpose in retelling the event, an insuperable task. His narrative employs hyperbole to cover inadequacy, for this all-important event solidifies, even recreates, the community, a new court, founded on chivalric values, on loyalty to a new king, and on his promise of protection to his vassals. We look to the adventure of the "Joie" and realize that Érec, the liberator, freed his people to live in a strongly protected society as he freed himself to live up to this protector role.

Thus Chrétien uses allegory in "la Joie de la Cort" episode to summarize and disclose the key to the entire romance. The word *joie* echoes throughout his text in contraposed contexts, provoking us to interpretation, to deduction of its significance. As Robert Guiette describes this medieval device: "l'esprit allégorique on symbolique se préoccupe des mots, propose des etymologies, se montre sensible à la sonorité verbale" ("the allegorical or symbolic mind is engaged with words, proposes etymologies, shows sensitivity to verbal resonance").[11] Érec realizes and unwittingly recovers true joy in a single symbolic battle. All the "joies" of the romance, of love, of familial and friendship ties, of recognition, of victory, of celebration receive their greatest force when joined to a sense of community and integration in courtly society. Érec breaks the isolating spell, reunites a court, and hence becomes bearer of "la Joie de la Cort," for his own court as well as for Evrain's.

11. Robert Guiette, "Symbolisme et 'senefiance' au moyen age," *Romanica gandensia: Questions de littérature,* 8 (1960), p. 35; my translation.

HOLLY WALLACE BOUCHER

Metonymy in Typology and Allegory, with a Consideration of Dante's *Comedy*

For now we see in a mirror dimly, but then face to face.
Now I know in part, then I shall understand fully.
    I Cor. 13:12

In both metonymy and metaphor a poet says something other
than what he means. By so speaking he may seem to decorate
or even hide his meaning; usually he actually manages to expand his meaning. Metonymy and metaphor are tropes: the
Greek word *trope* is defined as manner or style and so connotes embellishment of language. The root, however, signifies
turn or change. A trope is a turn of phrase that puts a twist in
meaning. Depending on the poet's purpose metonymy or metaphor may snatch meaning from the reader's grasp or turn a
new facet to the reader's view.

Quintilian, the classical authority, defines metaphor as a
trope shorter than the simile, for in the simile, "comparatur rei
quam volumus exprimere" while in the metaphor "pro ipsa re-
dicitur," the object is substituted for the thing rather than simply compared.[1] The trope metonymy consists of the replacement of one name by another, "nominis pro nomine positio"

1. H. E. Butler, *The Institutio Oratoria of Quintilian* (New York: G. P. Putnam's Sons, 1922), 8. 6. 8–9. All further references to this work are to this
edition and will be cited in the text.

(8. 6. 23), by association or reference, such as the name of the invention by that of the inventor, or a possession by the possessor. Closely related to the metonymic trope is the synecdoche, which refers to the part by the whole, or the whole by the part, or something omitted by what is included (8. 6. 19–21). Following the examples of Roman Jakobson and Jacques Lacan, synecdoche will be considered as a species of the genus metonymy in this paper.

We generally think of allegory as extended metaphor, but Isidore of Seville defined allegory simply as *alieniloquium*,[2] or speaking-other. Thus, allegory includes irony, where the poet says one thing but implies another. Ian Bishop reminds us that personification, which we generally associate with allegory, is not classically defined as allegory at all.[3] Further, Quintilian gives examples of both metaphoric, "translatio continuata," and nonmetaphoric allegory. The nonmetaphoric kind consists of disguising the sense by using other words or figures, "aliud verbis aliud sensu ostendit," or irony, "etiam interim contrarium."[4] The ancient definition, then, allows for other ingredients in allegory besides metaphor. Since both metonymy and metaphor are tropes that twist meaning and speak-other, then allegory, or particular kinds of allegory such as typology, may consist of a continued metonymy.

Roman Jakobson has studied the phenomenon of figural expression from a linguistic perspective. In his article on metonymy and metaphor (which is based on study of the mental disease aphasia), he describes the two tropes as opposite mental processes.[5] Metonymy is based on contiguity between words, metaphor on similarity between words; metonymy on referring and association, metaphor on signifying and substitution. According to Jakobson metonymy characterizes the logical fabric

2. Robert Hollander, *Allegory in Dante's Commedia* (Princeton: Princeton University Press, 1969), p. 236.

3. Ian Bishop, *Pearl in Its Setting* (Oxford: Basil Blackwell, 1968), pp. 62–63.

4. See Bishop's discussion of the matter, ibid.

5. Roman Jakobson, "The Metaphoric and Metonymic Poles," in Jakobson and Morris Halle, *Fundamentals of Language* (The Hague: Mouton, 1956), pp. 76–82.

of prose. Indeed, Jacques Lacan calls metonymy "the properly signifying function . . . in language."[6] Morton Bloomfield points out that syntax is fundamentally metonymic:[7] there are certain *syncategorematic* words of which the entire function is connective or, in Jakobson's terms, metonymic. Realism, as opposed to symbolism and other metalingual tendencies in literature, is particularly metonymic in its attempt to reproduce the observed continuities and relations of human experience.

Jakobson asserts that while metonymy is the basis of prose, metaphor underlies poetry. Indeed, as a vision poem the *Divine Comedy* may be considered one extended metaphoric trope: Dante says he is engaged in *"figurando"* the beyond.[8] As a satiric poem, however, the *Comedy* may be considered an extended ironic trope.[9] The *Comedy* is satire, in the sense that Dante wishes to criticize (even damn) the condition of this world by minutely describing the state of the next. As we shall see in consideration of Dante's *Inferno,* the irony of satire is constructed of metonymic relations. Satire employs ellipsis (a type of synecdoche), exaggeration, and dense realistic detail to prove its moral point. These literary techniques involve metonymic processes of reduction, expansion, and association. Jonathan Culler recognizes irony as a metonymy of juxtaposition: "Situational or dramatic irony is thus a device of cohesion which knits together incidents and gives them a meaning

6. Jacques Lacan, "The Insistence of the Letter in the Unconscious," English trans. in F. and R. DeGeorge, *The Structuralists: From Marx to Lévi-Strauss* (Garden City, N.Y.: Doubleday, 1972), p. 300.

7. Morton W. Bloomfield, "The Syncategorematic in Poetry: From Semantics to Syntactics," in *To Honor Roman Jakobson: Essays on the Occasion of His Seventieth Birthday* (The Hague: Mouton, 1967), pp. 309–317.

8. Dante Alighieri, *La divina commedia,* ed. C. H. Grandgent, rev. by Charles S. Singleton (Cambridge, Mass.: Harvard University Press, 1972). 23. 61. All further references to the *Comedy* are to this edition and will be cited in the text; translations are based on John D. Sinclair's version (New York: Oxford University Press, 1939).

9. I will not, in this paper, consider Dante's own views on the genre of the *Comedy.* Nor will I discuss Dante's ideas on allegory, as this perplexing problem has been fully treated elsewhere. See Jean Pépin, *Dante et la tradition de l'allégorie,* Conférence Albert-le-Grand, 1969 (Montreal: Institut d'Etudes Médiévales, 1970).

by relating them to a law of the world."[10] The situational irony of episodes in the *Inferno*, such as Dante's stance as confessor to the writhing feet of Pope Nicholas III, operates on a principle of inverted comparison, or reverse typology.

Both the evidence of traditional definitions of allegory and of contemporary linguistic theory suggest that we seek metonymy in Dante's allegory, where only metaphor has been sought before. I want to argue that Dante's whole typology, even beyond its ironic and realistic qualities, consists of metonymic relationships. Perhaps the long-sought secret to Dante's allegory lies not in the traditional extended metaphor of fourfold allegory, but in a typology dependent on a metonymy of historical continuity and particular *exempla*. A danger lies here, as in any discussion of style or figures of speech. The figure in question begins to be found everywhere and to make all language in its own image. If one seeks irony too assiduously, every bald declarative becomes subtly ironic. This danger is particularly present for study of metonymy because, as a colleague once exclaimed in exasperation, "Reality is metonymic!" There is a need to be precise, then, about what qualities make Dante's typology metonymic; one may at least be encouraged by the fact that Jakobson and Lacan see metonymy as characteristic of prose, metaphor of poetry. Thus metonymy ought to be a *rara avis* in the menagerie of the *Comedy's* tropes; yet one finds it everywhere.

What is metonymic about Dante's typology? At root, I think, it is the concept of time. More specifically it is the Christian concept of time which is metonymic. Time or history in itself may be arbitrarily considered continuous or discontinuous, linear or cyclic. There are exceptions, but if we consider it generally, the Christian concept of history lends time a peculiar shape. It is a shape related to the Platonic, and a product of the Hebrew, but distinct from both. In the Judeo-Christian view time is not perpetual but has a beginning and an end. Each event in time possesses an individual quality because it cannot be repeated; time is not cyclic but linear, so that each historical event is peculiar and particular. But conversely each

10. Jonathan Culler, *Flaubert: The Uses of Uncertainty* (Ithaca: Cornell University Press, 1974), p. 187.

historical event participates in a vast divine design. Each moment is part of a whole with which it is contiguous and to which it is essential. How can these opposites coexist? They coexist because they are the complementary terms of God's purpose, which requires particularity and continuity to lend history both meaning and direction. As A. C. Charity explains in his discussion of Christian typology, the norm for history is an act of God, "not a general idea, but an event, in history."[11] Charity argues that history gains its continuity from the unbroken thread of God's act and man's response: "To God's acts, or at least to his fulfilling act, whether promised or past . . . all events are related and related historically. They have the same ultimate causes as it, and they all share together with it in the one order of contingent cause and effect, in the same history of act and response."[12] History provides the arena for a continuing dialectic of divine and human action.

   Christian typology consists of the "science of history's relations to its fulfillment in Christ."[13] Typology is the perception of God's acts in history as consistent (in biblical terms, steadfast), therefore as interrelated and mutually illuminating; but also as each new, individual, and particular. Typology is continuous not simply because of the continuity of cause and effect in history, but because purpose is lent by history's author, God. According to this view God makes each event a partial revelation of his whole purpose and a term relative to the absolute fulfillment in Christ. God constructs history as a tightly written book where every episode depends on the episode before and refers to the episode ahead: "Divine activity, its purpose and its consistency, is basic to all genuine typology."[14] Frank Kermode perceives, in both the Gospels and the *Comedy,* an understanding of history as the prototypical book which possesses complex references among its pages: "There was a need for realism [in these books], and an equal need for

   11. A. C. Charity, *Events and Their Afterlife: The Dialectics of Christian Typology in the Bible and Dante* (Cambridge: Cambridge University Press, 1966), p. 5.
   12. Ibid.
   13. Ibid., p. 1.
   14. Ibid., p. 83.

testimonia, so that this sequence of events should seem a piece or even the crown of an historical development perceptible to the eye of the interpreter and written into the structure of the world, now seen as a book, now as a codex."[15] The legible continuum of time, it seems, is basic to the referential quality of all meaningful events.

After time and God, man provides the third aspect of continuity in typology. Man stands as the subject of typology as it unfolds in history. Unavoidably man participates in history, and inescapably he must accept or deny the claims of God's acts: "For man is at all times a part of the history which he interprets: he is involved inescapably in it."[16] The reason for man's involvement is crucial, because it coincides with God's involvement. The absolute term of history, the fulfillment of every event and the point to which all others, before and after, refer, is God's incarnation as man. Saint Augustine perceived that the basic factor which distinguished Christians from the Platonists and other wise men was not the concept of the Word but the incarnation of the Word in flesh. Hollander notes that the extended metaphor of allegory is the appropriate trope for Platonic truths, whereas (as I suggest) the extended metonymy of typology is the trope of Christian revelation, because Christian truth involves the particularity of history and the concreteness of the individual person.[17] In the Christian view the Incarnation transformed history not in the sense that it transcended time but in the sense that it redeemed time and invested history with purpose. The Incarnation became history's axis by entering history and centering history on God. Events in history are types of the Christ event "by virtue of their relation to a revelation that is fulfilled in him."[18]

How may the general concept of typology in history be applied to the specific episodes of the *Comedy?* Auerbach, Charity, and Hollander have all argued convincingly (if variously) that in the *Comedy* the individual person is judged by God in

15. Frank Kermode, *The Genesis of Secrecy: On the Interpretation of Narrative* (Cambridge, Mass.: Harvard University Press, 1979), p. 121.

16. Charity, *Events and Their Afterlife,* p. 8.

17. Hollander, *Allegory,* p. 5.

18. Charity, *Events and Their Afterlife,* p. 150.

terms of his own history. Thus each individual in death is the
antitype of his life in history; at the same time he is the type to
the antitype of Christ. Typology applies not only to great historical events but to the minutiae of everyday life. Charity
finds in Saint Paul the conviction that "both the existence
which the Christian possesses in the present, and all that is still
outstanding, still to be attained . . . are related, organically
and dialectically to the creative 'past' of God's action in
Christ."[19] Judgment, which is the subject of the *Comedy,* involves a typology because each person is judged against the
demand of the antitype of Christ. The verdict is rendered by
the individual himself. He confronts his own essence in death
as God confronts him, and the indelible truth of the earthly career is revealed. As Dante explains, "In voi è la cagione, in voi
si cheggia" ("In you lies the reason for evil, in you let it be
sought" *Purg.* 16. 83). If the soul has departed in sin from the
antitype of Christ to conform to the antitype of Satan, Adam,
and other deniers of God's plan, the moment of death reveals
this ironic denial as the sum of the soul's history. It is irrevocably separated from God in Hell. If the soul has cleaved in faith
to the antitype of Christ and affirmed God's purpose, then in
the moment of death he joins the fellowship of those who made
Christ the final term of their life. Necessarily, the individual's
life represents a "subfulfillment" of the life of Christ, not by
imitation but by partaking in Christ.[20] As Charity points out,
"all 'genuine' typology is 'applied' ";[21] by definition, typology
is incarnate. In the *Comedy* typology is applied in judgment.

The Word of God is the only word with historical existence,
as Hollander explains.[22] In the Platonic conception the spiritual truths are shadowed by the unreal visible world. But to
Christianity the unbridgeable gap between Creator and creation has been bridged by the Word made flesh. Creation itself
becomes part of God's truth, because God has become part of
concrete experience. The visible world does more than represent truth, it partakes of truth: "The relationship which typol-

19. Ibid., p. 87.
20. Ibid., p. 152.
21. Ibid., p. 159.
22. Hollander, *Allegory,* p. 21.

ogy embodies is . . . a dialectical rather than a directly representational one [in contrast to Platonic allegory]. One thing
does not mean another in typology: it involves it, or has infer-
ences for it, or suggests it . . . there is a real, existential,
parallel, as well as a certain historical dependency and continuity between the events which typology relates."[23] If metaphor, which consists of one thing represented or signified by
another distinct thing, serves to figure Platonic truths, then
metonymy, which represents a whole by a part which belongs
to it, or a part by the whole which contains it, or one thing by
another integrally connected to it, is the appropriate figure for
Christian typology. Coming close to this notion Charity calls
the tropes of the *Comedy* "images, references, and evoca-
tions," and "allusive rather than simply allegorical methods."[24]

Turning from the general subject of Christian typology as a
metonymic structure to the study of typology and metonymy
as discovered specifically in the *Comedy,* we find that several
salient aspects of Dante's journey may be described as metonymic. The first is the journey, the second the *exemplum,* the
third the *contrapasso* or retribution, and the last the representation of vice. The text itself best reveals these elements; we
will consider *Inferno* 5, the meeting with Paolo and Francesca.

> Così discesi del cerchio primaio
> giù nel secondo, che men loco cinghia,
> e tanto più dolor, che punge a guaio.

Thus I descended from the first circle down into the second, which
bounds a smaller space and so much the more of pain that goads to
wailing. (*Inf.* 5. 1–3)

Dante's journey has been described as type, image, figure,
symbol, allegory, metaphor, representation—almost any

23. Charity, *Events and Their Afterlife,* p. 199. See also Hollander, *Allegory,* p. 5, and the descriptions of metonymic structure in Jakobson "Metaphoric and Metonymic Poles," and Lacan, "The Insistence of the Letter."
24. Charity, *Events and Their Afterlife,* p. 247.

trope except metonymy. But that is how I would like to explain it, as metonymy.

David Lodge's description of the metonymic continuity of film applies to the progressive flow of Dante's pilgrimage: "We move through time and space lineally and our sensory experience is a succession of contiguities."[25] For Dante's journey is at once continuous within itself (as the uninterrupted traversal of the three realms of the beyond), with Dante's own life (for it is represented as a concrete event in that life and depicts Dante's concrete life experiences), and with Christian history. Dante has taken great care to make his journey refer to Christian history (as reflected in typology, liturgy, and theology) at every step. But his references to the general succeed only because the referent itself inheres in a concrete and particular experience. It is easy, but inexact, to call Dante's means of representation symbolism, as do Singleton and Gilson. Auerbach is more precise in calling it *figura,* by which he means that Dante's journey represents a typological fulfillment. Gilson agrees that each character met on the journey is not "a mere symbol: that the coefficient of reality . . . does much to make them live for us."[26] Hollander suggests that Dante uses allegory, symbolism, and metaphor in a peculiar way, because like the ancient use of *allegoria in factis,* Dante uses a verbal figuralism. He "treated the very words of his own poem as things."[27] Singleton has described the journey perceptively. He sees it as both metaphor and not metaphor: "The whole journey beyond exceeds metaphor. It is irreducible to the kind of allegory in which it had its origin."[28] Finally, Charity considers it crucial that the journey is extended in space, because the souls are lent a coherence to each other and within the design of God: their "locations cast light back on the living per-

25. David Lodge, *The Modes of Modern Writing: Metaphor, Metonymy, and the Typology of Modern Literature* (Ithaca: Cornell University Press, 1977), p. 84.

26. Etienne Gilson, *Dante the Philosopher,* trans. David Moore (London: Sheed and Ward, 1948), p. 70.

27. Hollander, *Allegory,* p. 264.

28. Charles S. Singleton, *Dante Studies I: Commedia, Elements of Structure* (Cambridge, Mass.: Harvard University Press, 1954), p. 12.

son who, by decisions taken when his will was still mutable, has committed his soul to this place."[29]

Each of these critics realizes that the journey is not adequately described as metaphor. I suggest that is because the journey depends on a principle of coherence of time and space and person which belongs only to metonymy. The journey stands as a part of the whole of Dante's life; but it reveals much more. It reveals how each of the depicted lives takes part in the whole plan of salvation; yet this unencompassable whole must be described only in part as we, the whole audience represented by a single pilgrim, meet a few of the souls in death. How better to describe this inherence of the whole in the part and participation of the part in the whole, than as metonymy?

Canto 5 opens with the striking image of Minos, the demon judge who weighs the gravity of each particular sin and sends the sinner to his particular punishment: "Vanno a vicenda ciascuna al giudizio, / dicono e odone e poi son giù volte" ("They go each in turn to the judgment; they speak and hear and then are hurled below," 14–15). As we have seen, the judgment is inseparable from the sin, and in ironic juxtaposition to the virtue. The punishments that Dante shows are not signs or metaphors for the state of souls after death but an integral result of the soul's life. As Auerbach perceived, the souls met on the journey are not mere shades of a more complete earthly life but the reverse: in death a person is eternalized in his essence and "we behold an intensified image of the essence of [his] being."[30] In death God has "never destroyed an individual form but on the contrary has fixed it in his eternal judgment . . . and wholly revealed it to sight."[31] In earthly experience we see but a part of the whole individual that confronts us beyond death. In "Figura" Auerbach explains his theory that the dead encountered in the *Comedy* are typological fulfillments of the promise (good or ill) of their lives. Thus each soul participates in a personal typology. Yet this whole can only be

29. Charity, *Events and Their Afterlife*, p. 198.

30. Erich Auerbach, *Mimesis: The Representation of Reality in Western Literature*, trans. Willard Trask (Princeton: Princeton University Press, 1953), p. 167.

31. Ibid., p. 168.

suggested by the few concrete attributes a person may reveal in the brief meeting.

When Dante has passed Minos he enters the second circle of tormented spirits and peers into the obscurity of "la bufera infernal" (31), the hellish storm which buffets a myriad of wailing souls. They rush in a "schiera larga e piena" ("a broad, dense flock," 41), which Dante compares to the flight of starlings or cranes. Especially in the *Inferno,* but also in the rather underpopulated *Paradiso,* Dante will confront crowds of the dead, and ask that one or two individuals be distinguished from the rest as examples. In every circle, terrace, or sphere, a few souls serve as *exempla* for a whole category of people. This is a common didactic technique; it is also a form of metonymy. The working of this metonymic device presupposes that the whole soul may be revealed by a few concrete characteristics; it also assumes, in the *Inferno,* that the soul may appropriately be condemned to the punishment of a single sin as the expression of the soul's whole nature. When Vergil descries and names several of the sinners in the horde of the lustful, he chooses a part to represent the whole: "E più di mille / ombre mostrommi e nominommi a dito" ("And he showed me more than a thousand shades, naming them as he pointed," 67–68). Each soul, in turn, is wholly represented by the punishment of a single, representative, sin.

The punishment of the sins by the *contrapasso* also exemplifies metonymy. For "the analogy between sin and punishment is direct . . . the latter is seen to consist in the perpetual continuance of the sin itself."[32] In fact, the *contrapasso* is not analogy at all, but a continuation of the sin, projected into eternity. As we have seen it is through the realistic attributes of each soul vis-à-vis the punishment that there occurs "an otherwise impossible degree of self-disclosure on the part of the shades."[33] The *contrapasso* makes explicit what was only implied in the person's earthly conduct—the blindness of earthly sin is ironically revealed in the light of eternity.

Metonymy is particularly appropriate to the description of

32. Charity, *Events and Their Afterlife,* p. 190.
33. Ibid., p. 189.

the sinful life (where things are always in disproportionate relation), especially here to the depiction of violent lovers. They
are described metonymically, "noi che tignemmo il mondo di
sanguigno" ("we who stained the world with blood," 90). This
image is a kind of double metonymy: as the stain of blood is
merely an emblem of all the effects of violent crime, so these
lovers shirked the responsibilities of all but one human relationship. As the society affected by the crime is a part represented by the whole, "il mondo," so these sinners allowed one
relationship to swallow all of life.

Accordingly, Paolo and Francesca confront Dante as spirits
driven, "di qua, di là, di giù, di sù" ("hither, thither, downward, upward," 43) by a dark storm. The punishment possesses a peculiar irony. In death they suffer physically and un-
endingly the torment their wills so eagerly embraced in life
when their intellects succumbed ("la ragion sommettono al ta-
lento," 39) to lust. The lovers clasp each other in an inseparable embrace: as they cleaved together willfully in life, here
they are condemned never to part. The *contrapasso* represents
the sin by an emblematic crystallizing of corruption into its attributes. Cohering to the earthly life of the individual, the *contrapasso* sums up that life externally.

Throughout this canto the motive power is love. Love has
driven these souls from life ("ch'amor di nostra vita dipartille," 69). Dante invokes Paolo and Francesca by the love that
leads them ("per quello amor che i mena," 78). They come as
doves summoned by desire ("dal disio chiamate," 82), borne
by their will ("dal voler portate," 84). Love is metonymic in
the sense that it drives people into association and contiguity.
Paolo and Francesca represent this aspect of love as they
clutch each other in a permanent embrace.

Jakobson discovered the aptness of metonymy for expressing repressed wishes; metonymy characterizes the censored
letters of prisoners, for instance, because the prisoners speak
of privation and desire but must express their lack by association and oblique reference. Jakobson's findings would seem
fertile for investigation from the Freudian perspective; indeed,
Jakobson's work informs studies by Jacques Lacan. Lacan attacks the Saussurean view that the signifying word designates

the signified meaning only arbitrarily. He claims, "No meaning is sustained by anything other than reference to another meaning."[34] Lacan sees metonymy and metaphor as the "two slopes of the incidence of the signifier on the signified,"[35] two ways in which the meaning of words is slanted, obscured, expanded, clarified. Whereas metaphor is the replacement of one word by another,[36] metonymy is based on the "word-to-word connection."[37] Because metonymy works by association and contiguity, by taking the part for the whole or referring to the part by the whole, it possesses the "power to bypass the obstacles of social censure."[38] Metaphor addresses the question of being, Lacan suggests, while metonymy poses the question of lack and of desire. Desire itself is a metonymy,[39] for metonymy expresses itself as "eternally stretching forth towards the desire for something else."[40] This stretching forth, when it occurs on the moral level, is called love or lust, and it is expressed on the linguistic level as a seeking of word to follow word in prose, or specifically, in metonymy.

The metonymy of love may be expressed in theological language. To Saint Augustine love is the motive force of all creation. Everyone loves the good and therefore ought finally to love the greatest good, which is God. But people are often diverted and love only lesser, created goods. This perversion, or inversion of love, is sin, where reason is subjected to desire. In sin a soul chooses a part of creation and loves it instead of loving the whole and end, which is God. Rightly directed love will lead a soul from good thing to good thing to the greatest good, love of God. God will be partly revealed by all of his creation and finally wholly loved. But wrongly directed love or lust will take the part, pleasure or money, for the complete good, salvation. Dante explains that the child "volentier torna a ciò che la trastulla" ("turns eagerly to what delights it," *Purg.* 16. 90).

34. Lacan, "The Insistence of the Letter," p. 292.
35. Ibid., p. 305.
36. Ibid., p. 301.
37. Ibid., p. 300.
38. Ibid., p. 303.
39. Ibid., p. 323.
40. Ibid., p. 313.

At first "di picciol bene in pria sente sapore" ("it tastes the savor of a trifling good," 91), and from there it is tricked and diverted ("quivi s'inganna, e dietro ad esso corre," 92).

Francesca describes love as a power, latent in the heart, which seizes the soul and attaches it irrevocably to the object of desire:

> Amor ch'a nullo amato amar perdona,
> mi prese del costui piacer sì forte,
> che, come vedi, ancor non m'abbandona.

Love, which absolves no one beloved from loving, seized me so strongly with his charm that, as thou seest, it does not leave me yet. (103–105)

Love has moved the lovers to desire only each other, so that they are diverted from the path which might lead them to God. The whole delight of Heaven that can be partially glimpsed and tasted in the joys of human love is forever replaced by this limited pleasure.

By what process does love seize and knit together the lovers' hearts in adulterous desire? As Francesca reveals, the process itself is metonymic. Love proceeds by association. As Christian conversion is often inspired by a book, whether it be the Bible, as with Saint Augustine, or the book of God's creation, so this love also begins with a book. If Dante's poem is an artifact imitating the poetic structure of creation,[41] and if to him words are things, then Dante must admit that words may bring forth sin as well as virtue. The love-inspiring book provides the emblem *par excellence* for the metonymic, associative quality of love. Paolo and Francesca read together from a book about Lancelot's love and of the tokens which lead to the full act of love. "Ma solo un punto fu quel che ci vinse" ("But one point alone it was that mastered us," 132): the lovers read of the kiss, and what that emblem was for Lancelot—a part of the desired whole—it becomes for them. As the words of a book are the medium of love, so do the eyes and mouth mediate the signs of desire:

41. Singleton, *Dante Studies I*, p. 25.

> Quando leggemmo il disïato riso
> esser basciato da cotanto amante,
> questi . . . la bocca mi basciò.

When we read that the longed-for smile was kissed by so great a lover, he . . . kissed my mouth.   (133–136)

Then Francesca and Paolo leave the book, which had led them to each other. It has done its work. We do not need to ask if its work was a metonymic function, because Francesca asserts that the book acted as the classic pander or go-between: "Galeotto fu'l libro e chi lo scrisse" ("A Galeotto was the book and he that wrote it," 137). The act of a pander exemplifies metonymy; the pander refers the love of one to that of another, bringing the two into contiguity by the exchange of tokens in promises or money. Francesca's words act, further, as a pander to Dante, who is overwhelmed by sorrow and pity, so that finally he participates in the lovers' torment and falls "come corpo morto cade" ("as a dead body falls," 142). The metonymy of love has seized even the poet, threatening to make him a participant in vice.

Dante's reaction to Francesca's speech implicates the poet not only emotionally but morally. For Dante's falling like a dead body is ironically juxtaposed to his real purpose on the journey, which is to be exalted to full life by the heavenly vision, not to faint dead away at the sight of sinners. The swoon recalls an earlier ironic juxtaposition, when Vergil points out the lovers whom love has separated from life, "ch'amor di nostra vita dipartille" (5. 69). As Dante hears that the heroes and heroines of the chivalric romances are damned he is crushed by pity, "fui quasi smarrito" (5. 72). Within the space of these four lines are repeated two phrases from the *Comedy's* opening sentence, "nostra vita" (1. 1), and "smarrita" (1. 3). Does Dante, in the ironic association of these two episodes, suggest that it was by a false, chivalric concept of love that he originally lost his way in life? In drawing a relation between the plight of these sinners and the loss of his way Dante ironically convicts himself of their sin. Yet in a further irony, since he is guilty only by association, he allows himself to suffer their damnation only by his compassion for them. Compassion acts, in turn, as the ironic conviction of the poet.

In this discussion of the Paolo and Francesca episode of the *Comedy* we have discovered that basic elements of the poem —the journey, the *exemplum*, the *contrapasso*, and vice—are represented in metonymic terms. Perhaps, then, it may be said of Dante's whole typology that it works not on metaphoric but on metonymic principles.

If Dante's typology is an extension of the metonymic trope, may other allegories be considered forms of metonymy as well? Certainly there are some that may not. In the area of allegorical interpretation Philo's allegorical exegesis of the Bible is built on metaphor. But as I have suggested most of the Christian exegetes, although influenced by the metaphors of Platonism, produce a biblical typology that is arguably metonymic. Personification allegory would seem antithetical to the metonymic construction because it consists of the substitution of one thing, an abstract quality, by another, a human character. But very often in personification human qualities are represented by the association of attributes. The golden-cowled hypocrites of *Inferno* 23 are personifications of this sort; the artistic representation of Avarice as distinguished by his moneybags might be considered a form of metonymy as well. Shall we consider the figure of Superbia in *Piers Plowman,* a figure named for a quality that is attributed to a certain kind of person, and recounting the particular sins in which this prideful person participates, a metaphor? It seems to me that Langland is not representing one thing, the quality Pride, by another thing, a prideful person, but that he exemplifies Pride by particular instances which inhere in the general category. And use of a particular to exemplify the whole we call metonymy.

The metonymic aspects of allegory may be approached from a perspective other than that of the use of attributes. Many political allegories, for instance, were conceived under threat of persecution. The theories of Lacan, Jakobson, and Leo Strauss[42] suggest to us that these censor-evading allegories

---

42. See Leo Strauss, *Persecution and the Art of Writing* (Glencoe, Ill.: Free Press, 1952), p. 24.

may possess metonymic structures. The parables and allegories of nineteenth-century Russian writers provide an example.

Finally, however, these suppositions as to the metonymic character of any allegory, including the *Comedy's*, can yield only relative conclusions. All language, as Jakobson has shown, is woven of both metonymy and metaphor. But an understanding of allegory on the level of grammar cannot fail to illuminate the still quite obscure questions, "what is allegory?" and "how does allegory work?" We have found that Dante's typological allegory is firmly rooted in the soil of historical circumstance; if such may be said about the allegory of other poets and of different types, perhaps allegory will no longer seem elaborately and gratuitously fictive but rather closely bound to historical and political necessity.

PATRIZIA GRIMALDI

Sir Orfeo as Celtic Folk-Hero, Christian Pilgrim, and Medieval King

Poor Turlygod poor Tom That's something yet:
Edgar I nothing am.
 King Lear 2. 3. 20

Sir Orfeo is one of many allegorizations of classical myths found in the Middle Ages. An allegorist, according to Frye and tradition, discusses one series of events when he is actually talking about another.[1] *Sir Orfeo* is an example of what Frye terms a "complex" allegory. Unlike many moral tales in which the allegory is simple and "the fiction wholly subordinate to the abstract moral,"[2] *Sir Orfeo* is complex because it employs an elaborate system of parallels to Celtic folklore and mythology, Christian morality, and political ethics.

Dante and many other writers in the Middle Ages, drawing upon patristic interpretation of the Bible, distinguish four (sometimes three) levels of interpretation: the literal level, the allegorical or History of the Church level, the tropological or

1. N. Frye, "Allegory," *Princeton Encyclopedia of Poetry and Poetics* (Princeton: Princeton University Press, 1965), p. 12. See also N. Frye, *Anatomy of Criticism* (Princeton: Princeton University Press, 1957), pp. 89–90.
2. N. Frye, "Allegory."

moral level, and anagogic or eschatological level.[3] I find this
doctrine of multiple readings extremely useful for the understanding of *Sir Orfeo*. The first (literal), because oldest in this
version, meaning of *Sir Orfeo* may be seen in a folktale pattern
based upon Celtic folklore and mythology; the second (allegorical and moral) meaning may be understood in terms of
Orfeo as a Christian pilgrim; the ultimate meaning (which is
usually "anagogic" but which I interpret as "social") lies in
considering Orfeo as a type of king who undergoes a political
education. Whether we view Orfeo's role as that of folk-hero,
pilgrim, or king, there is a major difference in the significance
of different episodes and in different stylistic elements.

I must begin by emphasizing that the main concern of the author is not Orfeo's great love for Heurodis. Vladimir Propp has
established that the basic unit of the fairy tale is not the character but the character's function in the plot.[4] The true significance of the poem, at all three levels of meaning, lies in the
trials undergone by Orfeo in his search for Heurodis. A Prop-
pian analysis, given below, reveals the pattern of action upon
which all three levels of meaning in the poem depend:[5]

I. *Process of abduction*
   1. ll. 1–55[6]   *Prologue:* The initial situation.
   2. ll. 55–69   *Violation:* Heurodis goes with her maid-
                       ens into the garden.
   3. ll. 69–76   *Victim submits to deception and thereby
                       unwittingly helps the enemy:* (definition:
                       complicity). No one lulls Heurodis to
                       sleep. She suddenly falls asleep by
                       herself to facilitate the villain's task.
   3. ll. 130–175   *The villain uses persuasion:* The knight

3. See, for instance, Dante's *Epistle to Can Grande,* ed. Giovan Battista
Giuliani (Savona: L. Sambolino, 1856), p. xxv.
4. As discussed in Victor Erlich, *Russian Formalism* (The Hague: Mouton,
1955), p. 217.
5. See Vladimir Propp, *The Morphology of the Folk Tale,* 2nd ed., rev. and
ed. Lewis A. Wagner, trans. Laurence Scott (Austin and London: University
of Texas Press, 1968), pp. 20–65.
6. All references to the text of *Sir Orfeo* are from A. J. Bliss, ed., *Sir Orfeo,*
2nd ed. (Oxford: Clarendon Press, 1966).

is sent to fetch Heurodis; later, the king takes her for a ride on his horse and shows her all sorts of beautiful things.

5. ll. 190–195   *The villain causes harm or injury to a member of the family:* (definition: villainy). The fairy king carries Heurodis away. This function is extremely important, since by means of it, the actual movement of the tale is created.

II. *Counteraction to abduction*

1. ll. 195–200   *Lack or insufficiency:* Orfeo loses Heurodis.

2. ll. 200–225   *Beginning of counteraction:* Orfeo makes the decision to leave his kingdom in search of Heurodis.

3. ll. 226–233   *Departure and the acquisition of magical agent:* Orfeo leaves home, with a harp that functions as a magical agent (not acquired, since it belongs to the hero).

4. ll. 281–355   *Hero transferred, delivered, or led to whereabouts of object of search:* (definition: spatial transference between two kingdoms). The fairy hunt actually guides Orfeo to the rock.

5. ll. 410–460   *Indirect combat of hero and villain:* The struggle here assumes its mild form in enchantment through the use of the harp.

6. ll. 460–470   *Initial misfortune or lack is liquidated:* Orfeo wins back Heurodis.

III. *Return of Orfeo*

1. ll. 477–478   *Hero returns:* (definition: return).

2. ll. 480   *Unrecognized arrival.*

3. ll. 530–550   *Difficult task:* Difficult task posed in this case to the steward, who functions as a substitute for the hero.

4. ll. 550–583   *Solution of task and the recognition of the hero:* The steward's heroic nature is recognized by his posing of the task.

5. ll. 584–586   *Transfiguration:* Orfeo reassumes his kingly appearance.

There is a folktale pattern here that the poet may or may not have consciously recognized which is a major governing agent of the poem.[7] The segmentation of the narrative reveals that the functions of the *dramatis personae* and the distributions of the functions among the *dramatis personae* of *Sir Orfeo* fits the pattern of the folktale as given by Vladimir Propp. Propp's description of the introduction and reintroduction of the folktale villain, for instance, precisely fits the introduction and reintroduction of the fairy king in *Sir Orfeo:* "First he makes a sudden appearance from the outside (flies to the scene, sneaks up on someone, etc.), and then disappears. His second appearance in the tale is as a person who *has been sought out,* usually as the result of guidance."[8] In lines 142–174 of *Sir Orfeo* the fairy king makes his sudden appearance before Heurodis, takes her for a ride through his kingdom, and informs her that the next day she must be under the ympe-tre to be taken away forever. The fairy king makes his second appearance in the tale at the end of Orfeo's search for the fairy kingdom.

The abstraction of the folktale pattern from *Sir Orfeo* reveals a neutral framework that serves to support multiple levels of interpretation. The Celtic elements added to this neutral framework define the journey of Orfeo, on the literal level, as one of a Celtic folk-hero. The Christian elements coalesce and build upon the folktale framework to form an allegorical representation of Orfeo as a Christian pilgrim. The notion of law that enters into the poem give rise to our consideration of Orfeo as a medieval king.

A few elements in the poem have attracted the attention of many critics for their strong ambiguity. I do not expect to unlock their "final" meanings but I will consider them as "open" signs susceptible to an interpretation of multiple meanings.[9] As

7. See Susan Wittig, *Stylistic and Narrative Structures in the Middle English Romances* (Austin and London: University of Texas Press, 1978), p. 135.

8. Propp, *The Morphology of the Folk Tale,* p. 84.

9. To attempt to discover "final meanings" is, in my opinion, a mistaken critical approach. For examples see Alice E. Lasaster, "Under the Ympe-tre: or Where the Action Is in *Sir Orfeo*," *Southern Quarterly,* 12, no. 4 (1974), 356–363; and Constance Davis, "Classical Threads in *Sir Orfeo*," *Modern Language Review,* 56 (April 1961), 161–166.

symbols they are *in limine* between two cultures and traditions, the Celtic and the Christian.

If we look at these ambiguities from the point of view of the
folktale they appear to be simply the magic objects of a collec-
tive imagination, having no great moral or social significance.
The much-discussed ympe-tre, for example, besides being related to the various trees of fairy tales, around or underneath
which magic events take place and which are symbols of fertility, is also closely related to the apple tree of the Celtic Other
World.[10] The Celtic element, however, lies not in the tree itself
(as it is not necessarily an apple tree) but in the fact that the
tree is simultaneously found both in the garden whence
Heurodis is abducted and in the fairy kingdom. The fact of the
ympe-tre being in two places at the same time signals its magic
qualities. As Eleanor Hull has pointed out, the most invariable
characteristic of the unseen world in Celtic myth is that objects
found there belong to the ordinary surroundings of every Irish
dwelling of any rank.[11]

I do not believe that the ympe-tre is related to Vergil's great
elm of dreams (*Aeneid*, 6. 281–284),[12] nor am I convinced by
the assertion that the Other World is the kingdom of Pluto and
that Heurodis is Proserpine.[13] The motivations of the abduction of Heurodis and Proserpine are not at all alike: the abduc-

10. As has been observed by A. J. Bliss, *Sir Orfeo*, p. xxxi; H. R. Patch,
The Other World According to Descriptions in Medieval Literature (Cambridge, Mass.: Harvard University Press, 1950), p. 37; and Drorena Allen,
"Orpheus and Orfeo: The Dead and the Taken," *Medium aevum*, 33, no. 21
(1964), 102–111.

11. In "The Idea of Hades in Celtic Literature," *Folklore*, 8 (1907), 121–
165. (The article is unannotated.)

12. Constance Davis, in "Classical Threads in *Sir Orfeo*," adopts Roman
mythology to explain the origin of the idea of the fairy kingdom in *Sir Orfeo*.
Besides assimilating the ympe-tre to the Vergilian *ulmus opaca*, Davis has a
less felicitous comparison to Roman architecture: "A tree was a common feature in the forecourt of a Roman house" (p. 165). She also believes that the
Other World in *Sir Orfeo* is the Roman Hades.

13. R. S. Loomis, in *Wales and the Arthurian Legend* (Cardiff: University
of Wales Press, 1956), pp. 132–177 and Eleanor Hull, in "The Idea of Hades in
Celtic Literature," p. 134, among other scholars, oppose the "casual assumption" that every Celtic fairyland was a *Totenreich* (Loomis, p. 142). Loomis
defines any analogy with classical traditions as "a gross misnomer" (p. 144).

tion of Proserpine was an act motivated by love to make her
queen of Hades; the abduction of Heurodis, on the other hand,
is both the fairy king's willful and capricious exertion of his
powers to interfere with human affairs and a manifestation of
his intention to test Orfeo. It is also quite clear that there is a
Queen of Fairy wholly distinct from Heurodis. According to
Celtic lore the fact that the same tree is found in the Other
World indicates either that the ympe-tre belongs there and that
Heurodis sleeping by it puts herself in the power of the fairies,
or that Heurodis herself is a fairy who belongs with the ympe-
tre and to the fairy kingdom. Heurodis might be considered a
fairy:[14] marriages between mortals and deities are common in
all mythologies, and it is an interesting fact that the ten years
spent in the Other World have not aged her. The story of
Heurodis' abduction in fact resembles that of the Irish legend
of Étaín, queen of Eochaid Airem, king of Ireland. Étaín was
herself one of the *side* or fairies; and one of Mider's reasons for
taking her away was that she had been his wife in a previous
stage of existence.

The Other World in *Sir Orfeo* is the Celtic *Sidh*. The description of fairyland is one of unfailing brightness and of inexhaust-
ible joy. Everlasting youth, brave men and lovely women,
music, drinking, and pastimes are widespread in Celtic legends. Walter Map and Giraldus Cambrensis have described the
lower realm as a fair, though dim, land, inhabited by high-
minded dwarves and abounding in treasure.[15] In the Celtic legends, however, as in many other mythologies, the location of
the Other World was a matter of conflicting traditions. One ancient conception seems to have placed it beneath the earth. A
poem in the *Book of Taliesin* (no. 7) contains the phrase "in the
Annwn below the earth, in the air above the earth"[16] (*Annwn* is
the Welsh designation for the Other World). In the same book
there is a poem usually called "Spoils of Annwn" (no. 30),
where Annwn is a name for Kaer-Siddi, the fairy fortress. In

14. A. J. Bliss, in *Sir Orfeo*, thinks that the poem does not provide enough
evidence to affirm such a thing (p. 35).

15. As discussed in R. S. Loomis, "*Sir Orfeo* and Walter Map's *De nugis*,"
Modern Language Notes, 51 (1936), 28–30.

16. R. S. Loomis, in *Wales and the Arthurian Legend*, p. 140, italics mine.

addition to the reference to a fairy fortress, other aspects of this poem are similar to those in *Sir Orfeo;* the fortress is also one of glass (the *Kaer Wydyr*) and the physical objects in the landscape, a gate and turrets, are similar. There is also a prisoner, Gweir, to be rescued.

A satisfactory explanation of the Other World in *Sir Orfeo* has not been given. In particular, the passage extending from line 387 to line 404 has given critics great difficulty.[17] This passage describes Orfeo's encounter with bodies "þouȝt dede, and nare nouȝt." The bodies are captured in the moment of their deaths and suggest the terrible consequences of warfare and a disordered Nature. Eleanor Hull's observation that objects that belong to the unseen world also belong to the ordinary world of the Celts, no matter how grim they are, seems relevant here. According to her, "As warfare and bloodshedding were essential to happiness in earthly life, they are at times reproduced in the Other World."[18] In both the Celtic and Christian cultures the meaning of this passage is that death, however peaceful it may appear to be, is a work of violence— a cutting down. The myths do not mitigate the impact of death with soothing words; they present it in its grimmest brutality.[19]

Despite the fact that there is not enough information to determine whether the Other World in *Sir Orfeo* is definitely Celtic, at the literal level the Other World in *Sir Orfeo,* just as in all Celtic myths, is the focal point of the poem. The narrative tension is directed toward Orfeo's finding the fairy kingdom, and the climax of the action takes place when Orfeo (the hero) meets the fairy king (the villain). While his ten years spent in the forest as a wild man are relevant to the understanding of the story as a Christian allegory, they are of only secondary

17. Bruce Mitchell in his "The Faery World of *Sir Orfeo*," *Neophilologus*, 2 (1964), 155–159, disposes altogether of lines 308–401 as a later addition to the poem and therefore not relevant. Dorena Allen, in her "Orpheus and Orfeo: The Dead and the Taken," p. 107, identifies the people suspended in the moment of their death as *taise*, which are wandering visible souls. This identification fails to establish the relationship of these *taise* to the Other World seen by Orfeo.

18. In "The Idea of Hades in Celtic Literature," p. 153.

19. As observed by Alwin Rees and Bringley Rees in their *Celtic Heritage* (London: Thames and Hudson, 1961), p. 341.

importance to the understanding of the poem as a folktale. On
the folk-hero level the meaning of the poem simply consists of
one man's initiation into life through experience. Like the
meaning of the voyage of Bran, the meaning of the ten years'
journey is not that of a pilgrimage nor is it connected with the
expiation of crimes.[20] The stories of "voyages" (*immram*) told
by Irish storytellers were the dramatizations of an initiation
process through experience into a more comprehensive view
of the world. Orfeo (the man), like Bran, son of Febal, or Cu-
chalain, is one of those elect mortals invited to the dwelling
place of the eternally young immortals. Like Bran or Oisin,
Orfeo and Heurodis return to earth only to die.[21] When Bran
returns to earth the lady in Mag Mell sings a lay that presents
Bran as a man set apart by his acquired wisdom:

> Not to all of you is my speech,
> though its great marvel has been known.
> Let Bran hear from the crowd of the world
> that of wisdom has been told to him.[22]

The wisdom gained by Bran is the kind of wisdom gained by
Orfeo.

The classical myth of Orpheus has often been used to illustrate unsuccessful human striving toward some ultimate goal.
In Christian times Orpheus was interpreted as a type of Christ
and his story as an allegory of the soul.[23] In what can be called
the textual tradition in the Middle Ages Orpheus exemplifies a
man fallen prey to his senses, who is forever looking longingly
back on earthly things. As Kenneth Gross Louis writes,
"Eurydice represents man's passion, constantly fleeing from
virtue and running through fields and meadows symbolic of
mortal desires, where the serpent is waiting to strike."[24]

20. See ibid., p. 316.
21. See E. Hull, "The Idea of Hades in Celtic Literature," p. 132, and Rees
and Rees, *Celtic Heritage*, p. 231.
22. Rees and Rees, *Celtic Heritage*, pp. 314–325.
23. See J. B. Friedman, "Eurydice, Heurodice and the Noon-Day Demon,"
Speculum, 41 (1966), 22–29.
24. Kenneth R. R. Gross Louis, "Henryson's *Orpheus and Eurydice* and
the Orpheus Tradition in the Middle Ages," *Speculum*, 41 (1966), 643.

Boethius identified Eurydice with *temporalia* and Hell, continuing the long tradition of Christian misogyny particularly
strong in the commentators of the *Consolatio*.[25] Pierre Ber-
suire, in his *Ovidius moralizatus*, not only interpreted Orpheus
as a type of Christ but also as a type of David, because both
were musician-kings.[26]

The author of *Sir Orfeo* expands two scenes that concentrate
upon moments of pathos into almost episode length.[27] The tone
of these scenes is markedly Christian and the author is clearly
trying to stir both terror and piety in his audience. The first
scene is the description of Heurodis' reaction to the news of
her impending abduction (ll. 76–95). Heurodis' reaction to her
"dream" is violent, and its violence can be associated with the
madness caused by demoniac possession.[28] On the other hand,
Heurodis' desperation is the dramatization of the struggle of
life against death, of virtue against vice. The second scene is
the moving dramatization of Orfeo's lament on the imminent
loss of Heurodis (ll. 95–130). Orfeo's lament is an impassioned
and shocked address of a loving husband to the beloved wife,
which adopts the form of Mary's lament over the dead
Christ.[29]

Sir Orfeo was doubtless perceived by Christian readers as an

25. See Friedman, "Eurydice, Heurodice and the Noon-Day Demon."

26. See Penelope B. R. Doob, *Nebuchadnezzar's Children: Convention of Madness in Middle English Literature* (New Haven: Yale University Press, 1974), p. 191.

27. Susan Wittig, in *Stylistic and Narrative Structures*, p. 136, has observed that a number of other poets have favorite scenes that they expand to almost episode length.

28. See Doob, *Nebuchadnezzar's Children*, p. 12.

29. Felicity Riddy, in her essay, "The Use of the Past in *Sir Orfeo*," *Yearbook of English Studies*, 6 (1976), 5–15, while recognizing the use of the form of Mary's lament, mistakenly defines Orfeo's lament as nostalgia. Riddy considers that the mourner is able to move imaginatively from the present to the past (which equals nostalgia in the case of Orfeo's lament for Heurodis) or is able to move imaginatively from the present to the future (which equals Mary's faith in Christ's resurrection in the case of Mary's lament for Christ). She does not grasp the realism implicit in the *lamentazione funebre*, which though expressed in the canonical language of ritual, is unidimensional in that this lamentation is rooted in and confined to the painful present, where the past is recalled dramatically simply to make the pain of the present more vivid.

allegory of the "progress of the soul," from sin to redemption through the expiation of the vice. Parallel to the progress of Orfeo as a mythological hero is therefore the *iter* of Orfeo as a penitent, a pilgrim to a certain shrine. In this context each episode takes on a new significance. Morality, which is extraneous to the fairy tale, becomes dominant as a set of norms guiding the individual in his relationship to God, and to a lesser extent, to society.

In this light many elements of the story acquire a new and grim significance. The ympe-tre becomes associated with the tree of knowledge and the fairy king with the Satan that strikes at noonday, the noonday demon of Psalm 90.[30] The abduction of Heurodis becomes the allegorical dramatization of the effects of man's sins. The departure of Orfeo—which in the folktale pattern is significant only as the first movement of the counteraction—becomes significant in its mode. The passage that describes Orfeo's transformation into a hairy anchorite, while irrelevant in the folktale pattern, is of the first importance in a Christian interpretation. His sufferings and humiliations become the central image of the story, which is about expiation through self-imposed suffering.

The strong ritualistic quality of the passage extending from line 205 to line 280, where there is an abundance of details both in the description of Orfeo's renunciation of his kingdom and of Orfeo's sojourn in the forest as a wild man, is reminiscent of the earliest Christian legends of the hairy anchorite. Like these early legends *Sir Orfeo* was probably meant "for the entertainment as well as for the moral encouragement of the monks."[31] And also like the early Christian legends, *Sir Orfeo* makes use of diverse sources, combining Celtic lore with Judeo-Christian elements.[32]

30. J. B. Friedman, in "Eurydice, Heurodice and the Noon-Day Demon," and *Orpheus in the Middle Ages* (Cambridge, Mass.: Harvard University Press, 1970), has given abundant documentation from the Midrashic commentaries on the subject of the noonday demon.

31. Charles Allyn Williams, "Oriental Affinities of the Legend of the Hairy Anchorite," *University of Illinois Studies in Language and Literature,* 11, no. 4 (1926), 57.

32. See Williams, "Oriental Affinities," and his "The German Legends of

Versions of the Christian legend are found in a collection of saints' lives known as the *Apophthegmata patrum. Aegyptiorum.* Other versions existed and circulated in Greek. Many are preserved in Latin form, along with Jerome's *Vita Pauli,* Athanasius' *Vita Sancti Antonii,* Rufinus' *Historia manoacorum in Aegypto.* These and other writings were included in a collection known as the *Vitae patrum,* which was used as source material by writers in various European countries in the Middle Ages.

One of the most popular Western tales of the hairy anchorite was that of John of the Golden Mouth (*Chrysostomus*). John lived as a hermit until one day he fell a victim to carnal temptation and became the worst of sinners. He violated the daughter of a king who had lost her way in the wilderness. Afterward, when he realized his sin, he threw her down from a rock. To this sacrifice he added a vow that he would live like a beast, like Nebuchadnezzar, crawling on his hands and feet and eating nothing but grass. One day when he was moving about in his penitent posture he saw in the distance a naked woman sitting near a rock and feeding a child. Unknown to him, the princess whom he had tried to kill had been miraculously preserved from harm, and the child she nursed was his own.[33] The resemblance between *Chrysostomus* and Orfeo lies mainly in the penance they both perform, in their physical aspects, and in their desiring a young woman. All the illustrations of Saint *Chrysostomus* represent a bearded man who crawls on the ground and looks longingly at a beautiful woman stretched out on the lawn and playing with a child. When Orfeo, kneeling at the fairy king's feet, asks to have Heurodis as a recompense to his ''glee,'' the reaction of the king is one of surprise and contempt:

> ''Nay,'' quath the King, ''that nought nere!
> A sori couple of you it were,
> For thou art lene, rowe and blac,

the Hairy Anchorite,'' *University of Illinois Studies in Language and Literature,* 39, no. 32 (1935), 9–134.

33. Taken from E. W., ''The Saint as a Monster,'' *Journal of the Warburg Institute,* 1 (1937–1938), 18.

> And she is lovesum, withouten lac;
> A lothlich thing it were forthi
> to sen hir in thi compayni."

(ll. 457–460)

The image of Orfeo as a wild man looking longingly at a beautiful woman is the same image of the saint painted by Dürer, Hans Sebald Beham, Johan Theodor de Bry, and Lukas Cranach the Elder. The poet of *Sir Orfeo* may have had the legend of Saint *Chrysostomus* in mind.

In her discussion about the "holy and unholy" wild man Penelope Doob says that while the "holy" wild man is not totally and continuously without reason, the "unholy" wild man is "truly mad having lost all use of reason as he endures the suffering that punishes and purges his sins."[34] If Orfeo, as a wild man, has temporarily lost his reason, the fairy hunt could simply be a hallucination.[35] It is less important, however, to be concerned with Orfeo's psychological state than to establish the affinities of the fairy hunt with the presence of hunters in the Christian legends of hairy anchorites. Charles Williams writes that "the discovery by a hunter of an anchorite, a hairy beast in appearance, is a normal element in the late medieval legends of the penitent hairy hermit."[36] There are also hunters in the legend of Saint *Chrysostomus,* for instance, who bring the young woman to *Chrysostomus'* retreat. In *Sir Orfeo* the grim hunters Orfeo sees "in hot undertides" (l. 282) are related to the noonday demons of the demonology tracts popular in the Middle Ages. Like the hunters in the *Chrysostomus* legend they perform the function of guides as well as reminders of Orfeo's former worldly existence.

It is obvious that in this poem, as in all European legends of hairy hermits, penance has an enormous importance. No critic, to my knowledge, has stressed the importance of

---

34. *Nebuchadnezzar's Children,* p. 169.
35. D. Hill, in "The Structure of *Sir Orfeo,*" *Medieval Studies,* 23 (1961), 136–153, speaks also about hallucinations but in the different context of a psychological analysis that I find too easy.
36. "Oriental Affinities," p. 123.

Orfeo's sin. In the interpretation of *Sir Orfeo* as a folktale there is no moral transgression on the part of Orfeo. There is no moral implication, therefore no implied penance, but instead a series of tasks. In the Christian interpretation of *Sir Orfeo* Orfeo's sin is allegorically represented by the yielding of the soul (when Heurodis wanders in the garden, falls asleep beneath the tree and consequently is abducted by the midday demon). The capital sin allegorically described is that of Accidia; the third sin here is Pride.

An analysis of Orfeo's transgression leads to a detail in the story that otherwise may be overlooked. Note the passage extending from line 179 to line 184 describing Orfeo's failed attempt to rescue Heurodis:

> He asked conseyl at ich man,
> Ac no man him help no can.
> A morwe the undertide is come,
> Ac Orfeo hath his armes ynome,
> And wele ten hundred knichtes with him
> Ich y-armed stout and grim.

Orfeo's men are wiser than their king, who believes that (like Étaín believes in the *Tale of Étain*) he can obstruct the will of the fairy king with military power. The sin exemplified here is pride.

The poem has a third level related both to the Celtic folktale and to the Christian allegory, in which Orfeo is portrayed as a type of king. We may define this level as anagogic in that it refers to an eschatological meaning. Morality serves here not only as a set of norms governing man's relationship to God but as a set of norms governing man's relationship to other men. The universal meaning of this level is not so much theological as political. The failure faced by Orfeo in his attempted rescue of his beloved wife brings him to understand that he is not omnipotent. Orfeo learns that he, a king, cannot defeat Death in the guise of the fairy king. Orfeo recognizes his sin of pride and decides to leave his kingdom and go into the wilderness to do

penance.[37] Pride is an especially injurious sin in a king. The
conduct of a proud king is not only condemned by God but also
on earth by the people under his rule.

The poem contains a strong concern with law: lines 200–217
show Orfeo, after his failed rescue, renouncing his monarchy
and entrusting his kingdom to a less exalted and more simple
man. Orfeo eventually wins Heurodis back not simply because
of the power of his music over the fairy king but because the
fairy king has given his word. The concern both for the ritual
and substance of law were common elements of the Celtic and
Christian culture. Orfeo, as an English medieval king, is a
product of both cultures. The third level of interpretation, in
which the happy ending is represented by the reorganization of
the kingdom, consists of a synthesis of the common Celtic and
Christian elements concerned with law and the end of time.

The sojourn of King Orfeo in the forest as a wild man and his
presenting himself at the gate of the bright kingdom as a monstrous minstrel are the stages of a journey that through self-imposed humiliations is intended to purge the sin of Pride from
Orfeo. When Orfeo first sees the fairy kingdom we are not
given a detailed description of the splendors he sees there, but
instead we are told that this "court of Paradis" is beyond any
man's ability to describe:

> No man may telle, no þenche in þought,
> The riche werk that ther was wroght;
> Bi al thing him think that it is
> The *proude* court of Paradis.
>
> (ll. 373–376, italics mine)

The author's recognition of the limits of his own powers reflects Orfeo's own sense of diminution before the splendor of
the fairy kingdom. The reason Orfeo ascribes pride to the
Other Kingdom is that he sees a kingdom very similar to his
own, but reproduced in a form more splendid than that of his
own court. That he attributes pride to the fairy court is a mea-

37. It is important to point out that the conception of Fortune is totally extraneous to this poem. For an opposing view see J. K. Knapp, "The Meaning
of Sir Orfeo," *Modern Language Quarterly,* 29 (1968), 263–273.

sure of his consciousness of his own sin of pride and foolishness in not having been humble before his own human limitations in actions and abilities. The designation of the court as proud also refers to the character of its king, who is aloof and invulnerable in his power over Life and Death. It is in his realization of his sin of pride and vainglory that Orfeo is educated by his ordeal.

To the interpretation of Orfeo as a medieval king is attached the imagery that gives the poem its historicity and stamps it as a literary work addressed to a sophisticated courtly medieval audience. The detailed account of Orfeo's kingdom in the prologue, the description of his military power (the one hundred knights) that takes place at the moment of his failed rescue, the crucial moment in the Palace Hall when Orfeo announces his decision to go into the wilderness, his return, his testing of the steward, and finally his coronation are all elements that, taken together, point out that this poem is as much a parable about power as it is a Celtic folktale and a Christian allegory. It is as a parable about power that the poem makes its bridge to history: all that we define as "medieval" in the poem (aside from the language), depends on the historical signs of this level. Orfeo is after all a medieval king and what he sees, be it real or imaginary, has the form of what he knows. We as readers see through Orfeo's eyes a world that is visually medieval: in the described landscapes, in the postures of the people that inhabit it, in the color of the sky and the forest, and in the contrast between a hideous reality and an absolute perfection that exist simultaneously side by side.

MAUREEN QUILLIGAN

Allegory, Allegoresis, and the
Deallegorization of Language:
The *Roman de la rose,*
the *De planctu naturae,*
and the *Parlement of Foules*

Allegory has recently become a very fashionable term, as dis-
tinctly modish as it used to be quite déclassé. Especially in the
context of contemporary Structuralist and post-Structuralist
methods of reading, it has become a major method of critical
discourse. With such overburdened words it is well to be as
careful as possible. Allegoresis, that is textual commentary or
discursive interpretation, has always enjoyed some critical
currency, and it is actually allegoresis rather than allegory itself which has come into fashion. Whether this growth in a
method of critical discourse sheds any light on actual allegory
—that is, on narrative peopled by personified abstractions
moving about a reechoing landscape of language—is another
question entirely. In *The Language of Allegory: Defining the
Genre* (1979) I have argued that there is a major distinction between allegory and allegoresis, between that species of text we
call allegory, which announces itself by a number of obvious,
blatant signals—most notably personification and wordplay—

163

to be about the magic signifying power of language, and that critical procedure I define as allegoresis which can, in fact, make *any* text (from Ovid's *Metamorphoses* to Rousseau's *Julie*), whatever its manifest literal meaning, appear to be about language, or any other (latent) subject.[1] It is with the ultimate purpose of distinguishing again in some concrete detail the process of allegory from the nature of allegoresis that I would like to consider the manner in which Chaucer in the *Parlement of Foules* has deallegorized his two sources, the *Roman de la rose* and the *De planctu naturae*.

Chaucer's process is essentially to transform the silent, unvoiced textuality of his allegorical sources into a dramatic, mimetic fiction of audible, voiced sound. Quite simply, he takes the static, embroidered birds of Alain's *Complaint* and in the *Parlement* makes them sing. More than merely vivifying Alain's inert figures or Jean's landscape, Chaucer radically alters the manner of presenting the text to the reader. Where Alain and Jean address a reader Chaucer addresses a fictive listener, an "auditor" who, unlike his predecessors' reader, is not asked to consider making judgments and interpretations about his own interpretive procedures. In other words, what Chaucer leaves out of his *Parlement* is any consideration of the danger posed his poem by the powers of allegoresis. Both Alain and Jean address the problem of allegoresis directly; their allegories are consequently protected against it. Because allegories, in effect, "deconstruct" themselves they leave no room for externally imposed interpretations. Unallegorical Chaucer is most vulnerable to that invasive interpretive force.[2]

---

1. *The Language of Allegory: Defining the Genre* (Ithaca: Cornell University Press, 1979), pp. 21, 26, 29–32, 224–225.

2. Older allegorizations of the *Parlement of Foules* focused on identifying the specific persons meant by Chaucer's birds. For a collection of these see *Chaucer's Works,* ed. F. N. Robinson (Boston: Houghton Mifflin, 1957), p. 791. A more recent allegorization in Bernard Huppé and D. W. Robertson, Jr., *Fruyt and Chaf: Studies in Chaucer's Allegories* (Princeton: Princeton University Press, 1963), pp. 101–145, reads the *Parlement* as Chaucer's criticism of the idolatrous unnaturalness of courtly convention, thus making it cohere exactly with Alain's and Jean's positions. Huppé and Robertson conclude their argument by saying, "Reading is the symbol of the good life. It delivers

The *Parlement* is a good poem in which to see at work the unallegorical quality of Chaucer's genius because the *Parlement* is very close to being an allegory. It is focused, as all allegories are, on a problem of language, specifically on the various and conflicting languages of love that can exist in a single society. Like the *Roman de la rose,* from which it takes its opening landscape, it has personifications. Like the *De planctu naturae* it is a dream vision. But it is not an allegory in the fundamental way in which Chaucer's sources are. For it is not a text self-conscious of itself as a text; rather it is a story told by a self-conscious storyteller.

Not that the *Roman de la rose* lacks stories, or eager storytellers. Many of its garrulous confabulators are so self-conscious of their charms they cannot stop talking. But Jean's main concerns in his part of the poem center very early on the interpretation of, rather than the mere retailing of, narrative. One of the first stories in the second section of the poem about the myth of the birth of Venus illustrates how Jean's self-reflexive textual and allegorical concerns take precedence over narration and may be said to bring it to a halt while "deconstructing" its verbal components. Because this story and the argument it causes are central to Chaucer's concern about love's language in the *Parlement,* it will be useful to look at Jean's text in some detail.

After the Lover has already pledged his allegiance to Amors, the god of love, Lady Raison descends from Heaven to remonstrate with him and woo him to her more reasonable attitude toward love. As she needs to define love for him she begins with the story of the birth of Venus, goddess of love. However, Reason makes a grave tactical error when she refers to the testicles from which Venus is born with the slang term *coilles* ("balls" might be a close equivalent in current English).[3] The Dreamer-Lover immediately objects to this nasty

---

the mind from the spears of desire and lifts it to the truth of heaven. Chaucer hopes to follow wisdom" (p. 145). My argument is that Chaucer's genius tends to make him seek that wisdom in other ways.

3. Guillaume de Lorris and Jean de Meun, *Le Roman de la rose,* ed. Félix Lecoy (Paris: Editions Honoré Champion, 1965), 3 vols., I, l. 5507; this edition hereafter cited in the text (translations are my own).

word and starts to argue with her about her diction. She should
have used "quelque cortaise parole," some courteous word or
polite euphemism. Their argument about diction persists
through nine hundred lines of the poem and ranges over a number of vast topics, but the main burden from Reason's point of
view is that it is the Lover's own squeamishness that makes
him object to her language. He would have found dirty *any*
word she might have used (for Reason named all things in the
first place); say she had used "relic" for instance: he would
have found even that word too low (ll. 7076–7084). Reason's
basic point is that had the Lover's attitude toward language not
been so corrupted by the god of love, he would have realized
that she had meant the word *allegorically*. "En ma parole
autre sen ot" (ll. 7129). Lady Reason explains that

> qui bien entendroit la letre,
> le sen verroit en l'escriture,
> qui esclarcist la fable occure.
>
> (ll. 7132–7134)

He who well understands the letter would see in the writing the
sense which illuminated the dark fable.

She also refers to the "integumanz aus poetes" of which, she
sneers, the Lover is obviously ignorant.

In mentioning here the moralization of Ovid, Lady Reason
refers to the wide practice of commentaries on Ovid's texts
that purported to extract from them profound and secret meanings. She refers in fact to the practice of allegoresis. We never
do learn exactly what other meanings Lady Reason intended
by those testicles, although they become an extremely important detail later in the poem when Genius tries his hand at telling the story of Venus (ll. 20002–20064).[4] The Lover is not at
all interested in this kind of discourse:

4. Of the many "integuments" of Ovid to which Jean may be referring here,
the most fascinating possibility is John of Garland's *Integumenta Ovidii, poe-
metto inedito del secolo XIII*, ed. Fausto Ghisalberti (Milan: Casa Editrice
Giuseppe Principato, 1933). The verses that refer to Venus' birth are these:

> Tempus quod sequitur secuisse virilia patris
> Dicimus inque maris precipitasse chaos.

> Mes des poetes les sentances,
> les fables et les methaphores
> ne bé je pas a gloser ores.

(ll. 7160–7162)

I don't care to gloss poets' fables and metaphors.

Outraged by her bawdy word, he rejects Reason and her kind of love. Reason, however, argues that his insistence on polite diction, on falsifying courtly euphemism, is only a demand for another kind of gloss:

> sui je coutumiere
> de parler proprement des choses,
> quant il me plest, sanz metre gloses.

(ll. 7048–7050)

I am accustomed to speaking directly about things when it pleases me, without giving glosses.

In the *Timaeus* Plato has taught us that the word must be cousin to the deed; thus the Lover can understand her words

---

> Tempus Saturnus, ubertas mentula, proles
>   Posteritas, venter est mare, spuma Venus.
> Iam propter varios effectus asserit error
>   Plures esse deos, est seges aucta mali.
> Non uno contenta deo patet etheris aula,
>   Sed tot divorum pondere pressa labat.
> Primo formavit statuam sibi Belus ut illam
>   Servus adoraret, paruit ergo timor.

(ll. 71–80, p. 41)

Clearly the time of chaos brought in by Saturn's castration was a time of polytheism and, most important, idolatry. In view of Jean's consideration of the idolatry later in the text in the story of Pygmalion (20787–21147), as well as in the word *relic* itself, I suspect Jean intended his readers to remember this particular reading of the word *coilles*.

For further discussion of idolatry in the *Roman* see Rosemond Tuve, *Allegorical Imagery* (Princeton: Princeton University Press, 1966), pp. 262–263. For a list of other moralizations of Ovid current in the twelfth century and later see J. de Ghellinck, *L'Essor de la littérature latine au XIIe siècle* (Paris: Desclée de Brouwer, 1946), I, 42n.

directly, without a gloss ("tout proprement, sanz glose metre" l. 7154). Jean takes great pains here to remind us that when the word is not cousin to the deed one is vulnerable to a perverted sort of love, such as the love offered by Amors; a love that relies on speaking in such delicate and refined terms about passion that one is never quite sure of the specifics of what Millament, in a much later argument, terms the "odious endeavors" of physical procreation. Such poetical and polite language, Jean shows in his vast critique of Guillaume de Lorris' diction, expresses a very dangerous attitude toward sexuality and absolutely undercuts the possibility of an allegorical understanding of love.[5]

The mere fact that Jean's Lover and Lady Reason argue about language demonstrates the fundamental allegorical quality of the work they inhabit. It is a text of language, about language. Yet it is most important in any comparison with Chaucer's bawdy diction for us to realize that Jean's defense of a slang term such as *coilles,* because it may help to illuminate a sacred truth, is a very different thing from the use of slang because the man or woman whose story you happen to retell would have used it. In this latter way Chaucer defends his low diction in the *Canterbury Tales,* referring to the same passage from Plato's *Timaeus* that Jean has Lady Reason cite:

> Whoso shal telle a tale after a man,
> He moot reherce as ny as evere he kan
> Everich a word, if it be in his charge,
> Al speke he never so rudeliche and large,
> . . . . .
> Crist spak hymself ful brode in hooly writ,
> And wel ye woot no vileynye is it.
> Eek Plato seith, whoso that kan hym rede,
> The wordes moote be cosyn to the dede.
>
> (ll. 725–742)[6]

5. For further discussion of this point see my "Words and Sex: The Language of Allegory in the *De planctu naturae, Le Roman de la rose,* and Book III of *The Faerie Queene,*" *Allegorica,* 2 (1977), 195–216.

6. *The Works of Geoffrey Chaucer,* ed. F. N. Robinson (Boston: Hougton Mifflin, 1957); all quotations of Chaucer are from this edition, hereafter cited in the text.

Chaucer defends his use of rude language by basing it on a criterion of verisimilitude—citing, of course, the relevant authorities as well. This is a very different controlling principle for diction than we find in allegory, where the words any given character speaks are controlled at least in part by the word that character *is*. So Lady Reason defends her bawdy language because it is reasonable to call a spade a spade. Plato was no fool.

Some eight thousand lines later in the *Roman de la rose* Jean again refers to Plato's remark that "les voiz aus choses voisines doivent estre a leur fez cousines" ("the words must be cousins to their deeds"; ll. 15161–15162). At this late point in the poem, long after Reason has been banished, the Lover's mad attitude toward language has full sway. Hence, even though the narrator apologizes for any low diction he may be forced to use in his extended description of a single act of sexual intercourse, there are absolutely no bawdy words. Jean, moreover, presents his apology specifically to readers who are asked to question their interpretations of the terms of the poem. Thus in the apology Jean promises to "gloss" the tale of a curious "rabbit" hunt (l. 15120). That the word for rabbit, *connin,* is close cognate to the slang term for female genitalia is a sly reference back to the central conflict about terms that dominates the argument between Reason and the Lover. The final episode is almost like a textbook demonstration of the effects of polite diction. The narration of the physical act itself takes the metaphoric form of an extended castle siege, followed by the final plucking of the "rose" of the poem's title. Notable among the words used here to refer to various genitalia is the term *relic*—the very word, in fact, which earlier Lady Reason had said she might have used to name testicles (ll. 7079 –7088, 21213–21217; 21553–21556). Thus the Lover is a pilgrim who yearns to worship relics specifically on his knees— an idolatrous position which easily translates into a position for sexual intercourse (ll. 21198–21205). Double entendres pile on top of one another; the final episode is a tour de force of witty innuendo, superficially polite, and quite obscene.[7] The words are not, however, cousins to the deeds.

7. See Tuve, *Allegorical Imagery,* pp. 278–279 for further discussion and for an explicit illustration of the physical facts (fig. 100).

Beyond the resonant humor of Jean's joke is a very serious point about the language of allegory. By the last episode Jean shows that to speak about sexuality in euphemisms is simply to limit the nonliteral meaning of language to the carnal, the merely erotic; to lift the veil of such metaphoric language is merely to lift up skirts. When, however, one uses the flesh itself as a veil—as Reason had tried to do in telling the myth of Venus—one may incarnate spiritual truths which reveal the connection between flesh and spirit, between the world and the Word of God. To do so depends, however, on verbal directness, on calling a spade a spade.

As his citation of Plato in the general prologue attests, Chaucer had read Jean's poem very carefully.[8] He recognized that the main problem Jean confronted there was the proper language for sexuality; what words should one use in order better to name the function sexuality serves in a divinely ordered cosmos? In the *Parlement* Chaucer does not answer this question; he simply rephrases it, presenting the problem in terms of a dramatic confrontation of heard voices. Chaucer does not mention the *Roman* by name in the *Parlement*. The source he does mention, Alain de Lille's *De planctu naturae*, had been a pivotal source for Jean's continuation of the *Roman:* Alain's prosimetric work had taken up the same question of diction and sexuality that forms the core concern of Jean's text. In citing Alain as a source then, Chaucer specifically singles out the source for the *Roman* that had most direct bearing on its linguistic concerns. Like his citation of Plato in the general prologue Chaucer's naming of Alain in the *Parlement* is compelling evidence that he had perceived Jean's allegorical concerns very clearly. And just as in the case of the *Roman*, to contrast Alain's statement of the problem of a proper diction for sexuality briefly with Chaucer's terms will help us to see how designedly *un*allegorical the *Parlement* finally is.

8. One other place Chaucer might have found Plato's remark quoted is Boethius' *Consolation of Philosophy*, 3. 12, where the necessary relation between word and deed has bearing on a philosophical argument. In view of the specific bawdiness of some of the *Canterbury Tales*, I think it much more likely that Chaucer was remembering the *Roman*.

In the *De planctu naturae* an elaborately personified Lady Nature complains to a Dreamer-Poet that man, alone of all her creatures, refuses to follow her laws enjoining procreation, replenishment, and resistance to death. Until recently most readers have assumed that the *De planctu* was a tract against various forms of perverted love, most notably sodomy.[9] But the curious terms in which Lady Nature couches her complaint raise another much more interesting possibility: that Lady Nature is less interested in sexuality per se and more interested in language. We notice that she consistently describes man's unnatural sexual practices in terms of grammar. The opening verse reveals the highly wrought rhetorical texture of her complaint:

> Praedicat et subjicit, fit duplex terminus idem,
>   Grammaticae leges ampliat ille nimis.
> Se negat esse virum, Naturae factus in arte,
>   Barbarus; ars illi non placet, immo tropus.
> Non tamen ista tropus poterit translatio dici;
>   In vitium melius ista figura cadit.[10]

[Man] is both predicate and subject, he becomes likewise of two declensions, he pushes the laws of grammar too far. He, though made by Nature's skill, barbarously denies that he is a man. Art does not please him, but rather trope; even that troping cannot be called metaphor; rather it sinks into viciousness.[11]

9. See R. H. Green, "Alain of Lille's *De planctu naturae*," *Speculum*, 31 (1956), 649–674; Winthrop Wetherbee, "The Function of Poetry in the *De planctu naturae* of Alain de Lille," *Traditio*, 25 (1969), 87–112. For a very recent discussion of the poem from the standpoint of its sexuality see John Boswell, *Christianity, Social Tolerance, and Homosexuality: Gay People in Western Europe from the Beginning of the Christian Era to the Fourteenth Century* (Chicago and London: University of Chicago Press, 1980), p. 259 and n. 60. I am indebted to Charlotte Morse for this reference.

10. Alain de Lille, *De planctu naturae*, ed. Thomas Wright, in *Anglo-Latin Satirical Poets and Epigrammatists of the Twelfth Century*, 2 vols. (Rolls Series, London, 1872), II, 429–522; hereafter cited in text.

11. Douglas Moffat, trans., *The Complaint of Nature*, Yale Studies in English, no. 36 (New York: Henry Holt, 1908); hereafter cited in text.

C. S. Lewis has remarked that it was with the "cold heart of
a stylist" that Alain was tempted to write about the problems
of perverted love because they offered "endless opportunities
for fantastic grammatical metaphor about the proper relations
of masculine and feminine, or subject and predicate in the
grammar of Venus." [12] In a sense Lewis is right. Grammar is a
perfectly legitimate metaphor when one is concerned with the
basic morality of poetry; Alain found grammar a particularly
attractive metaphor because he was concerned to show that
the corruption of language by irresponsible poets makes it impossible to conceive of the proper place of sexuality within the
divinely ordered cosmos. Thus, like the Lover and Lady Reason in the *Roman,* Lady Nature and the Dreamer-Poet in the
De planctu are having an argument about language and right
reading. Lady Nature describes Cupid's kind of love as one
that operates by a process *per antiphrasim*—"by antiphrase"
(Wright, p. 472); it is the "pax odio, fraudique fides, spes
juncta timori"—the hateful peace, the fraudulent faith, the
hope joined to fear—of conventional oxymoronic idiom. This
is the part of the *De planctu* that Jean de Meun simply translated and gave whole to Lady Reason in the *Roman de la rose.*
    Jean was doubtless interested in the metrum about Cupid
not simply because it was effective verse, but because it aimed
so directly at the linguistic concerns central to his own allegory
in insisting on the verbal perversion at the heart of Cupid's
power. *Per antiphrasim* Cupid corrupts the proper function of
language and of sexuality. Thus the proper joining of male and
female is as a pen writing on parchment leaves which creates a
replica of the Logos (Wright, p. 475). Under Cupid's false
power, however, men write astray: "For if the masculine
gender by some violent and reasonless reasoning should demand a like gender, the relation of that connection could not
justify its vice by any beauty of figure, but would be disgraced
as an inexcusable and monstrous solecism" (Moffat, p. 51).
Here the metaphor of grammar is not merely a polite way of
talking about sexual perversions; rather Lady Nature speaks

---

12. C. S. Lewis, *Allegory of Love* (1936; rpt. Oxford: Oxford University
Press, 1957), p. 106.

an allegorical language that insists upon the unifying analogy between fruitful sexuality and sane eloquence. What she needs to do is to teach the poet not only about right sexuality but about right reading. In the same way that Lady Reason in the *Roman* objects that she meant her use of the word *coilles* allegorically, so Lady Nature explains that there is a way of reading practiced by those of "loftier understanding": when the shell of the text is cast aside, "the reader finds within the sweeter kernel of truth" (Moffat, p. 40).

Of course, Lady Nature herself is a poetic figure that must be very carefully read. She duly explains for the Dreamer-Poet the significance of the great tear in her elaborate garment, a cloth woven of very precious material, which looks at various times to be red, green, white, and the color of air, embroidered with pictures of all animal creation. Lady Nature reads out the meaning of this garment: "From what we have touched on previously . . . thou canst deduce what the figured gap and rent mystically show. For since, as we have said before, many men have taken arms against their mother in evil and violence . . . themselves tear apart my garments piece by piece, and, as far as in them lies, force me, stripped of dress, whom they ought to clothe with reverential honor, to come to shame like a harlot" (Moffat, p. 41). This magic garment is itself an allegorical representation of natural creation considered as a fabric. But as a woven thing it is also an image of a text (*textus* = woven) that needs to be read, that is, to be interpreted—and so Lady Nature duly interprets it.[13] On this extremely significant garment Alain imagines pictures of birds. And it is in this elaborate list of fowls that most critics find the source for Chaucer's bird parliament in the *Parlement of Foules*. We should look at Alain's list in brief detail before analyzing how Chaucer deallegorizes these winged creatures when he introduces them into the *Parlement*.

13. J. A. W. Bennett, *Parlement of Foules, An Interpretation* (Oxford: Clarendon Press, 1957), p. 50 suggests that Alain may have taken the hint for Nature's robe from Macrobius' *Commentary on the Dream of Scipio* where it is argued that just as Nature "has withheld an understanding of herself from the vulgar sense of men by veiling herself with a variegated covering, [so she] has also wished to have her secrets handled by the wise through fables."

On Lady Nature's cloak in the *De planctu* "as a picture fancied to the sight," Alain explains there is "being held a parliament of the living creation" (Moffat, p. 11). Most notable are the birds. The pictures are not of static bits of embroidery, however; the birds are imaged in successive stages of change. "The eagle, first assuming youth, then age, and finally returning to the first, changed from Nestor to Adonis." The last two in the list are directly connected to their self-consciously poetic context: "The lark, like a high-souled musician, offered the lyre of its throat, not with the artfulness of study but with the mastery of nature, as one most skilled in the lore of melody; and refining its tones into finer, separated these little notes into inseparable chains. The bat, bird of double sex, held the rank of cipher among small birds." In closing this list Alain reminds the reader that it is a picture to be read: "Haec animalia, quamvis illic quasi allegorice viverent, ibi tamen esse videbantur ad litteram" (Wright, p. 439)—"These things, although as it were in allegory moving there, seemed to exist actually" (Moffat, p. 13). Moffat translates the *ad litteram* as "actually," a correct enough rendering; yet the tension between the two terms *allegorice* and *ad litteram* insists on a finely tuned awareness of the self-referential textuality of the context in which these birds appear. It would be easy to overanalyze the Chinese box-like arrangement of self-consciousness here, as the poet insists upon the literal liveliness of an ekphrastic description of the dress of an allegorical personification, in itself a representation of something else—the principle of aliveness in nature. Suffice it to say that what Moffat calls "actuality" in translating the phrase *ad litteram* indicates the complicated nature of relations between the literal and allegorical in the text immediately in front of the reader. The controlling metaphor of apprehension of this text is textuality itself. One reads the "text" of Nature's garment, literally and allegorically. One always stays firmly within the realm of the written, interpretable, readable word.

In direct contrast to the evident textuality of Alain's Nature is Chaucer's presentation of the goddess. The birds in the *Parlement of Foules* are not on her cloak; they crowd the landscape in which she stands.

> And in a launde, upon an hil of floures,
> Was set this noble goddesse Nature.
> Of braunches were here halles and here boures
> Iwrought after here cast and here mesure;
> Ne there nas foul that cometh of engendrure
> That they ne were prest in here presence,
> To take hire dom and yeve hire audyence.
>
> For this was on seynt Valentynes day,
> Whan every foul cometh there to chese his make,
> Of every kynde that men thynke may,
> And that so huge a noyse gan they make
> That erthe, and eyr, and tre, and every lake
> So ful was, that unethe was there space
> For me to stonde, so ful was al the place.
>
> And right as Aleyn, in the Pleynt of Kynde,
> Devyseth Nature of aray and face,
> In swich aray men myghte hire there fynde.
>
> (ll. 302–318)

The reference to Alain here follows directly upon a stanza in which Chaucer has most radically altered the method of presenting the goddess Nature. In Chaucer's version the noise made by the birds crowds the landscape so excessively there is no room for the narrator to stand. It is important to notice how Chaucer has given the fictive noise *volume* by making it take up *space*. This is no mere pun but a real sensory effect. The elision into location from auditory overload is a neat spatialization of the literary *textus* named by the reference to Alain. The effect is akin to that achieved early on in the poem when Scipio Africanus pushes the pudgy, inappropriate, reluctant narrator over the literary threshold specifically because the warning on the garden gates does *not* apply to him—though he does sojourn there to gain "mater of to wryte." In Chaucer's hands the literary landscape becomes a more realistic place; merely entering into the gates is not to define one's state of mind or one's character (as to be in the garden of Amors in the *Roman de la rose* is to enter into the specific mental state called being "in" love). Chaucer's narrator goes into the garden to gather material to write about; this is a very different verbal activity

from a fictive sojourn in the garden of love that is intended to
represent the intrapsychic process of falling in love—or, more
complicatedly, to instruct one in the abusive power of corrupt
poets to destroy the arts of language and thereby lead youth
astray.

Chaucer goes in the garden to listen, not to read—or to be
taught how to read and interpret. If Alain's living "parliament" is arranged on a silent textual surface which needs to be
read allegorically, Chaucer's vivification of that parliament is
to endow it with dramatic immediacy by giving it volume both
as three-dimensional space and as sheer noise.

> The goose, the cokkow, and the doke also
> So cryede, "Kek, kek! kokkow! quek quek!" hye,
> That thourgh myne eres the noyse wente tho.
> The goos seyde, "Al this nys not worth a flye!"
>
> (ll. 498–501)

Whether this part of the *Parlement* is in fact "allegorical" satire of the cacophonous methods of parliamentary procedure—
whatever the animal conducting it—or whether this is merely
a very lively presentation of a very lively group of birds, the
episode seriously undermines what had begun as a highly textual presentation of the problem of love. The noise of the parliament erases the textuality which marks Chaucer's source—
at just the moment which most clearly recalls Alain's highest
textual self-reflexiveness.

The first half of Chaucer's poem comprises the narrator's silent journey past an unspeaking series of personifications all
introduced by the rather readerly verb "I saw" (ll. 211–266).
This half of the poem ends appropriately enough with ekphrastic descriptions of the paintings on the walls of Venus' Temple:

> Semyramis, Candace, and Hercules,
> Biblis, Dido, Thisbe, and Piramus,
> Tristram, Isaude, Paris, and Achilles,
> Eleyne, Cleopatre, and Troylus,
> Silla, and ek the moder of Romulus:
> Alle these were peynted on that other syde,
> And al here love, and in what plyt they dyde.
>
> (ll. 288–294)

From this silent perfection—the readable realm of an exquisite literary landscape, which Chaucer sums up in the two-dimensional flatness of a wall painting—the poem moves swiftly into the dramatic conflict of the parliament. The speech and sound patterns of the strikingly noisy second half of the *Parlement* reflect individual personalities which, even though nameless, are less generic than Chaucer's dismissive list of named heroic lovers in the temple's frescoes. However typical of certain class attitudes each voice heard in the second half of the poem may be, it creates a distinct character and distinguishable personality. Readers remember Chaucer's bossy goose and demure formel.

A recent editor of the *Parlement* has argued that Chaucer owes virtually nothing to his source in the *De planctu* and that even though Alain, as we have seen, mentioned the parliament of living creation, Chaucer actually took the bird parliament from French love visions, in a number of which birds had figured largely as lovers.[14] Chaucer's treatment of the birds *is* very different from Alain's. Yet I think we should keep the *De planctu* as a major source for the *Parlement,* not so much because of the bird catalogue, but specifically because Alain's text concerns the same problems with language that dominate the last half of the *Parlement.* Like Alain and like Jean Chaucer questions the limits placed upon our attitudes toward sexuality by a literary language of love. Chaucer, however, makes his point very differently. His birds do not argue how to interpret; they argue what to do.

In the *Parlement* Lady Nature has called the birds together on St. Valentine's Day to choose up their mates for the year; she begins in an orderly manner, asking the highest-class birds to choose first, reminding them all that the female birds must give their consent—their "accord" (l. 668); this need for assent is, of course, the whole pivot of the plot, but it is no mere parodic ruse aimed at criticizing courtly convention. By "evene noumbres of acord" (l. 381) Nature has bound together the four elements into the natural world; the mating of the birds is only another instance of this ordering principle at work

---

14. *The Parlement of Foulys,* ed. D. S. Brewer (London: Thomas Nelson and Sons, 1960), p. 43.

in the common profit. That there are *uneven* numbers vying for
the hand of the formel eagle causes the whole problem; the
question is not merely which male bird should have the formel
for his mate but what the other two rejected suitors should do.
The problem is not merely practical, though many of the birds
think it is; rather it cuts to the center of the nature of love and
the function of sexuality and to the part these twin motives
play in the ordering of society. Most crucially in the context of
Chaucer's two allegorical sources, the problem is posed at the
outset by the very precise preference in diction by which the
royal eagle prefaces his choice. He says:

> Unto my soverayn lady, and not my fere,
> I chese, and chese with wil, and herte, and thought,
> The formel on youre hond, so wel iwrought,
> Whos I am al, and evere wol hire serve,
> Do what hire lest, to do me lyve or sterve.

(ll. 416–420)

Lady Nature specifically uses the two terms *fere* and *make*
to refer to *mate;* the royal eagle just as specifically refuses to
use them. His preferred diction for love is the vocabulary of
courtly compliment. It implicitly includes the whole constella-
tion of literary attitudes toward love that puts the ennobling
passion itself before any service it might do the common profit
by sexual reproduction of the species. The royal eagle talks
more of his willingness to die for love than his eagerness to reproduce. His is the kind of love whose language Lady Nature
had tried to correct in the *De planctu naturae;* the kind of love
which is the butt of Jean's critique in the *Roman de la rose.*
But here Lady Nature does not argue with the eagle or with
any other lover-birds; rather Chaucer deflates the birds' rhetoric by the familiar device of his narrator's naive praise; he
jokes rather than debates:

> Of al my lyf, syn that day I was born,
> So gentil ple in love or other thyng
> Ne herde nevere no man me beforn,
> Who that hadde leyser and connyng
> For to reherse hire chere and hire spekyng;

> And from the morwe gan this speche laste
> Tyl dounward drow the sonne wonder faste.
>
> (ll. 484–490)

The lower-class birds' response to such "gentil ple" is more direct, more comic, more deflating.

> The noyse of foules for to be delyvered
> So loude rong, "Have don, and lat us wende!"
> That wel wende I the wode hadde al toshyvered.
> "Com of!" they criede, "allas, ye wol us shende!
> Whan shal youre cursede pletynge have an ende?"
>
> (ll. 491–495)

The comedy of the parliament is not only a class conflict, it is a clash between a literary language of love and a brisk colloquial pragmatism which approaches the mating business for what it is, a necessary and joyous animal act.

Chaucer gives to the royal birds' literary attitudes a great deal of dignity and, unlike both his sources, he does not condemn their romantic posture. He suspends judgment, content to state the two opposing views. Thus, when the formel eagle finally chooses not to choose, Nature grants her a year's postponement. But like his sources Chaucer does keep to the fore the pivotal part language plays in the different attitudes toward love. The distance between calling a chosen mate a "soverayn lady" and not a "make" is a large one, involving two nearly cosmic dispositions toward the function of love in a God-ordered universe.

Summarizing the problems posed by the double nature of love in Bernard Silvestris' *De mundi universitate,* Winthrop Wetherbee explains:

The contrast between the brief animal act and the implication of divinity expressed by it suggest a deeper contrast . . . It expresses the uncertain and potentially tragic course of human life and at the same time recalls the transcient significance of the yearning for form . . . Thus generation is an appropriate symbol for the uncertainty of life. It is a godlike and humanitarian function—as Jean de Meun and Chaucer were to justify . . . It is also liable to degradation through the rejection of man's higher nature in favor of immediate and self-destructive pleasure.[15]

The *De mundi* would have been among the books the very bookish poet of the *Parlement* says he will go on to read, as he ends his poem with no conclusion to offer about the problem raised within it:

> And with the shoutyng, whan the song was do
> That foules maden at here flyght awey,
> I wok, and othere bokes tok me to,
> To reede upon, and yit I rede alwey.
> I hope, ywis, to rede so som day
> That I shal mete som thyng for to fare
> The bet, and thus to rede I nyl nat spare.
>
> (ll. 693–699)

As this final stanza so succinctly states the poet, in waking from the dream, wakes from the place of noisy life to the silent world of books. The song the birds sing at the end is not mere literary lyric, but verses of words set to actual music; the narrator is very careful to explain, "The note, I trowe, imaked was in Fraunce" (l. 677).[16] Such language lives in the vibrating air, not merely on the page. It lives in the same arena as the dramatic conflict between the language of heard voices in the parliament, and that is a different world from the world of words silently disposed in a text between the covers of a book. Dreamworlds can and do offer worlds where language itself becomes the actor in the drama—one thinks most immediately of *Piers Plowman*—but Chaucer's dreamworld is peopled by real creatures whose language is subordinate to personality (though this personality be the character of a class type). Although Chaucer may easily take up the same kinds of complicated linguistic questions about the proper language for love as his two allegorical sources do, he disposes of the debate in a fiction of real, heard noise.

It is in this oral rather than textual presentation of the prob-

15. Winthrop Wetherbee, *Poetry and Platonism in the Twelfth Century* (Princeton: Princeton University Press, 1972), pp. 184–185.

16. I am indebted to Marie Boroff for this point.

lem in the climactic second half of the *Parlement* that Chaucer
deliberately denies himself the opportunity for writing allegory. If this makes Chaucer a precursor of Shakespeare rather
than Spenser in the English Renaissance, it also indicates what
Spenser had to do to Chaucer to turn his master's narratives
back into allegory. What is one of the most wonderful, oral
style jokes in the *Canterbury Tales,* the tale of Sir Thopas,
Spenser takes with a wonderful genius of his own and makes
the basic fiction of *The Faerie Queene.* Harry Bailly's response to Chaucer-the-pilgrim's halting and lame minstrel version of a knight falling in love with the fairy queen is the brief
and comic "Thy drasty rymyng is nat worth a toord!" But
Spenser makes that rymyng the basis of Arthur's presence in
fairyland and therefore of the interlinking plots of six books.
He suppresses the parodic high jinks of the oral tale; he is deaf
to the joke.

The wittiness of Chaucer's Thopas tale lies in the very fictional frame of the *Canterbury Tales* themselves. That frame is
an oral operation that allows Harry Bailly's pithy "audience
response" the immediate power to stop the telling of the tale.
As fiction the entire work is oral performance. John Burrow
explains that a large measure of Chaucer's success with the pilgrimage frame derives from his exploitation of an old oral
style:

> In the *Canterbury Tales,* the older face-to-face relationship charac-
> teristic of an age when books were scarce, is internalized and fic-
> tionalized; and the corresponding features of style are thus accom-
> modated and given new justification within the poem's fiction, to
> which in turn they lend strength and authenticity . . . Chaucer ex-
> ploits the vigorous manner of the minstrels and their frank way with
> an audience in order to achieve a lively representation of the pil-
> grims telling their stories on the Canterbury road.[17]

Medieval texts were, of course, to be read from out loud, yet,
as Burrow also points out, the age of the mass production of
books had already dawned in Chaucer's day, and if books were

17. John Burrow, *Ricardian Poetry* (New Haven: Yale University Press,
1971), p. 36.

much rarer than they are now, they were less rare than they had been, and the silent reading experience must also have been more common. Against the background of this change in the physical absorption of literature we can sense the peculiar pressures of the unequivocally oral frame of the *Canterbury Tales,* and of the dramatic noise in the *Parlement of Foules.*

This orality not only is delightfully artful, it also seriously militates against the possibilities of allegory. If a work's fiction is that its narrative is heard in a pace of conversation, one is not invited—at least on the surface of the tale—to interpret, to gloss, to "read," whereas allegories are constantly concerned with the problem of interpretation: What did Reason mean by her bawdy word? What did poets really mean when they told stories of sodomite gods? What does the pardon from St. Truth sent to Piers Plowman really mean? What does the *A* in the *Scarlet Letter* really stand for? The contrast between Chaucer's dramatic orality in the *Parlement of Foules* and the self-conscious textuality of his allegorical sources bears out this essential distinction: one reads an allegory, one "listens" to Chaucer. Even when the substantive issue of narrative allegory is not itself glossing and reading, the narrative foregrounds the verbal surface of the text by puns and other obvious signals such as personification or Alain's grammatical metaphor. This signaling of the surface renders the text momentarily opaque, as it were; one can no longer see through the words to the narrative action but must stare instead at the vehicle which presents the action most immediately to the reader—the very words of the text.

By remaining in control of the reader's recognition of the textuality of the narrative (what, in another context, Geoffrey Hartman calls the "eclipse of voice by text"), allegory—as Northrop Frye noticed—frustrates the commenting critic by preempting his imposition of his own brand of allegoresis.[18] Allegory simply does not lend itself easily to "deconstruction" by allegorical critics. Texts so obviously aware of the difficulty of reading and interpretation—as the *Roman de la rose* and

18. Northrop Frye, *Anatomy of Criticism* (1957; rpt. New York: Atheneum, 1967), p. 90. See also my *Language of Allegory,* pp. 224–225.

the *De planctu naturae* —cannot be accused of rhetorical naiveté in need of a critic's demystification, as, rightly or
wrongly, one could accuse Shelley of mistaking the arbitrary
powers of language for the resources of his imaginative self.[19]
It is important to call attention to the difference because what
Paul de Man, for instance, calls the "grammatization of rhetoric" that deconstructive criticism applies to nineteenth-century texts is very much like the procedure used to generate
narrative by medieval (and Renaissance) allegory. Yet the differences between deconstructive allegoresis and allegory are
crucial.

Take, for instance, the argument about language between
Lady Reason and the Lover in the *Roman de la rose*. It is quite
similar to the argument about "referential authority" in the
second preface to Rousseau's *Julie;* this argument de Man sees
as the point of the novel's shift into the "allegorical mode" and
upon it he builds his fullest discussion of allegory in *Allegories
of Reading*.[20] According to de Man Rousseau's preface puts
into question the legitimacy of the referential verbal mode of
the preceding half of the text and renders it suspect. "In the
text of the Second Preface, the point at which the allegorical
mode asserts itself is precisely when R. admits the impossibility of reading his own text and thus relinquishes his power over
it" (p. 205). Jean de Meun's criticism of Guillaume de Lorris'
opening allegory occurs during the argument between Lady
Reason and the Lover about right reading. Yet there is a very
large difference. Lady Reason is a character *in* the narrative
while "R" and "N," the interlocutors of the second preface in
Julie, are fictionalized as commentators *external* to the text of
letters that forms this epistolary novel. This may seem a dis-

19. For a deconstructive reading of Shelley's "Triumph of Life," see Paul
de Man, "Shelley Disfigured," in *Deconstruction and Criticism* (New York:
Seabury Press, 1979), pp. 39–73. For a review of the book see Dennis Donoghue, "Deconstructing Deconstruction," *New York Review of Books,* 27
(June 12, 1980), 37–41. In the context of my discussion of Chaucer's orality,
Donoghue has very interestingly summarized the deconstructive enterprise as
a challenge to the "widely accepted vocal and acoustic character of poetry"
(p. 37).

20. Paul de Man, *Allegories of Reading* (New Haven: Yale University
Press, 1980), pp. 204–208.

tinction too literal and straightforward to be useful. Yet it is the difference between allegory and allegoresis; allegory includes its own self-querying commentary within the narrative, thus preempting a bit of the critic's freedom to impose meaning as he pleases. In her lessons on love, on allegoresis, and forthright diction, Lady Reason assumes a critical authority for the rest of the allegory which critics like de Man would need to appropriate for themselves. The strongest possible reading has already been stated by the poem itself.[21]

A thirteenth-century allegory never ends where a deconstructive reading (an allegoresis) of a lyric by Shelley or a novel by Rousseau might end, in the bleak insistence that there is no absolutely certain coherence between meaning and word. While allegoresis, no matter in what century it is practiced, needs to insist on the disjunction between meaning and word, between sign and signified, narrative allegory always pursues the goal of coherence. Thus de Man must argue that: "the innumerable writings that dominate our lives are made intelligible by a preordained agreement as to their referential authority; this agreement however is merely contractual, never constitutive. It can be broken at all times and every piece of writing can be questioned as to its rhetorical mode" (p. 204). Of an endless series of quotations "reaching as far back as the ultimate transcendental signified God, . . . none can lay claim to referential authority." Quite conversely, Lady Reason claims her authority to name (to assign contractual meaning—*relic* or *coilles* would equally have done for testicles) directly from God. The mere fact that she can appear in a fiction at all asserts the legitimacy of her (contractual) naming power; Reason named all things and presumably she named herself. When Reason's voice is silenced the poem becomes

21. For a discussion of the difficulty of imposing external allegorizations on the *Roman de la rose* see Tuve, chap. 4, "Imposed Allegory," in *Allegorical Imagery*, pp. 219–285. She flatly states: "We may not impose upon poems subjects their author did not choose. This is a basic problem in modern criticism and is the real reason why Molinet's allegorizing [of the *Roman*] was un-impos*able*" (p. 283). But allegoresis does serve a crucially important conservative function for culture: it keeps current in culture texts which are in danger of being lost. See C. S. Lewis, *Allegory of Love*, p. 62.

vulnerable to the Lover's fallacious attitude toward language, an attitude which insists (like allegoresis) on a polite disjunction between word said and meaning meant. Reason's language (like Lady Nature's grammar of Venus) insists on the congruence among word, physical fact, and divine intention.[22]

The impulse behind Jean's constant and witty innuendo in the last episode of the *Roman de la rose* is finally to disprove the insistence of allegoresis that the word can never be with "referential authority" cousin to the deed. When it is not, Jean tells us, the divinely ordained function of sexuality is unrecoverable. The last episode of the *Roman* is a self-conscious parody of allegoresis by means of which Jean warns the reader that to translate the real facts of physical sexuality into metaphoric terms is a form of idolatry. The ultimate result of reading the *Roman* ought to be to effect our choice, to make us take a more reasonable attitude toward sexual desire. Jean's laughter deflates high romantic notions of the religion of love to affirm the physical facts of coition that fulfill the divine plan.

De Man is right to say that "allegories are always ethical." But when he goes on to explain that "morality is a version of the same language aporia [confusion] that gave rise to such concepts as 'man' or 'love' or 'self,'" I doubt that few allegorists before the twentieth century would agree. However self-referential true allegorical narrative may be, its ultimate goal is to persuade the reader of the ethical effects of interpretations; right reading is ethical action.

Chaucer's *Parlement* reveals that he was a good reader of the *Roman*. He understood clearly that if language had become an idol for the poem's Lover it was not one for the author. Chaucer takes Jean's concern about language (the conflict between euphemistic and natural-reasonable diction) and dramatizes it with a chorus of voices that renders audible the community of creatures served by the ideal of a "commune profit" (l. 75). That Chaucer could so easily do this indicates the essentially social thrust of his predecessors' concern with language.

22. Allegory relies on a realist attitude toward language. For a fuller discussion of this basic fact see chap. 3, "The Context," of my *Language of Allegory*.

Although ranged in a silent textual space, the language of Alain
and Jean is meant to illuminate and instruct us in our true social responsibilities within a God-centered cosmos. Language
for them is a force that must move society toward the Word at
the center of the universe. Alain and Jean must be said to read
that word: Chaucer must be said to hear it in the voices of creation. To accept that in the *Parlement* Chaucer has deallegorized
his sources by transforming their silent textuality into audible
mimesis should not obscure the fact that for all three of these
medieval writers it was critically possible and morally vital to
perceive that Word in the world.

MILLA B. RIGGIO

The Allegory of Feudal Acquisition
in *The Castle of Perseverance*

Allegory is intimately associated with the society in
which the poet writes; it demands human
participation and must be explicable in social terms.
  Michael Murin, *The Veil of Allegory*

Fifteenth-century English morality plays characteristically
dramatize the process of Christian redemption as an allegory
of temptation, repentance, and divine mercy. Stripped of their
Catholic doctrine but retaining their predominant structural
features, sixteenth-century moralities often serve more obviously political purposes. By recognizing that allegorical
drama could deal simultaneously with political issues and spiritual matters "without self-contradiction," David Bevington
pointed the way to a clearer understanding of the transition
from religious to political allegory in morality plays. Bevington
traced this phenomenon to the second half of the fifteenth century, in particular identifying *Wisdom Who Is Christ* (c. 1460–
1480) as the first English morality play to contain an extended
political commentary.[1]

However, evidence suggests that this use of allegory dates
back at least to the early fifteenth century. The oldest extant

1. This argument was first presented in "Political Satire in the Morality *Wis-*
dom Who Is Christ," in *Renaissance Papers*, 1963 (Durham, North Carolina:

English morality play, *The Castle of Perseverance* (c. 1400–1425), contains a consistent substructure of allusions that associate economic and social abuse with feudal patronage.[2] I will show that this systematic set of references, which reflects certain very specific political realities and economic fears of the early fifteenth century, centrally reinforces the religious allegory of the play. In developing the central conflict between good and evil the play utilizes two different medieval concepts of kingship to illustrate the irreparable corruption of the world. Instead of reflecting a desire for social reform this critique of society provides a formal vehicle for the conservative Christian ideal of *contemptus mundi*.

Medieval Christian writers favored allegory because of its tendency to give universal sanction to a particular set of moral patterns and to transfer meaning consistently from one level of reality to another, features which accorded well with medieval theological ideals. As a result, specific allegorical motifs recur in medieval poetic and prose narratives, in sermons, in treatises dealing with social theory, and finally in vernacular religious drama. *The Castle of Perseverance* dramatizes four such traditional theological allegories: the pilgrimage of human life, the battle between the vices and the remedial virtues, the defense of a figurative castle, and the debate of the four daughters of God in the parliament of Heaven.[3] Its projection of a

---

University of North Carolina Press, 1964), pp. 41–51. The quotation in the text appears on p. 41. In a summary of this argument in David Bevington, *Tudor Drama and Politics* (Cambridge, Mass.: Harvard University Press, 1968), p. 35, Bevington mentions in passing that *The Castle of Perseverance* is "alive with incidental topical satire" but does not attempt to analyze the pattern of this satire.

2. *The Castle of Perseverance* is bound together with *Wisdom Who Is Christ* and *Mankind* in the Macro Manuscript. All quotations in this paper are taken from Mark Eccles, ed., *The Macro Plays,* Early English Text Society, OS, 262 (New York: Oxford University Press, 1969).

3. Studies which link separate allegories in *The Castle of Perseverance* with other literary traditions include: Wilhelm Creizenbach, *Geschichte des neueren Dramas* (Halle, 1893), Vol. II; W. Roy Mackenzie, *The English Moralities from the Point of View of Allegory* (Boston: Ginn, 1914), especially pp. 57–65 and 202–203; G. R. Owst, *Literature and Pulpit in Medieval England*

world controlled by these "universal" allegories of good and evil links this play not only with other fifteenth-century moralities but also with poetic and homiletic traditions. Each of the play's theological allegories has a literary history of its own. Dramatized in the play they establish the orthodox Catholic doctrine of confession and repentance as the key to salvation.[4]

But *The Castle of Perseverance* is more than a "formidable commonplace book of medieval dramatic allegory."[5] It is also an elaborate theatrical spectacle which echoes courtly traditions in its staging. Any attempt to separate the theatrical conventions from the religious allegory distorts the meaning of the play. The elaborate sets, festive costumes, half-comic and half-courtly battles do not merely gild the play's simplistically didactic purpose. By stressing the opposition between the brazen vulgarity of evil and the gracious dignity of divine good, the staging points to the ways the play goes beyond traditional theology in its use of allegory and becomes a reflection on the social order.[6]

(Cambridge: Cambridge University Press, 1933), especially pp. 85, 92, 526–547; Robert Potter, *The English Morality Play* (Boston: Routledge and Kegan Paul, 1975), pp. 16–29; Morris Roberts, "A Note on the Sources of the English Morality Play," *Studies by Members of the Department of English,* University of Wisconsin, No. 18 (1923), pp. 110–117; Roberta D. Cornelius, *The Figurative Castle* (Bryn Mawr, Penn.: n.p. 1930); Edgar T. Schell, "On the Imitation of Life's Pilgrimage in *The Castle of Perseverance,*" *Journal of English and Germanic Philology,* 67 (1968), 235–248; Hope Traver, *The Four Daughters of God* (Bryn Mawr, Penn.: n.p. 1907), pp. 135–138.

4. Described in the banns to the play as "mowthys confession and . . . hertys contricion," (The banns, ll. 127–128). For a discussion of the doctrine of penance in the medieval morality play see Potter, *The English Morality Play,* pp. 30–57. Eleanor Prosser, *Drama and Religion in the English Mystery Plays* (Stanford: Stanford University Press, 1961) makes a similar argument about the cycle plays, while at the same time tracing the development of the doctrine of penitence in the late Middle Ages.

5. Quotation taken from Michael R. Kelley, *Flamboyant Drama: A Study of* The Castle of Perseverance, Mankind, *and* Wisdom, (Carbondale, Ill.: Southern Illinois University Press, 1979), p. 29. Kelley, however, argues for the separation between the didactic substance and the theatrical form of the play.

6. The spectacular five-hour production of this play at the University of Toronto in August 1979 vividly emphasized the brazen splendor and brash acquisitiveness of Mundus' court and the dignified nobility of the courtly virtues, who were costumed in regal gowns that draped to reveal woven, armorlike un-

What is at stake—what motivates the action of each of the play's dramatized literary allegories—is the conflict of authority between the World and God. The pilgrimage of human life establishes the arena in which the World as a brazen feudal upstart challenges and finally loses to God's authority. The battle of the vices and remedial virtues pits a group of disorderly, ditch-digging sins against a courteous sisterhood of virtues who triumphantly fling roses, thus illustrating the distinction between the courtesy and valor of God's forces and the modish vulgarity of evil.[7] The central figurative castle serves as an emblem of true courtliness as well as a theological symbol, in this way furthering the contrast between the dignity of divine authority and the pompous spectacle of the worldly kingdom. As the struggle is waged during Humanum Genus' lifetime, God withholds his presence from the play. However, the concluding debate in the parliament of Heaven demonstrates the superiority of God's harmonious order over the litigious dissension fostered by the legal processes of the World.

The social underpinnings of the allegory are clear. All the major figures of evil are referred to as kings and lords. Flesh identifies himself, the World, and the Devil as "kyngys thre" (l. 267) and as "grete lordys" (l. 1007), designations echoed recurrently, as when the messenger Backbiter greets Flesh:

---

dergarments on the arms. During the judgment scene, which occurred at twilight, the setting sun illuminated God's throne in the East, conveying a sense of majesty and suggesting an additional dramatic advantage to the traditional symbolic placement of this throne. I am grateful to Alexandra Johnston and the records of Early English Drama staff at Toronto for access to their facilities during my research.

7. In the staging of the courtly *château d'amour* battles (especially popular in France), both sets of combatants—the ladies defending a central castle and the attacking gentlemen—fought with flowers. Whether any direct relationship exists between the play and the *château d'amour* tradition or not, arming only the courtly virtues in the castle with roses does emphasize the contrast between their courtliness and the vulgarity of the sins. For a discussion linking the *château d'amour* tradition to *The Castle of Perseverance* see Merle Fifield, "The Assault on the Castle of Perseverance—the Tradition and the Figure," *Ball State University Forum*, 16, no. 4 (Autumn 1975), 16–26.

> Heyl, Kynge, I calle!
> Heyl, prinse, proude prekyd in palle!
> Heyl, hende in halle!
> Heyl, syr kynge, fayre þe befalle!

(ll. 1791–1794)

Though each of these three "grete lordys" has a measure of separate authority, the World actually initiates the action and controls the forces of evil throughout. The primary tempter and dominant sin is Mundus' servant Covetousness, who successfully tempts Humanum Genus twice, in the second instance single-handedly defeating the virgin virtues after the other sins have all been repulsed in battle. Covetousness himself has an acting scaffold where the other sins gather at his request to influence Humanum Genus. Despite his prominence Covetousness persistently serves Mundus. He acts only on Mundus' commands, and when he fails temporarily Mundus gives him a sound beating.[8] Throughout his life of sin Humanum Genus too wears the "clothynge" (the livery) of Mundus—only one example of the social "cloth" of the allegory.

Further illustrating how inseparable Christian allegory is from social commentary, sin is dramatized almost entirely in the language of economic acquisition and associated persistently with the practices of feudal patronage. In his opening speech Mundus identifies himself not only as a king but more specifically as a feudal overlord, claiming to rule the world by feudal right:

8. J. McCutcheon, "Covetousness in *The Castle of Perseverance,*" in Fredson Bowers, ed., *English Studies in Honor of James Southall Wilson,* University of Virginia Studies, Vol. 4 (1961), 175–191, discusses the importance of Covetousness in this play. However, McCutcheon altogether dismisses the significance of Covetousness' position as a servant of the World. For references to Covetousness as the most important sin in the late Middle Ages see Morton Bloomfield, *The Seven Deadly Sins: An Introduction to the History of a Religious Concept* (East Lansing, Mich.: Michigan State College Press, 1952), p. 95; Lester K. Little, "Pride Goes before Avarice: Social Change and the Vices in Later Christendom," *American Historical Review,* 76 (1971), 16–49; and Russell A. Peck, *Kingship and Common Profit in Gower's "Confessio Amantis"* (Carbondale, Ill.: Southern Illinois University Press, 1978), p. 100.

> All þe world myn name is ment . . .
> All þese londys at myn avyse
> Arn castyn to my werldly wyse.
> My tresorer, Syr Coueytyse
> Hath sesyd hem holy to me.
>
> (ll. 165, 179–182)

Covetousness, the one sin Mundus controls directly, is called Mundus' "treasurer" (see ll. 164, 764), not his child, as are the sins of the Flesh and the Devil. As treasurer to the World Covetousness is an economic overseer who dispenses wealth to the World's retainers. Moreover, he is a knight who has bound a large number of countries to Mundus by feudal contract: *Sir* Covetousness has "sesyd" the world to Mundus. The verb itself has specific legal connotations. A term of land law widely current in the fifteenth century, the verb *sesyd* (seised) designates the feudal bond by which possession of a property is given to a tenant or a purchaser as a fee. A man in possession of property is "seised" (see l. 182); a man dispossessed is "disseised." Such possession, or "seisin" (see l. 763), presumes a continuing social contract and conveys certain complex rights and obligations, to which the play recurrently refers.[9]

In the course of the play the terminology of feudal vassalage and possession takes on abstract moral meaning. In a simple metaphor, for instance, Lechery describes herself as keeping a castle in Humanum Genus' loins (l. 971). In a more elaborate example of transferred meaning the verb *feffe* (enfeoff) consistently signifies the spiritual endowment of Humanum Genus by the forces of evil. The term *enfeoff* originally indicated only a gift of land but by the fifteenth century was used to describe the endowment of any form of property. In the play Humanum

9. Sources used to define legal terms and explain medieval land law include *Black's Law Dictionary*, 5th ed. (St. Paul, Minn. West Publishing, 1979); Paul S. Clarkson and Clyde T. Warren, *The Law of Property in Shakespeare and the Elizabethan Drama* (Baltimore: Johns Hopkins University Press, 1942); W. S. Holdsworth, *A History of English Law*, 4th ed. (1936; rpt. London: Methuen and Sons, 1976), Vol. II; Frederick Pollock, *The Land Laws*, 3rd ed. (London: Macmillan, 1896); C. H. Williams, ed., *Year Books of Henry VI: I Henry VI, A.D. 1422*, (London: The Selden Society, 1933).

Genus is "feffed" not only with worldly property and goods by Mundus and Covetousness but also with spiritual vices and fleshly indulgences by other sins (ll. 1026, 1151, 1158). Similarly, the term *entail,* a legal provision binding the inheritance of property, is used to describe the disposition of Mundus, who is "of þys entayle" (l. 2697), that is, in a mood to disinherit Humanum Genus spiritually as well as economically.

Words suggesting economic possession, such as *seisin, enfeoff,* or *entail,* are readily identified. However, other words and phrases more subtly reinforce the central economic allegory of evil. For instance, Humanum Genus places great emphasis on his "noble array." The word *array* not only refers to Humanum Genus' fancy new clothes but also indicates the rich trappings of his feudal lordship in a more inclusive sense. Having taken Mundus as a "good lord" has enabled him to attain a "rich (or great) array": a richly endowed social status which gives him lordly privileges of his own. In a speech directed primarily to the audience, Mundus' page Voluptas (or, as he is called in English, Lust-liking) directly links "aray" with feudal vassalage:

> Whoso wyl be fals and couetouse
> Wyth þis werld he schal haue lond and house . . .
>   [Voluptas descends into the platea]
> Pes, pepyl, of pes we you pray.
>   Syth and sethe wel to my sawe.
> Whoso wyl be ryche and in gret aray
>   Toward þe Werld he schal drawe . . .
>   Whoso wyl wyth þe Werld haue hys dwellynge
> And ben a lord of hys clothynge
> He muste nedys, ouyr al þynge,
>   Eueremore be couetowse.
>   (ll. 487–488, 491–494, 500–503;
>   stage directions are given in Latin in the text)

Other terms—*assize, enprise, trust, ure, owse,*—similarly weave a pattern of legalistic, economic language continuously through the framework of the allegory. In such a context even apparently neutral phrases take on a social coloration. The phrase *good entent,* for instance, would seem to signify nothing more than good intentions, as when the Good Angel says of human nature in general:

> Whyl Mankynd is in good entent
> His þoutys arn unhende.

(ll. 2028–2029)

However, in the process of the drama the word *entent* implies a degree of social recognition which may be employed by the forces of evil as well as those of good. Humanum Genus is told at the beginning of the play to "take the World to þine entent" (l. 389). And in lines 527–528, the Bad Angel encourages Lust-liking and Folye to "take to me good entent." Throughout *The Castle of Perseverance* terms like these clearly point in two directions—outwardly to social commentary and inwardly to spiritual ideals that are the mainstay of Christian allegory. Most important, on this level the play reveals no inconsistency of purpose: the language of Christian allegory and social commentary intersect in the dramatic moment.

Through such economic terminology *The Castle of Perseverance* consistently establishes feudal patronage as the primary metaphor for sin. The dramatic attack on feudal relationships and on economic acquisition constitutes more than a topical subtext in the play. The feudal imagery plays a precise structural role in the overall allegory, in which the corrupt feudal world is counterpoised against the sovereign harmony of God's reign. Both God and Mundus are depicted as kings. But only the world of sin—the kingdom of Mundus—is feudal in nature. No economic terminology is used to characterize the kingdom of God and none of the social concerns which preoccupy Humanum Genus in the feudal world have value to him as a subject of God. God rules alone. But though Mundus initiates much action, he must share his feudal authority with the other two "kyngs" of evil, the Flesh and the Devil. God's kingdom is undivided; the feudal world of sin is filled with dissension and disorder.

In setting up this central opposition the play drapes its Christian doctrine in two different medieval ideals of kingship: that of the feudal ruler and that of the absolute sovereign monarch. The medieval feudal contract called for personal loyalty to the overlord, but it implied a limited ruling power. The feudal king was the superior lord among many feudal lords, and his struggle to maintain his feudal rulership frequently created dissension. Various theories of absolute sovereign authority rivaled this concept of feudal lordship at different times during the Middle Ages. By the fifteenth century English political commentaries stressed the importance both of a sovereign ruler and of a unified national kingdom, which in legal theory was often called a patria. It is precisely this contrast which the play dramatizes allegorically. God is not just superior in authority to Mundus. Both the nature of his power as the absolute monarch of Heaven and the structure of his undivided kingdom differ in kind from the limited feudal power and fragmented social realm of Mundus.

It might seem initially that in establishing the contrast between the corrupt feudal world and the sovereign monarchy of God the play is simply following the conventional political theory of the fifteenth century. Such a line of reasoning might naturally assume that the topical references of the play reflect at least an implicit desire to support the secular structures of monarchical authority so prominently defended in the fifteenth century. However, the play does not bear out these assumptions. As Ernst Kantorowicz has pointed out, even when social theorists had favored the theoretically reciprocal feudal contract, God had consistently been described as an absolute monarch, omnipotently ruling over the "patria" of Heaven.[10]

10. Ernst H. Kantorowicz, *The King's Two Bodies: A Study in Medieval Political Theology* (Princeton: Princeton University Press: 1957), p. 234. Kantorowicz stresses the distinction made by late medieval theorists between feudal kingship and what he calls "polity-centered kingship," the sovereign authority of a king as ruler of a patria. Kantorowicz argues that from the thirteenth century on the subject's obligations to the sovereign king were increasingly placed above those to the feudal lord. For this entire discussion see pages 232–272. Useful sources of information on various medieval theories of kingship and their relative political weight include Henry de Brackton, *On the Laws and Customs of England*, trans., rev., notes Samuel E. Thorne (Cambridge, Mass.: Harvard University Press, 1968, 1976), especially Vol. II; and R. W. Carlyle and A. J. Carlyle, *A History of Medieval Political Theory in the*

By reducing the status of Mundus to that of a frivolous feudal overlord, whose power is petty in nature and whose kingdom is fragmented, the play actually supports a more conservative assertion of God's absolute supremacy. Developed in this way the blend of traditional Christian allegory and contemporary economic *exempla* carries with it an implied condemnation of the social world for which the fifteenth century provided a specific historical rationale.

Preserving the symmetrical balance between good and evil maintained throughout, Mundus opens and God closes the play. Each "king" delivers a long speech in which he claims to rule "all the werld" (ll. 165, 3615). However, Mundus boasts vaingloriously about his feudal power. He enumerates the countries he controls; he defines the relationships of his followers as economic; his law of acquisition is based on social principles; and perhaps most of all he claims authority only during the human lifetime:

> I do men rawyn on ryche rowe
> Tyl þei be dyth to dethys dent.
>
> (ll. 168–169)

In contrast, God allows Humanum Genus to make a free choice of good or evil during his lifetime. But God claims as his special prerogative the final judgment after death (ll. 3616–3623). Though he enumerates the social estates of men under his control

> Kyng, kayser, knyt, and kampyoun,
> Pope, patriark, prest, and prelat . . .
> Lytyl and mekyl, þe more and þe les,
>
> (ll. 3611–3612, 3614)

he has no interest in their social condition. Indeed, he does not appear until after Humanum Genus' death. A "kyng in ma-

---

West (London: W. Blackwood and Sons, 1903–1938), especially Vol. V. For a discussion of the importance of God's kingship in the cycle plays see Jerome Taylor, "The Dramatic Structure of the Middle English Corpus Christi, or Cycle, Plays," in Jerome Taylor and Alan H. Nelson, eds., *Medieval English Drama* (Chicago: University of Chicago Press, 1972), pp. 148–156.

jeste'' (l. 3483) who expresses concern only for the condition
of the human soul, God remains regally remote but also lovingly merciful. His sovereignty is absolute.

The entire play is organized around the confrontation between the feudal world of sin and the harmonious kingdom of
God. During the opening half of the play Humanum Genus is
welcomed ceremoniously into two specific communities: first,
the feudal court of Mundus and, second, the society of the virtues who take refuge in the Castle of Perseverance. The two
ceremonies of induction illustrate clearly the distinction between the concept of feudal patronage associated with the
World and the ideal of divine sovereignty which characterizes
the authority of God.

Humanum Genus becomes a liveried retainer of Mundus in a
lengthy and elaborate feudal ceremony which consists of two
parts: the feudal investiture at the scaffold of Mundus and the
further ceremonial endowment at the scaffold of Covetousness. The scene with Mundus (ll. 456–814) constitutes a formal
"conveyance" of Humanum Genus' "seisin." Such a conveyance in late medieval England involved more than a transfer of
land; it also established the feudal contract. "Seisin" itself implied "the completion of the feudal investiture, by which the
tenant was admitted into the feud and performed the rites of
homage and fealty."[11] The ceremony of investiture—called a
"livery of seisin"—served a vital role in the process of establishing a feudal relationship: "Essential to the validity of every
feoffment was the livery of seisin—which may be explained as
the formal delivery of possession . . . Proof of the conveyance depended upon the notoriety of the transaction, hence a
great deal of attention came to be paid to the *ceremony* of livery and the witnesses before whom it was performed."[12] At
the beginning of the ceremony in the play Mundus defines the
nature of his "servyse." His servants Lust-liking and Folye
are knights; his vassal "schal be kyng and were þe croun"
(l. 476); the reference, of course, is to feudal kingship. Mundus
offers both wealth and feudal power (see ll. 584–596). Lust-lik-

11. *Black's Law Dictionary*, p. 1218.
12. Clarkson and Warren, *The Law of Property in Shakespeare*, p. 113.

ing presents Humanum Genus as a "servant of nobyl fame" who wants to be "boþe ryche of gold and fee . . . be gret of name . . . be at gret honour . . . to rewle town and toure" (ll. 576, 572, 579–581). Having been thus presented as a candidate for feudal investiture Humanum Genus pledges his fealty to Mundus: "And þerto here my trewþe" (l. 609). At this point Mundus takes Humanum Genus "up" to his throne (l. 614) and sends him away with Lust-liking and Folye who clothe him in the livery of Mundus, a "nobyl aray" (l. 728) consisting of coin-bedecked garments and conveying status as well as gaudy decoration:

> Voluptas [addressing Mundus]: . . .
> In bryth besauntys he is bownde
> And bon to bowe to you so bolde.
> (ll. 700–702; "besauntys" are gold or silver coins)

Accepting service as a knight and retainer of Mundus, Humanum Genus pledges to defend Mundus without question, whether he be right or wrong:

> þou feffyst me wyth fen and felde,
> And hye hall, by holtys and hyll . . .
> I am kene as a knyt.
> Whoso ageyn þe Werld wyl speke,
> Mankynde schal on him be wreke.
> In stronge presun I schal him steke,
> Be it wronge or ryth.
> (ll. 740–741, 746–750)

Note the feudal verb *feffyst*. Mundus receives the pledge and confers a knighthood on Humanum Genus, at the same time conveying the seisin:

> I *feffe* þe in all my wonys wyde,
> In dale of dros tyl þou be deth . . .
> Here I gyfe þe wyth myn honde,
> *Syr,* an opyn *sesun.*
> (ll. 755–756, 762–763; italics mine)

The entire structure of this scene depends on the feudal ceremony to convey the message of the Christian allegory. By pledging his patronage only until death and offering Humanum Genus an "opyn sesun," Mundus has foreshadowed the dispossession of Humanum Genus which will take place at the moment of death. This disinheritance scene plays an important role in the overall allegory of the play. But for the moment a naively deceived Humanum Genus is led away by Sir Covetousness for the continuation of his feudal "feoffment." Maintaining the same ceremonial language Sir Covetousness "enfeoffs" him with riches: "Here I feffe the in myn hevene / wyth gold and syluyr" (ll. 889–900). Then Covetousness calls the other sins to his scaffold where they also "enfeoff" Humanum Genus with fleshly and spiritual vices at the request of Covetousness. Later in the play, after Covetousness has lured him from the Castle of Perseverance, Humanum Genus again pledges himself to the World: "Covetyse þou muste me sese" (l. 2750). Although no formal livery of seisin occurs at this point, the operative verb "sese" (seise) stresses the consistency with which the Christian allegory of bondage in sin is portrayed as a process of feudal investiture.

In contrast to this ceremony of fealty and feoffment, the virtues' reception of Humanum Genus into the castle assumes the character of a spiritual ritual (ll. 1602–1666). Despite the fact that Confession answers the plea of the Good Angel in the "name of felechepys olde and newe" (l. 1304), the virtues do not establish a feudal bond with Humanum Genus. Because of a gap in the manuscript the opening speeches of the virtues are missing from the play, but in the ceremonial welcoming speeches which remain five of the virtues deliver exhortations to good behavior with the dignity befitting their station as "ladys in londe, lovely and lyt" (l. 1667). The acquisitive impulse, the raucous behavior, the impression of brash, newly rich lordship, the modish clothes and French phrases which characterize the followers of the World, the Flesh, and the Devil and which have been associated with feudal patronage are replaced by a sober definition of Christian duty which does not imply a feudal bond but which nevertheless gracefully reflects *genuine* courtly manners. Even the metaphor of royalty has shifted. The virtues invoke the Virgin Mary as their highest figure of authority. But in contrast to Mundus, who frivolously calls himself a "lykynge lord" who "trotte[s] and trem-le[s] . . . [and] hoppe[s]" (ll. 461, 457, 458), the Virgin is a "curteys qwene" (l. 1632) whose sovereign power is imperial rather than feudal in nature: she is the "Emperes" of Heaven (l. 1706).[13]

Just as the ceremonies of reception emphasize the spiritual poverty of Mundus' feudal kingdom, so, too, do Mundus' laws and forms of "justice" parody the very concept of law itself. The chief agent of disorder in the feudal world of sin, Mundus' law of acquisition has but a single governing principle, repeated by Covetousness and Humanum Genus in a rhapsodic duet: "More and more . . . more and more . . . more and more" (see ll. 2700–2777). As listed by Covetousness the specific tenets of Mundus' law invert God's commandments and reflect the worst abuses of economic acquisitiveness as it is illustrated by all social estates: covet more than you need; depend on simony, extortion, and false assize; give no help; do not pay your servants; destroy your neighbors; do not tithe; do not help beggars; cheat when dealing with merchandise; swear by deception; buy and sell according to false weights (ll. 835–854).

This law itself rewards cheating and removes all hierarchy of spiritual authority; it can be carried out only by policies of betrayal and methods of economic manipulation. The impression the play thus creates of subverted law accords well with descriptions historians give of the early fifteenth century as a period in which law "has become a tool adaptable to the purposes of the unscrupulous."[14] Although by this time the

---

13. The medieval concept of *empery* resembles the ideal of an absolute sovereign king in that both the emperor and the sovereign monarch rule absolutely over a large consolidated kingdom, in contrast to the feudal king. This same distinction is dramatized in *Wisdom Who Is Christ,* in which Wisdom appears in imperial robes in contrast both to the devil who is costumed as a gallant and to the retainers of the evil figures, who wear feudal liveries.

14. See Williams, *Year Books,* p. xvii for quotation, which refers to general conditions in early fifteenth-century England. This characterization of lawless-

feudalistic contracts of bondage and indenture had largely been replaced by a system of monetary leases and sales of property, the practice of feudal patronage as depicted in *The Castle of Perseverance* was still extensive. Law had replaced theology as the major study for ambitious young men, and legal maneuvers in the various secular and ecclesiastical courts could tie up family property for years. Under such circumstances land disputes were frequently settled by armed invasion rather than by legal process. To take an example: in 1411 a justice of the King's Bench invaded a property to settle a land dispute and, when charged by Parliament to explain the invasion, pleaded ignorance of the law![15] In such an environment the support of a powerful "good lord" was essential even for small landholders; the system of "maintenance" and the manipulation of the courts which figure heavily in the list of social complaints in the second half of the fifteenth century were both securely established by the first decades of that century. In focusing on such abuses *The Castle of Perseverance* reflects the economic realities and political fears of its period.

In contrast to the legal processes of Mundus, which foster only dissension and disorder, God not only fulfills the natural law; in Thomistic terms he even transcends that law. However, it is significant that he does not offer any form of corrective for the economic abuses of the play. Consistent with the theological indifference to social welfare illustrated throughout the play, the final judgment of God simply but emphatically ignores the economic difficulties. During the debate of the four daughters, Justice (an elder daughter) demands the fair process of law:

---

ness in the early fifteenth century is widely shared by social historians of this period. See, for instance, F. R. H. DuBoulay, *An Age of Ambition: English Society in the Late Middle Ages* (London: Thomas Nelson and Sons, 1970), especially pp. 31–60 and 128–142; or J. R. Lander, *Conflict and Stability in Fifteenth Century England* (London: Hutchinson University Library, 1969).

15. The case of Robert Tirwhit, Justice, is described in Williams, *Year Books,* pp. xvi–xvii. Cases involving such invasions appear frequently throughout this period. The Pastons, a prominent East Midlands family, suffered at least three invasions stemming from property disputes during their turbulent family history.

> If þou mans kynde from peyne aquite,
>   þou dost ageyns þyne owyn processe . . .
>   þou dost wronge, Lorde, to Trewth and me
>   And puttys us fro oure devnesse.
>   (ll. 3383–3384, 3433–3434)

In response Mercy and Peace plead for God to forgive Humanum Genus, thus sacrificing the idea of fair process to the more generous concept of forgiveness. The two younger daughters win the debate, and Peace announces that "Mankynd schal haue grace" (l. 3547). However, the argument that carries the day is not Mercy's quasi-legal plea for Humanum Genus but Peace's assertion that unless they agree on forgiveness, they themselves "schuld . . . euere [be in] dyscorde here" (l. 3515). Thus, the debate in Heaven is resolved not by means of litigious process but through reconciliation. In the kingdom of Mundus legal process creates discord and disorder. In the patria of God legal process itself gives way to the establishment of an eternal order in which economic issues have no meaning.

Such divine harmony is achieved, however, at a cost. Having no good works to his credit except that implied by his final penitence, Humanum Genus has not earned anything which he can claim as his by right. Humbly acknowledging his guilt and sin, he must depend entirely upon the favor of God's grace for his redemption. The concept of grace itself implies subjection and connotes social as well as theological significance. As a legal term *grace* may be defined as "a favor or indulgence as distinguished from a right."[16] And in the play King Mundus possesses the royal prerogative of "grace" as well as God. However, whereas God grants grace to an undeserving sinner, Mundus uses his royal power to despoil his loyal retainer through "hys grace" (l. 2937). Betraying Humanum Genus unfairly, Mundus implicitly denies the rights to which his feudal patronage should have entitled Humanum Genus. In thus discounting the value of the feudal contract the play also ignores the emerging social ideal of individual right within so-

---

16. *Black's Law Dictionary,* p. 628.

ciety.[17] Instead, it reasserts the conservative Christian definition of the individual as an unworthy subject of God, a sinning member of the *congregatio fidelium*. In this sense the "topical" satire of Mundus and the "universal" allegory of God merge into one dramatic whole. They work indistinguishably together to dramatize the specific theological ideal of *contemptus mundi* upheld throughout the play.

The final economic *exemplum* of the play focuses the allegory of acquisition even more sharply on an issue of great concern in the early fifteenth century: the difficulties connected with property inheritance. Having been struck by Death's dart, Humanum Genus calls for help from Mundus in the name of "felechepys olde and new" (l. 2861)—that is, in precisely the same terms to which Confession earlier responded to the Good Angel (l. 1304). However, unlike Confession, Mundus betrays the trust of "fellowship," and he uses the law of inheritance to effectuate his betrayal. He tauntingly announces that he has *entailed* Humanum Genus' property away from Humanum Genus' heirs, and, gloating that he will serve Humanum Genus as he has served thousands before, he sends a ragged vagabond called "I-Wot-Neuere-Who" to confiscate the estate (see ll. 2843–3007). Two aspects of this dispossession may claim our special attention. The first is the degree to which the preoccupation with inheritance and the emphasis on entails reflect the social realities of the early fifteenth century. The second is the extent to which the presence of this social issue serves only to negate the value of society.

A complex social problem of inheritance has been condensed in the single character of "I-Wot-Neuere-Who." Since he has been designated as heir, this unknown boy represents the passing of inheritance out of Humanum Genus' family. In

17. Walter Ullman, *The Individual and Society in the Middle Ages* (Baltimore: Johns Hopkins University Press, 1966) discusses the connection between the political ideal of individual rights, which gained emphasis in the late Middle Ages particularly in England, and the practices of English feudalism and the nature of the feudal contract. Ullman also emphasizes the importance of the medieval definition of the Christian as a "subject" of God in preserving the Catholic hierarchy.

addition, by offering Humanum Genus an expiatory funeral
party before tossing him into a lake (seeing him off to Hell),
"I-Wot-Neuere-Who" assumes a task previously defined in
the play as belonging to an executor.[18] Largitas (ll. 1660–
1662), Abstinentia (ll. 2605–2608), and Castitas (ll. 2609–2612)
have all warned Humanum Genus that "sekatours" will make
merry and give large feasts with his carefully guarded goods.

Both the loss of family property and the difficulties with
unreliable executors accurately mirror fifteenth-century economic realities. As a result of a larger cash flow and a smaller
population, the sale and rental of land increased rapidly during
the late fourteenth and early fifteenth centuries. Thus, although property holdings often increased in size, continuous
ownership and hereditary continuity on the land were less consistently maintained during this period than they had been previously. Especially in the East Midlands where *The Castle of
Perseverance* was probably composed,[19] the sudden new mo-
bility of small landowners in the early fifteenth century
(c. 1410–1440) created a virtual crisis of inheritance, temporarily altering the patterns of hereditary land descent.[20] By mid-

18. The use of feasts as rituals of social expiation has historical precedent.
For instance, the punishment meted out to Robert Tirwhit, Justice, for his
armed invasion of property included providing a large feast for the parties involved: "Supplying two tuns of Gascon wine and two fat oxen and twelve fat
sheep to provide a dinner," Williams, *Year Books,* p. xvii.

19. There seems little doubt that *The Castle of Perseverance* was written in
or near Norfolk. However, since no records exist of performances of this or
any English morality play in the fifteenth century, it is difficult to discuss the
composition or early performance of the play with any certainty. See John
Wasson, "The Morality Play: Ancestor of Elizabethan Drama?" *Comparative
Drama,* 13, no. 3 (Fall 1979), 214.

20. Cicely Howell, "Peasant Inheritance Customs in the Midlands 1280–
1700," in Jack Goody, Joan Thirsk, and E. P. Thompson, eds., *Family and
Inheritance* (Cambridge: Cambridge University Press, 1976), pp. 112–155. See
also Paul Murray Kendall, *The Yorkist Age* (London: George Allen and
Unwin, 1962), p. 213. The Paston fortunes further exemplify the difficulties
with inheritance, especially in the East Midlands. As long as John Paston's
benefactor, Sir John Fastolf, lived, the Paston fortunes rose. However, when
Fastolf died and left his property to John Paston, troubles began. Paston was
twice jailed by coexecutors in his legal attempts to obtain possession of his
property, which he was expected to defend in court in London at the same
time that he defended the property itself in the East Midlands. See H. S. Ben-

century a measure of stability had returned to the estates of the East Midlands with regard to family possession and inheritance, but during the period in which *The Castle of Perseverance* is assumed to have been written, family properties were often dispersed. At this same time, lawyers were finding ways to break entails on wills, a manipulation necessary if the sales of entailed property were to convey permanent ownership. By showing Mundus as playing tricks with the idea of entailed property the play reflects the social preoccupation with this question. Both the process by which property was inherited and the breaking of an entail, however, led to abuse, since they frequently depended on the good will of executors or other outside parties. In centering the final spiritual crisis of the play around the question of inheritance *The Castle of Perseverance* once more makes use of contemporary economic problems to establish its spiritual allegory.

However, the play's emphasis on these timely issues does not imply a desire to reform social abuse. Instead it exemplifies both the unimportance and the inadequacy of the World at the same time that it stresses the need for penitence as the key to salvation. One of the most interesting aspects of the disinheritance scene is the subtle way it negates the significance of social bonds. The dialogue which occurs between Humanum Genus and the unknown heir (ll. 2921–2994) momentarily introduces a whole new set of relationships into the play. For the first time we learn that Humanum Genus has a family. He says that he had expected his wife and children to inherit his hard-won property (ll. 2971–2981) and suggests that even his cousins and nephews would be better heirs than a ragged unknown boy (ll. 2943–2951). The discovery of his dispossession occasions Humanum Genus' most serious lament:

> I Wot Neuere Who! so welaway!
> Now am I sory of my lyf.
> I haue purchasyd many a day
> Londys and rentys wyth mekyl stryf . . .
> To myne chyldyr and to myn wyfe
> In dethe whanne I were dyth . . .

nett, *The Pastons and Their England* (Cambridge: Cambridge University Press, 1951), pp. 1–26; and Kendall, *The Yorkist Age*, pp. 194–243.

> Now alas, my lyf is lak . . .
> þe Werld hathe ordeynyd *of hys entayle*
> I Wot Neuere Who   to be myne eyre.
> (ll. 2969–2972; 2976–2977; 2983; 2993–2994; italics mine)

At this point Humanum Genus offers himself to the audience as an *exemplum* of sin and with his final breath calls for mercy (ll. 2982–3007). In effect, Humanum Genus' death has been held back for several hundred lines and the entire dialogue about his family introduced only to allow for his repentance, his confession, and his last-minute cry for mercy. This cry saves him, for without it Mercy could not plead her case before God. Thus, indirectly Humanum Genus is saved because of the disinheritance of his family. The family passes back into oblivion; presumably they remain disinherited, for we never hear of them again. Neither Humanum Genus' social obligations to his family nor the economic welfare of his kindred matter in this play. Viewed from the perspective of inevitable death, only the condition of the soul is of consequence, and that is not a social issue. The only family of significance in the play is the family of God, considered as a spiritual abstraction. The only society which gains favor is that of the church and even it is treated as a mystical entity, not a social institution. The confession which makes possible Mercy's intervention on Humanum Genus' behalf is accomplished without the aid of priests and clergymen. Such internalization of penitence reflects the theological discourse of the fifteenth century, just as the economic allegory of sin catalogues contemporary abuses.[21] But in a century in which the acquisition of property and the redefinition of feudal relationships played an intense role in the lives of Englishmen beginning to regard themselves as citizens, this play discounts all concern with social well-being as an *exemplum* of sin.

21. See Ullman, *The Individual and Society in the Middle Ages,* pp. 143–145. According to Ullman "the direct link between the individual and divinity, without the mediatory role of ecclesiastical officers, became the pivotal point of man's religious life," p. 145. David Bevington, *Tudor Drama and Politics,* p. 35, also refers to the minimal role of clergy in *The Castle of Perseverance,* though his explanation for the noticeable absence of clergy differs from mine.

Though in orthodox Christian theology the salvation of the single soul consistently takes precedence over other issues, total renunciation of the world represents only one strand of Christian thought. Christian allegory can depict salvation as compatible with social progress. In the late fourteenth century allegories which emphasized the importance of social well-being were, in fact, particularly popular. Such a pilgrimage allegory as, say, *Piers Plowman* stresses individual salvation but at the same time indicates that concern over the soul does not necessarily negate belief in social perfection. Like *The Castle of Perseverance*, *Piers Plowman* weaves a language of economic acquisition throughout its conventional Christian allegories. However, this poem exhibits a continuous interest in social law, in family welfare, in the industrious accumulation and right use of worldly goods totally lacking in *The Castle of Perseverance*. To take one instance which compares well with the dispossession of Humanum Genus in the play: in passus 5 of the B text of *Piers Plowman* Repentance addresses Covetousness as if he were an errant sinner, capable of reform. Repentance tells him that unless he repents of his greediness his estates will be sacrificed to unscrupulous executors. The implication in this passage, as throughout the poem, is that economic acquisition can serve good as well as bad purposes. There is true as well as false "mede." Should he repent, Covetousness could presumably save both his property and his soul.[22] No such possibility exists in *The Castle of Perseverance*. The play treats social corruption as the given norm of society—its only possible condition. From this perspective earthly wealth cannot be industriously gotten or well used. Humanum Genus can save his soul only by losing his property and consequently disinheriting his family.

22. Walter W. Skeat, *The Vision of William Concerning Piers the Plowman* (Oxford: Clarendon Press, 1886), p. 152. For discussions of *Piers Plowman* as a document assuming the possibility of social perfection or stressing the common good, see Morton W. Bloomfield, *Piers Plowman as a Fourteenth Century Apocalypse* (New Brunswick: Rutgers University Press, 1961); and Donald R. Howard, "Body Politic and the Lust of the Eyes," chap. 4 in *The Three Temptations: Medieval Man in Search of the World* (Princeton: Princeton University Press, 1966), pp. 161–213.

The Castle of Perseverance focuses attention on the chaos evident in the acquisitive economic climate of the fifteenth century. And in doing that the play contains a dimension of social satire. The conflict of power between secular and spiritual authority belongs to the economic and social history of the fifteenth century as well as to the theological and philosophical disputes of this period. But despite the topical nature of its moral *exempla*, the play does not open the door to social reform. In its resolution it more simply reaffirms the orthodox Christian hierarchy in which the individual is defined as unworthy subject of God, altogether dependent on the undeserved favor of divine grace for salvation. Reminded of sin and convinced of the need to obey God, a chastened fifteenth-century audience was expected to see in the allegory of feudal acquisition, and by extension in its own acquisitive impulses, an *exemplum* of disobedient godlessness, not a possible program of reform.[23]

23. The research for this article was supported by a sabbatical leave extension grant from Trinity College.

JOHN L. KLAUSE

George Herbert, *Kenosis,*
and the Whole Truth

"Dare to be true. Nothing can need a ly." This moral exhortation in George Herbert's "Church-porch"[1] does high honor to the truth, which ought to be served despite inconvenience or danger, and in whose service the Christian can be false neither to himself nor to any man. Indeed, is not God himself Truth itself, and the source of our imperative to seek it? Does he not, through his power, in accordance with his promises, guarantee that the truth will prevail, that its adherents will be rewarded? A man of faith like Herbert need not be uneasy on the subject. Besides, truth is reliable on its own. Herbert devoutly believed that "all Truth [is] consonant to it self" (*The Country Parson,* [hereafter *CP*] ch. 4, p. 229),[2] so that it allows, for example, no contradictory precepts in the Scripture, forbids even God him-

1. Line 77. All citations from Herbert's writing will be from *The Works of George Herbert,* ed. F. E. Hutchinson (Oxford: Clarendon Press, 1941).
2. On the self-consistency of truth see Edward Herbert's *De veritate,* trans. M. H. Carré (Bristol: University of Bristol, 1937), pp. 84–88. Lord Herbert dedicated the manuscript of this work to his brother George. See Joseph Summers, *George Herbert: His Religion and Art* (Cambridge, Mass.: Harvard University Press, 1954), p. 33.

self to be "untrue" to his own nature—as the poet often reminds his divine interlocutor:

> Thou canst no more not heare, then thou canst die.
> ("Prayer [II]," 6)

> Thou canst not choose but see my actions.
> ("Obedience," 23)

> Thy promise now hath ev'n set thee thy laws.
> ("Artillerie," 24)

Similarly assured the pastor likes to console his troubled flock:
"As Creatures, [God] must needs love [us]; for no perfect Artist ever yet hated his owne worke" (*CP* 34. 283). Whether
through faith or reason Herbert also strives to find a fundamental "consonance" between truth and other values. In a number
of poems ("Love [I and II]," "Jordan [I and II]," "A true
Hymne," "The Forerunners," and the two "Sonnets" from
Walton's *Lives*) he suggests more or less explicitly that beauty
is a depiction of the truth, however defined, the truest art being
ceteris paribus the most beautiful. And throughout *The Temple*
he assumes that moral virtue is action upon the truth, which
has been sifted from the "false glozing" promises of sin ("Dotage," 1) and made to inform "true remorse," "true desires,"
"delights more true / Then miseries are here" ("The Water-
course," 8; "Love [II]," 4; "Dotage," 17–18). If sin is forgetting ("Miserie," 62; "The Banquet," 31), salvation is learning:
an opening, mending, wiping, and drying of eyes, so that they
may enjoy the vision of "such a Truth" that quickens, heals,
and "ends all strife" ("The Pearl. Matth. 13. 45," 32; *CP* 24;
"The H. Scriptures. I," 9; "Ungratefulnesse," 17–18; "The
Banquet," 45–46; "The Dawning," 14; *Lucus,* no. 35; "The
Glance," 21; "The Call," 3). To be constant to the truth, then,
is to "dare" only from the perspective of one whose lack of
nerve leads him to doubt what in the abstract he knows must
be so.

The authentic risk for one who loves the truth is to place
oneself in the position of forgoing it. And Herbert's meditations on the necessity, even the desirability, of such a venture

are among his most impassioned. The humanist in him would cling to the notion that every truth, the whole truth, is compatible with the aesthetic and moral good he seeks to promote. The Christian in him, who would be a humanist insofar as he may, must acknowledge that in this finite, fallen world, *bonum* and *verum* are often in competition, to the distress of the latter. Of the "many spiritual conflicts" that occasion his poetry,[3] none is more acute than that which requires him to surrender his "eyes" ("Submission," 20) for the sake of his heart.

This conflict Herbert earnestly attempts to resolve, recording the effort in poetry that is dramatic, argumentative, and symbolic. Although each mode is important for his purposes, it is through symbols, finally, that he is able to speak most succinctly and suggestively about his conclusions. We must examine briefly some of these symbols, but only after trying to be more precise about the problems they are meant to illustrate.

That the truth does not contain within itself the same absolute imperative as does (moral) goodness was clear to Herbert upon the kind of simple reflection that produced his Outlandish Proverb, "All truths are not to be told" (no. 89).[4] Whereas every departure from a moral standard is in some degree criminal (one may not "do evil, [even] that good may come of it" [*CP* 37. 287]), a withholding or distortion of, a failure to act upon the whole truth may be legitimate and salutary. God himself has withheld much truth from us in good causes. Either to try or to punish he has for a time denied us that full vision of himself which would preclude error, withdrawing so completely sometimes that one may doubt his presence at all:

> My knees pierce th'earth, mine eyes the skie;
> And yet the sphere
> And centre both to me denie
> That thou art there.
>
> ("The Search," 5–8)

3. Walton's *Lives* (New York: Scot-Thaw, 1903), p. 303.

4. See *CP* 12. 245. The Parson "allows his Charity some blindnesse . . . ; especially since of the two commands, we are more enjoyned to be charitable, then [than] wise." See also 7. 233; 33. 278; *Outlandish Proverbs* (hereafter *OP*), nos. 3 and 86.

Some truth God veils in order to protect us:

> O that I could a sinne once see!
> . . . . .
> But God more care of us hath had:
> If apparitions make us sad,
> By sight of sinne we should grow mad.
>   ("Sinne [II]," 1, 6–8; compare "Vanitie [I]," 10–14)

Some truth he holds back in order to create in us a "restless-ness" that will drive us to him ("The Pulley") or to our fel-lows: "Neither hath God opened, or will open all to one, that there may be a traffick in knowledg between the servants of God, for the planting both of love, and humility" (*CP* 4. 229. Compare 24. 263; *Orationes* no. 3, p. 450. See Augustine, *De doctrina Christiana*, Prooem. 6). Most astonishingly, how-ever, though he cannot choose but see, God somehow closes his *own* eyes:

> Blest be the God of love,
> . . . . .
> Who gave me sight alone,
> Which to himself he did denie:
> For when he sees my waies, I dy.
>   ("Even-song," 1, 5–7)

God "hath forgotten" the sins of those whom he will save (*CP* 37. 288) forbearing to treat his chosen according to their de-serts, imputing to them a value not their own:

> When creatures had no reall light
> Inherent in them, thou didst make the sunne
> Impute a lustre, and allow them bright.
>   ("Faith," 33–35)

If the Author of truth may choose to neglect or be chary of it, there are clearly times when a man ought to do so as well. Herbert inevitably finds that in his moral and devotional life he must often resort to a "holy" falsification, of the kind that he complains about in "Conscience":

> Peace pratler, do not lowre:
> Not a fair look, but thou dost call it foul:
> Not a sweet dish, but thou dost call it sowre:
> Musick to thee doth howl.
> By listning to thy chatting fears
> I have both lost mine eyes and ears.
>
> (1–6)

Although the "pratler" is to be silenced by Christ's blood (16), this conscience is not, as one might think, simply an errant one. It is, rather, the same zealous moral sentinel that is at work throughout Herbert's meditations seeking to assure right action at whatever cost to the whole truth. Just as God is forever *enticing* man to good ("The Church-porch," 295; "Affliction [I]," 1; "Ungratefulnesse," 22; and especially *CP* 11. 243–244), so conscience has its "stratagems to catch us in" ("Sinne I," 7) and does not hesitate to use them. It can "wink" the world and "woman-kinde" into "a blacknesse and distaste" to prepare the soul for renunciation ("Home," 38–40; compare "The Collar," 26). Through deliberate inattention to the greatness of Man (celebrated by Herbert in the poem of that title), it can, to foster humility and patience, dwell on the thought that the glory of God's creation is but "clay," "dust," "a silly flie" ("Complaining," 5, 8). Because certain acknowledgments are God's due from us, our debt of gratitude requiring that we should be thankful not only "when it pleaseth" ("Gratefulnesse," 29), conscience may dictate "insincere" expressions in prayer or in poetry.

Now a *dévot* may maneuver through the truth in this way without the slightest compunction. Intent on the *unum necessarium,* he may gladly abandon a troublesome loyalty to the truth that would save it to its last ounce and inch. But Herbert could not dispense with any truth without a struggle. And we can see how intense and how crucial the struggle may have been by considering one of the most important themes in his work, the biblical concept of *kenosis,* or "emptying."

For a Christian the injunction to imitate his Lord can be as difficult to understand as it is to obey. Everywhere in his work Herbert recognizes that he is obliged to "follow" Christ in his "resigning," who

> did freely part
> With [his] glorie and desert,
> Left all joyes to feel all smart.
>
> ("Dialogue," 29–31)

If the precedent meant only that one should endure pain with resignation, then Herbert might single-mindedly pray and strive for the gift of conformity to Christ's example. But the matter is not so simple. The Epistle to the Philippians (which Herbert was fond of referring to and quoting from)[5] describes a mystery that transcends mere stoicism: "Let this mind be in you, which was also in Christ Jesus: Who, being in the form of God, thought it not robbery to be equal with God: But made himself of no reputation [*heauton ekenosen*, 'emptied himself'], and took upon him the form of a servant . . . And being found in fashion as a man, he humbled himself, and became obedient unto death, even the death of the cross" (2:5–8). The "emptying" of which St. Paul speaks (and which seems to embarrass the translators of the Authorized Version into a euphemism)[6] is more than an acceptance of suffering. It is a self-diminishment that involves a deliberate departure from the truth: Christ, as Herbert says, freely parts with his "desert," ignoring what he is and ought to be to become what he is not. How a divine being can accomplish so radical a metamorphosis is surely beyond human understanding; Paul nevertheless urges Christians to be of Christ's mind and to imitate him. Herbert tried to "follow" this "resigning," mysterious as it was in its origins and meaning. But he could not practice self-denial without demurrals that he was too honest to conceal.

What might Christ's *kenosis* require of one who would imitate it? Religious authorities through the ages have suggested a form of self-annihilation, in the knowledge that Jesus himself

5. Compare, for example, "The Sacrifice," 63, 221–223, and "Dialogue," 29–30, with Phil. 2:6. And *CP* 19. 253; *Valdesso's Considerations,* ad 49. 313; *Letters,* pp. 366 and 380, with Phil. 4:8.

6. Paul probably quotes here from an early liturgical hymn (see *Peake's Commentary on the Bible,* ed. Matthew Black, and H. H. Rowley [London: Thomas Nelson and Sons, 1962], p. 986), which in its lack of precision seems more true to the mystery of the Incarnation than the less exceptionable English redaction (which was originally Tyndale's).

prevailed upon his disciples to "deny" and "lose" themselves (Luke 9:23–24) and that St. Paul fervently obeyed: "I am crucified with Christ: nevertheless I live; yet not I, but Christ liveth in me" (Gal. 2:20). Christian theologians have not always agreed on the philosophical implications of this essentially poetic, devotional language (hence all the disputes about the nature and operation of grace); but Herbert's understanding of it has been defined, most notably by Stanley Fish, as a literal one: before God Herbert believes that he must seek "the undoing of the self as an independent entity, a 'making of no thine and mine' by making it all thine, a surrender not only of a way of seeing, but of initiative, will, and finally of being (to say 'I am' is to say amiss)."[7] Such a blithe insistence on the absolute sovereignty of God and the utter nothingness of man—an emptiness that the deity should come to fill—may describe with some accuracy the mystical impulse to surrender or lose the self in a Transcendental Infinite. It may by various qualifications be made acceptable to the Christian mind. It does not, however, do justice to the complexity of Herbert's thought, and it fails even to hint at the fact that for Herbert *kenosis* is an intellectual as well as a moral problem.

The problem, as has been suggested, is one of saving the truth, and there is much that Herbert desires to preserve. He recognizes, of course, that God demands the extirpation of the "selfishness" that is error: of the pride that persuades us that we are more than we are or deserve more than is our due; of the egocentric passion that seeks satisfaction in "sugred lies" ("The Rose," 2). At the same time Herbert knows of a self "most true" ("Constancie," 3), with its own value and rights, which he cannot believe God wishes to see dissolve.

Herbert has a very strong, Augustinian sense that being is good *in se*. Even the devil, he says, "hath some good in him"

---

7. *Self-Consuming Artifacts* (Berkeley, Los Angeles, and London: University of California Press, 1972), p. 158. Richard Strier, in "Humanizing Herbert" (*Modern Philology,* 74 [1976], 78–88), criticizes Helen Vendler's description of Herbert's "self-acceptance" (*The Poetry of George Herbert* [Cambridge, Mass.: Harvard University Press, 1975], p. 161 and *passim*). None of these studies distinguishes properly between "true" and "false" selves.

("Sinne [II]," 3), for despite the privation of goodness in
Satan's character, he is at least good in his substance. *Bonum
convertitur cum ente*.[8] By creating beings other than himself,
then, God assured that in his universe, although he would be
the source of all value, he would not be the *only* good; and the
Creator can hardly be jealous of other selves, who are distinct
from him *because* he is generous. Thus when Herbert prays,
"make no Thine and Mine!" ("Clasping of hands," 20), he
does not mean "let there be no I and Thou." On the contrary,
in his humblest expression there lurks an appreciation of the
value of the self's separateness: "Lesse then the least / Of all
Gods mercies" may be his constant "posie" ("The Posie,"
11–12; see also "The Printer to the Reader"); but these are
very like the words of Jacob after he *wrestled with* the Lord
(Gen. 32:10; see "Decay," 2; "Sion," 16; "The Crosse," 8).
Herbert liberally avails himself of the privilege of asserting
himself against God, sometimes conducting a lover's quarrel in
which submission, always difficult, is dramatic ("The Collar")
or poignant ("The Search," "The Crosse"), less frequently
allowing to stand his complaints that the meager prerogatives
of the self have been ignored or violated ("Hope," "Longing"). If, as Rosemond Tuve has claimed, the author of *The
Temple* learned "the distinction between love and the desire to
be valuable,"[9] he also believed that this desire need not be unholy. He does not retract such expressions of it as "Employment [I and II]," "The Starre," and "The Odour"; and he
dares to remind God that the loss (to perdition) of a creature
whom the Creator has made valuable is true loss indeed
("Gratefulnesse," 6–8; "The Pulley," 14–15; "L'Envoy,"
5–10).

Herbert could not explain how it is possible that "nothing is
our own" ("The Holdfast," 7)—existence, ability, virtue are

8. See Hutchinson's commentary on "Sinne [II]," p. 498. For suggestions
of this outlook elsewhere in Herbert's writings see "Ephes. 4. 30," 22; "The
Elixir," 13–16; "The H. Communion," Williams MS., 21–22; *CP* 25. 263; *CP*
34. 283; *OP* 520.

9. See "George Herbert and *Caritas*," in *Essays by Rosemond Tuve*, ed.
Thomas P. Roche, Jr. (Princeton: Princeton University Press, 1970), p. 196.

all God's gifts—and yet much is genuinely "ours" (12). This was as great a mystery as Christ's presence in the Eucharist, which one must believe without understanding ("Divinitie," "The H. Communion," Williams MS.). But whatever the conceptual difficulties it was important for Herbert not to let these truths go: that "Obedience" is meaningless if the obedient self is only a cipher or fiction; that "Praise" and "Prayer" are vain if they are only God's breath returning through an empty vessel to its origin; that redemption and punishment cannot without absurdity be given to marionettes. *Kenosis* is not self-annihilation.

It is, however, a form of denial—even of the truth and of the "true" self. The emptying required by Christ's example is not merely humility, or a perception of one's true lowliness before God (in Herbert's poem "Humilitie," that virtue is pre-eminently clear-eyed and intelligent). *Kenosis* is not merely the sensible, therapeutic pruning of excess ("Lent," "Paradise," "The Size") nor a logical consequence of finitude (*Valdesso's Considerations,* ad 49, p. 313). Although Christ's passion, and by extension ours, is indeed a kind of emptying, symbolized by the outpouring of the Savior's blood to the last drop (*Passio discerpta,* no. 3; "The Bunch of Grapes," 28), suffering is a symptom rather than a formal cause of the *kenosis* implied by the Incarnation; for, as we have seen, before Christ could suffer he had to forget.

Self-forgetfulness is *kenosis* in the most eminent sense, a sense convincingly illustrated by the parable of the Good Samaritan. It was when "a certain lawyer" asked him, "Who is my neighbour?" that Jesus told that story, concluding it with a deft and significant rephrasing of the original question: "Which . . . was neighbour unto him that fell among thieves?" (Luke 10:36). The neighbor has moved from the circumference of the circle, where the legal mind, jealous of its own rights, has placed him, to the center, replacing "me" or "my" as the object of attention and concern. Just so, Herbert feels, did Christ ignore his "glorie and desert" ("Dialogue," 30), neglect his very life ("vitam, quam negligis," "In natales et pascha concurrentes," 5), in his utter preoccupation with the needs of those whom he loved:

He so farre thy good did plot,
That his own self he forgot.
Did he die, or did he not?[10]

("Businesse," 23–25)

Christians too are called upon to "pass" their "right[s] away" ("The Rose," 12) in a "forgetting of themselves" (*CP* 26. 267). And the forgetting, occasioned as it is by love of another—by devotion to the will of God or by attention to the needs of a neighbor—has, strictly speaking, nothing to do with the goodness or evil of what is renounced in the process. Herbert knows very well St. Paul's charter for the Christian humanist: "Whatsoever things are true, whatsoever things are honest, whatsoever things are just, whatsoever things are pure, whatsoever things are lovely, whatsoever things are of good report . . . , think on these things" (Phil. 4:8). He is also aware that this humanism (advocated in the same Epistle as is *kenosis*), when considered not as a system of values to be contemplated but as a program for moral choice, can only be tentative. "A man is to embrace all good," he says, commenting on the passage just cited, "but because he cannot doe all, God often chuseth which he shall doe" (*Valdesso's Considerations,* ad 49. 313). The *man* must choose as well, and love may dictate that he leave uncultivated, unharvested, and untasted much that is noble and beautiful. A buried life at Bemerton, which closed off many possibilities of self-development, was far from the greatest of love's abnegations.

Weak flesh must surely rebel against an idealism so thorough that it forbids one, because even self-accusatory thoughts can be subtly egocentric, to dwell upon his own unworthiness ("Dialogue," "Love [III]"). A mind like Herbert's may also, out of strength, resist the necessity for ignorance and deprivation, seeking means to fill what has been emptied, to recover as much as possible of the whole truth that has been lost in loving. Herbert had to accommodate to the ideal of *kenosis* two of

10. The relationship of love to knowledge is the main concern of Anders Nygren in his survey of "The Christian Idea of Love," *Agape and Eros,* trans. A. G. Hebert, and Philip Watson, 2 pts. in 3 vols. (London: Society for Promoting Christian Knowledge, 1932–1939). Is the highest love bestowed where there is no desert, thus no knowledge possible of the value of the beloved?

his most basic instincts: that value is created by building rather than destroying and that "there is a Justice in the least things," so that "everything" is to be given "its end" (*CP* 26. 265).

Herbert finds value coextensive with being and displays none of the romantic's or modern's fascination with *die Nichtigkeit*. For him the "vertuous soul" is like "season'd timber" —solid, substantial ("Vertue," 13–14); only evil would turn it "to bubbles straight" and make it "vanish into a winde" ("Nature," 9–11). He was himself a builder, having undertaken the repair of three churches in his later years.[11] And in his *Temple* he thinks of both "Heart-work" and "Heaven-work" as processes of edification.[12] God is, after all, an "Architect" ("The Church-floore," 19) who piles up blessings ("The Pulley") with which to "furnish & deck [the] soul" ("Christmas," 13). The "stately habitation" thus fashioned ("Man," 2) "Sinne" and "Death" may "raze . . . to the very floore" ("The World," 16–17); but "Love" and "Grace" and "Glorie" can rebuild a still "braver Palace" on the same foundation (19–20). Man's own greatest work is through the power of grace to "reare" the altar of his heart, God himself cutting the "stones" to be "cemented" ("The Altar"). Furthermore, God loves to *fill* what he creates, in the Eucharist to feed man even with himself ("Whitsunday," 8; "The Priesthood," 27; "The Invitation," 5–6; "The Banquet"; "Love [III]"). It is evident that Herbert's prayers reflect these truths. But how is the self-attention implied by his entreaties that he be built ("Affliction [IV]," 29) and filled ("Good Friday," 29) compatible with *kenosis?*

And how is the precept of forgetfulness to be welcomed by one who finds virtue in the counsel "Slight not the smallest losse" ("The Church-porch," 343)? The accountant in Herbert is so prominent that it sometimes has to be rebuked. He advises his reader to keep a spiritual ledger:

> Summe up at night, what thou has done by day;
> And in the morning, what thou hast to do.

11. See Amy M. Charles, *A Life of George Herbert* (Ithaca: Cornell University Press, 1977), pp. 128–129, 146–154.

12. See Richard Baxter's *The Saint's Everlasting Rest,* quoted in Hutchinson's introduction, p. xliv.

> Dresse and undresse thy soul: mark the decay
> And growth of it: if with thy watch, that too
>   Be down, then winde both up; since we shall be
> Most surely judg'd, make thy accounts agree.
>
> ("The Church-porch," 451–456)

But this "book" can work against true piety if it leads one to a
false sense of his net deficits in the divine service ("The Collar") or to a futile effort to square accounts on his own ("The
Thanksgiving") or to despair when that futility is appreciated
("Dialogue"). Tallies have to be transcended or forgotten
("The Pearl," "The Discharge," "Judgement," "Love
[III]"). On the whole, however, Herbert feels that one would
fail "Justice" not to attend to and care for the value in "the
least things." There is a comprehensiveness in his concern.
"Not one poore minute" goes without its blessing ("Even-
song," 30–31), and this ought to be recognized. "Praise [God]
to the full / Each day, each houre, each moment of the week"
("Love unknown," 68–69). By the same principle not one
grain of dust ought to be unaccounted for at the general resurrection ("Faith," 41–44). The priest dares to hope that every
soul may come to the sacred "feast":

> Lord I have invited all,
>   And I shall
> Still invite, still call to thee:
> For it seems but just and right
>   In my sight,
> Where is All, there All should be.
>
> ("The Invitation," 31–36)

"It is an ill Mason that refuseth any stone," says the country
parson (*CP* 4. 228), and Herbert will refuse none. To him
everything seems to have a place, therefore a purpose, therefore a value beyond that in its mere being: "Nothing is little in
God's service"; the most ordinary things (as *The Temple* is
meant to demonstrate) may "be washed, and cleansed, and
serve for lights . . . of Heavenly Truths" (*CP* 14. 249; 21.
257). In strict and less strict senses the world is sacramental:
bread, wine, water, sunbeams, windows, floors, pulleys, locks

and keys, clocks and boxes and bags, ceremonies, shapes of words on a page, all can mediate between God and man. Evil too has its uses: "Ev'n poysons praise" the Lord ("Providence," 85); "jealousie" may "spurre" to good ("The Church-porch," 263); "sinnes" may "plead" for redemption ("Church-lock and key," 11). If Herbert is eager to search out the most tenuous of goods and allow them their worth— "Should a thing be lost? / Should creatures want for want of heed their due?" ("Providence," 85–86)—can he forget with complacency his own poor, truant self, whom Christ died to save and continues to dote upon?

Herbert meets the threat that *kenosis* poses to his instincts and values in the only way he can, with faith—faith that the deprivations brought about by self-neglect are somehow only illusory. When we forget ourselves, he believes, a God who cannot fail "remembers for [us]," insuring that our true interests will be realized in spite of our inattention to them ("The Holdfast," 14; *CP* 26. 267). What appears to be denial is affirmation. Barns are and can only be filled by being kept vacant:

> We talk of harvests; there are no such things,
> But when we leave our corn and hay.
>
> ("Home," 55–56)

Thoughts that renunciation is definitive, that both the way and end are "tears" ("The Pilgrimage," 28), are temptations to be resisted, for God will not allow us to go empty of the good he yearns to lavish upon us. He will overcome our strong suspicions that we strive without purpose, achievement, and fulfillment ("Employment [I and II]," "Hope," "The Crosse"); he will "answer" the conscience which demands that each good be given its "due" ("The Quip"; "Constancie," 5). "Take one from ten, and what remains? / Ten still" ("Charms and Knots," 15–16). Since, however, love often obliges us to forget all thought of "gains," and when we do look for them, losses seem at least as real as they, our "treasure" will be built up in *secret* ("Coloss. 3. 3").

Herbert senses that in a limited way reason may assist faith in rescuing the truth and value that appear to be casualties of the cross. When he thinks of *kenosis* as a means rather than an end he may take comfort from the knowledge that a methodological renunciation (like Descartes' methodological doubt, we might say) is something of a fiction: one cannot really unknow the truths or unappreciate the goods that are winked away. More significant, Herbert's understanding of truth as a *process* emphasizes the tentativeness, the incompleteness of any given moment in its realization. "Call me not an olive, till thou see me gathered," his proverb says (*OP*, 301). Call nothing truth, either, or renunciation, until its whole story has been told. Fulfillment will come for the individual only at the end of time ("Faith," 41–44; "Man," 51; "Mans medley," 5–6; "The Size," 13–24; "The Glance," 19–24; "Dooms-day," 25–30), when that realization of potential will be *the whole truth,* the culmination of discrete moments of which *kenosis* has been only a transient one. Time is a gardener, not an executioner, his scythe a pruning knife, not an axe ("Time").

To embody in his poetry the religious paradoxes we have been considering Herbert had only to make use of symbols that his faith provided. The Eucharist is for him the bread and wine of sacrifice, wheat ground and grape pressed as Christ was, who was "broken" and emptied himself for our sakes ("The Agonie," 13–18; "Peace," 39; "The Bunch of Grapes," 22–28; "The Banquet," 25–30). Yet the sacrament is clearly food, a filling good ("The H. Communion," 7–8, 37–40; "The Invitation," 4–12). The altar is both a sacrificial stone and a banquet table, the temple a place of destruction and of nourishment.[13] The stones in Herbert's *Temple* are, of course, his

13. Herbert's emphasis on the sacrificial character of the Eucharist puts him at odds with radical Protestantism. He probably did not believe with Roman Catholics, however, that the Eucharist renews or reenacts the sacrifice of Calvary. On the distinction between "renewal" and "representation" see Robert Ellrodt's discussion of Herbert's eucharistic theology in *L'Inspiration personnelle et l'esprit du temps chez les poètes métaphysiques anglais,* 2 vols. in 3 pts. (Paris: Corti, 1960), I, i, 324–342.

M. M. Ross contends that in Herbert's treatment of the Eucharist we see "analogical symbol" (which affirms "the presence in the sign of the thing signified") dissolving into "simple metaphor" (a sign wholly other than the thing signified). See *Poetry and Dogma: The Transfiguration of Eucharistic Symbols in Seventeenth-Century English Poetry* (New Brunswick: Rutgers University

poems; and these can themselves be considered symbolic of
the filling that preempts *kenosis*. Each poem represents a moment in the making of a temple spiritual, there being Sundays
of joy in the soul, Fridays of humiliation (*CP* 10. 241), Christ-
mases, Easters, Whitsuntides, and Lents. All are *ad aedifican-
dum*, even moments of abnegation. "Life" may be born of
"Mortification"; and art may be created out of the absence,
even the renunciation, of art ("Jordan [I and II]," "A true
Hymn,")—if, that is, artlessness is seen as only a moment in
a whole process of creation, as a discordant note may be resolved in harmony ("Deniall") or as a protestation that "sparkling notions" have fled may grow into a sparkling notion
("The Forerunners"). The temple may rise on pillars that
should for the Christian be ephemeral, but that retain somehow a mysterious substantiality even when the builder rejects
them: moods of recrimination ("Hope"), perplexity ("The Pilgrimage"), doubt ("The Search," 5–8), and bitter longing
("Longing," 55–72). Although these thoughts and sentiments
must be mastered and forsworn, they and the poems which
they help to construct are anything but "self-consuming,"[14]
Protests can be recanted and errors corrected, but they cannot
disappear, for they are part of the whole truth to which the
temple stands as a monument.

The truth is that Herbert has loved and praised and thanked
his Lord, has misunderstood, slighted, doubted, betrayed him
and pleaded for mercy. He has also wrestled with him until his
"threatenings" lay "bleeding on the ground" ("The Crosse,"

Press, 1954), pp. 28–54, 178–182. But compare Ellrodt, *L'Inspiration personnelle*.

14. They are not (to use another of Fish's metaphors) ladders to be dis-
pensed with after being used to climb to a *moment* of insight and conversion.
Fish seems to believe that the self-subversion of the poem parallels and sym-
bolizes the self-annihilation of the poet. But at the end of his discussion of Herbert he admits "the difficulty, if not impossibility, of the self-consuming enterprise of Herbert's art" (p. 233). For a thoughtful review of *Self-Consuming
Artifacts* see Joseph Summers, "Stanley Fish's Reading of Seventeenth-Century Literature," *Modern Language Quarterly*, 35 (1974), 403–417. In his new
book on Herbert (*The Living Temple* [Berkeley, Los Angeles, and London:
University of California Press, 1978]) Fish turns his attention to the mysterious
"building" of God's temple spiritual.

12). He has seen himself emptied, requested that he be filled; prayed that he might love without the least thought of self-interest—"Let me not love thee, if I love thee not" ("Affliction [I]," 66)—and allowed himself to be loved with complete devotion ("A true Hymne," 20; "Love [III]"). He has closed his eyes, yet he is sure he will not have missed a thing. The whole story must be told and *stay on the record* (as the poet's complaints do after they are "taken back"), for it is all part of the final triumph of Justice.

> Ah my deare angrie Lord,
> Since thou dost love, yet strike;
> Cast down, yet help afford;
> Sure I will do the like.
>
> I will complain, yet praise;
> I will bewail, approve:
> And all my sowre-sweet dayes
> I will lament, and love.

("Bitter-sweet")

Herbert is anything but smug about his appropriation of the whole truth, however. His faith comes to him in spiritual combat, through episodes of doubt. In his poetry one senses a magnificently strong will at work, which refuses to believe that a grain of true good will be lost, but must live without an exact knowledge of how loss may be avoided. How can the priest who is punished "in his Ministry" (*CP* 8. 235) deny the injury to a good that exists apart from him, except with a faith that remains inarticulate? How can the priest who would "invite all" to the divine supper ("The Invitation") accept the "loss" of the non-elect, but with a stoical refusal of commentary on the action of a God

$$\text{who gives to man, as he sees fit,} \begin{cases} \text{Salvation.} \\ \text{Damnation.} \end{cases}$$

("The Water-course," 10)

Since a will can buckle and fail if, as Herbert would say, God withdraws his favor, the soul's drama remains tense until the protagonist is "past changing" ("The Flower," 22).

Some might think that Herbert's ideal of "Submission" of mind and will must in crucial ways damage his poetry. David Cecil, in his preface to *The Oxford Book of Christian Verse,* has berated the religious writer who "does not say what he really feels, but what he thinks he ought to feel."[15] But the naiveté of the critic's program of "truth to feeling" is surely evident in Herbert's case. One of the reasons that *The Temple* is so compelling is that it records the travail of a soul who perceives an ideal to which his feelings must be made to accord, of a soul not content with what is given but struggling toward a truth beyond momentary facts and appearances. Henry James thought it probable "that if we were never bewildered there would never be a story to tell about us."[16] Does not the story become more interesting when one labors under the (perceived) necessity of refining bewilderment into faith? Even if a worshipful Herbert sometimes expresses gratitude when feeling resentment, or admiration when a part of him would blaspheme, this is no ultimate falsification, for he has shown us how *The Temple* with its capstone of submission has been built. He would have been less than honest had he failed to reveal, in individual poems and in the *oeuvre,* his conviction that the whole truth and the true good may be gained only by their partial suppression.

15. P. xiii. For a discussion of this problem see Helen Gardner, *Religion and Literature* (London: Faber and Faber, 1971), pp. 122–142.

16. Preface to *The Princess Casamassima* (New York: Scribner's, 1908), p. lx.

PRUDENCE L. STEINER

A Garden of Spices in New England: John Cotton's and Edward Taylor's Use of the Song of Songs

New England rarely resembles a garden of spices. To be sure, Francis Higginson's diary of his voyage from England in 1629 described the landfall off Salem glowingly: "Now what with fine woods and green trees by land and these yellow flowers [of seaweed] painting the sea, made us all desirous to see our new paradise of New England, whence we saw such forerunning signals of fertility afar off."[1] Nonetheless, he warned prospective settlers in 1630 that they should bring not only oatmeal and aqua vitae, but also pepper, cloves, mace, cinnamon, nutmegs, and fruit.[2] John Winthrop told his son, who was preparing to come in 1631, to bring pepper, ginger, and conserve of red roses.[3] Governor Bradford of Plymouth remembered (some ten years later) his first, December, view of Cape Cod like this:

1. Francis Higginson, *Journal of His Voyage to New-England,* in *The Founding of Massachusetts: A Selection from the Sources,* ed. Stewart Mitchell (Boston: Massachusetts Historical Society, 1930), p. 72.
2. George Francis Dow, *Every Day Life in the Massachusetts Bay Colony* (Boston: Society for the Preservation of New England Antiquities, 1935), p. 3.
3. John Winthrop, *The History of New England . . . ,* ed. James Savage (Boston: Little, Brown, 1853), I, 454.

"For summer being done, all things stand . . . with a
weather-beaten face, and the whole country, full of woods and
thickets, represented a wild and savage hue."[4] Edward Johnson's early history of New England, *Wonder-Working Providence of Sion's Saviour in New England,* is explicit about the
thickets and thorns, not to mention the sweet fern, "whose
scent [in summer] is very strong so that some herewith have
been very near fainting."[5] Edward Taylor himself set out from
Cambridge for Westfield, Massachusetts in November 1671
and found the journey extremely difficult because: "the snow
[was] above Mid-Leg deep, the way unbeaten, or the track
filled up again . . . Mr. Cooke of Cambridge told us it was the
desperatest journey that ever Connecticut men undertook."[6]

To the perception of these first settlers, then, New England
was not a garden of spices. Some have argued that John Cotton
and Edward Taylor, transplanted from England to New England, turned their attention to the Song of Songs as a way of
compensating for their bleak surroundings. On the other hand,
both these wayfaring and rigorous Calvinists could well have
approved the encouragement John Winthrop offered his wife a
month after he arrived in Massachusetts: "And howsoever our
fare be but coarse in respect of what we formerly had (pease,
puddings, and fish being our ordinary diet) yet He makes it
sweet and wholesome to us, that I may truly say I desire no
better."[7] It is unlikely that geography influenced their choice
of texts; furthermore, Cotton's first explication of Canticles
was written in England before he left his well-established community in Boston to come to the Massachusetts Bay Colony.
Rather, both preachers turned to the Song of Songs because it
is a text well suited to the kind of commentary that their theol-

    4. William Bradford, *Of Plymouth Plantation: 1620–1647,* (New York:
Alfred A. Knopf, 1953), p. 62.
    5. Edward Johnson, *Wonder-Working Providence of Sion's Saviour in New
England* (London, 1654), ed. William F. Poole (Andover, Mass.: Warren F.
Draper, 1867), p. 81.
    6. Edward Taylor, *The Poems of Edward Taylor,* ed. Donald E. Stanford
(New Haven: Yale University Press, 1960), p. xli.
    7. John Winthrop, Letters, etc., in *Winthrop Papers,* 1628–1630 (Boston:
Massachusetts Historical Society, 1929), II, 303.

ogy required. Each had a theory of exegesis, and their explications of the Song of Songs demonstrated how each theory was to be applied.

Certainly the Song of Songs invites exegesis, a process that may have begun soon after it was first written down. There is evidence that the Synod of Javneh, which met in A.D. 90 to establish the canon of the Jewish Bible, was uneasy about the Song of Songs. Tradition holds that it was Rabbi Akiba who persuaded its members to include the Song in the Bible, saying, "All the writings [Hagiographa] are holy, but the Song of Songs is the Holy of Holies."[8] The same synod adopted the thesis that the Song of Songs described the loving relationship between the Lord and Israel, his bride.[9] One of the Targums proposed that the Song is a picture of the history of Israel before and after the Babylonian captivity.[10]

These sober interpretations were accompanied by explicit warnings. "Our Rabbis taught: He who recites a verse of the Song of Songs and treats it as a [secular] air, and one who recites a verse at a banqueting table unseasonably, brings evil upon the world."[11] It was a book to be taken seriously, and with great caution.

Jewish commentary on the Song of Songs flourished through the centuries; English-language equivalents were encouraged by Reformation translations, which opened up new kinds of language and imagery to theologians and laymen alike. Increasingly readers began to ask questions, to quarrel about interpretations, to use bits and pieces of the Bible as aids to prayer and meditation. The Song of Songs did not escape this process.[12]

8. *Babylonian Talmud,* trans. I. Epstein (London: Soncino Press, 1935–1952), *Yadaim,* III, 5, p. 559.

9. *The Jewish Encyclopedia* (New York and London: Funk and Wagnalls, 1906), "Song of Songs," XI, 466.

10. Song of Songs, *The Soncino Books of the Bible,* ed. A. Cohen (London: Soncino Press, 1952), p. xi.

11. *Babylonian Talmud, Sanhedrin* 101a, p. 684.

12. An enormously comprehensive and thoughtful study of this question is Barbara Kiefer Lewalski's *Protestant Poetics and the Seventeenth-Century Religious Lyric* (Princeton: Princeton University Press, 1979).

Like the Synod of Javneh, English Protestants had to confront the puzzles of the Song of Songs, a holy book that does not mention God but dwells lovingly and at length on the natural world and the beauty of the beloved. "How fair and how pleasant art thou, O love, for delights! This thy stature is like to a palm tree, and thy breasts to clusters of grapes."[13] It is hard to fit this sort of thing into the Bible without exegesis. John Cotton, Teacher to the First Church of Boston from 1633 and Overseer of Harvard from 1637 until his death in 1652, and Edward Taylor, member of the Harvard class of 1672 and minister in Westfield from December 1671 until a few years before his death in 1729, each in different ways came to terms with the Song of Songs and incorporated it for himself into his larger pattern of religious belief and analysis.

Both of them, of course, believed in the unity of the Scriptures, believed that the same Holy Spirit animated all parts of it, and that it was the duty of the sincere believer to understand that unity, even though it might not be apparent at first. But whereas John Cotton looked through the Bible to something that lay beyond, Edward Taylor looked directly at it; this difference shapes their treatment of the Song of Songs.

Seventeenth-century American Puritanism did not escape some of the less attractive kinds of controversy that had disturbed the development of the Reformation in England since the beginning of the reign of Queen Elizabeth. Quarrels about the appropriate vestments for the clergy, about whether one could baptize in salt as well as in fresh water, about how and to whom communion could be given, about the proper forms of church governance, were part of the larger questions about the proper conduct of a godly life. Cotton, although he was engaged in some of these specific arguments and never denied their importance, insisted that regenerate man should be able to look beyond the ordinances of the church, comforting and helpful as they may be, to the God who was the inspiration of those ordinances, to the truth behind the symbol, so to speak. Not that he was indifferent to the proper forms of these ordinances, but that he was able to keep a curious double vision—

13. Song of Songs, 7:6–7.

to look at these matters and at the same time to see through them to something more universal.[14]

This double vision is apparent in Cotton's commentaries on the Song of Songs. There are two versions of this *Brief Exposition on the Whole Book of Canticles,* one written in Boston, England, before Cotton crossed the Atlantic, published in 1642, and a second, printed in 1655, longer, dryer, more systematized than the first. At the beginning of the first version Cotton states his thesis: the Song of Songs is "a heavenly marriage song between Christ and his Church."[15] More specifically, it is a history of the estate and condition of every church (here he means the community of the faithful, whether Jewish or Christian) from Solomon's time to the Last Judgment.[16] No sooner has Cotton offered this explanation than he qualifies it: "Neither are all the passages of the estate of the Church in every age here described, (for how can that be in so short a song?)"[17] This is the framework, the text behind the text that Cotton explicated to his congregation—an explication that worked on two levels.

Cotton's approach is illustrated by his commentary on Song of Songs 2:9, 11: "My beloved is like a roe or a young hart: behold, he standeth behind our walls, he looketh forth at the windows, shewing himself through the lattice . . . For lo, the winter is past, the rain is over and gone."

These verses, says Cotton, describe the return of Israel from the Babylonian captivity. For lo, the winter is past: "To wit both the naturall Winter, the stormy rain whereof might have hindred travell: and also the metaphoricall Winter of *Babels* captivity was now expired, and all the storms of it was blowen over, whence the Chaldee word . . . is here used to signify this winter, and not the common Hebrew word . . . : Chal-

14. John Cotton, *Christ the Fountain of Life* (London: Robert Ibbitson, 1652), sermon 2, pp. 21–29.

15. John Cotton, *A Brief Exposition of the Whole Book of Canticles . . .* (London: Printed for Philip Nevil, 1642), p. 4. This is, of course, very close in spirit to the interpretation of the Synod of Javneh.

16. John Cotton, *A Brief Exposition with Practical Observations upon the Whole Book of Canticles . . .* (London: Printed by T. R. and E. M. for Ralph Smith, 1655), pp. 1–2.

17. Cotton, *Canticles* (1642), p. 5.

dee words are fittest to express Chaldee things."[18] Verse 9 is not the bride's description of the bridegroom, who standeth behind our walls, but Israel's description of the coming of Cyrus to destroy the Babylonia of oppression.

Cotton, however, did not stop there. Following the author of the Book of Ezra, who wrote that the Lord stirred up Cyrus to encourage the return to Jerusalem, Cotton instructed his congregation to see through the events of history to what lay beyond them. Does the beloved show himself through the lattice? This is Cyrus appearing through the broken walls of Babylon, and Christ manifesting himself through his human instrument. "See here the Church looks not at Cyrus so much but at Christ in him."[19]

This is the most intricate of Cotton's explanations. A different method of exposition, one that stays quite close to the classic form of the Puritan sermon, is used for the first verse of chapter 2: "I am the rose of Sharon."

> The rose, though it be, First, fair and orient for colour and beauty. Secondly, fragrant; and pleasant for smell, of all flowers. Thirdly, wholesome and medicinable for use; yet it is also seen fading: continueth but a while, not to be seen above a moneth or two, all the year long, but in some conserves or syrups made of it . . .

> The Church [the Jewish people] . . . was as a rose, yet not as a rose in a Garden enclosed and fenced, but lying in open fields exposed to be cropt, or trod down of the beasts of the field, sometimes the Babylonians, sometimes the Ægyptians . . .

> Doctrine. The church . . . is . . . even in her worst times as a rose of the field . . .

> Reason. From want of open flourishing and conspicuity but as a rose which flourisheth, for a moneth, and yet is secretly kept in conserves all the yeare . . .

> Use. For comfort to Churches in their lowest estates; For 1. [The Lord] will preserve a remnant. 2. This remnant shall be as fragrant

18. Cotton, *Canticles* (1655), p. 45.
19. Cotton, *Canticles* (1642), p. 73.

as roses . . . 4. [The Lord] will conserve us, when our flourishing is past.[20]

Every detail is examined, each spice and fruit is identified according to its medicinal properties and then used as a symbol for the history of God's people. Cotton's examination of the Song 4:3, is a case in point.

Thy temples are like a piece of pomegranate . . .

Pomegranates are commended by Fernelius [a sixteenth-century French physician]
   First, for repressing the heat of Choler,
   Secondly, the malignity, rottenness and agrimony of feavers,
   Thirdly, the looseness of the belly . . .
   The Ecclesiasticall governours of the Church doe performe to it; they repress the heat of fallings out among brethren, the notorious abuses, the looseness, or distempredness of the people; they comfort the feeble, and bind up the weak, and are therefore fitly resembled by Pomegranates.[21]

Cotton was well aware of the wealth of materials in this Song, as his introduction to the 1642 edition indicates. "The first Reason why this Song is more excellent than others is, because this song speaketh not onely of the chiefest matter . . . but also . . . with more store of more sweet and precious, exquisite and amiable Resemblances, taken from the richest Jewells, the sweetest Spices, Gardens, Orchards, Vineyards, Winecellars, and the chiefest beauties of all the works of God and man."[22] It is worth noting the word *resemblances;* for Cotton and his congregation the whole Song could only be understood as a resemblance of something that lay beyond it. "[4:4: Thy neck is like the tower of David.] The very nature of the comparison cleareth it, that *Solomon* here speaketh not of *Pharaohs* daughter, nor of any *Shulamite,* nor any other wife or concubine of his. For it were an uncomely and monstrous resemblance, to compare the neck of any woman to a Tower."[23]

20. Cotton, *Canticles* (1655), pp. 35–37.
21. Cotton, *Canticles* (1642), pp. 107–108.
22. Ibid., p. 9.
23. Cotton, *Canticles* (1655), p. 86.

Some resemblances cause more difficulties than others. Aware of this, Cotton warned his congregation of the importance of the proper kind of reading, reassuring them that:

> the amourousness of the dittie will not stir up wantonnesse in any age, if the words be well understood: but rather, by inflaming with heavenly love, will draw out, and burne up all earthly and carnall lust, and, even as fire in the hand is drawn out by holding it to a stronger fire, or as the light and heat of the Sunne extinguisheth a kitchin fire, so doth heavenly love to Christ extinguish base kitchin lusts.[24]

Having thus armed himself, Cotton advanced on those verses most susceptible of being misread.

> [1:13: He shall lie all night betwixt my breasts.] The breasts are those that give milke; the sincere milke of the word to the Churches children, to wit, the Priests and Levites.[25]

> [4:5: Thy two breasts are like two young roes that are twins.] The breasts give milk to Babes, and signify the . . . Church-officers . . . It is a great part of the beauty (or Fairness) of the Church, when their Officers walk one to another, in equality . . . It implieth . . . [that these officers] will not be single, but two and two go together: as Pastour and Teacher in a settled Church . . . It is a beauty to a Church, when their ministers want not society, and equality one with another . . . [The verse is] to teach Churches, to look at it, as a deformity to have but one Minister. A Church with one Minister is as a wife with one breast.[26]

Cotton seems to be putting out the coals of fire and vehement flame of this book by choosing an unemotional rhetoric. This sobriety is consistent with almost all of his preaching and writing. Cotton gave notice of his "conversion" by Richard Sibbes in 1609 in a sermon he preached in St. Mary's Church, Cambridge. "Scholars crowded the church, expecting to hear a pretty play of wit," wrote one biographer. "Instead, Master

24. Cotton, *Canticles* (1642), p. 8.
25. Ibid., p. 39.
26. Cotton, *Canticles* (1655), pp. 84–85, 198–200.

Cotton preached a plain sermon upon the doctrine of repentance. The wits openly showed their disgust."[27] One of Cotton's notes to the Canticles explains by implication his own technique.

> Thy lips are like a thread of scarlet, and thy speech is comely [4:3]. Both signifying the delivery or utterance of the Doctrine of the Church . . . which was First, as a thread slender . . . not plump or swelling with humane eloquence, but savouring of Fisher-like tenuity and simplicity.

> Ministers are to learn to frame themselves to be amiable in God's sight . . . by not affecting carnall eloquence but gracious and deep-dyed powerfull utterance; for swelling words of humane wisdome make mens preaching seem (as it wer) a blubber-lipt ministry.[28]

Cotton's Puritan orthodoxy included a healthy distrust of "swelling words"—rhetorical flourishes that revealed more of human pride than the Holy Spirit. "Gods altar needs not our polishings," said the preface to the *Bay Psalm Book;* whether or not Cotton wrote that preface the idea was congenial to him, as his commentary on Canticles makes clear.[29] The Holy Spirit was free to use "sweet and precious, exquisite and amiable Resemblances," but man was obliged to subdue the destructive vanity of carnal eloquence as well as the baser kitchen lusts. Cotton's style reinforces his commentary; both instruct the reader to read his explication the same way he reads Canticles—to look not at but through the text to the meaning and force that produced it.

Whereas Cotton looked through the Song of Songs, Edward Taylor looked at it. One of the reasons for this difference is set

---

27. Samuel Eliot Morison, *The Founding of Harvard College* (Cambridge, Mass.: Harvard University Press, 1935), p. 101.

28. Cotton, *Canticles* (1642), pp. 106, 112.

29. *The Bay Psalm Book,* (1640; facsimile rpt. Chicago: University of Chicago Press, 1956). The sentence quoted appears in the last paragraph of the preface. For an argument that Cotton may have written this preface see Zoltan Haraszti, *The Enigma of the Bay Psalm Book* (Chicago: University of Chicago Press, 1956), p. 27.

out in a sermon Taylor preached to his congregation in Westfield, Massachusetts in August 1703. "The great Calvin affirms . . . that the vaile being remooved we shall see God
openly reigning in His Majesty. Christs Humanity shall [be no
longer] the Medium which detains us from any Sight of God
beyond it."[30] This may have reminded Taylor's congregation
of Paul's first Epistle to the Corinthians, in which he wrote,
"For now we see through a glass, darkly, but then fact to face;
now I know in part, but then I shall know even as also I am
known." Classicists will recognize in Paul's letter echoes of
the Platonic myth of the cave; we can read Taylor's sermon as
a statement of his belief that man in this world can only see
heavenly things when they are in what he calls a "medium." It
is this that governs, in part, Taylor's approach to the Song of
Songs.

In the course of more than forty years Taylor wrote over two
hundred "Preparatory Meditations," poems that reflect some
of the major themes of his sermons and that were designed to
put his soul in order before he celebrated communion; they
were, so to speak, sermons that had himself as the congregation. Seventy-six of these are based on texts from the Song of
Songs. In several cases he wrote more than one poem on a
text: three on "I am the lily of the valleys," two on "My beloved is mine and I am his," two on "While the king sitteth at
his table, my spikenard sendeth forth the smell thereof." The
images in the poems vary, as is understandable in poems separated by almost forty years. But they are consistent in their illustration of the way Taylor's poetry reflects his theology.

It is well known that Taylor's poetic practices make difficulties for his readers and editors. The poems were not published
during his lifetime, and his handwriting was anything but clear,
so that there is some problem in establishing a text. Possibly
Taylor would have disentangled some of the rougher rhythms
and altered some of the false rhymes if he had prepared the
text for publication. Though he had read other poets of England and New England, he himself was only privately a poet.

30. Edward Taylor, *Christographia*, ed. Norman S. Grabo (New Haven:
Yale University Press, 1962), p. 412.

First of all he was a minister to the soul—and the body: contemporary evidence suggests that he was obliged to know
something about medical matters, and at least one poetical
meditation reads in part like a pharmacopoeia.[31]

His poems suggest that Taylor was aware of his poetical ina-
dequacies. They contain not one but three types of disclaimer.
The first is the most noticeable—a couplet or so at the end of
almost every poem acknowledging his inability to sing unless
he is in a state of grace.

> My heart thy Viall with this spicknard fill.
> Perfumed praise to thee then breath it will.
>
> When thou unto thy praise my heart shalt tune
> My heart shall tune thy praise in sweetest fume.[32]

This concluding statement of self-deprecation is such a persistent element that after a while one is tempted to discount it. But
it is reinforced by two less mechanical disclaimers. One is Taylor's confession of his poetical inadequacy,[33] and another is his
suggestion that language itself is inadequate to the task.[34]

> Words are Dear Lord, notes insignificant,
>   But Curled aire when spoke Sedan'd from the Lip
> Into the Eare, soon vanish, though don't Cant,
>   Yea run on tiptoe, and hence often trip
> Sometimes do poother out like th'Chimney Smoake
> Hence often smut the matter, and nigh Choake.[35]

Written in August 1723, this is very close to part of a letter
Taylor wrote to his first wife almost fifty years earlier.

---

31. Taylor, *Poems,* pp. xlvi, lvi, and Meditation 67b, 2nd Series, pp. 204–
207.

32. Ibid., Meditation 62, 2nd Series, p. 193, and Meditation 145, 2nd Series,
p. 346.

33. Ibid., Meditation 32, 1st Series, p. 51, and Meditation 12, 2nd Series,
p. 101.

34. Ibid., Meditation 43, 2nd Series, p. 159, stanza 2, and Meditation 146,
2nd Series, p. 347, stanza 1.

35. Ibid., Meditation 162, 2nd Series, p. 382.

My love [is] a Golden Ball of pure Fire rolling up and down my Breast, from which there flies now and then a Spark like a Glorious Beam from the Body of the Flaming Sun. But I alas! striving to catch these sparks into a Love Letter . . . find that by what time they have fallen through my pen upon my Paper, they have lost their shine, and fall only like a little Smoke thereon instead of gilding them.[36]

If we take these elements as part of a serious examination, rather than simply as mock modesty, and combine them with Taylor's belief that we cannot see God's glory directly but only through a medium, we can begin to understand Taylor's use of the Song of Songs, which he called a source of "rich and Weighty Metaphors [that] emblemize the eminency of the Operations" of the Divine Nature.[37]

There is a form of gematria to which students of literature sometimes succumb that produces computerized concordances to the poets, analyses of the number of lines that end with consonants, and other mathematical tazzles and snicksnarls (two of Taylor's more vivid synonyms for difficulties). Taylor himself was not immune to this disease; one of his poems devotes four stanzas to the "rich mystery" of the number seven.[38] In the concordance to Taylor's poetry, one of these devices of learned bibliomancy, the word *word*, is listed as appearing eighty-eight times, usually in one of two ways. Either Taylor is mourning the inadequacy of his own words or he is praising God's Word that restores "the garden of [his] Soul."[39] Over and over Taylor is trying to come to terms with those problems of language that are also mysteries of theology. The opening words of the Gospel of John are, "In the beginning was the word." John's simple declaration of a complicated mystery is complicated further by his later statement: "And the word was made flesh"—a line that Taylor used as the text for a meditation that begins by acknowledging the in-

36. Quoted in William B. Goodman, "Edward Taylor Writes His Love," *New England Quarterly*, 27, no. 4 (December 1954), 513.

37. Taylor, *Christographia*, p. 444.

38. Taylor, *Poems*, Meditation 21, 2nd Series, pp. 116–117.

39. Ibid., Meditation 136, 2nd Series, p. 329.

adequacy of language itself. For Taylor to abandon the word-made-flesh in his sermons to himself would have run counter to one of the most important tenets of his theology. Yet staying too close to the word produced difficulties of which he was and we are all too aware.

Cotton saw the rose of Sharon as an emblem of the chosen people and explained both the reasons this was a proper resemblance and the spiritual uses to be made of it. Taylor wrote one of his longer meditations on the same verse, but his manipulation of it is very different. The rose for him represents Jesus, and even the traditional narrative of Jesus' life is elaborated in details that conform to the image.

> But, oh! alas! that such should be my need
>> That this Brave Flower must Pluckt, stampt, squeezed bee,
> And boyld up in its Blood, its Spirits sheed,
>> To make a Physick sweet, sure, safe for mee.
>> But yet this mangled Rose rose up again
>> And in its pristine glory, doth remain.[40]

Instead of moving away from the image to the idea behind it, Taylor reinforces the image by elaborating it, dwelling on each imagined element of this imagined rose.

Sometimes this technique fails, as Taylor admits.

> And hence these Metaphors we spirituallized
>> Speake out the Spouses spirituall Beauty clear:
> And morallizd do speak out Enemies.[41]

Chapter 7, verse 2 of the Song of Songs poses dreadful problems: "Thy navel is like a round goblet, which wanteth not liquor: thy belly is like a heap of wheat set about with lilies." The Babylonian Talmud used the first part of the verse as an instruction on how many of the Sanhedrin must be present to decide certain matters.[42] John Cotton saw it as an image of the true doctrine of the church, which nourishes the believer. But Taylor, who could neither simply cite the verse as support for

40. Ibid., Meditation 4, 1st Series, p. 13.
41. Ibid., Meditation 151, 2nd Series, p. 356.
42. *Babylonian Talmud, Sanhedrin* 14b, p. 68.

some other discussion nor break away from it, fell back on explanation. These were not real navels and bellies, they were

emblems of Santifying Grace most high . . .

Hereby is shown [the church's] spiritual growth in Grace
    Whereby she able rises to bring forth
Her spirituall offspring of a spirituall race
    Her Saints, and Sanctifying, Grace their growth.
    Her Spirituall Navill buttoning all her Store
    Of Liquor rich; the Spirits Wine fat pure.[43]

In thirty-eight consecutive lines of this meditation he used the word *spirit* or *spiritual* sixteen times, sometimes twice in a line, as if he despaired of making either sense or poetry out of such uncompromising material.

These hideous examples are only part of Taylor's poetry. His place in the canon of American poets is by no means dependent on the fact that he was something of a *lusus naturae*. "Huswifery," "The Ebb and Flow," and Meditation 6 of the First Series, "Am I Thy Gold? Or Purse, Lord" are often anthologized and deservedly so. Sometimes a stanza shines out of an otherwise undistinguished meditation, as if Taylor were able briefly to put aside his doubts and let the "Flakes of flaming glory" fall unencumbered on the page.

You Holy Angells, Morning-Stars, bright Sparks,
    Give place: and lower your top gallants. Shew
Your top-saile Conjues to our slender barkes:
    The highest honour to our nature's due.
    Its neerer Godhead by the Godhead made
    Than yours in you that never from God stray'd.[44]

When Taylor failed it was partly because of his diffidence but also partly because of the text he chose. The more precise, vivid, explicit the text, the more it hampered him. Doubtful of his own worth as a poet, doubtful even of the validity of lan-

43. Taylor, *Poems,* Meditation 149, 2nd Series, p. 353.
44. Ibid., Meditation 44, 2nd Series, p. 162.

guage, Taylor kept so closely to the rich and weighty metaphors that his poetical meditations often collapsed under them.
  Simple chronology may have something to do with his difficulties. Taylor was born into the third generation to grow up
with the Word of God as it was diligently translated by learned
scholars in 1611. Almost half of that "new" translation was
material kept from earlier translations; some of it in fact went
back to William Tyndale's prose of 1530. The language of the
Authorized Version, "the noblest monument of English
prose," as John Livingston Lowes called it, was thus not the
language of Edward Taylor or his congregation. Taylor's sermons in the series *Christographia,* preached between 1701 and
1703, are mixtures of biblical phrase and paraphrase with a balanced, formal, sober style that has little in common with the
rhythms or vocabulary of the King James Bible.

> Its rationall to thinke that [Satan] Concluded he had blockt up the
> Passage of Divine Favour from Mankinde, Subverted the Design of
> Glory to God, Stopped the Current of all Holiness and Happiness
> for Man: and had open'd the Floodgates of the Curse for everlasting
> vengeance to come tumbling down there thro' upon the head of all
> men to all Eternity.[45]

> And here, I say, all Created Wisdom is in Christ: This Created Wis-
> dom is that light that is Seated in the Intellectuall Faculty filling the
> Eye of the Soul with a Cleare Sight into all things that are the proper
> objects thereof.[46]

  Side by side with the biblical paraphrase and the measured
prose is another element of Taylor's language: his use of
homely, country dialect, of words that he perhaps coined himself, and of the technical vocabularies of theology, medicine,
"huswifery," or metallurgy.[47] He knew Hebrew and Greek
and probably consulted the Bible in its original languages as
well as in translation when he prepared his poetical medita-

45. Taylor, *Christographia,* p. 118.
46. Ibid., p. 122.
47. See for examples Taylor, *Poems,* Meditation 107, 2nd Series, p. 277,
stanza 1; Meditation 67b, 2nd Series, pp. 204–205; Meditation 45, 2nd Series,
p. 163, and "Huswifery," p. 467; Meditation 49, 2nd Series, p. 169.

tions.[48] But neither the ancient tongues nor the standard translations were his own language, and this foreignness of idiom
may well have put an additional strain on his ability to see
through the imagery, to transcribe his visions or hopes in his
own terms.

For Cotton the chronological situation was different. Like
Taylor he was learned in Hebrew and Greek, but his own En-
glish idiom was much closer to that of the Geneva and the King
James Bibles.

> There is another combination of virtues strangely mixed in every
> lively holy Christian and that is, Diligence in worldly business, and
> yet deadness to the world; such a mystery as none can read, but
> they that know it. For a man to rise early, and go to bed late and eat
> the bread of carefulness, not a sinful, but a provident care, and to
> avoid idleness . . . go any way and bestir himself for profit, this
> will he do most diligently in his calling, and yet be a man dead-
> hearted to the world.[49]

An awareness of these accidents of linguistic evolution may
be necessary for an understanding of differences between Cotton and Taylor, but it is surely not sufficient. One must add, for
example, the innate difference between a prose explication of a
song and a poetical response to it; the form itself has an influence on the way the text is treated. More important still is the
difference of attitude toward human language itself. Although
he had misgivings about his own abilities and occasional fears
that any language might be inadequate, Taylor did not deny the
appropriateness of man's words as an instrument to respond to
God's grace.

> I fain would have a rich, fine Phansy ripe
>   That Curious pollishings elaborate
> Should, Lay, Lord, on thy glorious Body bright
>   The more my lumpish-heart to animate.[50]

48. See, for example, the headnote to Taylor, *Poems*, Meditation 117, 2nd
Series, p. 296.
49. Cotton, *Christ the Fountain*, p. 119.
50. Taylor, *Poems*, Meditation 74, 2nd Series, p. 217. See also Meditation
92, 2nd Series, p. 248, stanza 2; Meditation 101, 2nd Series, p. 263, stanza 2.

Cotton, as we know, felt differently. "Humane wit and authorities added to [the word of God] do but adulterate it, like as Paint does marble, or as honey and wine in children's minds; as painted glass windows darken the light," he wrote in his commentary on Ecclesiastes.[51] Only a "man that is enlightened with the knowledge of God's Will, and the mystery of Salvation may lawfully in his meditations make use of diverse Creatures or Things, that are apt and fit to represent Spirituall things unto him."[52]

Despite their reservations Cotton and Taylor held fast to the Song of Songs. It was not a longing for pomegranates in Boston or Westfield that sent these Puritans to the dangers and delights of Canticles. Rather it was a need to understand the mystery that animates language, to test their understanding of it, to respond to that mystery as best they could.

51. John Cotton, *A Brief Exposition with Practical Observations upon the Whole Book of Ecclesiastes* (London: Anthony Tuckney, 1654), p. 269.

52. John Cotton, *Some Treasure Fetched Out of Rubbish* (London: 1660), p. 29.

JAMES ENGELL

The Modern Revival of Myth:
Its Eighteenth-Century Origins

The eighteenth century sets the patterns of thought for romantic and modern concepts of myth. In criticism and poetry eighteenth-century writers are the first to claim that classical mythology, passively received and used largely for stock ornament and allusion is, in Coleridge's later phrase, "exploded mythology." The new critical maturity is summed up in Johnson's disdain for Granville's poetry: "He is for ever amusing himself with the puerilities of ancient mythology."[1] The Renaissance, which revived, explored, and embellished classical myths, and romanticism, which—as Emery Neff says—created the "classics of the modern world," flank the comparatively thin bar of the eighteenth century like two massy weights. But picking up this bar we extend the Renaissance tradition and also grasp the rise of the modern approaches to mythology with all their creative and cultural potential.[2] And the century connecting the two great mythopoeic

1. *Lives of the English Poets by Samuel Johnson,* ed. G. B. Hill, 3 vols. (Oxford: Clarendon Press, 1905), II, 294.
2. The best anthology, with detailed introductory essays to individual authors and a superb bibliography, is *The Rise of Modern Mythology 1680–1860,*

periods is thin only if we are looking at poetry alone,[3] for in sharp contrast to the conventional view of it as a valley between two Olympuslike summits, the eighteenth century rethinks literary and critical assumptions of mythology and transforms them into modern views.

The eighteenth century neither blindly worshiped nor utterly rejected the gods. As Frank Manuel said, it confronted them.[4] Its many intellectual premises concerning mythology were exactly those from which the romantic poets gained direction and confidence. Historical research, comparative mythology, the sociology and anthropology of myth, its linguistic and psychological origins, and the figure of the poet as mythmaker, engaged critics and poets themselves. Such a thorough and multiple investigation was intensified by a dilemma faced for the first time in the eighteenth century, a dilemma we have not escaped: what can we do as we find it increasingly difficult to create original myths of the kind we admire in earlier, popular writers, when, at the same time, we find it just as hard to retell those old myths because—for the purpose of the poet writing at the present time—they are "exploded" and unoriginal?[5] Does a premium on literary originality spell doom for an enduring modern mythology?

---

ed. Burton Feldman and Robert D. Richardson (Bloomington: Indiana University Press, 1972); see pages 1–295 for the eighteenth century.

3. Although it discusses primarily poetry and not prose criticism and commentary, still indispensable is Douglas Bush, *Mythology and the Romantic Tradition in English Poetry* (Cambridge, Mass.: Harvard University Press, 1937; rpt. New York: Pageant, 1957). The neoclassic age, says Bush, witnessed "almost fruitless generations" in its attempts at mythological poems and "is almost completely barren, at least of good ones" (pp. xi, 5).

4. Frank Manuel, *The Eighteenth Century Confronts the Gods* (Cambridge, Mass.: Harvard University Press, 1959) is the best extended and focused treatment of the cultural and religious character of mythology in the eighteenth century. Manuel also examines crosscurrents of mythography between France and England.

5. This question, expanded to the whole range of English poetry and literature in the eighteenth and early nineteenth centuries, forms the subject of W. J. Bate's *The Burden of the Past and the English Poet* (Cambridge, Mass.: Harvard University Press, 1970). Bate discusses "the neoclassic dilemma" of admiration without the hope of original imitation in chapter 2 (pp. 29–57), especially pages 34–36.

However we classify the various eighteenth-century treatments of mythology (they are woven from many connected threads, like the huge tapestries of Alexander at Hampton Court), we discover, as writers then discovered, that each approach is a matter of emphasis. Bishop Warburton could not demonstrate the divine legation of Moses, a religious and even dogmatic conclusion, without attention to historical evidence. When Lowth discussed the "sublime" quality of the Hebrews' "mystical allegory," he engaged an aesthetic sense of style immediately applicable to contemporaneous poetry. Newton constructed his historical chronology with deep curiosity about the possibility of literal belief in ancient religious myths. The relation of critics and poets to mythology became like Keats's address to the urn: it is a "sylvan historian," a record of the past, but around its shape also haunts a "leaf-fring'd legend" engaging the beholder's imagination to create more than the eye can see. Hume might have been on the utterly skeptical side of all mythology, whether pagan, Christian, Jewish, or Chinese, but he analyzed beliefs to understand myths.

Then again some, like Blackwell and later Hazlitt, held that myths originally were not necessarily stories of the gods that were meant either to entice or to oppress the unlettered majority into religion. Instead, myths could be seen as the original and poetic vehicle of speculative philosophy, of all ideal discourse concerning nature and its first cause. Psyche, a myth about the nature of the human mind and inner spirit, was, after all, introduced by Apuleius' *Golden Ass* in the second century as the last goddess. Classical mythology had at last symbolized its more self-conscious introspection. Bacon himself indicated that philosophic wisdom, not religion, was the key; for him, as Blackwell noted in *Letters Concerning Mythology* (1748), mythologies were the "Wisdom of the Ancients" and "a constant Source of Pleasure to a speculative Man, as they represent some of the grandest Ideas in Nature and Art."[6] Mythology, said Blackwell himself in the *Proofs* (1748) following his earlier *Enquiry into the Life and Writings of Homer* (1735), is actually the grand and universal allegory of nature, the imagi-

---

6. Thomas Blackwell, *Letters Concerning Mythology* (London, 1748), p. 5.

native narrative of the cosmos, the world's creation in narrative form. It became the "majestick Method" of the poet's creative power.[7]

THE END OF AN EPOCH

Paradoxically, the rapid increase in literacy in the eighteenth century diluted rather than strengthened the force of classical mythology. The new reading public was more modern (*modo, just now*): knowledge of the original tongues of mythology often meant grammar and a smattering of popular texts. The young Wordsworth and some others still immersed themselves in Ovid's *Metamorphoses* (for which Wordsworth maintained a lifelong preference over Vergil), and Keats translated the *Aeneid* as a schoolboy.[8] (Interestingly, all the major romantic poets did study classical mythology in the original, at least in Latin.) But Wordsworth admitted in a note on the *Ode to Lycoris* (1817) that in the seventeenth century "an importance and a sanctity were at that period attached to classical literature . . . that can never be revived. No doubt the hacknied and lifeless use into which mythology fell towards the close of the seventeenth century, and which continued through the eighteenth, disgusted the general reader with all allusion to it in modern verse."

Yet what Wordsworth said had already been noted repeatedly—and more acutely—by eighteenth-century critics and poets frustrated with classical mythology in contemporary writing. With Akenside, as with most (and later with Wordsworth himself), this disgust mixed with nostalgic admiration. But the essence of nostalgia is irretrievability. Poets and readers familiar with previous borrowings knew that to borrow again was pointless, and that to change a borrowing slightly

7. Thomas Blackwell, *Proofs of An Enquiry into the Life and Writings of Homer* (1748), pp. 36–38; Blackwell, *An Enquiry into the Life and Writings of Homer* (1735), p. 148.

8. Charles Cowden Clarke, in his *Recollections* of John Keats (pp. 123–124), says Keats knew basic handbooks: Andrew Tooke's *The Pantheon* (1698), John Lemprière's *Bibliotheca classica; or, a Classical Dictionary* (1788), and Joseph Spence's *Polymetis* (1747): "This was the store whence he acquired his intimacy with the Greek mythology."

would not give novelty but only offend expectation, violate custom, and appear idiosyncratic. This feeling Johnson hammered home repeatedly. Waller, he said,

> borrows too many of his sentiments and illustrations from the old mythology, for which it is vain to plead the example of ancient poets: the deities which they introduced so frequently were considered as realities, so far as to be received by the imagination, whatever sober reason might even then determine. But of these images time has tarnished the splendor. A fiction, not only detected but despised, can never afford a solid basis to any position, though sometimes it may furnish a transient allusion, or slight illustration. No modern monarch can be much exalted by hearing that, as Hercules had had his *club,* he has his *navy.*

Even "of the ancient poets" Johnson contended, "every reader feels the mythology tedious and oppressive." It was, quipped Johnson, a "school boy's" subject (though Keats would later make great imaginative use of his relatively simple handbook learning). Alternately bored and offended, we recoil at "the inefficacy and incredibility of a mythological tale."[9]

Johnson was writing this when Wordsworth was at Hawkshead Grammar School and Coleridge was soon to enter Christ's Hospital. Even earlier, in 1746, Akenside admitted in his note "MM" to *Hymn to the Naiads* that "the mere genealogy, or the personal adventures of heathen gods" has no place in new poetry and is "but little interesting to a modern reader." As Johnson put it, not even sharing Akenside's wistful attempt to give naiads British citizenship as protectresses of the Thames, the renovation of classical and even gothic deities and fairies smacked of an enervated culture and a literary heritage unable to face "real life." In T. S. Eliot's transposed key, "The nymphs are departed." Even in Gray's Welsh *Bard,* which made a case for the genius and power of the individual poet, Johnson denigrated "the puerilities of obsolete mythology."[10]

9. Johnson, *Lives,* I, 295, see Addison's *Spectator* no. 523; *Lives* I, 213; II, 17.

10. Johnson, *Lives* III, 436; II, 204.

In the critique of Wordsworth and poetic diction in the *Bio-graphia*, Coleridge states that Gray should be censured in his "Sonnet on the Death of Mr. Richard West" not for outmoded diction, as Wordsworth had done in the Preface to *Lyrical Bal-lads*, but for the use of "an exploded mythology."[11] (The line in question was Gray's "And reddening Phoebus lifts his golden fire.") Yet Coleridge is only echoing Johnson's phrase that Thomas Tickell's *Kensington Garden* is populated by "Grecian deities and Gothick Fairies" in which "neither spe-cies of those exploded beings could have done much."[12] Coleridge himself was castigated by his own schoolmaster James Boyer (an eighteenth-century man of true common sense who taught Charles Lamb, too) for mythological allu-sions in his juvenile poetry: "*Harp? Harp? Lyre? Pen and ink, boy, you mean! Muse, boy, Muse? Your Nurse's daughter, you mean! Pierian spring? Oh aye! the cloisterpump, I sup-pose!*"[13] Yes, Wordsworth had a point, after all. Mythological allusion usually implied an archaically trite diction. That was Boyer's exact complaint, too. James Beattie, in *Essays on Po-etry and Music* (1778), scoffed that with certain authors "a country-maid becomes . . . a *nymph of the groves;* if flattery sing at all, it must be a *syren song;* the shepherd's flute dwin-dles into a *oaten reed,* and his crook is exalted into a *scep-ter.*"[14] In his Preface, Wordsworth followed the reverse proce-dure and italicized Gray's diction that did *not* offend. Classical mythology became a deadweight encumbering the develop-ment of a natural language of passion.

Throughout the eighteenth century the successful use of classical mythology and the most striking allusions to it sur-faced in comic or mock-heroic work. *The Rape of the Lock;*

11. Samuel Taylor Coleridge, *Biographia Literaria* (1817), ed. J. Shaw-cross, 2 vols. (Oxford: Oxford University Press, 1907), II, 58–59.

12. Johnson, *Lives,* II, 311.

13. Coleridge, *Biographia,* I, 5.

14. James Beattie, *Essays on Poetry and Music, as They Affect the Mind,* 2nd ed. (Edinburgh, 1778), p. 259. Beattie had apparently learned something since the failure of his lifeless poem *Judgment of Paris* thirteen years earlier in 1765. See Emerson Marks, "In Search of the Godly Language," *Philological Quarterly,* 54 (Winter 1975), 289–309.

The Dunciad; Joseph Andrews, that "comic epic in prose" where Fielding spoofs the idolatry of Homer; and *Tom Jones,* where comically inflated chapter openings parody not the openings of books of the *Iliad* but Homer's mechanical imitators—all this is in fun and it works. Eliot could still achieve this effect in *The Waste Land* simply by changing words. Lines from the *Parliament of Bees* by John Day (1574–c. 1640),

> A noise of horns and hunting, which shall bring
> Actaeon to Diana in the spring,

become

> The sound of horns and motors, which shall bring
> Sweeney to Mrs. Porter in the spring.

It was in the eighteenth century that serious allusions to myth began to fail regularly. Dryden's *Astraea Redux,* echoing Vergil's fourth *Eclogue,* pleased in 1660, but, as Wordsworth said, the next century grew impatient with contrivance and parallelism. Granville's *Heroic Love,* Spence's *Polymetis,* and Prior's *Solomon* were received as tepidly as Rowe's *Ulysses,* Gay's *The Fan,* and Thomson's *Agamemnon.* This last trio Johnson dismissed with similar judgments: to show heroes such as Ulysses "as they have already been shown is to disgust by repetition; to give them new qualities . . . is to offend by violating received notions"; *The Fan* "is one of those mythological fictions . . . of little value. The attention naturally retires from a new tale of Venus, Diana, and Minerva"; and *Agamemnon* "had the fate which most commonly attends mythological stories, and was only endured, but not favoured."[15] The repellent nature of common mythology in modern poetry became a constant theme of Johnson's *Lives.*

The success of "mythological works" with a serious tone nearly vanished. In the Preface to *A Tale of a Tub,* Swift poked fun at those who in a "Grand Committee" had "mythologized" the meaning of his "tub" and explained it as a diversion

15. Johnson, *Lives,* II, 68, 283; I, 291; see *Rambler* 37: "Mythological allusions," especially in pastorals, are an "absurdity."

thrown to Hobbes's *Leviathan!* Only the mock-heroic and satiric inversions, or—as Johnson admitted—the frolicsome inventions of Pope's *Rape of the Lock,* supported the machinery
of supernatural beings.[16] Abstract personifications (Fame, Avarice, Hope, and so on) feebly replaced the gods. And ironically, what Peter Gay calls the "pagan" Enlightenment was
modern enough to reject pagan deities (except for ornamenta-
tion), yet religious enough to feel uneasy about Christian mythological fiction that strayed beyond the Bible. We shall return
to the crucial question of faith, for the flight of the "damned
crew" of deities from the divine-human Jesus in Milton's
Hymn signaled what Johnson saw as the end of "mythological
allusions . . . with sentiments which neither passion nor reason could have dictated, since the change which religion has
made in the whole system of the world."[17] This change, combined with the new literacy and new premiums on originality
and on the representation of "real life," knelled the end of an
epoch. The importance of this cannot be overstressed. The literary world was thrown into a kind of paralytic trauma, and
poets and critics struggled to regain their coordination.

As the century progressed an escape route developed. It was
not, after all, the stock diction, the frozen or hackneyed
images, or even the narrative line, the "fable" of classical mythology that captured admiration. What was important was the
individual poet's ability, the spirit or the genius that invented a
work of power. In Yeats's metaphor it was not the "circus animals" that counted, but the "foul rag-and-bone shop of the
heart." The poet's ability to make myth out of experience and
the materials at hand—that was what surpassed the names,
however wonderful and resonant, of ancient gods. The poet's
power to create myth was highlighted, for instance, in a series
of critical articles in the *British Magazine* (1762) for which both
Goldsmith and Smollett have received credit.[18] Instead of a
cultural heritage of common values and images, "mythology"
began to be seen as a call to natural individualism, even to a

16. Johnson, *Lives,* III, 233.
17. Johnson, *Rambler,* 37.
18. René Wellek, *The Rise of English Literary History* (Chapel Hill: University of North Carolina Press, 1941), p. 70.

rebellious will that spurned a mechanistic, commercial society and, as with Blake's "Ratio," inverted the notions of right reasoning and viewed them as oppressive. This attitude is echoed in Wordsworth's cry, "I'd rather be a pagan suckled on a creed outworn."

HISTORICISM AND THE HELLENIC REVIVAL

To recapture the ideal of the mythmaking poet who followed natural rather than artificial impulses the yoke of Rome had to be cast off. Roman models could not revive the mythmaking power in modern form. The tenor of early eighteenth-century literature had been, on balance, more Roman than Greek. Dryden tried on Vergil's helmet, Twickenham became a rough equivalent to the Sabine Farm, and Johnson turned to Juvenal for the pattern of his two great longer poems. The Roman world had passed on all the ancient mythologies. Agrippa's Pantheon at Rome remains the most perfectly preserved of all major public buildings of the Empire. No other exterior better exemplifies that Augustus found the city brick and left it marble.[19] But the gods inside were Greek in origin and Aeneas himself was Priam's son. As far as original, *inventive* strength was concerned, the Roman legacy had, for the eighteenth century, moved into satire and contemplative verse. When the high satiric mode waned in the 1740s, poet-critics turned to Greece. After *The Vanity of Human Wishes* (1749) no major poem of the century overtly derives from a Roman model.

Since the late seventeenth century Longinus and Pindar had been centers of critical attention. Fénelon's *Avantures de Télémaque* proved highly popular[20] and—aside from influencing Andrew Ramsay's *Travels of Cyrus*—it prompted Thomas Russell's excellent sonnet on Philoctetes, *Suppos'd to be Written at Lemnos.*[21] Ramsay, also known as the Chevalier de

19. Perhaps the modern companion comes from William Alfred's poem "In Memory of My Friend Robert Lowell." Alfred speaks first, then Lowell:

> Where you are Christ only knows. I'm in Harvard Square.
> "We found it brick; we're leaving it prefab."

20. For instance, Blackwell, *Life and Writings of Homer,* pages 60–61, discusses Fénelon's work.

21. Bush, *Mythology and the Romantic Tradition,* p. 40n.

James Engell

Ramsai and not to be confused with his countryman Allan
Ramsay, communicated with Nicolas Fréret, the famous
French mythographer, knew Fénelon personally, and, in his
Conversations with Fénelon, claimed a kind of conversion ex-
perience. His new religious sensibility shines through the *Trav-
els of Cyrus* and informs two important essays Ramsay affixed
to the *Travels,* "Of the Mythology of the Antients" (1728) and
"A Discourse upon the Theology and Mythology of the
Pagans" (1730), essays to which we shall return later. Under
the Grecian influence William Whitehead, following Akenside's *Hymn to the Naiads* (1746), produced *Hymn to the
Nymph of Bristol Spring.* It is significant that Blackwell's
Memoirs of the Court of Augustus proved far less successful
than his studies of Homer. Addison's *Cato* gave way to Thomson's *Agamemnon,* and Aeschylus became something of a
rage, his most colorful admirer being Parson Adams. Swift's
retelling of Greek myths counterpointed his Horatian satires.
Psyche became the subject of Gloster Ridley's poem *Psyche*
(1747), as well as of the notable mythological chapter "The Vision" in Abraham Tucker's *Light of Nature Pursued* (1768–
1777). Collins tried to mythologize the passions collectively
and separately in his odes and asked British poets to look to
Greece and "confirm the tales her sons relate!"[22] The progress
poems of Gray and others began with Greece and ended with
Britain. John ("Estimate") Brown took Greece as his model
for the rise of poetry in primitive societies. He abhorred the
standard of Augustan Rome.[23] When to this Hellenic revival
we add the rising interest in Hebrew poetry and myth reflected
as early as Milton and carried through Ramsay's *Travels,* Warburton's *Divine Legation of Moses Demonstrated* (1737–
1742), and Lowth's *Lectures on the Sacred Poetry of the
Hebrews* (1753), we see that Hebraism and Hellenism were
ousting Augustanism. This helped greatly to generate a new
view of mythology.

But the Hellenic revival, at its best, declined any *close* imita-

22. "The Passions: An Ode for Music," l. 188.
23. Wellek, *Rise of English Literary History,* p. 77; see Howard D. Wein-
brot, *Augustus Caesar in "Augustan" England* (Princeton: Princeton University Press, 1978), p. 127.

tion of Greek (or other ancient) mythology. As Edward Young stated in his famous dictum, quoted as frequently in his own day as in histories now, "To imitate the *Iliad* is not to imitate Homer." In fact in 1735 Blackwell himself had pointed this out in his *Life and Writings of Homer,* where he criticized Trissino's blank verse *L'Italia liberata* (1524) as a noble failure precisely because it imitated the *Iliad* and not Homer's genius.[24] The aim of imitation should be more ideal than formal. The power of invention, not old gods or heroes, was what was wanted. Horace's advice in the *Ars poetica* that "it is better to dramatize the *Iliad* into acts than to offer a subject unknown and unsung" no longer sat very well. The Greek cast of mind and its mythopoeic force, not the myths themselves, became the higher object of emulation. Although Young's *Conjectures* (1759) is filled with allusions to classical mythology, his real point was that, despite Pope, nature and Homer are *not* the same. Look to nature, said Young, for "the true Helicon" is not earlier literature but "the breast of Nature." The goal is not another *Iliad* but "a capacity of accomplishing a work so great." Granted, direct imitations of Greek fable endured, but as Johnson said, they were more endured than favored.

The turning to Greece resulted in an increased historical consciousness of mythology. The rise of modern mythology and the rise of systematic literary history go hand in hand. Moreover, the fables not only were *older* by the streams of Helicon than by the Tiber, they seemed more genuine and less borrowed, however much of Greek mythology itself was derivative of cultures that thrived centuries earlier. Yes, pushed further, even Greece could be seen as young. "To allegorize," said Blackwell, "is an Egyptian invention."[25] All one had to do was open the *Timaeus* and read Solon's conversation with the Egyptian priest (or Hesiod's *Theogony* for that matter). By the Nile the myths seemed oldest of all. A kind of historical one-upmanship operated. Blackwell expressed it in his *Letters Concerning Mythology:* "The Greeks and Romans had their Religion at second hand from powerful and knowing Nations,

24. Blackwell, *Life and Writings of Homer,* p. 32.
25. Ibid., p. 86; see pp. 136–137.

but who had departed from their first Establishment, before their Intercourse with European People. It is not therefore to be expected, that *these* should be wiser than their Masters, and exercise a Purity they had never received.''[26]

It was comforting to view Greece as a latecomer by hundreds, even thousands of years in the field of mythology. It offered hope that to be first was more accident than distinction (so Johnson on *Paradise Lost:* it "is not the greatest of heroic poems, only because it is not the first"). The still-undeciphered Egyptian hieroglyphs exuded a sense of mystery. Ramsay and Warburton tried to explain them in terms of symbol and myth. In 1730 Ramsay mentioned the famous Persian scholar Thomas Hyde (1636–1704), who helped bring to light Persian mythology. Ramsay also extended himself into a discussion of the Vedas, the Yking (the Chinese *I Ching*), and even North American myths. Already Bernard Fontenelle had studied Peruvian myths. The historical approach led to comparative mythology. Antoine Banier (1675–1741) had claimed that all myth, unlike allegory, has a historical basis.[27] Ramsay's historical curiosity, in his *Discourse upon the Theology and Mythology of the Pagans,* revealed a more syncretist approach: "We see then that the doctrines of the primitive perfection of nature, its fall and restoration by a divine Hero, are equally manifest in the Mythologies of the Greeks, Egyptians, Persians, Indians and Chinese."[28] And later Johnson himself projected a *History of the Heathen Mythology, with an explication of the fables, both allegorical and historical, with references to the poets.* He also admitted "good reasons" for reading mythological romances, primarily the poet's "fertility of invention" and "beauty and style of expression."[29]

The very idea of "pastness" then, if not essential to myths, seemed to enhance them. Clio was the muse of history *and*

26. Blackwell, *Letters Concerning Mythology*, p. 372.

27. Ibid., pp. 405–411, 372; Andrew Ramsay's *Discourse upon the Theology and Mythology of the Pagans* (1730), pp. 79–88. The *Discourse* is appended to the *Travels of Cyrus* (1728).

28. Ramsay, *Discourse*, p. 88.

29. *Critical Opinions of Samuel Johnson,* ed. J. E. Brown (Princeton: Princeton University Press, 1926), pp. 159–160.

epic poetry. The temporal enemies of the mythmaking imagination are a historical sense based purely on fact and—at the other extreme—an antihistorical stance proclaiming the relevance of the modern only. So Blackwell regretted the "meer *historical* Use (setting aside higher Considerations)" of comparative mythology. A speculative admixture open to literary style, philosophy, and religion was needed. Spenser—and Chatterton—knew the value of a generalized sense of the past as it affected poetic language. Sidney admitted in his *Apology* that he loved to hear some old crowder singing the "Ballad of Percy and Douglas," and that while in Hungary he heard oral poets reciting stories generations old. In both Marlowe's and Goethe's *Faust* the hero immerses himself in dusty tomes and searches for secret knowledge locked in the past. (Thomas Mann's Adrian Leverkühn resorts to medieval magic squares and an arcane, private alchemy of symbols and mathematical relationships.) Somewhere between a factual knowledge of history and complete ignorance of it lay the suggestive and partial awareness conducive to myth. Alfred North Whitehead remarked that the Renaissance knew about classical mythology just enough as was good for it. The eighteenth century knew more, but its historical interest now also swung in the critical direction of the poet's ability to create myth in the first place.

Primitivism

The Hellenic revival and much of the historical approach to mythology were symptomatic of something larger and harder to define, primitivism. Blackwell prefaces his *Letters Concerning Mythology* with an engraving of the bust of Homer and contends that all great poets have had "a *simple country* Look," like the "*plain rustick* Look," of this bust. (Much to Coleridge's dismay, *rustic* was the word Wordsworth later stressed in his Preface.) Blackwell even praised the Appalachian Indians for their primitive mythology: "Their daily Worship is simple and pure."[30] Had complexities of civilization choked mythology? Were not Blake's "dark satanic mills" simply negative images of "the green and pleasant" pastoral

30. Blackwell, *Letters Concerning Mythology*, pp. 12, 406.

world often associated with myths? When the curtain goes up on Goethe's *Faust,* the great man turns from his books and wishes himself away from esoteric learning. He wants to escape into a clear, direct, and inviting pastoral world.[31] In Keats's 1817 volume of poems his dedicatory sonnet to Leigh Hunt (who himself made notes in Blackwell's *Life and Writings of Homer*) expresses the link between a primitivistic pastoral setting and the power to make myths. Although "Glory and loveliness have passed away" from a world where there is "no crowd of nymphs" and where "Pan is no longer sought," Keats hopes—as the remaining poems in the volume testify—to revive the magic of myth and nature. Hazlitt also hypothesized that the pastoral world originated mythology, but lamented, "We have few good pastorals in the language."[32]

Underneath this all lay a grand paradox: primitivism reflected, as Arthur Lovejoy has noted, "the discontent of the civilized with civilization." Yet no self-respecting poet, as Keats and others before recognized, wanted to revive the mummies of parched fable. One could try to negate the course of history that was debilitating classical mythology by reviving the myth of a *timeless* golden age, one so old as to be perennial. But by the eighteenth century this myth was itself becoming trite. An alternative was the glorification of the child, the only "civilized" being not spoiled by civilization. Wordsworth addressed the child as "thou best philosopher," and Novalis proclaimed, "*Wo Kinder sind da ist ein Goldnes Zeitalter.*" Later, in Dickens, Melville, and Twain, settings devoid of (or opposed to) the pressures of commercialized society and a focus on childhood (frequently on an orphan—even Ishmael becomes one) add to the archetypal and mythic dimension of their work. Coleridge could, with some nostalgia, invoke the "fair humanities of old religion" and wish their return, despite his later criticism of an "exploded mythology." Wordsworth's

31. *Faust,* 1. 392–397.

32. William Hazlitt, *Complete Works,* ed. P. P. Howe, 21 vols. (1930–1934), XX, 296, 61; IV, 18–19, 34; see James Engell, *The Creative Imagination: Enlightenment to Romanticism* (Cambridge, Mass.: Harvard University Press, 1981), pp. 211–212.

sonnet "The world is too much with us" is, as Douglas Bush states, "the keynote of a mass of mythological poetry of the nineteenth and twentieth centuries; the old antagonism between Pan and Christ has become a contrast between the ugly materialism of our commercial and industrial civilization and the natural religion, the ideal beauty and harmony, of Hellenic life."[33] As early as Akenside's *Hymn to the Naiads* (Bush calls it "the most remarkable mythological poem of the century"), the poet hoped to escape the "unhallow'd rout" and "profaner audience" of modern civilization. But it was before the cult of primitivism reached epidemic proportion; Akenside's nymphs were to encourage British commerce, its getting and spending, and to provide for "the maritime part of military power." Gray, Goldsmith, Cowper, and Blake would all become less sanguine about the bonds linking myth, money, and power.

For all its vaunted virtues of simplicity much primitivism arrived on the back of arduous historical scholarship. The prizing of the *Volk* could be an easy sentiment, but the work of Gray and Percy came painstakingly. (It was to be one of Wordsworth's great strengths as a poet that he was born into and grew up surrounded by the rustic; he did not learn it from books.) Academic and antiquarian research created a thirst for a new mythology based on earlier, "purer" times. In a sonnet written in a copy of Dugdale's *Monasticon*, Thomas Warton styled himself "of painful Pedantry the poring child," but envisioned the pedant soon melting into the pensive bard; it is true that much of the antiquarian research, such as Stukeley's, was more inventive than accurate. Like Gray and Collins (see *Ode on the Popular Superstitions of the Highlands*), Warton turned not only to Greece but to Britain for new mythology. The conclusion of Warton's *Pleasures of Melancholy* rejects the Greeks(!) and praises the Druids. His sonnets "Written at Stonehenge" and "On King Arthur's Round Table at Winchester" reveal a primitivistic, mythic urge. Warton had read William Stukeley's *Stonehenge, a Temple Restor'd to the Brit-*

33. See Coleridge, *Wallenstein*, pt. 2 (*The Piccolomini*), 2. 4. 123–131; Bush, *Mythology and the Romantic Tradition*, pp. 58–59. Bush connects Wordsworth's sonnet to Thomas Taylor's translation of Proclus in Taylor's *Plato;* compare *The Excursion*, IV, ll. 717 ff., 847 ff.

ish Druids (1740), and the Druidic line continued through Blake. Although "early English poetry was still too near to fall completely under the category of 'primitive',"[34] a poem such as Collins' *Ode on the Death of Mr. Thomson* gives a sense of this ancient British mythology. The last stanza combines nostalgia, a pastoral world long lost, and a mythological poet (Thomson himself) as the object of a yearning for British mythology:

> Long, long, thy stone and pointed clay
>   Shall melt the musing Briton's eyes;
> "O! vales and wild woods," shall he say,
>   "In yonder grave your Druid lies!"

Yes, the British past could seem mythic. As Richard Hurd related in *Letters on Chivalry and Romance* (1762), Milton wrote *Paradise Lost* only after abandoning "his long-projected design of Prince Arthur" (letter 12).

RATIONAL INQUIRY

A contemporaneous and not always sympathetic analysis probed the validity of primitivism. As early as 1690 Sir William Temple's *Of Poetry* and *Essay upon the Ancient and Modern Learning* used the age-old theory of cyclical cultural change to explain current literary development.[35] Cultures reaching a sophisticated plateau looked back to times when there were giants in the earth. The irony was that the ancient literary periods that were objects of longing for modern primitivism suffered backward glances themselves. Much "ancient" mythology, in fact, was about earlier fables and heroes. Even the gods experienced a cultural revolution, the Olympians supplanted the Titans. Temple asked, will poor mankind never learn? Must the imagination streamline history to make it conform to the simple patterns of strong, archetypal emotions? Alas, even cultured man, concluded Temple, must—like an aging child— be amused before the sleep that rounds his last dreams.

---

34. Wellek, *Rise of English Literary History,* p. 123.
35. Ibid., pp. 35–44, 70–71.

In the *Life and Writings of Homer* Blackwell divided mythology into "natural" and "artificial," the latter being the result "of great Search and Science." But "natural" mythology "is the Faculty that . . . invents and creates it." Blackwell felt his own century largely "artificial," with polished manners and apparently degenerate literary power. In his dedication he remarked that heroic poetry belongs to a rougher age; he was persuaded that in all likelihood "*we may never be a proper Subject of an Heroic Poem.*"[36] Blackwell, whose *Enquiry* Gibbon called "an effort of genius," became influential in Germany through Herder.

In 1763, the year James Macpherson purveyed *Temora*, his second translation of Ossian (the first was *Fingal* in 1761), John Brown's *Dissertation on the Rise, Union, and Power, the Progressions, Separations, and Corruptions of Poetry and Music* reinforced cyclical theory with an argument taken from Greece, the prototype of which might be Hesiod's *Theogony*, which Blackwell himself had discussed.[37] *Ossian* tended to vindicate such theories: it was, in Brown's words, a "noble confirmation" of an earlier, mythologically superior age. But of course there were opponents. Aside from not having seen original manuscripts, Johnson was probably suspicious because he knew Percy's genuine research. The myth of the noble savage rankled Johnson as well. He already scoffed at Rousseau and took the view that this was old stuff indeed—a culture hoodwinking itself, developing a New Style calendar with one hand and turning back the clock with the other. Rousseau's points were not new. Dryden's triplet from the *Conquest of Granada*, nearly ninety years before, revealed a vision already popular:

> I am as free as Nature first made man,
> Ere the base laws of servitude began,
> When wild in woods the noble savage ran.

36. Blackwell, *Life and Writings of Homer*, pp. 148, 28–32; see also pp. 167–168, 213.

37. See Wellek, *Rise of English Literary History*, pp. 74–81; Bate, *Burden of the Past*, pp. 55–58. Blackwell, *Life and Writings of Homer*, p. 99.

William Duff explicitly made the connection with mythology that lurked behind the debate about primitivism. The last section of his *Essay on Original Genius* (1767) defends its long title: *That original Poetic Genius will in general be displayed in its utmost vigour in the early and uncultivated periods of Society, which are peculiarly favorable to it; and that it will seldom appear in a very high degree in cultivated life.* Early societies, Duff argued, had an advantage in composing mythologies and inventing symbols. Life was simpler, emotions and ideas more forcefully expressed. Greek mythology, "a system of ingenious fiction," and the "remarkable boldness of sentiment and expression . . . the most poetical figures of speech" in Eastern and Egyptian mythologies were attributable to the "primitive" state of those societies.[38]

Hume, believing like Blackwell that mythology was originally used to exploit the fear of common people and to control them (anticipating Marx's "opiate of the masses"), resurrected arguments of Velleius Paterculus, the first-century rhetorician.[39] Cultures follow cycles, said Hume, in his *Essay on the Rise and Progress of the Arts and Sciences.* Perfection in the arts will "necessarily decline." Like "decadence," the idea of primitivism was becoming more important because the eighteenth century self-consciously began to think of *itself* in such terms. And the fact that Hume could revive a seventeen-hundred year-old argument favored that very argument's premise; the question remained whether a new mythology could be created in the face of predetermined cycles that controlled literature.

Rational inquiry into primitivism and mythology thus cut two ways. It could deflate or buoy up. The point is that there was genuine debate. Kames, for instance, attacked Paterculus in his *Sketches of the History of Man.* The Highland Society of Scotland, perturbed and embarrassed by the *Ossian* controversy, established a commission to pass judgment on the work —and not to render the Scottish verdict of "not proven." In

38. William Duff, *An Essay on Original Genius in Philosophy and the Fine Arts, Particularly in Poetry* (1767), pp. 124, 192–193n, 181, 186–187.

39. Blackwell, *Life and Writings of Homer,* p. 78; see Bate, *Burden of the Past,* pp. 82–84; Wellek, *Rise of English Literary History,* pp. 72–73, 39.

1805 the commission's report, compiled by Henry Mackenzie, was generally favorable. But that same year Malcolm Laing, who five years earlier had already attacked Macpherson, produced a heavily annotated edition of *Ossian* revealing echoes of not only Homer and Vergil, but Waller, Prior, and Pope.

Perhaps an inevitable cultural cycle did grind out an age of myth and was now grinding or "polishing" down a veneer. At any rate, a "revolution" had occurred. The century found itself entering a new cycle and no one would deny it. Thomas Warton, in *Observations on the Faerie Queene* (1754) called Spenser "a *romantic* poet," the last champion of allegory. Then, after Milton's sublimity, "imagination gave way to correctness" (sec. 10, "Of Spenser's Allegorical Character"). In 1762 Hurd repeated the lament: "What we have gotten by this revolution, you will say, is a great deal of good sense. What we have lost is a world of fine fabling, the illusion of which is so grateful to the *charmed spirit* that, in spite of philosophy and fashion, *Faery* Spenser still ranks highest among the poets." Hurd felt that cultural determinists ignored the human factor. The *"charmed spirit"* meant more than good sense. One might put it in Thoreau's later words: "This lament for a golden age is but a lament for golden men." The problem was to stir the poet to heroic action, not to fiddle with theories that minimized his power as a free agent.

CRUCIAL TERMINOLOGY

When Hurd said the "revolution" in poetry left "fine fabling" by the wayside, he really meant "mythmaking." The eighteenth century and the romantics never spoke of *myth* or *myths*. The closest usage often was *fable*. Not until the 1820s and 1830s did *myth* and *mythic* enter the language.[40] For the eighteenth century *mythology* carried assumptions often overlooked. It implied a body of interconnected creations and, according to Johnson's *Dictionary*, their "explication." The con-

40. See Harry Levin, "Some Meanings of Myth," *Daedalus*, 88, no. 2 (Spring 1950), 223–231, rpt. in *Myth and Mythmaking*, ed. H. A. Murray (New York 1960). For *myth* and *mythology* see Robert D. Richardson, "The Enlightenment View of Myth and Joel Barlow's *Vision of Columbus*," *Early American Literature*, 13 (1978).

nected creations give each other resonance and meaning (Duff's "*system* of ingenious fiction"). Forgetting this fact makes it a pernicious one. Yet although myths isolated from other myths did not yet really exist for the eighteenth century, the new historical and comparative awareness was eroding traditional unity. Modern pluralism of culture was beginning to destroy the old sense of mythology and to foster myth instead. A "myth" is more easily understood. It is one story—or even an ideology, often not literally true in expression. So Theseus says, "I never may believe / These antique fables, nor these fairy toys." But "mythology" is, properly speaking, what it last was for the eighteenth century and for the romantics, a whole narrative or series of stories so layered that their connection becomes something of *universal* import. Hippolyta gently corrects her consort:

> But all the story of the night told over,
> And all their minds transfigur'd so together,
> More witnesseth than fancy's images,
> And grows to something of great constancy,
> But, howsoever, strange and admirable.[41]

Although *myth* was not yet a word, the eighteenth century employed many terms and frequently debated their slippery meanings. The value of these discussions seems to have been less in forming clear definitions than in providing critical tools and interpretations. No norm or standard was reached, but the nature of mythology acquired a contour and surface relief from the pressure of these increasingly acute and learned debates. Ephraim Chambers' *Cyclopedia* (which Rousseau rightly noted was the original for Diderot's and d'Alembert's *Dictionnaire encyclopédique,* "at first to be only a sort of translation of Chambers"),[42] contains in its 1728 and later editions a struc-

41. *MND* 5. 1. 23–27. Perhaps for this reason Douglas Bush says that as far as English literature is concerned, everyone interested in mythology sooner or later collapses in the bosom of Shakespeare or, it might be added, in the bosom of Arthur, which Falstaff did—and Milton nearly followed.
42. *Confessions,* bk. 7 (1747–1749). Booksellers had conceived translating Chambers. Of course Diderot greatly expanded that plan.

tural definition of *fable* as plot or narrative, the essence of which "is to be a symbol" itself, "to signify somewhat more than is expressed by the letter." Influenced by Banier, Chambers subdivided fables into rational, moral, and mixed types.

A dozen years later Warburton conceived of mythology as a vast system of allegories, each of which uses various "symbols," themselves nothing more than "improved hieroglyphics." In turn, hieroglyphics are "tropical"—or "proper"— the simplest kind of literal pictures. The teaching of the ancients often involved feigning "a *divine original* for hieroglyphic characters," in other words, backtracking to develop larger allegories from single symbols instead of letting these symbols emerge from one original allegory. Of special interest, this suggests a method of composition in which the poet invents an allegory or narrative to explicate or to place in context an already received, though obscure, symbol. Such a narrative becomes an explication or exegesis in the form of fiction.[43] And Andrew Ramsay, while agreeing with Banier that allegory and mythology are different, questioned Banier's conviction that mythology must have a historical basis. Already the battle lines of later debates—such as Creuzer's religio-allegorical school versus Loebeck's historical interpretations— were being drawn. In his *Discourse* prefixed to Fénelon's *Avantures de Télémaque,* Ramsay decried that symbol, allegory, and hieroglyph were all degenerating and, by a process of critical secularization, losing their religious import.[44]

The discussions extended into the romantic period. Coleridge's famous distinction between symbol and allegory is a continuation of them, and we are still continuing them today. Schelling, who himself made a distinction similar to Coleridge's (and later praised Coleridge's for its deeper insight), left suggestive remarks still unfamiliar to most English read-

43. William Warburton, *The Divine Legation of Moses Demonstrated,* 2 vols. (1737–1742), II, bk. 4, sec. 4.
44. Ramsay's *Discours sur la poésie épique* (1797 ed.), p. 11 (prefixed to Fénelon's *Avantures*). On "secret symbols" and on allegory versus parable see Blackwell, *Life and Writings of Homer,* pp. 84–86, and *Letters Concerning Mythology,* pp. 56–57, 76.

ers.[45] Some are worth repeating, for they reveal the close theoretical attention often behind the great romantic achievements.
Schelling defines *schema* as the presentation of a class of individual particulars by a generalized one; conversely, *allegory*
presents a general idea, value, or concept by an individual
character or image; and a *symbol* mediates perfectly between
these two. It is the perfect equilibrium of an intellectual world
of eternal, universal ideas and a material world of transient,
particular individuation. Mythology is the totality of nature living in the human mind, the existence of nature expressed as
the mind's independent poetic or imaginative existence. "Mythology" is thus a *state of mind*—and then it generates literary
works. It is "the first condition and necessary material of all
art."[46]

Perhaps the most important effect of the eighteenth-century
and romantic debates and definitions was to create an atmosphere in which the concepts seemed crucial and relevant to
literature, an atmosphere in which the aspiring poet would
want to create a new mythology and new symbols. Yet in
doing this the poet would inevitably have to handle the questions of religion and modern philosophy.

THE CHANGES OF RELIGION AND PHILOSOPHY

Milton felt an uneasy truce between Pan and Christ, and afterward, as we have seen, classical mythology began to break
down. The "damned crew" of old gods fled, but "time," as
Milton hoped, did not "run back, and fetch the age of gold." In
the greatest of English epics—and of course great by the standards of all literatures of all times—Milton had expressed the
essential Christian myth, but with the exception of Blake later

45. See Coleridge's *Statesman's Manual,* in *Lay Sermons,* ed. R. J. White,
in *The Collected Coleridge,* ed. Kathleen Coburn and Bart Winer, 16 vols.
(Princeton: Princeton University Press, and London: Routledge and Kegan
Paul, 1969–   ), pp. 29, 30, 30n, 73, 79; see also Coleridge's *Miscellaneous
Criticism,* ed. T. M. Raysor (Cambridge, Mass.: Harvard University Press,
1936), pp. 28–29; and his *Notebooks,* ed. Kathleen Coburn, 4 vols. (New
York, Princeton, and London: Bollingen Foundation and Princeton University
Press, 1957–   ), III, 3325, 4183, 4498 and nn.
46. F. W. Schelling, *Sammtliche Werke,* ed. K. F. A. Schelling, 14 vols.
(Stuttgart and Augsburg, 1856–1861), V, 399–423; I, 406.

poets failed to regenerate its power. Deists and pantheists produced a spate of epics, odes, and effusions in the eighteenth century, most of which have been deservedly ignored. They are too abstract and full of moralizing.[47] *The Seasons,* while one of the excellent long poems in the language, is simply not "myth." In philosophic poetry the tendencies of natural religion secularized and intellectualized the mythological elements. *Ossian* puzzled admirers and critics alike by what Thomas Warton called a "perplexing and extraordinary circumstance": *Ossian* handled the problem of religion by having none at all![48]

Johnson objected that no writer could break the taboo of mixing profound religious truths with literary fiction. In a sense, the Christian religion had thus killed off the religious content of myth. One could try to smile with the ancient authors (let alone Renaissance poets) who smiled indulgently at the suggestion that they believed their stories to be literally true. But, among other considerations, they had no Bible always putting literary treatments to the litmus test of one holy text. Or one could argue endlessly about the religious origins of ancient myths, but of what real use was this to the struggling poet writing at the present time? In Johnson's words, "The change which [the Christian] religion has made in the whole system of the world" changed our view of mythology. Yet while someone devout, or simply familiar with the Bible, might be offended or bored by inventive fables of Jesus, Moses, or St. John (by and large, Blake avoided using biblical figures in his myths), one "Christian" character could always be treated mythologically—the devil. This fact is behind Blake's remark that Milton was of the devil's party, for the devil is the one who leaves elbowroom for the imagination. Both Wordsworth in the 1815 Preface to *Lyrical Ballads* and Coleridge in his Shakespeare Lectures, to exemplify how the imagination works in poetic description, selected passages from *Paradise Lost* that portray the devil and death.

Overall, however, the problem was that myths not believed,

47. See Blackwell, *Letters Concerning Mythology,* p. 395.
48. Wellek, *Rise of English Literary History,* p. 187.

or "half" believed, enjoyed a pleasing quality, a distance, a "pastness" or quaintness, but myths held devoutly to be true suffered because they did not elicit that wonderful and exciting "willing suspension of disbelief," but instead demanded a willing suspension of belief itself.

While Hurd maintained that "fashion and philosophy" had banished the "charmed spirit" of fable and allegory, Blackwell and others saw modern philosophy as a possible counterpart to mythology. Bacon, after all, had considered mythology as "the wisdom of the ancients," and Fontenelle linked early philosophizing to early myths. If philosophy were only to turn away from extremes of rationalism and empiricism and pay more attention to the imagination, what Blackwell called the "creative Faculty,"[49] then there would be less conflict between the "charmed spirit" of the poet and that of the philosopher—and more chance for new myths. This is exactly what began to happen in the early eighteenth century and continued throughout it.[50] By the romantic period Blake, Keats, Goethe, Novalis, and in some moods Shelley and Wordsworth effectively showed that to philosophize in poetry *is* to create myth. Although this attitude takes for granted that neither the philosophy nor the poetry is abstract and theoretical, but narrates human life and direct experience, the optimistic Blackwell even suggested that systems such as Descartes' and Gilbert's could serve as "modern" analogues to ancient myths. (If they were weaker it was only because they relied on but "one Principle of their own invention"[51] rather than being an interlocking series of major principles: they were like single myths rather than a unified body or system of mythology.) By putting the study of mythology into contact with currents of contemporaneous philosophy and psychology Blackwell was helping to revive the stature and relevance of the mythmaking faculty of the poet itself.

Sapere aude, dare to think independently, is the famous motto of Kant's *Was ist Aufklärung?* But this phrase from

49. Blackwell, *Letters Concerning Mythology,* p. 301.
50. See Engell, *The Creative Imagination,* chaps. 2, 3, 6–12, 16, 19.
51. Blackwell, *Letters Concerning Mythology,* pp. 231–233, 283.

Horace's *Epistles* occurs as an intellectual battle cry in 1748. Blackwell uses it in *Letters Concerning Mythology* to promote a sympathetic and multifaceted inquiry into mythology. Regretting the "meer *historical*" as well as the purely skeptical, and the religiously dogmatic uses of ancient mythology, he envisions "higher considerations." Is there one basic impulse that explains mythmaking? By a "sympathetic Intercourse" with mythology Blackwell feels we can learn about ourselves. Myths still "work," he implies; that is, they continue to fascinate us—they work on some deep-seated psychological principle. As Blackwell explains it, this principle engages the imagination, the mimetic faculty, judgment, and philosophic wisdom all at once.[52]

Blackwell's tolerant optimism was wise. He could laugh gently at the wild syncretist Postelli (author of *Pantheosia . . . That is Universal Unity, or the Sound of the last Trumpet save one*): "The best Key to this Conduct, is to tell you, that this great Man was, at times, a little crazy, though with some lucid Intervals." Yet even in "crazy" theories Blackwell saw an affirmation that mythology was an inevitable and fascinating human pursuit. It always surfaced, its impulse an ineradicable part of human nature. What appeared remarkable, as Vico and Herder pointed out also, were the different manifestations and cultural identities of mythology. So Blackwell could say that "*Human Life* is the veriest *Proteus* in the World."[53] This may not sound like a conclusion of the Enlightenment, of *sapere aude*, for it seems to deny the immutability and consistency of human nature. But Blackwell's point is that indeed myth *is* consistent. It is found everywhere and will continue to raise its wonderful protean head. Life in ancient times, he says, was just as diverse. It is only that ancient mythologies permit us to grasp that diversity imaginatively without choking on detail. He ends *Letters Concerning Mythology* with the already famous "the lunatic, the lover, and the poet" speech of Theseus. It is the human imagination that remains constant, and when it dares to think or to create independently, then the result may be Blake's *Jerusalem* as well as Kant's *Critiques*.

52. Ibid., pp. 155, 349–350, 23–24, 119, 283; see also pp. 130–131.
53. Ibid., pp. 387–388, 408.

THE NEW POET

> *Wer sichert den Olymp? vereinet Götter?*
> *Des Menschen Kraft im Dichter offenbart.*

> Who makes Olympus sure, and gives the gods one life?
> The power of humankind, as in the bard revealed.
>   *Faust* 1. 156–157

We have seen that with every major consideration of mythology faced by the eighteenth century—with religion, philosophy, poetic language and diction, and with the newer ideal of originality—the poet was being asked to perform a great deal in a growing atmosphere of self-conscious critical demand. It was no wonder that a myth of the poet as genius, seer, prophet, sage, and hero developed again, more fully than it had since classical times. Such a myth was formative, yet it could weigh heavily, too. To invent modern heroes seemed as hard as to be one. Coleridge, so learned and so philosophically and critically acute, seemed stymied at the thought of finishing something as short as *Christabel*. But Keats, who according to Charles Cowden Clarke had little more than a schoolboy's handbook learning of mythology and what it meant, was able to sail into the trade winds of creating new mythology and, given his short career, make astonishing headway.

As poetic creativity itself began to take on the proportion of mythological heroism, the poet as hero—as the subject of his own poetry—and the power of mythmaking itself, as much as any specific myth, became valued. Mythology in the romantic period would often take on the general tincture of autobiography. *Don Juan, The Prelude, Faust, Prometheus Unbound, Milton,* the second *Hyperion, Lamia,* and even *The Rime of the Ancient Mariner,* these were all about the poet's experience. Often they faced up to Johnson's criterion of "real life" and avoided a hollow use of classical mythology. And without becoming bogged down in Christian doctrine they often explored religious experience and the problem of evil. In many respects the hope fulfilled was a hope of the eighteenth century. As early as 1735 Blackwell had urged that the potential poet "be indulgent . . . to his *Imagination,* which is the prime Faculty of a Mythologist. It is this, that distinguishes the *real Poet.*"[54]

54. Blackwell, *Life and Writings of Homer,* p. 154.

JOHN A. HODGSON

Transcendental Tropes: Coleridge's Rhetoric of Allegory and Symbol

More than any of his German precursors Samuel Taylor Coleridge takes a rhetorical approach to defining the concepts of allegory and symbol. While his critical strategy in broaching the subject, to affirm the Goethean valuing of symbol over allegory, is unexceptionably derivative (from A. W. Schlegel or Schelling, perhaps, no less than from Goethe), his tactics, recurring to fundamental rhetorical figures, are novel. He not only revives the classical and Renaissance notion of allegory as extended metaphor, he also initiates a parallel association of symbol with synecdoche as a means of discriminating the two modes: "The Symbolical cannot, perhaps, be better defined in distinction from the Allegorical, than that it is always itself a part of that, of the whole of which it is the representative. — 'Here comes a sail,'—(that is, a ship) is a symbolical expression. 'Behold our lion!' when we speak of some gallant soldier, is allegorical."[1] The nature of his approach here, moreover, appears to remain generally constant throughout his mature

1. *Coleridge's Miscellaneous Criticism,* ed. Thomas Middleton Raysor (London: Constable, 1936), p. 99.

life: it is strongly implicit in his writings from the 1790s on and, once formulated in 1816, is frequently explicit thereafter. Indeed, during his last decade, as Coleridge increasingly concentrates his attention on the Bible—a book, he finds, "so strangely written, that in a series of the most concerning points, including . . . all the peculiar tenets of the religion, the plain and obvious meaning of the words . . . is no sufficient guide to their actual sense or to the writer's own meaning"[2]—a philosophy of rhetoric, of the turnings of literal meanings, becomes an absolutely necessary prerequisite for his critical endeavor.

Whatever interest in the rhetoric of allegory and symbol Coleridge has traditionally provoked by the sheer force of his own abiding interest, however, he has also effectively stymied by the apparent simpleness of his definitions and the desultoriness of his applied criticisms. The frustration is unfortunate, for these appearances are incomplete and misleading. Coleridge may initially state his argument rather simplistically, but though he adheres almost formulaically to his original terminology thereafter, his essential argument, over time, becomes increasingly sustained, sophisticated, and complex. He is indeed guilty, I shall argue, of serious lapses; but at the same time he is responsible for some of the finest rhetorical analyses of his age. Both his lapses and, far more regrettably, his accomplishments remain generally unappreciated. His later analyses of metaphor and allegory in particular—not those for which he is generally known—constitute a remarkably insightful investigation of the mode which the romantics, though many of them often maligned it, did so much to redeem for European literature. It is time to examine Coleridge's work on allegory and symbol anew.[3]

2. Samuel Taylor Coleridge, *Aids to Reflection,* ed. Henry Nelson Coleridge, 4th ed. (1840; rpt. Port Washington, N. Y.: Kennikat, 1971), p. 116. Hereafter *AR*.

3. I would like to acknowledge two important essays that have greatly stimulated my thinking here: Paul de Man, "The Rhetoric of Temporality," in *Interpretation: Theory and Practice,* ed. Charles S. Singleton (Baltimore: Johns Hopkins University Press, 1969), pp. 173–209; Tzvetan Todorov, "On Linguistic Symbolism," *New Literary History,* 6 (1974), 111–134.

As numerous critics have noted, Coleridge's advocacy of a
symbolic, synecdochic mode of writing, though first specified
only in 1816 in *The Statesman's Manual,* is in fact strongly implicit in his writings as much as twenty years before. In the
"one life" philosophy that dominated his thinking throughout
the late 1790s synecdoche is the very essence of man's (and
nature's) participation in godhead:

> 'Tis the sublime of man,
> Our noontide Majesty, to know ourselves
> Parts and proportions of one wondrous whole!
> . . . . .
> . . . But 'tis God
> Diffused through all, that doth make all one whole.[4]

In a pantheistic world view, of course, man's—and any
thing's—place in the cosmos is innately, definitionally synecdochic: "In this faith *all things* [not only those customarily associated with the sublime, such as 'rocks or waterfalls, mountains or caverns'] counterfeit infinity!"[5] Coleridge's stance is
notable, however, for its easy movement from ontological to
rhetorical applications of this principle. In his well-known September 1802 letter to William Sotheby, for example, the comments prompted by his dissatisfaction with William Lisle
Bowles's latest volume of poetry refer equally to both the
seer and the sayer, both the apprehender and the communi-
cator:

> There reigns thro' all the blank verse poems such a perpetual trick
> of *moralizing* every thing . . . never to see or describe any inter-
> esting appearance in nature, without connecting it by dim analogies
> with the moral world, proves faintness of Impression. Nature has
> her proper interest; & he will know what it is, who believes & feels,
> that every Thing has a Life of it's own, & that we are all *one Life*. A
> Poet's *Heart & Intellect* should be *combined, intimately* combined

4. "Religious Musings," ll. 126–131, in *The Complete Poetical Works of
Samuel Taylor Coleridge,* ed. Ernest Hartley Coleridge (Oxford: Oxford University Press, 1912), I, 113–114.
5. *Collected Letters of Samuel Taylor Coleridge,* ed. Earl Leslie Griggs
(Oxford: Clarendon Press, 1956), I, 349. Hereafter *CL.*

& *unified,* with the great appearances in Nature—& not merely held
in solution & loose mixture with them, in the shape of formal Simi-
lies. (*CL*, II, 864)

So too in his letters Coleridge more than once shifts naturally
from a similar statement of this philosophic precept to an apt
poetic *exemplum* (*CL*, I, 334, 349–350, 397–398).

Coleridge's recognition of the appropriateness of synecdoche, the basic trope of immanence, to a philosophy of pantheistic monism marks the beginning of a rhetorical theory of poetry. This beginning is rudimentary, to be sure, and internally
undiscriminating in the same ways as is pantheism itself (for
like all things, all synecdoches would seem indifferently valid
figures of the universal Presence). Coleridge would soon leave
both the philosophy and the rhetorical theory behind. The nat-
uralness of their relationship, however, the perfect suitedness
of the rhetorical and philosophic principles to one another,
suggested a critical ideal which thereafter became a continuing
force in his thought.

When Coleridge took up the questions of allegory and symbol in *The Statesman's Manual* in 1816 he was writing in the
context of a quite different set of philosophic concerns. Most
important, where before he had looked primarily for the evi-
dences of divine immanence, now he pursued "the transcendental philosophy" and its accommodation to Christianity.
"The statesman's manual," we must not forget, is the Bible;
Coleridge subtitles his pamphlet "The Bible the Best Guide to
Political Skill and Foresight: A Lay Sermon . . ." Coleridge's
attitude here, then, even in dealing with literary questions, is
not merely critical but polemical; correspondingly, however,
he is concerned to develop critical techniques which will be
adequate not merely to lesser works of literature, but also to
the supremely privileged and truthful—and challenging—
Book. "Religion," he once wrote, in some sense "is the poetry of mankind";[6] and the critical definitions of *The States-*

6. *Coleridge on Shakespeare: The Text of the Lectures of 1811–1812,* ed.
R. A. Foakes (London: Routledge and Kegan Paul, 1971), p. 88 (lecture 8).

man's Manual serve purposes no less literary for being at the
same time unabashedly theological. Ideally, he believes, one
should "read the Bible as the best of all books, but still as a
book; and make use of all the means and appliances which
learning and skill, under the blessing of God, can afford
towards rightly apprehending the general sense of it."[7]
The notions of symbol and allegory Coleridge now pro-
pounds, in many respects simply by paraphrasing or expanding
upon the 1802 letter to Sotheby, represent an attempt to adapt
his earlier rhetorical analysis to the greater demands of his new
philosophy:

> It is among the miseries of the present age that it recognizes no me-
> dium between *Literal* and *Metaphorical*. Faith is either to be buried
> in the dead letter, or its name and honors usurped by a counterfeit
> product of the mechanical understanding, which in the blindness of
> self-complacency confounds SYMBOLS with ALLEGORIES. Now an
> Allegory is but a translation of abstract notions into a picture-lan-
> guage which is itself nothing but an abstraction from objects of the
> senses; the principal being more worthless even than its phantom
> proxy, both alike unsubstantial, and the former shapeless to boot.
> On the other hand a Symbol (ό estin aei tautegorikon) is character-
> ized by a translucence of the Special in the Individual or of the Gen-
> eral in the Especial or of the Universal in the General. Above all by
> the translucence of the Eternal through and in the Temporal. It al-
> ways partakes of the Reality which it renders intelligible; and while
> it enunciates the whole, abides itself as a living part in that Unity, of
> which it is the representative. The other are but empty echoes
> which the fancy arbitrarily associates with apparitions of matter,
> less beautiful but not less shadowy than the sloping orchard or hill-
> side pasture-field seen in the transparent lake below. Alas! for the
> flocks that are to be led forth to such pastures! "*It shall even be as
> when the hungry dreameth, and behold! he eateth; but he waketh*

7. Samuel Taylor Coleridge, *The Table Talk and Omniana,* ed. T. Ashe
(London: Bell, 1909), p. 153. See Coleridge's marginalia criticizing interpreters
of the Book of Revelation for "their utter want of . . . all Eye Taste and Tact
for Poetry generally . . . Hence, they forget . . . that the Apocalypse is a
POEM, and a Poem composed by a Hebrew Poet, after the peculiar type of
Hebrew Poetry." (Cited in Coleridge, *On the Constitution of the Church and
State,* ed. John Colmer, The Collected Works of Samuel Taylor Coleridge, 10
[Princeton: Princeton University Press, 1976], p. 140n.)

> *and his soul is empty: or as when the thirsty dreameth, and behold*
> *he drinketh; but he awaketh and is faint!"* (ISAIAH xxix.8)[8]

We find Coleridge apparently still quite settled here in discriminating allegory from symbol as metaphor from synecdoche;
but now his characterizations of these two tropes, in their
greater particularity, acquire also a new complexity which
seems reactively to confound the very impetus of clarification
it exists to serve.

An allegory, as Coleridge here defines it, is typically abstract
and arbitrary.[9] A symbol, the far more admirable trope, is
pointedly the opposite: we might call it real and determined.
But more than this, Coleridge's notion of symbol involves a
larger, even cosmic set of assumptions. First, the universe
comprises a great, ultimately transcendent hierarchy: individuals, species, genera, universals, God.[10] Second, through its
sudden recourse to the notion of translucence, the symbolic
synecdoche is now identifiable, figuratively (N.B.), as the synecdoche of light; absolutely, this is to say, as the synecdoche
of signification or intelligibility itself.[11] Taken together, moreover, these two larger assumptions inevitably suggest the presence in Coleridge's argument of a fundamental, if modified,
Neoplatonism—with what ramifications and consequences,
we shall presently try to see.

8. Coleridge, *The Statesman's Manual,* in *Lay Sermons,* ed. R. J. White,
The Collected Works of Samuel Taylor Coleridge, 6 (Princeton: Princeton
University Press, 1972), pp. 30–31. Hereafter *SM.*

9. There is a succinct illustration of Coleridge's meaning in his "Notes on
the Book of Common Prayer" in *Literary Remains,* as he describes "the doctrine of the Sacramentaries, according to whom the Eucharist is a mere practical metaphor, in which things are employed instead of articulated sounds for
the exclusive purpose of recalling to our minds the historical fact of our Lord's
crucifixion; in short . . . just the same as when Protestants drink a glass of
wine to the glorious memory of William III!" (*The Complete Works of Samuel
Taylor Coleridge,* ed. W. G. T. Shedd, V [New York: Harper and Brothers,
1884], 23. Hereafter *LR*).

10. The absolute comprehensiveness of this hierarchy, only implicit in the
present passage, becomes quite explicit in the exactly contemporary *Theory of
Life;* see Coleridge, *Miscellanies, Aesthetic and Literary,* ed. T. Ashe (London: Bell, 1885), pp. 384–385, 409–424.

11. Coleridge's use of *translucence* here has confused some commentators

This famous *Statesman's Manual* passage, Coleridge's most sustained commentary on symbol and its difference from allegory, is also very possibly his most evasive and misguided. My misgivings about it, I hasten to add, are for the most part supported by evidence of Coleridge's own. He was continually qualifying and revising its assertions in his later writings; and the queries I raise now all anticipate reactions he would himself eventually begin to make.

To begin very simply: how real—more accurately, how free from abstractness—will a Coleridgean symbol necessarily be? As long as the symbolic trope is merely that most basic and trivial kind of synecdoche, the representation of a concrete whole by an actual part (a sail as a symbol of a ship), this issue of abstractness does not even arise. But in the *Statesman's Manual* passage Coleridge is obviously accepting as potentially sumbolic the full range of synecdochic figures—not only the part-for-whole trope, but also all varieties of member-for-class: individual-for-species (Adam as a symbol of mankind; see *AR*, pp. 265–266), species-for-genus, and the like.[12] And these very notions of species, genus, kind bring an element of

---

who have taken the word, in accordance with modern usage, to refer to a medium through which light imperfectly passes. Coleridge's actual meaning, however, is "shining through," referring not to the medium but to the light passing through it. An instance from the *Table-Talk* confirms this unambiguously: "As to what Captain Hall says about the English loyalty to the person of the King—I can only say, I feel none of it. I respect the man while, and only while, the king is translucent in him: I reverence the glass case for the Saint's sake within; except for that, it is to me mere glazier's work—putty, and glass, and wood" (p. 106).

12. In line with his notion of the universal hierarchy Coleridge actually imposes a qualification on these latter tropes: a lower form or species may symbolize a *higher* in the same kind (*AR*, p. 243n). Correlatively, then, no form of a species may symbolize a "lower" in the same kind, and only the "lowest" form may symbolize the entire genus. These restrictions derive straightforwardly from Coleridge's unempirically hierarchical, chain-of-being notion "that the definition of a genus or class is an adequate definition only of the lowest species of that genus: for each higher species is distinguished from the lower by some additional character, while the general definition includes only the characters common to all the species. Consequently it describes the lowest only" (*AR*, p. 232). See Coleridge, *The Friend,* ed. Barbara E. Rooke, The Collected Works of Samuel Taylor Coleridge, 4 (Princeton: Princeton University Press, 1969), I, 467n. Hereafter *Friend*.

abstractness into the conceptions of part and whole.[13] Some of Coleridge's own examples clearly illustrate this: thus, "the instinct of the ant-tribe or the bee is a symbol of the human understanding," since "the understanding in itself, and distinct from the reason and conscience, differs in degree only from the instinct in the animal" (*AR*, p. 243n).

A second basic crux in Coleridge's argument simply counterpoises the first on the other side of his symbol-allegory distinction: will an allegory necessarily be arbitrary? Here Coleridge's characteristically Platonic and Neoplatonic images for allegory's abstractness—shadows, echoes, reflections— dramatically counter his assertion: traditional figures of abstractness and insubstantiality they certainly are, but there is nothing arbitrary about the relation of a reflection to its original, or a shadow to the object which casts it. And if an allegory might thus relate determinedly to the concept it represents, the seeming antithesis of allegory and symbol begins to suggest instead the ambivalence or reciprocity of a common signifying gesture: symbol will be to allegory as light is to reflected light, or alternatively as light is to a shadow cast from it by some object.

Light reflected from what surface? Shadow cast by what object? Coleridge does sometimes extend his meditations to these considerations, even in these or similar images. Thus in an important 1818 insertion for *The Friend* he queries, if the appearances of the world are actually mere "Nothings," unreal appearances, yet "what is that inward Mirror, in and for which these Nothings have at least a relative existence?" (*Friend,* I, 522n). Again, correspondingly using images of substance and shadow instead of mirror and reflection, he writes in a contribution to his and Southey's *Omniana,*

> I am firmly persuaded, that no doctrine was ever widely diffused, among various nations through successive ages, and under different

13. "Can a Generic Idea as far as it is Generic have existence? No—why not? Because it wants the entire determinateness or particularity which all existing things have; therefore out of the mind every Generic Idea is a nonentity" (*Coleridge on Logic and Learning,* ed. Alice D. Snyder [New Haven: Yale University Press, 1929], p. 141).

religions (such as is the doctrine of original sin, and redemption . . .), which is not founded either in the nature of things or in
the necessities of our nature . . . I do not however mean, that
such a doctrine shall be always the best possible representation of
the truth, on which it is founded, for the same body casts strangely
different shadows in different places and different degrees of light;
but that it always does shadow out some such truth and derives its
influence over our faith from our obscure perception of that truth.[14]

Somewhat similarly, in marginalia distinguishing between the
mode of acquiring and the mode of communicating knowledge,
he characterizes the latter as "the *art* of reasoning, by acts of
abstraction, which separate from the first ['Intuition, or immediate beholding'] are indeed mere shadows, but, like shadows,
of incalculable service in determining the rememberable out-
lines of the Substance."[15]
    To follow Coleridge through such speculations, however,
would be an ultimately frustrating quest. For as these quotations no less than their numerous Neoplatonic prototypes illustrate, the ultimately elusive—and abstract—factor is not
shadow at all, or even that which casts a shadow, but rather
the light source itself. As Coleridge himself soon remembered
to acknowledge, "Consciousness itself, that Consciousness of
which all reasoning is the varied modification, is but the Reflex
of the Conscience, when most luminous" (*Friend,* I, 523n).[16]
The light source is God; it and its shining, in whatever aspect
—conscience, reason, revelation—are *a priori* propositions.
This source of revelation, moreover, is no trope but the ef-
facement of all tropes, the ineffable which only a trope can

    14. Robert Southey and Samuel Taylor Coleridge, *Omniana, or Horae Otio-
siores,* ed. Robert Gittings (Carbondale, Ill.: Southern Illinois University
Press, 1969), p. 180. A slightly changed version appears in *Friend,* I, 430.
    15. Marginalia to Boehme, *Works;* quoted in Richard Haven, *Patterns of
Consciousness: An Essay on Coleridge* (Amherst, Mass.: University of Massachusetts Press, 1969), p. 14.
    16. See a notebook passage quoted in James D. Boulger, *Coleridge as Reli-
gious Thinker* (New Haven: Yale University Press, 1961), p. 227: "The Light
from God (i.e. God's revelation of his Being and Attributes generally and of his
Will relatively to Man) must have been introductory to the Light of Reason in
the Conscience, and the Light of Reason in the Conscience to the Light of Reason in the understanding."

even attempt to intimate. "With the silence of light, it describes itself and dwells in *us* only as far as we dwell in *it*. The truths, which it manifests are such as it alone can manifest, and in all truth it manifests itself" (*Friend*, I, 515–516). The finite synecdoches of part for whole, individual for species, species for genus are all genuinely symbolic in Coleridge's sense, representing a fact or truth of an order immediately higher than their own, "partak[ing] of the Reality which [they] render intelligible." But the translucence, the ultimately transcendent light, simply allegorizes this very quality of intelligibility, and as such represents only itself—not a truth, but truthfulness itself. Thus Coleridge's expanded synecdochic definition of symbol in *The Statesman's Manual* is in part corrupt—corrupt precisely where its rhetoric is impure, in the clandestine introduction of a metaphoric figure.[17]

Once we dismiss the red herring of "translucence" in the *Statesman's Manual* passage, the reality and determinedness of a symbolic synecdoche would seem, as before, to be functions of its essential immediacy: the effective symbol will be not merely a part, but recognizably an immediate, characterizing part, of the whole it would represent. This prescription presents difficulties, though, once we undertake to figure specifically transcendent concepts; for is it indeed possible to offer genuine symbols, substantial and immediate parts, of reason, or God, or the mysteries of faith? That Coleridge himself improperly instances light as just such a trope is hardly reassuring. And our unease can only increase when we read, in his continuation of the *Statesman's Manual* passage, his ostensibly symbolic alternative to the wages of allegorizing. This Scripture-colored exclamation, a passage consistently ignored by those who would take Coleridge's definition of symbol at face value, immediately follows the quotation from Isaiah: "O! that we would seek for the bread which was given from

17. See Jerome C. Christensen, "The Symbol's Errant Allegory: Coleridge and His Critics," *ELH*, 45 (1978), who argues that "in Coleridge the undeniable and pervasive wish for a metaphysical continuity that is involved in his promotion of the symbol is typically breached by a discourse that divulges the obdurate discontinuities of signification. Coleridge's metaphysical symbolism is transgressed by a discursive allegory" (p. 644).

heaven, that we should eat thereof and be strengthened! O that we would draw at the well at which the flocks of our forefathers had living water drawn for them, even that water which, instead of mocking the thirst of him to whom it is given, becomes a well within himself springing up to life everlasting!'' (*SM*, p. 31). Here Coleridge is imaging transcendent concepts, certainly; but is his language truly symbolic, according to his own accompanying definition? How are we to distinguish it from the very allegorizing to which Coleridge so ostentatiously opposes it? That in fact we cannot distinguish it demonstrates the inadequacy of Coleridge's present definitions to his transcendental purposes. Nevertheless, Coleridge unshakably believes that there is a meaningful distinction to be made here, that these biblical images of bread and water are somehow too real and determined to be considered mere metaphors. As he continues in his later writings to press this point he develops what we must recognize, though he did not, as a deeply revisionary theory of rhetoric, keeping his customary synecdoche-metaphor contrast as its basis but radically changing the implications of these terms.

To return for a moment to the central question informing Coleridge's endeavor, is it possible to find genuinely substantial and determined tropes for transcendent concepts? The *Statesman's Manual* passage, as we have seen, as much as says ''in synecdoche and symbol, yes; in metaphor and allegory, no''—and immediately gives us strong causes to mistrust both answers. Those causes, however—the abstractness of light, the determinedness of reflection and shadow—are themselves only metaphoric. Before we can test them further we need to ''return'' them, if possible, in order to learn what kind of actual relationships between a transcendent concept and its representation might occasion these tropes. By 1825 in his *Aids to Reflection*—the title itself punningly intimates as much—Coleridge is undertaking precisely such a rhetorical ''returning.''

The ''Introductory Aphorisms'' of *Aids to Reflection* waste no time in driving to a first basic rhetorical clue: reflection figures reflection; mirroring figures thought. As Coleridge soon

observes, "In order to get the full sense of a word, we should
first present to our minds the visual image that forms its primary meaning" (*AR*, pp. 80–81n). More important to our concerns than this venerable mirror-of-thought figure itself, however, is the contextual transition it implies, which appears
clearly in Coleridge's cunning appropriation of the trope:
"Suppose yourself fronting a mirror. Now what the objects behind you are to their images at the same apparent distance before you, such is reflection to fore-thought" (*AR*, p. 68). Here
the objects spatially behind the man observing them in the mirror figure events which are temporally behind him, incidents
which belong to his history and experience. And this is a significant further clue to the answer we are seeking: the figure of
reflection shows how a determined spatial relationship can represent a determined temporal one.

A similar situation obtains with respect to Coleridge's alternative determined figure for allegory: shadow figures shad-
owing—it figures, that is, either foreshadowing or following,
both of which are determined temporal relationships. In imaginatively reviewing the creation week of Genesis 1, for example, Coleridge exclaims, "who that hath watched their ways
with an understanding heart, could as the vision evolving still
advanced towards him, contemplate the filial and loyal bee; the
home-building, wedded, and divorceless swallow; and above
all the manifoldly intelligent ant tribes . . . and not say to
himself, Behold the shadow of approaching humanity, and the
sun rising from behind, in the kindling morn of creation!" (*AR*,
p. 140). This kind of trope or something very like it is, of
course, familiar to us as the essence of Christian typology,
wherein God is discovered repeatedly to have determinedly
and substantially allegorized his own Incarnation in the actual
persons and events of history. So the figure of shadow, like
that of reflection, can represent a determined temporal relationship as a determined spatial one.

A determined no less than an arbitrary allegory, then, has
the potential for temporal development. This observation in itself affords no new practical guidance to imaging the transcendent; for as Coleridge readily recognizes, "Before and after,
when applied to such subjects, are but allegories, which the

sense of imagination supplies to the understanding" (*AR*, p. 110). Thinking about such imaging in temporal terms may, however, aid our recognition of its essential nature by sensitizing us figuratively to the issue of priority.[18] Just as spatial relationships suggest temporal ones, so do temporal relationships suggest logical ones. And what is it that makes any temporal or spatial allegory determined? One thing: a cause-effect relationship. That which is logically prior determines that which is loglogically consequent. We may determinedly allegorize the transcendent, which is *a priori*, by means of its consequences —and in no other way.

Coleridge still in *Aids to Reflection* ostensibly maintains his familiar oppositions of symbol and allegory, synecdoche and metaphor. "There is, believe me, a wide difference between symbolical and allegorical" (*AR*, pp. 284–285n). The nature of symbols and symbolic expressions, he reaffirms, "is always tautegorical, that is expressing the same subject but with a difference, in contra-distinction from metaphors and similitudes, which are always allegorical, that is, expressing a different subject but with a resemblance" (*AR*, p. 204). Emphatically he insists that the similarity yoking a metaphor's tenor and vehicle is only superficial, the difference separating them fundamental: "All metaphors are grounded on an apparent likeness of things essentially different" (*AR*, p. 158; taken from *Friend*, II, 280). Repeatedly he censures "the (I had almost said dishonest) fashion of metaphorical glosses" in Scriptural exegesis (*AR*, p. 123; see also pp. 166, 189, 285n, 349). When he prepares to analyze the rhetoric of Paul's writings on Christ's redemption of mankind, however, he readily acknowledges it to be metaphoric. But by metaphor Coleridge now suddenly means not the arbitrary, fanciful similitude he has heretofore been decrying, but something far more precise and quite unfamiliar. Paul's judiciously selected figures are distinctive and privileged in that they are determined: they do indeed alle-

18. See Coleridge, *Biographia literaria*, ed. J. Shawcross (Oxford: Oxford University Press, 1907), II, 207: "The sense of Before and After becomes both intelligible and intellectual when, and *only* when, we contemplate the succession in the relations of Cause and Effect."

gorize a transcendent cause by way of some of its consequences.

In Coleridge's newly restrictive sense of the term, a metaphor is a surprisingly complex figure of speech. It represents

> an act, which in its own nature, and as a producing and efficient
> cause, is transcendent; but which produces sundry effects, each of
> which is the same in kind with an effect produced by a cause well
> known and of ordinary occurrence. Now when I characterize or
> designate this transcendent act, in exclusive reference to these its
> effects, by a succession of names borrowed from their ordinary
> causes: not for the purpose of rendering the act itself, or the matter
> of the agency, conceivable, but in order to show the nature and
> magnitude of the benefits received from it, and thus to excite the
> due admiration, gratitude, and love in the receivers; in this case I
> should be rightly described as speaking metaphorically. (*AR*, pp.
> 204–205)

Specifically, Coleridge finds in the Pauline texts four basic
metaphors for the Redemption: sacrificial expiation, reconciliation or atonement, ransom from slavery, and satisfaction of a
creditor's terms by a vicarious payment of the debt. He absolutely denies that these (or any) metaphors can properly characterize the essential nature of redemption or that Paul ever intended them to be so understood, and he goes to some lengths
to show that the last of them, the vicarious satisfaction of a
debt, is in its literal sense irreconcilable and incongruous with
Christian doctrine. The Redemption itself is necessarily unut-
terable, "a spiritual and transcendent mystery, *that passeth all
understanding*" (*AR*, p. 297, quoting Paul in Phil. 4:7). But it
does have various effects—"sanctification from sin, and liberation from the inherent and penal consequences of sin in the
world to come," with accompanying "feelings of joy, confidence, and gratitude"—which are "the same for the sinner
relatively to God and his own soul, as the satisfaction of a debt
for a debtor relatively to his creditor; as the sacrificial atonement made by the priest for the transgressor of the Mosaic
Law; as the reconciliation to an alienated parent for a son who
had estranged himself from his father's house and presence;
and as a redemptive ransom for a slave or captive" (*AR*, pp.

297, 291). A Pauline metaphor for the transcendent act of redemption thus means to be illustrative only of one or a few of the act's consequences, not of their unknowable cause. It figures that cause only at a remove, by way of this resemblance of effects, and does not imply any identity with or similarity to the transcendent cause itself.

What Coleridge is here terming metaphor, then, is in fact but a remarkable subclass of the trope; by some definitions, indeed, it is not a true metaphor at all. We might most accurately, if clumsily, describe it as a particular way of combining two cause-effect metonymies: a familiar act or agent, a known cause, serves as a trope for its known effect; while this effect conversely images a different, transcendent cause of which it is alternatively a consequence.[19] The complete trope itself, despite its seeming complexity, is by no means unnatural or esoteric; it is, however, but infrequently recognized. As I am not aware that it has a name, I shall simply call it determined metaphor, meaning thereby to distinguish it from the more familiar kinds of metaphor, which are indeed, as Coleridge asserts, arbitrary.[20]

Thus guided by Coleridge's analysis, it is now possible to propose another rhetorical principle of allegory: just as metaphor is the fundamental trope of allegory, so is determined metaphor the fundamental trope of determined allegory.

To return to the consideration of how Coleridge extends or revises his rhetorical theory of the symbol in *Aids to Reflection,* it is well to begin by taking note of a certain cautious evasiveness in his argument. At the center of this evasiveness, as

19. If the effects in question are similar but not identical, this figurel combination becomes even more complex: it will now also contain in its middle a metaphoric figuration of one effect by the other.

20. They are arbitrary—illogical or alogical—because they are formed from two conversely related synecdoches, and thus involve the sophism of transition into a new kind. On metaphor as a combination of synecdoches see Jacques Dubois et al., *Rhétorique générale* (Paris: Larousse, 1970), especially pp. 106–112, and the brief summary by Jonathan Culler, *Structuralist Poetics* (Ithaca: Cornell University Press, 1975), pp. 180–181. For Coleridge on the sophism involved see *SM,* p. 99 and n; *AR,* pp. 216, 287.

of the argument itself, is his new emphasis on and understanding of the trope of analogy.

Clearly Coleridge intends analogy here to share the burden of meaning which earlier had been borne by the symbol alone. His association of the two terms is most explicit: "The language is analogous, wherever a thing, power, or principle in a higher dignity is expressed by the same thing, power, or principle in a lower but more known form . . . These analogies are the material, or (to speak chemically) the base, of symbols and symbolic expressions; the nature of which is always tautegorical, that is expressing the same subject but with a difference" (*AR*, p. 204; see also pp. 290, 299). Analogy in this sense is thus but another name for that kind of synecdoche wherein "a lower form or *species* [symbolizes] a higher in the same kind" (*AR*, p. 243n).

Coleridge's appropriation of analogy for his present transcendental purposes prompts two questions. First, is it even possible to image synecdochically the transcendent by the perceptible? (This is, of course, the question which Coleridge begged by his sophistic use of light and translucence in the *Statesman's Manual* passage.) Can a transcendent fact, that is, also be in part—and be known to be—a phenomenal fact? Metaphysically, as Coleridge would have learned from Kant, the answer must be no.[21] Theologically, however, Coleridge would find two occasions for answering yes: the Incarnation and the Eucharist. Hence his privileging of the Johannine "bread of life" and "living water" as symbolic, something we have already seen in *The Statesman's Manual*. Any other instance of such a trope, however, would seemingly have to be illicit. Coleridge himself, moreover, several times says as much: "All the mysteries of faith . . . are intelligible *per se*, not discursively and *per analogiam*. For the truths are unique, and may have shadows and types, but not analogies" (*LR*, p. 402; see also *SM*, p. 67; *Friend*, I, 515).

Second, is analogy indeed, as Coleridge here assumes, a way of representing one thing by another *in the same kind?* In fact quite the contrary is true. As Coleridge himself had earlier

21. See the *Critique of Pure Reason*, B294–315; *Prolegomena to Any Future Metaphysics*, secs. 30, 34.

realized, "Analogy always implies a difference in kind and not merely in degree."[22] His example demonstrates his meaning very clearly: "It is the sameness of the end, with the difference of the means, which constitutes analogy. No one would say the lungs of a man were analogous to the lungs of a monkey, but any one might say that the gills of a fish and the spiracula of insects are analogous to lungs" (*Theory of Life*, p. 404; see also *NB* I, 2319). Countering the lucidity of his example, however, Coleridge's immediately prefatory theoretical statement cannot but give us pause: "It is the sameness of the end, with the difference of the means, which constitutes analogy." As a description of analogy this is somewhat unusual, not to say skewed; but how very aptly it describes what we have just been learning to recognize as determined metaphor! There is all the more reason, then, to explore the relationship of these two tropes.

Let me first adduce as a replacement for Coleridge's a description of analogy with which he was certainly quite familiar. I take it from Kant's *Critique of Judgment*, footnoting section 90: "*Analogy* (in a qualitative signification) is the identity of the relation between reasons and consequences (causes and effects), so far as it is to be found, notwithstanding the specific differences of the things or those properties in them which contain the reason for like consequences (i.e. considered apart from this relation)."[23] Kant here helps us to appreciate that the root trope of analogy is again the cause-effect metonymy. Where a determined metaphor turns on the similarity of two effects, however, an analogy turns on the similarity of two relations between cause and effect—turns, that is, on the similarity of two ratios. Thus analogy, distinct from determined metaphor yet rhetorically cognate with it, constitutes an alternative means of determinedly imaging the transcendent.

As Kant goes on to suggest in some of the passages just

22. *The Notebooks of Samuel Taylor Coleridge*, ed. Kathleen Coburn (Princeton: Princeton University Press, 1957–   ), I, 2319. Hereafter *NB*.

23. Immanuel Kant, *Critique of Judgment*, trans. J. H. Bernard (New York: Macmillan, 1951), p. 315. The entire footnote and the paragraph to which it is appended are relevant, as are Kant's brief discussions of analogy in section 59 of this same *Critique* (pp. 197–200) and in section 58 of the *Prolegomena to Any Future Metaphysics*.

cited, it is quite possible, even traditional, to use analogy to image transcendent concepts. But that Coleridge actually is, as he claims, talking about analogy in *Aids to Reflection* is not at all apparent. Ostensibly he is trying, along the lines of his earlier distinction of symbol from allegory, to demonstrate the presence in the Bible of two alternative modes of representing the spiritual mysteries of Christianity, taking as his examples of analogy and metaphor the Gospel of John (preeminently John 3:6, "That which is born of the flesh, is flesh; that which is born of the Spirit, is Spirit") and the writings of Paul, respectively. His presentation of John 3:6 as an analogy, however, seems notably sophistic. "The latter half of the verse contains the fact asserted; the former half the analogous fact by which it is rendered intelligible" (*AR*, p. 204). But as an analogy this is not tautegorical; it is merely tautelogical, and therefore trivial—like saying that lungs are analogous to lungs. We can analyze Christ's statement to Nicodemus more meaningfully than this, though, by recognizing in it two distinct causes productive of two similar or identical effects: flesh regenerates, spirit regenerates. We can, in other words, take rebirth as a common effect rather than as a common ratio. And despite his vehement denials this is clearly what Coleridge is doing: "The interpretation of the common term is to be ascertained from its known sense, in the more familiar connexion— birth, namely, in relation to our natural life and to the organized body, by which we belong to the present world.— Whatever the word signifies in this connexion, the same essentially (in kind though not in dignity and value) must be its signification in the other" (*AR*, p. 299). But this is, after all, simply to read John 3:6 as a determined metaphor. Once again, as before in *The Statesman's Manual,* Coleridge's great rhetorical opposition, now ostensibly of analogy versus metaphor, ultimately resolves into a common figure.

Coleridge's too-hasty valuation of symbol over allegory in *The Statesman's Manual* may perhaps best be understood as symptomatic of his more fundamental ambition at that time to honor imagination over fancy. Certainly he explicitly identifies the imagination as "that reconciling and mediatory power, which . . . gives birth to a system of symbols . . . consubstantial with the truths, of which they are the *conductors*," even as he correspondingly sees allegories as "empty echoes which the fancy arbitrarily associates with apparitions of matter" (*SM*, pp. 29, 30). Such an excuse seems irrelevant to the parallel and similarly flawed distinction of analogy from metaphor in *Aids to Reflection,* though, for obviously Coleridge does not regard Paul's tropes as abstract or arbitrary—indeed, he cites Paul frequently in *The Statesman's Manual* as exemplary of the Bible's excellence (see especially p. 44).

Let me offer a different explanation for Coleridge's strategy in *Aids to Reflection.* Although the Johannine and Pauline tropes are not, after all, different in kind, they may, I think, be considered to differ in degree. Paul's metaphors tend to be determined by relatively few effects; Coleridge, in fact, typically speaks of a Pauline metaphor as figuring Christ's redemption by way of a single effect only. John's metaphor of rebirth, on the other hand, has the special virtue of yielding simultaneously a great many determined effects, some of Paul's among them: "In the redeemed it is a regeneration, a birth, a spiritual seed impregnated and evolved, the germinal principle of a higher and enduring life, of a spiritual life . . . [It is] an assimilation to the principle of life, even to him who is the Life . . . [It is] at the same time a redemption from the spiritual death" (*AR*, p. 290). I would propose, then, the following distinction: where Paul's tropes are determined metaphors, John's central trope is an overdetermined metaphor. Though the distinction is not Coleridge's, he did in fact figuratively anticipate it years before, in the *Omniana.* I have already cited a passage which may be taken as illustrative of determined metaphor: "The same body casts strangely different shadows in different places and different degrees of light; but . . . it always does shadow out some such truth." But presently Coleridge follows this image up with another: "Let a body be suspended in the air, and strongly illuminated. What figure is here? A triangle. But what here? A trapezium . . . and so on. The same question put to twenty men, in twenty different positions and distances, would receive twenty different answers: and each would be a true answer. But what is that one figure, which being so placed, all these facts of appearance must result, according to the law of perspective . . . ? Aye! this is a different question . . . this is a new subject" (*Omniana*, pp. 180, 181). The new subject, we can now recognize, is that of a highly overdetermined metaphor.

The famous romantic opposition of symbol and allegory, whatever its value in analyzing the rhetoric of ordinary thought, nevertheless in transcendental rhetoric is but an irrelevancy. Coleridge, who made this opposition a commonplace, has misled us badly. But his errors, volitional all, did indeed, as Stephen Dedalus says they would, prove to be the portals of discovery. Beneath the false issue of synecdochic versus metaphoric tropes there lay hidden a genuine, significant crux, that of determined versus arbitrary figuration, the true and inescapable issue for any rhetoric that would strive to be transcendental. And the critic who so frequently and successfully worked to depreciate the practice of allegory became, in his last decade, the one who more than any other began finally to understand and reveal the uniquely privileged status of the mode.

PETER ALLAN DALE

Sartor Resartus and the Inverse Sublime:
The Art of Humorous Deconstruction

Two responses to *Sartor Resartus,* one Victorian and one
modern, will serve to illustrate the sort of reading this work
has characteristically attracted. First, T. H. Huxley's "conversion" experience, as he described it in 1868: "Kicked into
the world—a boy without moral or religious guidance; what
was the agent of my redemption?—Not the hope of immortal-
ity or future reward. It was *Sartor Resartus* that led me to
know that a deep sense of religion was compatible with the entire absence of theology."[1] Next, A. J. LaValley's existentialist account of Carlyle's relation to modern thought, published
more than a century after Huxley's remarks, in which he says
of *Sartor* that "Carlyle's faith issues in Tillich's terms from the
deepest part of the self, where it is in contact with both being
and nonbeing . . . Within the self both the Ideal, the power
of being, as well as the impediment, the threat of nonbeing
exist. Hence it is this self which alone must fashion the new
myth for the society to be reborn in the phoenix death-re-

1. Leonard Huxley, *Life and Letters of T. H. Huxley* (New York: D. Apple-
ton, 1900), I, 237.

birth."[2] Widely separated in time and philosophic outlook as
these two readings are, they still have in common two things.
Both treat *Sartor* as if it were a book primarily about ideas, the
idea of a religion without theology in Huxley's case, of a religion of the self, in LaValley's; and both treat these ideas as if
Carlyle had offered them in the most earnest imaginable manner. Neither is at all concerned with what is certainly the key
question of the book, the question woefully posed by Teufelsdröckh's long-suffering editor, of why a man with "real
Thoughts to communicate" should resolve to "emit them in a
shape bordering so closely on the absurd?"[3]

I shall urge another sort of reading altogether, a reading according to which *Sartor* is a book not about ideas but about the
symbolic forms that convey ideas, and according to which the
humorous element, far from being incidental, is organically involved in the writer's attempt to understand the peculiar status
of symbolic form in the early nineteenth century.

On what grounds do I contend that the book's central problem is the problem of form? To begin with, there is the nature
of Carlyle's two protagonists—and there are, of course, two
protagonists, two quite distinct personalities that govern the
development of the book, the philosopher Diogenes Teufelsdröckh and the man who is writing about him, the nameless
narrator or "Editor." Both men are writers. Teufelsdröckh
has written a volume, which he calls the *Philosophy of
Clothes,* and is in the process of writing a sequel, the *Palingen-
esie der menschlichen Gesellschaft (Newbirth of Society).* He
has also written, although not for publication, a great quantity
of disconnected autobiographical information. The Editor is
writing a book (*Sartor Resartus*) that is an interpretation of
Teufelsdröckh and his opinions. Both men—and this is the

2. A. J. LaValley, *Carlyle and the Idea of the Modern: Studies in Carlyle's
Prophetic Literature and Its Relation to Blake, Nietzsche, Marx, and Others*
(New Haven and London: Yale University Press, 1968), p. 84.
3. Thomas Carlyle, *Sartor Resartus,* in *Sartor Resartus and Selected Prose,*
ed. Herbert Sussman (New York: Holt, Rinehart, and Winston, 1970), p. 265.
All further citations will be to this, the most recent, edition of *Sartor* and will
be in the text.

main point—see their vocation as writers specifically in terms
of a responsibility to *organize* or *shape* their respective materials. Teufelsdröckh's material is the confused mass of "things
in general," of reality itself. Everywhere he looks he sees a
"chaos" of experience which can no longer be contained by
the forms of thought that once made it intelligible. It is his special mission in life to give this chaos a new form. "In times like
ours," runs the "half-official" Weissnichtwo statement of his
professional responsibilities, "when all things are, rapidly or
slowly, resolving themselves into Chaos," a professorship is
needed to "facilitate" the "bodying forth" again of "somewhat" in the way of order (46). For the Editor Teufelsdröckh's
effort at order is itself a chaos. The Volume on Clothes and the
fragments of autobiography suffer from "an almost total want
of arrangement" (59). Thus does he "sit . . . deciphering
these unimaginable Documents . . . endeavouring to evolve
printed Creation out of a German printed and written Chaos"
(96). In short, then, we have a book, *Sartor Resartus,* the express purpose of which is to re-form the confusion of another
book, which itself is attempting to re-form the confusion of
reality.

A second reason for seeing *Sartor* as a book about form lies
in the nature of the Clothes Philosophy itself. This is, if one
thinks about it, essentially a philosophy about the way men
structure their experience. Clothes, in Teufelsdröckh's highly
metaphoric way of thinking, represent forms of thought and
perception. The "deepest" meaning of clothes, says the sage
of Weissnichtwo, who like his creator has apparently dipped
into Kant, is as the Space and Time "Thought-forms" (240)
through which we receive our most immediate experiences,
forms "spun and woven for us from before Birth itself" (238).[4]
Beyond this all language, all signs, all social, political, and economic organization (81–82, 91, 237–238) are seen by Teufelsdröckh as varieties of clothes in the sense that they give

4. Carlyle had read approximately a hundred pages of the *Critique of Pure
Reason* and had a rudimentary understanding of the "transcendental aesthetic." The best discussion of Carlyle's knowledge of Kant is in René Wellek's *Immanuel Kant in England* (Princeton: Princeton University Press,
1931), pp. 183–202.

visible shape to an otherwise inchoate experience. Most important, there are "Church-clothes," which are " 'in our vocabulary, the Forms, the *Vestures,* under which men have at
various periods embodied and represented for themselves the
Religious Principle' " (201–202). Teufelsdröckh is, in fact,
quite a modern philosopher. He is not concerned at all with
constructing a particular belief system. What fascinates him,
rather, are the constantly changing structures of belief, or
more precisely, the symbolic presentations of belief that man
relies upon to interpret himself and his world.

The conception of *Sartor* rests on what its author takes to be
a fundamental and unending opposition in experience between
chaos and form. We are constantly told by the Editor and still
more impressively by Teufelsdröckh that man exists as a consciousness in the midst of an "immeasurable circumambient
realm of Nothingness and Night" (36), a boundless, orderless
flux.[5] What we must do in the face of this chaos, indeed, what
we instinctually do do is attempt to counteract it or render it
tolerable by various intellectual constructions of our own. We
strive to establish "habitable colonies" of the mind in the
midst of the immeasurable and unintelligible (36).

The concept of form for Carlyle is essentially a concept of a
clear, if arbitrary, delineation of experience. Through form the
"inarticulate" is rendered "decisive" and "discernible."
Form is not something that is, as it were, always there ready to
be discovered, as it is with Plato, but something—and this is
the key point—that emerges dialectically through time. His
concern is with the *process* of formation, with the way order
derives from and gradually "articulates" experience. The
chemical metaphor which he uses to describe the Editor's enterprise, like the "hourly advancing" shape of the book itself,
nicely expresses this sense of form as becoming rather than
being. "As in some chemical mixture, that has stood long

5. The experience of chaos is expressed on many levels in the book. The
entire universe for Carlyle is in flux, as is society (50), as is the individual self
(160), and, of course, the text and style of the book itself constantly aim at
conveying the impression of disorder.

evaporating, but would not crystallize, instantly when the wire or other fixed substance is introduced, *crystallisation commences . . . Form rose* out of void solution and discontinuity; *like united itself with like* in definite arrangement; and soon . . . the image of the whole Enterprise had shaped itself, so to speak, into a solid mass" (40–41; italics mine).

The tendency to see form as a process is a characteristic Carlyle shares with the romantics. Where he differs from them (and most notably from Coleridge) is in his insistence on regarding the formative process not as a spontaneous or organic one analogous to the growth of a plant, but as a fundamentally factitious, man-motivated and -controlled process. The clothes-forms by which we govern our lives are expressions of man's "'Tool-using'" nature (65–66); they are his "works," his "victory of Art over Nature" (80); they are, that is, neither natural nor divine, but decisively *cultural* phenomena. The significance of this distinction becomes clearer if we consider for a moment the concept of the imagination which for Carlyle, as for his romantic predecessors, was a concept intimately associated with the formative process.

Imagination for Coleridge, whom I will take as my exemplar of romantic theory, is the distinctively formative power. It is "that reconciling and mediatory power, which incorporates the reason in images of the sense, and organizes (as it were) the flux of the senses by the permanence and self-circling energies of the reason."[6] Similarly, Carlyle in *Sartor* tends to locate the formative power in man's capacity imaginatively to project a shape on experience. There are, he says, "outflashings of man's Freewill" that "lighten, more and more . . . the Chaotic Night that [threatens] to engulf [him] in its . . . horrors" (199). These "outflashings" are leaps of the mind into the realm of the "fantastic" (205) where it envisions the shape of things to come. Imagination constructs the "symbols" by which the inexpressible is expressed; it weaves "'Garments, visible Bodies, wherein the else invisible creations and inspira-

6. S. T. Coleridge, *The Statesman's Manual*, ed. R. J. White, in *The Collected Works*, ed. Kathleen Coburn (London and Princeton: Princeton University Press, 1969–   ), VI, 28–29.

tions of our Reason are, like Spirits, revealed, and first become all-powerful' " (91).

The difference between the two men's thought lies essentially in the degree of reality each is prepared to allow to the imagination's projections, to the forms—or as each tends to think of them, the *symbols*—into which the mind organizes experience. In Coleridge's case it is quite clear that imagination is an expression in the finite mind of a divine force making for unity in both the human and natural world. Accordingly, the forms or symbols which the imagination produces are real in the Platonic sense that they express the actual order, the God-given order, that exists behind the appearance of things. "[Imagination] gives birth to a system of symbols, harmonious in themselves, and consubstantial with the truths of which they are the conductors."[7] In Carlyle's case there is no such clear assertion that the imagination is a divine expression or that its symbols are "consubstantial" with the true order of the world. For him the imagination's order is imaginative or fantastic very much in the sense of being unreal. To create form is a constant necessity of the mind, but Carlyle makes absolutely no claims for the reality or universality of the forms the mind creates. On the contrary, the whole point of the clothes-making rather than the organic metaphor for the formative process is to insist upon the artificial, temporary, and superficial nature of the forms in which we place experience.

Thus as we move from Coleridge's concept of the formative process to Carlyle's, we are moving from a process that is safely anchored in the divine and consequently in the reality of things, to a process that has implicit in it a very strong element of unreality or fictiveness. Man makes his own forms, and because it is he that makes them and not God or nature or any other absolute these forms have no necessary existence. Their existence is contingent upon the times and conditions under which they were constructed.

An inevitable corollary of this position is a preoccupation with the radical instability of form. The forms that man makes have their day, but they cannot last; it is in their manmade na-

7. Ibid.

ture to decay or "wear out" with time. Thus even as he urges the necessity of form Carlyle accepts—indeed, is preoccupied by—the fact that form once achieved has nowhere to go but toward dissolution. Everywhere, he says, we find the "'tatters and rags of superannuated worn-out Symbols . . . dropping off'" (211). So much a part of experience is this instability of form that we need a "Legislator"-critic (the contrast with Shelley's legislator-poet is undoubtedly intended) who will help us carry the inadequate forms off when they no longer serve, one "who can tell when a Symbol has grown old, and gently remove it" (211).

Carlyle's formative process, as we can now begin to see, may best be described as a historical dialectic. The finite imagination of man erects certain structures, "colonies of the mind," which enable him to cope with experience. These structures, far from being permanent or real in any religious or metaphysical sense, are time-bound and as such must inevitably wear out and decay. As this happens, the imaginative ingenuity of man again comes into play and, as it were, in self-defense constructs other more viable forms to replace the outmoded ones, and so on from one age to another. It is this *historicization* of the concept of form that finally most distinguishes Carlyle's thought from that of his major English romantic predecessors.

Implicit in what I am calling the historicization of form is a potential for skepticism or irreverence that does not exist, for example, in Coleridge. If one is struck, as Carlyle is so forcibly struck, by the fictiveness, the instability of form, one can be rather more offhand about it than if one believes that it is part of the inherent nature of things.

Teufelsdröckh's plan for re-forming the chaos of his experience is regarded by Editor and, *a fortiori*, author alike with the utmost irony. Indeed the whole point of introducing the Editor is to keep the reader's attention firmly fixed on the unreality of Teufelsdröckh's formative mission. "The Editor [must] give utterance to a painful suspicion, which through late Chapters, has begun to haunt him . . . It is a suspicion . . . confirmed almost into certainty by the . . . humoristico-satirical tendency of Teufelsdröckh . . .: a suspicion, in one word, that these Autobiographical Documents are partly a mystification! What if many a so-called Fact were little better than a Fiction'' (192). And, of course, even without the Editor's constant hesitations we have a text that everywhere undermines the seriousness of its characters' activity. For an obvious example, how can we take seriously the philosophic efforts of a man named Diogenes Teufelsdröckh?

Plainly there is potential in Carlyle's historicized concept of form for a skepticism that extends to despair. One has only to look at what happens to the concept farther down the Victorian road, for example, in the Tennyson of the pessimistic sections of *In Memoriam,* the Arnold of *Empedocles,* the George Eliot of *Mill on the Floss,* and so on. But in Carlyle's case and at this relatively early point in his career, the more disturbing aspects of the historicity of form are largely suppressed. The dominant mood is decidedly humorous. The stumbling efforts of men to place an intelligible order on experience, the inevitable dissolution of the orders they create are the occasion here for laughter and sympathy, not tears and anxiety.

Exactly what is it that is funny in *Sartor?* What we laugh at in the book is, in a word, an elaborate breakdown in communication. Humor, as Carlyle's mentor in these matters, Jean Paul Richter, has said, is primarily a matter of misunderstanding (*unverständige*);[8] Don Quixote, for example, is ridiculous charging windmills because there is a discrepancy between his understanding of reality and that of the rest of mankind. If the communication between Don Quixote and his own world, or between Don Quixote and his reader were better, we would laugh a good deal less. In *Sartor* the misunderstanding resides almost exclusively on the structural and linguistic levels. Teufelsdröckh's heroism is expressed not, like Quixote's, in knight-errantry, but, like that of his romantic predecessors, in poetic prophecy. His mission is ultimately to deliver his fellow man from the Age of Unbelief by weaving for him a new reli-

8. J. P. Richter, *School for Aesthetics,* trans. Margaret Hale under the title *Horn of Oberon* (Detroit: Wayne State University Press, 1973), pp. 76–81. See also Hale's introduction, pp. xxvii–xxix.

gious mythus, a new vestiture of the Infinite. His medium, as he continually tells us, is the "miracle" of language. His great problem is to transmute his vision of the Infinite into a suitable symbolic form: "'How paint to the sensual eye . . . what passes in the Holy-of-Holies of Man's Soul; in what words, known to these profane times, speak even afar-off of the unspeakable?'" (180). What makes a suitable symbolic form as far as Carlyle is concerned is, simply, that form's ability to convince others and carry them along in belief: "'Mystical, more than magical, is that Communing of Soul with Soul, both looking heavenward: here properly Soul first speaks with Soul . . . How true is that of Novalis: "It is certain, my Belief gains quite *infinitely* the moment I can convince another mind thereof"'!'" (202).

This, of course, is a common view of the romantic hero: he is the poet-prophet who must not simply *see* the Infinite but contain it in a symbol, a mythus, which others can understand and believe in. Thus Shelley, for a notable example, insists that the poet must not only "participate" in "the eternal, the infinite, and the one" but that he must also "redeem" this otherworldly experience from "decay" by expressing it in some allegorical or metaphoric form, some "picture of integral thought," which will in turn "produce the moral improvement of man."[9] Common too is the romantic poet-prophet's need for another, a friend who will alleviate his doubts over whether, in fact, he is making himself understood.

Against this background we see that Teufelsdröckh approaches being something very like a parody of the romantic poet-prophet (just as Quixote is a parody of the knight-errant). He, or rather his situation in *Sartor,* embodies all the fears that one finds among romantic mythmakers about being misunderstood, about being taken for a fool or a madman. Indeed, the single most important characteristic of the sage of Weissnichtwo is that he cannot be understood. The overall form of his book is a chaos, and his language is a "mystification": "A wild tone pervades the whole utterance of the man, like its keynote

9. P. B. Shelley, "A Defence of Poetry," in *The Complete Works,* ed. R. Ingpen, and W. E. Peck (London and New York: Gordian Press, 1965), VII, 111–112, 117.

and regulator; now screwing itself aloft as into the Song of Spirits, or else the shrill mockery of Fiends; now sinking in cadences, not without melodious heartiness, though sometimes abrupt enough, into the common pitch, when we hear it only as a monotonous hum; of which hum the true character is extremely difficult to fix" (57). "No man's actions appear ridiculous to himself," says Richter, "except an hour later when he has already become a second self."[10] The Editor is Teufelsdröckh's second self, and his function is not, as it would be in high romantic poetry, to reassure the hero that he is making sense, that he is *believable* (as in Wordsworth's use of Coleridge in *The Prelude*). His function, rather, is precisely what Richter suggests: to provide a second ironic, "misunderstanding" perspective in the light of which all the hero's most earnestly held convictions become just a little and often more than just a little ridiculous.

Carlyle, then, has created something of a romantic antihero in Teufelsdröckh, for the latter is an outlandish failure as a poetic mythmaker, as a maker of form and of language, in an era in which such a maker was for many the supreme ideal, the hero for the times. The creation of such an antihero might in other circumstances be taken as an expression of extreme skepticism over the validity of the whole romantic mythopoeic program for the revitalization of belief through the vision of imaginative genius. In the case of *Sartor,* however, we stop well short of such a conclusion. Although Teufelsdröckh has failed himself to achieve the sublime romantic mission, he (like his creator) still believes in the possibility of such a mission (see 232–233). More to the present point, however, the prevailing humorous tone of the book persistently defeats any potential movement toward despair. The humor, the essentially friendly and sympathetic rather than satiric laughter that Teufelsdröckh and his Editor inspire, keeps the reader constantly in mind of the fact that the ultimate aim of the book is not Denial but Affirmation.

What Teufelsdröckh stands for, in the end, is not the impossibility of the romantic enterprise, but the comic inversion of

10. Richter, *Aesthetics*, p. 79.

it, just as Quixote, stood for the comic inversion of the chivalric enterprise. The comic inversion of a dominant literary-cum-spiritual ideal does not represent a failure of faith in that ideal. What is involved, rather, is a mature recognition of the realities that tend to undermine or block the ideal, and the hope of somehow redeeming that ideal by indirection, by the act of comic criticism, or as I say in my title, humorous deconstruction. Teufelsdröckh's function, then, is not so much romantic mythmaking or prophecy as it is "'rag-gathering'" and "'rag-burning'" (233) in preparation for genuine prophecy.

The humor in *Sartor,* as I have said, resides almost exclusively on the structural and linguistic levels. What this means may best be understood by considering what Carlyle has taken from the German humorist Richter. Carlyle knew Richter's work intimately and, in fact, introduced it both through translation and critical commentary to the English reading public. No one who reads the two men's works together can fail to observe that the German's style, his characters, and much of his general understanding of life have inspired *Sartor.*[11]

Of the many things Carlyle learned from Richter about humorous style, the most important, to my reading, was the art of "sporting" with the text. In Richter, as later in Carlyle, this sporting takes primarily two forms. On the one hand there is an intensely self-conscious disruption of the overall structure of the text by constant editorial or narratorial comment; on the other there is the creation of an outrageous form of language, which becomes the most distinctive characteristic of the humorous character.

In Richter the disruption of overall literary structure in-

11. A number of scholars have written on the influence of Richter on *Sartor.* The most complete study is J. P. Smeed's excellent "Thomas Carlyle and J. P. Richter" (*Comparative Literature,* 16 [1964], 226–253). Smeed, however, while he is very thorough in tracing stylistic influences, tends to discount Carlyle's understanding of the philosophical aspects of Richter's concept of humor (Carlyle "ignores the basically metaphysical view of humor" in Richter [p. 228]). One of the main points of my own argument is that Carlyle, in fact, understood very well and to a large degree reproduced Richter's metaphysical concept of humor in *Sartor.*

volves an ironic commentator who periodically stops the development of the story (much in the manner of Carlyle's Editor) to draw attention to the difficulties of writing and organizing a text and ultimately to the absurdity of the bookmaking process itself. Thus in *Schulmeisterleins Wutz,* an example which I choose because of its close parallel to *Sartor's* situation of one writer self-consciously trying to organize the life and opinions of another, Richter will do things such as this: "I would really have known little about the whole man [Wutz] if [his wife] had not been standing at the door as I went by last year on the twelfth of May. As she saw me writing in my notebook while I walked, she asked me if I was not also a maker of books. 'Of course, dear lady,' I replied, 'I produce one every year and present it to the public.' In that case, then, she asked, would I come into the house and spend some time with her old man, who was also an author." Or this: "While I am in this frame of mind, please don't ask me to tell you about the Schoolmaster's many happy moments, as he himself describes them in his *Book of Joy* . . . Perhaps they may appear in a postscript on some future occasion, but not today!"[12] For another instance, here is Richter's narrator commenting on the textual confusion of *Schmelzles Reise nach Flätz,* an example I choose partly because Carlyle translated it and partly because it foreshadows another characteristic device of *Sartor,* an editor's desire for "conveniency and order" gone madly astray.

> [I] must . . . apologize for the singular form of this little Work, standing as it does on a substratum of Notes . . . But the truth is, this line of demarcation, stretching through the whole book, originated in the following accident; certain thoughts (or digressions) of my own, with which it was not permitted to disturb those of the Army-chaplain, and which could only be allowed to fight behind the lines, in the shape of Notes, I, with a view to conveniency and order, had written down in a separate paper; at the same time, as will be observed, regularly providing every Note with its Number, and thus referring it to the proper page of the main Manuscript. But

12. J. P. Richter, *Life of the Cheerful Schoolmaster Maria Wutz,* trans. J. Grayson, in *Nineteenth Century German Tales,* ed. A. Flores (New York: Doubleday, 1959), p. 30.

in the copying of the latter, I had forgotten to insert the corresponding numbers in the Text itself . . . Well, the thing at any rate is done, nay perpetuated, namely printed.[13]

The second of Richter's principal ways of sporting with the text, the creation of an outrageous language, involves a number of things: for example, abundant use of neologisms and compound words, and a disruption of syntax that repeats the larger disruption of the text's overall structure (recall Teufelsdröckh's "quite broken-backed and dismembered" sentences [57]). But the real heart of Richter's humorous language is the highly self-conscious and highly strained use of metaphor.[14] The "metaphorical sensuous style," he writes in his *Vorschule der Ästhetik,* is the style peculiar to the humorous: the humorous "representation should overflow with images and with witty and imaginative contrasts,"[15] thus one finds Richter's humorous characters constantly crowding their speech, as one of them puts it, with "metaphorical *ricochet-shots,*"[16] linguistic diversions that send the mind flying every which way from the subject at hand and, in this, contribute further to the comic disruption of form (in this case linguistic form) that we saw in the case of the editorial interventions. Here, for example, is a passage from *Quintus Fixlein,* also translated by Carlyle:

In the choir, this Free-haven and Ethnic Forecourt of stranger church-goers, [Quintus] smiled on all parishioners; and, as in his childhood, standing under the wooden wing of an archangel, he looked down on the coiffed parterre: His young years now inclosed him like children in their smiling circle and a long garland wound itself in rings among them, and by fits they plucked flowers from it and threw them in his face. Was it not old Senior Astman that stood there on the pulpit Parnassus? . . . [And] was there not a church-

13. J. P. Richter, *Schmelzle's Journey to Flätz,* in *German Romance,* trans. T. Carlyle (Boston, 1841) II, 144–145.

14. This point is made of Richter by Wolfdietrich Rasch in *Der Erzählweise Jean Pauls* (Munich: Hanser, 1961), pp. 31–41.

15. Richter, *Aesthetics,* pp. 99–100. See also Hale's introduction, p. xxiv.

16. J. P. Richter, *Hesperus,* in *Werke* (Munich: Hanser, 1960), I, 578: "'Sie konnte unmöglich metaphorische *Rikoschet-Schusse* in diese Zeile laden.'"

library of consequence . . . lying under the minever cover of pastil dust . . . And could he not at present . . . have wished to cast this alphabetic soft-fodder into the Hebrew letter-trough whereto your Oriental Rhizophagi (Rooteaters) are tied?[17]

Carlyle in the writing of *Sartor* was, like Richter, very much preoccupied by the use and meaning of metaphor. We see this in explicit statement—"Metaphors are [the] stuff [of language]: examine Language; what, if you except some few primitive elements (of natural sound), what is it all but Metaphors, recognised as such, or no longer recognised; still fluid and florid, or now solid-grown and colourless? . . . Metaphors [are Language's] . . . living integuments" (91)—and see it as well in Teufelsdröckh's and the Editor's own metaphoric "ricochet-shots" which are almost certainly themselves rebounding off Richter's distinctive style. As the Editor says it is the nature of Teufelsdröckh that "if he can but set [his thought] on the back of a Figure, he cares not whither it gallop" (193). " 'Wondrous indeed is the virtue of a true Book [writes Teufelsdröckh]. Not like a dead city of stones, yearly crumbling, yearly needing repair; more like a tilled field, but then a spiritual field: like a spiritual tree, let me rather say, it stands from year to year, and from age to age . . . ; and yearly comes its new produce of leaves (Commentaries, Deductions, Philosophical, Political systems . . .), every one of which is talismanic and thaumaturgic, for it can persuade men' " (169–170).

Through the model of Richter, then, we see more clearly the essential "mechanics"—if you like—of Carlyle's humorous composition. Stylistically, humor depends, with the Englishman as with the German, on what we may call the unexpected disruption of our normal expectations about literary and linguistic form. We expect things to move in a particular order and according to customary rules. When this order and these rules are violated there is an immediate potential for humor, as there always is in situations of significant incongruity, the incongruity in this case being between what we are accustomed to in the way of convention and what is actually hap-

17. J. P. Richter, *Quintus Fixlein,* in *German Romance,* trans. T. Carlyle, II, 223.

pening before us on the page. Obviously such a disruption of
expectations need not necessarily be funny. But when, as in
the case of both these writers, the disruption is at once naive,
in the sense of proceeding from apparent ignorance of the fact
that conventions are being violated, and harmless, in the sense
of being so clearly eccentric as to present no real threat to accustomed order, then the result is humorous.

Carlyle, however, was fascinated not simply by the mechanics but also by the meaning of the German humorist's
unique style. For Carlyle, as, indeed, for Richter himself, one
could not separate style from overall outlook on life. Richter's
work was formally and linguistically intriguing and not a little
disconcerting. It was on the surface an "Indian jungle, a
boundless unparalleled imbroglio, nothing on all sides but
darkness, dissonance, confusion." Yet, Carlyle believed, it
had some central order, some higher meaning than met the
eye: "The farther we advance into [Richter's work], we see
confusion more and more unfold itself into order, till at last,
viewed from its proper centre, his intellectual universe, no
longer a distorted incoherent series of air-landscapes, coalesces into compact expansion; a vast, magnificent and vari-
gated scene . . . the anarchy is not without its purpose."[18]
I do not think Carlyle understood at the time he wrote this
essay (1827) exactly what that order within apparent confusion
was. He knew from Richter's own theoretical works that it had
something to do with what the latter called the "inverse sublime," but he was not prepared to articulate what that meant.[19]
What one does see in the essay on Richter is a recognition
that the German's "confused," "dissonant" style has something to do with a reaction against the ordinary channels or
forms in which the thought of his day was conveyed. Thus Carlyle complains of minds "forcibly crushed into foreign

18. T. Carlyle, *Works,* ed. H. D. Traill (London, 1896–1899), XXVI,
14.
19. Carlyle's comments on the inverse sublime in the 1827 essay (*Works,*
XXVL, 16–17) suggest no real understanding of what Richter was saying
about it in the *Vorschule.* Hence, perhaps, Smeed's belief that Carlyle was ignorant of the metaphysical implications of Richter's theory of humor.

moulds," of men who "move smoothly in the old-established railways of custom." Against this tendency to be contained by unsatisfactory forms he sets what he calls the "true law of culture," the law, that is, which Richter exemplifies: "Let each become all that he was created capable of being; expand if possible to full growth, resisting all impediments . . . and show himself at length in his own shape and stature, be these what they may."[20] In short, Richter's eccentricity of style is interpreted as an expression of the individual spirit's efforts to throw off uncongenial forms, to escape the "beaten paths of Literature" to find that new shape or structure that most suitably expresses his needs.

A similar opposition between received cultural forms and the efforts of the free spirit to move beyond these is, as I have already amply indicated, at the heart of Carlyle's philosophic, as opposed to stylistic, enterprise in *Sartor*. The process, again, is what Teufelsdröckh's Clothes Philosophy is all about: the threadbare clothes-forms of society must go up in phoenix flames so that the soul may be free to express itself anew.

How exactly the "confused" and "dissonant" style that Carlyle found in Richter and reproduced in *Sartor* functions to free the spirit, to bring it closer to the so-called true law of its being, may be briefly indicated. What Carlyle has called "sporting" with the text has the effect of keeping the reader constantly mindful of the radical instability and artificiality of both literary and grammatical-cum-semantic form.

This is readily apparent in the case of the disruption of the overall structure of their books. For both writers this disruption involves primarily the use, or rather the overuse, of the narrator. This narrator, absurdly self-conscious of his responsibility to order his text and at the same time terribly insecure about his competence to do so, constantly projects himself on the reader's attention. The effect is clear. As Richter puts it, it is in the nature of the humorist to allow the editorial insertions to play the primary role in his story, and his purpose in doing this is precisely to draw attention to the limitations of received forms and the awkwardness of trying to contain the freedom

20. Carlyle, *Works*, XXVI, 19–21.

and vitality that is life itself within them: "Hence with every humorist the 'I' plays the primary role; wherever he can, he drags his personal circumstances into his comic theater, although only in order to annihilate these poetically."[21] The poetical "annihilation" Richter is talking about here involves, as I understand him, the self-conscious destruction of that clarity of shape which constitutes not only personal identity but every structure on which identity depends and which, however reassuring, still keeps the spirit from expanding, from fully expressing its infinite potential, its "true law."

Similarly, if we examine what Carlyle is doing with language in *Sartor* and particularly with Teufelsdröckh, whose language is the most interesting thing about him, the essence of his humoristic character, we find that what concerns him is, again, the need to disrupt normal structures of communication. Thus an opposition is set up between Teufelsdröckh's "exaggerated" speech and the more or less plain style of the Editor (although, as the Editor says, his speech becomes progressively infected by Teufelsdröckh's). As far as the Editor is concerned Teufelsdröckh's language is an abuse of "plain words" (180) and the "purity" of thought and form that he associates with normal English speech (265).[22]

The most distinctive quality of Teufelsdröckh's effort to break out of the "prison-speech" he has inherited is, again, the use of outlandish and excessive metaphor. Metaphor, says Richter is the "transubstantiation of spirit," the embodiment in concrete and communicable form of one's thought, and as such it is the basic stuff of all language usage, a point with which Carlyle, as we have seen, is in agreement. The humorous use of metaphor, however, is more than this. It is metaphor calling excessive attention to itself as a destroyer of normal categories of thought, as that which yokes together things

21. Cited by Rasch, *Der Erzählweise Jean Pauls,* pp. 8–9, my translation. See also Richter, *Aesthetics,* pp. 91–99.
22. The case for plain language is carried on in a number of treatises on language in the late eighteenth and early nineteenth centuries. According to George Campbell in *The Philosophy of Rhetoric* (2nd ed. [London, 1801]), a major source of poor communication is excessive and heterogeneous metaphors (II, 60, 161).

we ordinarily think of as separate, for example books and tilled
fields, leaves and philosophic tracts, speech and Pandemonian
lava, the word of God and man's force of free will. The principal metaphor of *Sartor* is, of course, the metaphor of clothes
for ideas or forms of thought. To say that forms of thought,
especially religious beliefs, are like clothes is to disrupt in a
profound way our normal categories of thought about religion.
It is to make religion mean something quite different from what
we are accustomed to having it mean; a concept that is normally associated with the transcendent and imperishable we
are now being asked to associate with the superficial and tran-
sitory. Of this effect of humorous metaphor in Richter, Wolfdietrich Rasch, from whose splendid study of the German
writer's art I have learned a great deal that has helped me to
understand what Carlyle is doing in *Sartor,* writes, "Metaphor, the exchange of names, the transmutation of things, has
the power of loosening up and dissolving the rigidity of the objective world. 'Chemica non agunt nisi soluta' (i.e., only fluidity allows the freedom necessary to form a new organization—
or: new shapes come only from liberated bodies). Therefore
metaphor, which has value as a figure of speech and also as a
place filler, has value as well, in itself, as a poetical principle."[23] Metaphor liberates the rigidity of experience as customarily received and in doing so makes possible the imagination of new shapes.

In summary, then, we can say that *Sartor* not only in the
Clothes Philosophy that it conveys but also in its self-regarding
literary form and in the distinctive language of its principal
character is an exercise in structure drawing attention to itself,
the point of which is to emphasize the ephemerality or, again,
the historicity of all form. The historicization of the concept of
form, which is the burden of Carlyle's "real Thought," invites
the humorous mood; the particular expression of that mood is
a style that wonderfully supports the larger philosophic point.

To leave the argument here would be to give an essentially
aesthetic answer to the original question of why Teufelsdröckh
expresses "real Thoughts" in such an absurd shape. He does
so because his creator sees what his Editor does not: the shape

23. Rasch, *Der Erzählweise Jean Pauls*, p. 31, my translation.

of his style, absurd as it may seem, nonetheless conforms quite nicely to the meaning of his philosophy. But is the aesthetic answer enough? I think not, particularly in the case of this writer, for Carlyle was notoriously adverse to merely aesthetic explanations. The aim of his humor, like the aim of the romantic mythopoeic enterprise it rests upon, like the aim of his work in general, is ultimately directed beyond the text toward the transformation of the world itself. Carlyle sports with the forms that others take for granted as part of the nature of things. He makes the reader laugh at these forms with the intention of freeing him alike from their restraints and the fear of their dissolution. Humor or laughter thus becomes a *gentle* (the word in this context is Carlyle's own) deconstructing agent in a social and intellectual, literary and linguistic context in which the author is convinced that deconstruction is absolutely essential if society is to advance to a more satisfactory form of spiritual deliverance.

We come back again to Richter's notion of humor as the "inverted sublime" or, as he also calls it, "negative infinity." Humor, he says, "annihilates . . . the finite through its contrast with the idea. It recognizes no individual foolishness, no fools, but only folly and a mad world. Humor annihilates both great and small because before infinity everything is equal and nothing."[24] This definition of humor follows, in fact, from Richter's definition of the romantic. A romantic consciousness for him is one that seeks "beauty without limit." The basis of romanticism is an "all-animating religion that breaks down the world of sense by breathing a spirit into it." One may find the voice of romanticism throughout Richter's work: "By Heaven! it is no wonder that man rises and will go on; for . . . does not Freedom's breath blow on the ever-varying Eden, when released from the neck- and heart-breaking chains of narrow circumstances, we fly freely and gladly, as in dreams, over ever new scenes . . . [My Friend], nothing is confined in so many prison-walls as is this our human-self."[25] There is no irony, no humor here, only an earnest, essentially

24. Richter, *Aesthetics,* p. 88. See the entire discussion of the subject, pp. 88–94.

25. J. P. Richter, *Campaner Thal,* trans. Juliette Bauer, in *Campaner Thal and Other Writings* (New York, 1864), pp. 23–24.

Platonic longing to escape the bonds of the senses, and one may, of course, find exactly the same "romantic" longings throughout Carlyle.[26]

The humorist shares with the romanticist this longing for the infinite, this sense of the oppressiveness of finitude and all limiting forms. But he is a romanticist manqué. He lacks the ability to satisfy his needs by creating a positive vision of infinite beauty. All that he can do is play with, disrupt, and ultimately "annihilate" through laughter the forms that fail to satisfy or that oppress him. This is his inverse route to the Infinite. The process of annihilation, while less satisfactory than the process of reconstruction, nonetheless, remains for him a cheerful process, for he annihilates in the faith that beyond all forms there is finally a spiritual force, a sublime entity that survives their destruction and fuels the next generation's efforts to achieve the ideal. As Richter puts it, humor is a kind of mock apocalypse; it can sport with chaos in supreme confidence of spiritual rebirth: "Insofar as a Day of Judgment precipitates the material world into a second chaos, simply in order to hold divine judgment, humor would conceivably seem to approach madness, which naturally renounces the senses and common sense . . . and yet like the philosopher retains reason; humor is a raving Socrates as the ancients called Diogenes."[27] Like Richter's ancient Diogenes, Carlyle's modern one has given us a chaos that—to recur to Carlyle's own early judgment on Richter's style—has "its proper center," its proper purpose, once we look at it from the right perspective.

26. For instance, quite unironically expressed, in *Heroes and Hero Worship*, Carlyle, *Works*, V, 9–10, 82–85.

27. Richter, *Aesthetics*, p. 99. It is not unlikely that this passage influenced Carlyle's choice of the name and character of his hero in *Sartor*.

HARRIET RITVO

Gothic Revival Architecture in England and America: A Case Study in Public Symbolism

In 1834 fire destroyed the Houses of Parliament. They needed to be replaced, it was generally agreed, by a building not only commodious and convenient, but expressive of the historic significance of Parliament in English society and of the place of the English nation in the world. The conflagration provided English architecture, according to one recent historian, with "the finest opportunity since the Great Fire of London."[1]

One year later an equivalent chance offered itself in America. In 1835 the Congress of the United States formally accepted the bequest of an Englishman named James Smithson, who left all his property "to found at Washington *an establishment for the increase and diffusion of knowledge among men.*"[2] Congress voted to create the Smithsonian Institution in fulfillment of these terms in 1846. The physical incar-

1. M. H. Port, "The Old Houses of Parliament," in *The Houses of Parliament,* ed. M. H. Port (New Haven: Yale University Press, 1976), p. 5.
2. George Brown Goode, *An Account of the Smithsonian Institution: Its Origin, History, Objects and Achievements* (Washington, D.C.: n.p., 1895), n. pag.

313

nation of this first national intellectual institution was perceived as an important symbol of the independent cultural
progress of the new republic.

These two structures were the most significant public buildings erected in their respective countries during the early Victorian period. As a national civic monument each carried a
heavy weight of patriotic pride. All aspects of their planning
and construction attracted wide attention and inspired public
discussion, attack, and justification. In each case concern focused on the style of the building as the quintessential expression of its national symbolism. In the 1830s and the 1840s, although they shared a common heritage and a common
language, England and the United States were very different
states—one a constitutional monarchy with deep historical
roots, the other a self-consciously progressive republic. Alexis
de Tocqueville, who traveled in both countries during the
1830s, characterized the United States as a democracy in
which the judgment of the multitude—the mass of ordinary
people—dominated. English society, on the other hand, still
retained some aristocratic features; and opinion, like power,
emanated from a superior class.[3] Despite such differences, the
same style was selected for both buildings. In each case politi-
cians sensitive both to symbols and to the responses of their
audiences chose to recreate medieval architecture in the manner that has become known as Gothic Revival.

Why, then, if architectural style is the vehicle of meaning,
and if the national ideologies of Great Britain and the United
States differed so markedly during the first half of the nineteenth century, did the political leaders of both countries
choose to embody their central beliefs in the same symbol?
What was it about the Gothic Revival style that made it seem
an appropriate symbol for divergent public cultures?

Architecture communicates meaning through a building's
style, form, size, location, materials, and relation to other

3. Tocqueville's accounts of his journeys are available in *Democracy in
America*, ed. Phillips Bradley and Henry Reeve, 2 vols. (New York: Vintage,
1945) and *Journeys to England and Ireland*, trans. George Lawrence and K. P.
Mayer, ed. K. P. Mayer (London: Faber and Faber, 1958).

parts of the spatial environment. Thus architecture functions as a language. Many of its elements, like those of verbal language, are culture-specific; the association between any individual component of a building and its meaning is conventional, not intrinsic.[4] Style is among the most prominent elements of what may be called the architectural code, usually easy to identify and to isolate from other elements. The style of a building is normally determined by a process in which meaning, rather than function or even appearance, is especially important. Style is also the aspect of a building most comprehensible or readable to the lay observer.

More often than not the style of a building reflects the style of past buildings, and not simply in the way that a work of literature or a painting, as the temporary culmination of a long tradition, incorporates the styles of distinguished predecessors. Architecture, the aesthetician Roger Scruton notes, is peculiarly prone to revivals. Perhaps because of the habitual respect accorded surviving monuments, a style can be resurrected in detail without either the irony or the preciousness that would be the inevitable effect of such a return in another art.[5] Indeed, the history of the nineteenth-century Gothic revival shows that academic revivals of antiquated architectural styles need not be static or sterile. They can dramatically expand the symbolic vocabulary of their time.

Critics who deplore the featurelessness of much modern architecture see the nineteenth century as a time when, "dressed in historical styles, buildings evoked explicit associations and romantic allusions to the past to convey literary, ecclesiastical, national or programmatic symbolism."[6] The eclectic historicism of Victorian architectural style represented the attempt of architects to communicate with a consuming public that was

4. For an extended exploration of this proposition see Donald Preziosi, *The Semiotics of the Built Environment: An Introduction to Architectonic Analysis* (Bloomington: Indiana University Press, 1979).

5. Roger Scruton, *The Aesthetics of Architecture* (London: Methuen, 1979), p. 16.

6. Robert Venturi, Denise Scott Brown, and Steven Izenour, *Learning from Las Vegas: The Forgotten Symbolism of Architectural Form,* rev. ed. (Cambridge, Mass.: MIT Press, 1977), p. 7.

observing buildings with increasing interest and interpreting their symbolism with increasing sophistication. This was a public that looked for iconography in buildings; architects provided it by developing an elaborate system of historical references. The High Anglican Ecclesiological Movement, which prescribed correct medieval models for nineteenth-century English and American churches, best exemplified this tendency, but it influenced even the design of private and informal buildings.[7] In *The Architecture of Country Houses,* for example, a popular American manual of 1850, Andrew Jackson Downing included not only plans for cottages, farmhouses, and villas in the Gothic, Italian, and several other styles, but suggestions about the kind of person and way of life for which each style would be most appropriate.[8]

The range of symbolic meaning in the public architecture of both Victorian England and Victorian America was defined in political forums and open to comment by concerned citizens. This greatly complicated the process of stylistic expression. Major buildings were seen and, in one way or another, criticized by a broad sample of the electorate. So, unlike a painter or a poet, a public architect could not imagine that he was working for a self-selected clientele. If it were to be widely appreciated, a building had to speak in language that could be generally understood.[9]

His dialogues with an extended audience constrain the architect of public monuments. A poem or a symphony, even if it has been commissioned by the state, is the product of countless decisions about form and tone, image and meaning, made by the artist alone, perhaps even unconsciously, and certainly without consulting self-appointed representatives of his audi-

7. James F. White, *The Cambridge Movement, the Ecclesiologists, and the Gothic Revival* (Cambridge: Cambridge University Press, 1962) and Phoebe B. Stanton, *The Gothic Revival and American Church Architecture: An Episode in Taste, 1840–1856* (Baltimore: Johns Hopkins University Press, 1968) contain detailed discussions of the impact of the Gothic Revival on Victorian church building.

8. Rpt. New York: Dover, 1969. In the fifteen years after its publication *The Architecture of Country Houses* went through nine printings and sold over 16,000 copies.

9. Scruton, *Aesthetics of Architecture,* p. 13.

ence. Every stage in the planning and construction of a public building, on the other hand, is open to discussion by those who have commissioned it—people who have invested a great deal of money and, often, emotion and prestige. Whether their motives are aesthetic or emblematic, pragmatic or financial, they may dictate not only basic specifications (how large a building, for what purpose, in what location) but also its form, its materials, its decorations, its style.

The result is a kind of protracted public negotiation about aspects of creation normally inaccessible to consumers of art. This makes public architecture the most participatory of the arts. The choice of the style of a public building, along with the definition of the meaning of that style, normally reflects a quasi-political consensus, not an individual's aesthetic judgment. The public contribution to this process of aesthetic decision making should ensure that the resulting symbolism will be generally accepted and understood. As with other public acts, however, there is always a possibility of misunderstanding that distorts the dialogue between decision makers and audience.

The symbolic versatility of the Gothic Revival style may reflect its diffuse and ambiguous historical roots. Unlike some of the revivals that succeeded it—the Queen Anne Revival of the 1870s, for instance[10]—it did not appear all at once in a relatively coherent form, but emerged slowly during the eighteenth century. Charles Eastlake, the major contemporary chronicler of the Gothic Revival and an enthusiastic advocate, argued that "revival" was actually a misnomer because the style had persisted since the Tudor period in the obscure vernacular buildings of rural England, as well as in the "baronial" residences of the Scottish upper class.[11] Indeed, Gothic parish churches were built into the last third of the seventeenth century.[12] And although Eastlake notes sadly that Gothic monu-

10. Roger Dixon and Stefan Muthesius, *Victorian Architecture* (New York: Oxford University Press, 1978), pp. 65–69.
11. Charles Eastlake, *A History of the Gothic Revival* (1872; rpt. Leicester: Leicester University Press, 1978), pp. 45; 58–59.
12. Kenneth Clark, *The Gothic Revival: An Essay in the History of Taste* (1928; rpt. New York: Holt, Rinehart and Winston, 1962) p. 20.

mental architecture received its "death-blow" in 1633, when "the first stone was laid for a Roman portico to one of the finest cathedrals of the Middle Ages," he also claims that the antiquarian interest in medieval buildings that was to produce a miscellany of archaeological studies and handbooks during the next two centuries began to surface at approximately the same time.[13]

Not all the antiquarians, nor all who read their books, shared Eastlake's ideological devotion to Gothic as the best form of architecture, both morally and aesthetically. Those who built Gothic structures in the eighteenth century—the first people to use the style in a consciously imitative way—simply found it amusing and attractive. Most famous are the extravagant country houses built by two noted aesthetes and eccentrics: Horace Walpole's Strawberry Hill, an older mansion remodeled and enlarged in stages from 1753 to 1776, and William Beckford's Fonthill Abbey, begun in 1796. Neither gentleman was concerned with historical or archaeological accuracy, still less with the resurrection of medieval piety. Both viewed the Gothic style as a dramatic departure from dull classical norms, an unregulated style that offered the opportunity to express their flamboyant personalities.[14] Fashionable architects like Humphrey Repton valued the style for its picturesqueness as well as its exotic associations; it became part of their standard repertory. The history of Corsham Court in Wiltshire, an Elizabethan mansion that was remodeled in various styles by a series of revival architects, shows the emergence of the taste for Gothic decoration. The 1750 restoration was Palladian, but that of 1797 was in a Gothic that seemed "the very acme of contemporary taste."[15]

At the same time that the Gothic style was being revived as a fanciful and elegant means of self-expression it was also collecting—or reaffirming—a set of historicized associations.

13. Eastlake, *History of the Gothic Revival,* pp. 12–16, 59, 66–71.

14. Clark, *The Gothic Revival,* pp. 46–65, 86–91.

15. Frederick J. Ladd, *Architects at Corsham Court: A Study in Revival Style Architecture and Landscaping, 1749–1849* (Bradford-on-Avon, Wiltshire: Moonraker Press, 1978), pp. 86–90, 115.

When the House of Lords commissioned renovations in 1799 it chose Gothic plans. This lent a new dignity and a new meaning to the style; despite the authentic medieval character of the old Houses of Parliament, all previous eighteenth-century renovations, as well as all serious proposals for an entirely new structure, had been classical. The Lords' decision expressed not official susceptibility to the vagaries of fashionable taste, but a sense (inaccurate) that Gothic was an indigenous English style expressive of traditional English political virtues. Therefore it seemed an appropriate expression of national identity and will during the protracted struggle with Revolutionary France.[16]

The public symbolism most familiarly associated with Gothic architecture before the new Houses of Parliament were built was not political or civic, but religious. The architectural remains of medieval Catholicism survived in great quantity all over Great Britain, in the form of cathedrals, parish churches, abbeys (some ruined, others converted to private dwellings), and educational institutions. When early nineteenth-century Britons thought of built religion they imagined it in medieval form. The torpor of the eighteenth-century Anglican church meant that, outside of rebuilt London, relatively few new churches offered alternative images of religious structures.

Nineteenth-century church builders reemphasized the religious associations of Gothic architecture. When, in the 1830s, the Oxford Movement arose to cleanse the Church of England of the practices and doctrines that had developed in the previous two centuries, it looked to the Middle Ages as a time of purer and more effective faith; appropriately, the churches built to express this program of reform and return emulated the style of that earlier time. The Cambridge Camden Society, later called the Ecclesiological Society, acted as the architectural wing of the Oxford Movement. Ecclesiological architects like George Gilbert Scott and William Butterfield believed that the brilliant artistic achievements of the Middle Ages had been sustained by the virtue and piety of medieval society. They hoped that their careful imitations of these buildings half a millennium later would help reverse the social process; perhaps

16. Port, "The Old Houses of Parliament," pp. 5–7.

architecture would sustain a renewal of religious consciousness.[17]

Roman Catholicism produced a parallel movement with similar architectural symbolism, following the liberal legislation
that lifted many restrictions on Catholics in the 1820s and
1830s. For English Catholics medieval architecture was even
more resonant than for Anglicans. It recalled not only an age of
faith, but a time of Catholic ascendancy. Augustus Welby
Northmore Pugin, who collaborated with Charles Barry on the
designs for the Houses of Parliament, was the leading exponent of this movement, which was less rigid in its stylistic pre-
scriptions than were the Ecclesiologists and more open to Con-
tinental influence and inspiration.[18] Nevertheless, he shared
their conviction that there was a strong connection between
Gothic architecture and social morality. Further, he urged
that, in addition to churches, secular public and domestic architecture should reflect the Gothic Revival.[19]

Although in 1843 Pugin pronounced the Houses of Parliament to be the only recently erected public building in England
"that it is not painful to contemplate as a monument of national art,"[20] the concerns symbolized by its Gothic design
were not religious. Indeed, the Houses of Parliament may be
seen as the first stage of an attempt to do not what Pugin desired, but its opposite: to secularize the Gothic Revival style
by dissociating it from its traditional religious context. The obvious choice of style for a major government building would

17. Stanton, *The Gothic Revival and American Church Architecture*, pp.
5–8.

18. Dixon and Muthesius, *Victorian Architecture*, pp. 182–188.

19. Pugin made this point strongly in the ironical oppositions of his drawings
in *Contrasts: Or a Parallel between the Noble Edifices of the Fourteenth Century, and Similar Buildings of the Present Day: Showing the Present Decay of
Taste* (London: Dolman, 1841), as well as in his many polemical tracts. Other
ecclesiastical Gothic Revivalists agreed with him. See, for example, G. G.
Scott's catalogue of the "many classes of public buildings to which few would
dispute the applicability and appropriateness of Gothic Architecture," in *Remarks on Secular and Domestic Architecture, Present and Future* (London:
John Murray, 1858), pp. 200–202.

20. *An Apology for the Revival of Christian Architecture* (London: John
Weale, 1843), p. 9.

have been one of the classical varieties—Greek or Italian— that had characterized virtually all the monumental architecture of Europe since the Renaissance. The selection of so unlikely an alternative was an implicit declaration that Gothic was their equivalent in civic prestige and seriousness.

This triumph for the Gothic Revival came after a long, slow decay in the dominance of classical architectural styles. The importance of the Houses of Parliament crystallized public awareness of the implications of this shift. The proprietors of Corsham were merely following a fashion in changing the mansion from Palladian to Gothic. Applied to public buildings, however, the same decision constituted a profound revolution in the symbolic language of architecture.

The introduction of such a style, upsetting venerable preconceptions of how public buildings should look and what they should say, was bound to be controversial. Major debates erupted over the style chosen for the Houses of Parliament. Commentary often circled around issues of abstract aesthetics or simple pragmatism, but the fundamental argument was about symbolism. And the argument was all the fiercer because the Gothic style could say so many different things. Freighted with a miscellany of nationalistic, antiquarian, exotic, and religious associations, Gothic Revival architecture offered a varied and even sometimes self-contradictory vocabulary.

The style of the Houses of Parliament was essentially an exercise in historical association. Charles Barry's design won first prize in a competition limited to entries in Gothic or Elizabethan style. Because the latter was much less widely understood and appreciated in 1835 than the Gothic (of over eighty entries in the competition only a few were Elizabethan), it was clearly the intention of the Parliamentary Committees on Rebuilding to eliminate classical designs that would inevitably link the new building with a long line of European governments, stretching back to Rome and Greece.[21] They wished to

21. M. H. Port, "The Houses of Parliament Competition" and appendix I, in *The Houses of Parliament*, pp. 39, 310–311.

ensure that the Houses of Parliament expressed the national spirit in Gothic idiom.

The impact of the symbolic statement made by the medieval style of the new Parliament building is the more remarkable in view of its many archaeological lapses. Barry's design was intended to be Perpendicular, a choice criticized by later Gothic Revivalists because it reflected an unfortunately late period of medieval architecture, but the details were not consistently Perpendicular, or even medieval. Some were taken from Tudor building styles. Even Pugin, who made detailed designs for the interior and exterior decoration, ultimately repudiated the building on archaeological grounds: "All Grecian, Sir, Tudor details on a classic body."[22] Indeed, Barry, who had been trained in the classical tradition, would have designed the Houses of Parliament in an Italianate style had the competition been completely open.[23] The general plan of the building as well as the regularity of the elevations ("the strong tendency to long unbroken horizontal lines," according to Eastlake)[24] reflected classical architectural patterns. Nevertheless, despite the reservations of the experts, public responses to the Houses of Parliament focused on its medieval character.

Looking back in 1872 Charles Eastlake asked, "Who knows how far the taste for Medieval Art might have been developed at all but for the timely patronage of the state?"[25] After the appropriate styles had been proclaimed, and even after Barry's design won the competition, advocates of classicism made determined attempts to reverse the decision. W. R. Hamilton, one of many pamphleteers in this rearguard cause, contrasted classical civilization with medieval barbarity and superstition and queried the fundamental legitimacy of all revival architecture. Classical styles, he argued, had been used so continuously and variously that they had become modern, whereas Gothic was an alien style artificially grafted onto the culture of the nine-

22. B. Ferry, *Recollections of A. W. N. Pugin and His Father Augustus Pugin* (London: Stanford, 1861), p. 248.
23. Dixon and Muthesius, *Victorian Architecture*, p. 156.
24. Eastlake, *History of the Gothic Revival*, p. 183.
25. Ibid., p. 184.

teenth century.[26] In the *Quarterly Review* George Vivian, dismayed that the nation would be represented by what he viewed as a "disordered" architecture, suggested the "Roman" style for the new Houses of Parliament.[27] More pragmatically, a writer in the *Westminster Review* protested that classical architecture not only better represented a free people, but also was cheaper and less likely to be defaced by London grime.[28]

Such voices represented the urbanity of Enlightenment culture, the sense of belonging to a unified European civilization that had originated in classical antiquity and that was once again flourishing after a prolonged setback in the "dark" medieval period. Exponents of a rationalistic, liberal philosophy, critics of Gothic Revival architecture wished to place Great Britain's governmental institutions in the mainstream of this steady human progress. The voices on the other side, not content to identify the present as the acceptable outgrowth of the recent past, wished to place Great Britain somewhere else.

Like their opponents, apologists for the Houses of Parliament could muster a panoply of arguments. Gothic architecture was widespread in Britain before the island could boast any classical buildings; it therefore linked modern government to an earlier era of English history, an era already represented near the site of the new building by Westminster Abbey. The style was, according to a writer in *Blackwood's Edinburgh Magazine*, "adapted to the Gothic origin and time-worn buttresses of our constitution."[29] Because it was so ancient the Gothic style seemed peculiarly English, peculiarly representative of the native genius that had also produced parliamentary government.[30] Finally, Gothic was a natural style. Its appear-

---

26. Hamilton wrote a series of three pamphlets on this theme in 1836 and 1837, cast as *Letters to the Earl of Elgin on the propriety of adopting the Greek style of architecture in the construction of the new Houses of Parliament*.

27. "Review of Hope's *History of Architecture*," *Quarterly Review*, 53 (1835), 340.

28. W. E. H., "Mr. Barry's Design for the New Houses of Parliament," *Westminster Review*, 25 (1836), 409–424.

29. A. Alison, "The British School of Architecture," *Blackwood's Edinburgh Magazine*, 40 (1836), 283.

30. The misconception that Gothic architecture was an appropriate national style because it had originated on home soil was widespread among European

ance was well adapted to the gloomy English climate, and its
forms were derived from nature. One theory traced the Gothic
vault to the meeting of branches over a forest path.[31] Because
it was organic it was also flexible; according to Henry Noel
Humphreys, writing for professional builders and serious ama-
teurs in the *Architectural Magazine,* "the Gothic, in what may
be termed its *natural existence,* suited itself with wonderful
pliability to every new purpose to which it was applied."[32]

What all this meant was a redefinition of Great Britain's national image. It included a self-confident revaluation of English
culture in comparison with that of France and the Mediterra-
nean. But it also revealed serious doubts about contemporary
Britain, shaped by the Enlightenment and the Renaissance. As
opponents of the Gothic Houses of Parliament realized, to
adopt a medieval style for the building that housed the most
characteristic and important national political institution was
to reject, in some way, the nineteenth-century nation. And
such nostalgic sentiment was, apparently, widespread; according to the most serious modern historians of the Houses of Parliament, "public opinion liked Barry's synthesis."[33]

Revival architecture can be seen as a kind of pastoral, expressing the desire to replace a complex present with a simpler
past. Britain in the 1830s was adjusting with difficulty to social
and economic changes. In general groups which traditionally
had been silent began to be heard, and this, perhaps as much as
the problems that inspired them to speak, produced an uneasy
public sense of potential tears in the fabric of society. Widespread economic distress sparked agricultural riots throughout
England in 1829 and 1830, while in the North industrial work-
ers pondered the grievances that led to the Chartist Movement
of the late 1830s and 1840s. The passage of the Reform Bill of
1832 signaled a redistribution in the balance of political power

nations until later in the century, when it was generally acknowledged that
only France could legitimately make this claim.

31. Port, "The Houses of Parliament Competition," pp. 30–32.

32. "Suggestions relative to the best Models of Style to be adopted in designing the new Houses of Parliament in the Gothic Taste," *Architectural
Magazine,* 5 (1838), 51.

33. M. H. Port and Phoebe B. Stanton, "Select Committees and Estimates:
The Collaboration Continued," in *The Houses of Parliament,* p. 80.

between the upper and the middle classes, and between rural and urban areas. Although its immediate effects were hardly cataclysmic, the agitation it provoked in the general election of 1831 emphasized the existence of strong antagonisms within British society.

The Gothic style of the Houses of Parliament sought to deny all this; in a sense it rejected not only nineteenth-century problems, but liberal nineteenth-century solutions. It resurrected a mythic time when the social order seemed stable, when responsibility accompanied authority, when there were no large cities, and when—although the rich had more and better—the poor had enough. This was not exactly an aristocratic image, but it certainly excluded the middle classes. (Indeed, English architects could find few indigenous civic and mercantile buildings to copy. Models for structures built for middle-class activities existed only on the Continent.) Nor was nostalgic Gothic imagery confined to architecture. It occurred frequently in early Victorian literary culture; in the writings, for example, of Thomas Carlyle and William Cobbett (who often used an architectural metaphor—the empty or ruined parish church—for the decline of the traditional countryside).[34] Thus the controversy over the style of the Houses of Parliament was part of a larger national debate about which historical associations were appropriate to nineteenth-century England—a debate in which Gothic was, for a time, so successful that, according to a recent critic, it seemed "the basis for a new universal style."[35]

The Houses of Parliament established the legitimacy of the Gothic style for public and even commercial architecture, and many Victorian builders made use of it. It always retained its quasi-political character, combining a yearning for the past with an attempt to make the present more palatable by masking its least acceptable aspects, such as industrialization and class conflict. The Midland Grand Hotel, for example, was designed by G. G. Scott in 1868 in a grandiose "cathedral Gothic" style. It completely obscured the train shed of St.

34. See, for example, Cobbett's *Rural Rides,* first published in 1830, and Carlyle's *Past and Present,* first published in 1843.
35. George L. Hersey, *High Victorian Gothic: A Study in Associationism* (Baltimore: Johns Hopkins University Press, 1972), p. 43.

Pancras Station behind it, which was a much admired triumph of Victorian engineering.[36] Thus the symbol of the dynamic present was disguised by the symbol of the static and reassuring past.

Scott's design for the Midland Hotel leaned heavily on designs he had prepared for the Foreign Offices competition of 1856. Although he did not exactly win the competition, he received the commission—in part because in February 1858 Palmerston's Liberal administration was replaced by Lord Derby and the Tories, who were eager to emphasize the Gothic roots of English government. But Lord Derby's government lasted little more than a year, not long enough for building to begin. When Palmerston returned to office he rejected the symbolism of the medieval designs and insisted that the offices be built in an Italian style.[37] Even after two decades, during which the meaning of its symbolism had been diluted by rather miscellaneous applications, Gothic Revival architecture still projected a recognizably conservative message.

If in an English setting Gothic Revival public architecture evoked the Middle Ages and reassuringly harnessed modern dynamism to traditional patterns of life, it evoked something different in the United States. Of course, some eighteenth-century Americans, like their English contemporaries, were attracted by the romance and picturesqueness of Gothic. Even Thomas Jefferson thought of decorating a mountaintop near Monticello with a battlemented tower; he also considered adorning his family graveyard with "a small Gothic temple of antique appearance."[38] Several generations later American Ecclesiologists enthusiastically adopted the High Anglican program for church architecture formulated by the Camden Society.[39] Nevertheless, Americans seldom identified their po-

36. John Summerson, *The Architecture of Victorian London* (Charlottesville: University Press of Virginia, 1976), p. 47 and *Victorian Architecture in England: Four Studies in Evaluation* (New York: Norton, 1971), p. 38.

37. Dixon and Muthesius, *Victorian Architecture*, pp. 158–164.

38. Wayne Andrews, *American Gothic: Its Origins, Its Trials, Its Triumphs* (New York: Vintage, 1975), p. 13.

39. See Stanton, *The Gothic Revival and American Church Architecture*, chaps. 2 and 3.

litical institutions with the feudal English past. The classical style, symbolizing not the courts of Renaissance Europe, but republican Rome and the civic democracies of Greece, was the obvious choice for American governmental buildings; the federal Capitol, which set the pattern for state legislative buildings, exemplified this style, as did the White House. The classical plan for the city of Washington, prepared by Pierre Charles L'Enfant, a product of the French Enlightenment, symbolized the rational order and political freedom of the new nation, which would herald an age of unprecedented progress for humanity.[40]

The Smithsonian Institution was, according to its enthusiastic apologist Robert Dale Owen, "the first edifice in the style of the twelfth century and of a character not ecclesiastical, ever erected in this country."[41] Yet its symbolism has nothing to do with religion, nor much in common with the symbolism of the Houses of Parliament. Its appearance was a bold departure — an attempt, on Owen's part, to define a national style that would be neither classical nor conservative. That Owen, an English émigré who had been elected as a progressive congressman from southern Indiana, turned to Gothic Revival in this attempt testifies to the freedom that he felt he had gained by leaving Britain. He and his father, the utopian social reformer Robert Owen, were just the kind of people who deplored the traditionalist implications of the Gothic designs for the Houses of Parliament. In America, however, the younger Owen felt that architectural styles, like people, were loosed from the fetters of the past.

Located on the southwest edge of the then-empty Mall, the Smithsonian Institution was designed to be a noticeable structure. As an early historian of the Smithsonian noted, its congressional advocates stressed the necessity of an "important

40. L'Enfant's plans, which had been commissioned by George Washington, were not implemented for almost a century after they were made. Because he antagonized Jefferson and various members of Congress L'Enfant was dismissed in 1792.

41. *Hints on Public Architecture, Containing, among Other Illustrations, Views and Plans of the Smithsonian Institution* (New York: George P. Putnam, 1849), p. 109.

building"—even "a large and showy building"—on a prominent site.[42] Such a monument would both dignify and publicize
the work of the new institution, which apparently enjoyed a
ready public of admirers. When the cornerstone was laid on
May 1, 1847, a public holiday was declared, and six thousand
to seven thousand people gathered on the Mall for the ceremonies.[43]

This was the culmination of two decades of political struggle, for Congress had doubted first whether it was consistent
with American independence to accept such a bequest from an
Englishman (this took approximately ten years to decide), and
second (requiring an additional decade) what kind of institution would most effectively and usefully increase and diffuse
knowledge among men. In their debates congressmen and sen-
ators took the progressive mandate of Smithson's will very
seriously. John Quincy Adams held out stubbornly for a research observatory,[44] and there were advocates for educational institutions of many kinds—most insistently for an ex-
perimental agricultural college. The stipulation that the
"establishment" be located in Washington also sparked discussion; legislators were understandably eager to ensure that
the new institution be truly national. The building represented
the resolution of these conflicts. Architectural specifications
were mentioned in each of the competing legislative proposals
in approximately the words of the compromise bill that was finally enacted: "A suitable building, of plain and durable materials and structure, without unnecessary ornament, and of
sufficient size."[45] In 1847 the *Report of the Organization Committee* defined the functions of the Smithsonian Institution in
terms of the required components of its physical structure: a

42. George Brown Goode, *The Smithsonian Institution 1846–1896: The
History of Its First Half Century* (Washington, D.C.: n.p., 1897), pp. 55, 251.
   43. Ibid., pp. 255–256.
   44. See Adams' address, presented in 1839 to the Quincy Lyceum and to the
Boston Mechanic Apprentices' Library Association, and reprinted as lecture 1
in *The Great Design*, ed. Wilcomb E. Washburn (Washington, D.C.: Smithsonian Institution, 1965), pp. 43–64.
   45. William Jones Rhees, ed., *The Smithsonian Institution: Documents Relative to Its Origin and History, 1835–1899* (Washington, D.C.: Government
Printing Office, 1901) I, 432.

library, a museum, a chemical laboratory, lecture rooms, and an art gallery.[46]

Thus the importance and complexity of the Smithsonian's politically negotiated mission were represented by the size and internal diversity of its building. But how was its Norman style to symbolize the progress and spread of learning in a quintessentially modern nation? Owen, who served as chairman of the Building Committee, addressed this issue in *Hints on Public Architecture,* a remarkable book prepared at the suggestion of the Smithsonian's Executive Board to explain the requirements of American public architecture and how the building designed by James Renwick, also the architect of Gothic churches and prominent among American Ecclesiologists, fulfilled them.

Owen began by denying the general validity of revival styles: "It is among the conditions of a true Architecture . . . that it mould itself to the wants and the domestic habits and the public customs and the political institutions and the religious sentiment of its country and its age . . . an Architecture of another age and another country may be eminently deserving our admiration . . . and yet be wholly unworthy of imitation."[47] He identified the specific unsuitability of the Egyptian style ("we need no time-defying pyramids"), the Grecian style (ill-adapted "to the wants of a later age, of a more northern climate, and of a more advanced civilization"), and the Gothic style (emblematic of "titled robbers" and "an oppressed peasantry").[48] What Owen rejected was the penumbra of historical association that surrounded each style. Yet he also doubted that the American culture of his time could generate an original, distinctive national architecture. His task, therefore, was to strip a style of its historical associations, replacing them with a symbolism appropriate for republican America.

He started not with aesthetic criteria, but with a set of functional requirements for a truly American style. It had to be flexible in external form and in the arrangement of its parts,

46. (Washington, D.C.: Blair and Rives, 1847), p. 7.
47. Owen, *Hints on Public Architecture*, p. 12.
48. Ibid., pp. 2, 5, 7.

and capable of adaptation to America's diverse climates. It could not be elaborate or expensive, and its effect should depend on its striking form rather than on decoration. Such a style, both dynamic and expansive, could fittingly be characterized as republican.[49]

Owen reexamined the major historical styles, once again rejecting the classical as too formal, too expensive, unsuited to a cold climate, and uncomfortably associated with a single kind of building, the temple.[50] Instead, he accepted Gothic architecture as the basis of an American style, because of "its truth, its boldness, its lofty character, its aspiring lines . . . the independence with which it has shaken off the shackles of formal rule . . . its changeful aspect."[51] Although it is not inconsistent with the appearance of a Gothic building, this was hardly the message conveyed by the Gothic style of the Houses of Parliament.

The symbolism Owen attributed to Gothic architecture ignored its historical context. Indeed, he preferred not to call the various styles by their historicist names, instead discussing Greek under the functional heading of post and lintel architecture, and Gothic under that of arch architecture. Thus the turreted and battlemented outline of the Smithsonian roof evoked not images of a castle or a cathedral on a hill, and the way of life associated with them, but the independence of the American spirit, its resistance to regimentation, and, not least important, its need, in a severe climate, for chimneys, air shafts, and heating ducts.[52] Unlike the English revivalists, with their concern that all the elements of Gothic Revival building be taken from a single period of medieval architecture, Owen was willing to mix periods to enhance symbolism. He characterized the Smithsonian building as designed primarily in the style of

49. Ibid., pp. 8–10.
50. Ibid., pp. 31–46.
51. Ibid., p. 63.
52. Owen also stressed the relative cheapness of Gothic architecture in comparison with classical, which he attributed to the fact that Gothic structures did not require marble, but could be built of inexpensive locally available stone. The table on page 98 of *Hints on Public Architecture* shows the cost per cubic foot for Gothic buildings as between 9 and $17^1/_4$ cents, while that for classical buildings varies from $33^1/_3$ to 126 cents.

the late twelfth century, but with a "general feeling
. . . especially in the principal towers . . . of a somewhat
later period, when all lingering reminiscences of the Post and
Lintel manner had been carried off."[53] It added the grace of
the late medieval pointed arch to the health and purity of the
Norman or rounded arch manner, while maintaining the honest, republican impact of the earlier style. Borrowing a point
from the more pragmatic apologists for the Houses of Parliament, Owen also stressed the organic nature of medieval architecture, which made it flexible. It was adaptable to any site,
and it allowed for growth, perhaps especially important in a
young nation pursuing its "manifest destiny." Since symmetry
was not required, additions could be made without destroying
the plan of the building.

Owen's attempt to replace the vocabulary of historical reference normally associated with Gothic Revival architecture
with a vocabulary derived solely from function and appearance
was at least partially successful. The Smithsonian Institution
building was commissioned and built in that style, as were,
subsequently, several neighboring buildings. But Owen's argument appears to work better in the absence of the building that
exemplifies it. English visitors have always been puzzled by
the appearance of the Smithsonian. The ironic James Fergusson, a contemporary architectural historian, derided the pride
of nineteenth-century Washingtonians in the "rude, irregular"
building;[54] in the twentieth century the politer Nikolaus
Pevsner, in general an appreciator of Victorian medievalism,
laconically noted that the Gothic style was "an odd choice."[55]
The message of the building and the symbolic language with
which it was expressed have seemed to be in conflict.

Contemporary American observers registered similar confusion. Although they may have shared Owen's understanding of
the mission of the Smithsonian and the character of the American nation, they often failed to read the style of the Smithson-

53. Owen, *Hints on Public Architecture*, p. 104.
54. *History of the Modern Styles of Architecture* (1862; rpt. New York:
Dodd, Mead, 1891) II, 336–337.
55. *A History of Building Types* (Princeton: Princeton University Press,
1976), p. 134.

ian according to his intention. Historicism would creep in. With the best will in the world, Joseph B. Varnum, the author of a midcentury guidebook to Washington, proclaimed that the style of the building "continues to recommend itself for structures like this, to the most enlightened judgment"; he admired its strength and the variety of its parts, its uniqueness and its versatility. Even as he admired, however, Varnum thought of "the fortified monasteries of former times," and, in the end, he found it hard "to discover any special use for all these towers."[56] The sculptor Horatio Greenough, himself both an ardent nationalist and an exponent of functionalism as the appropriate American style, reacted with more vigor. It was, perhaps, the American analogue of the English appreciation of the Houses of Parliament. He understood the building's symbolism in historical terms and therefore rejected it. Walking in Washington one night after a protracted absence during which the Smithsonian had been built, Greenough was shocked by the appearance of the building, especially in comparison with the neighboring Capitol: "All that medieval confusion . . . dark . . . complication . . . It scared me . . . It seemed to threaten . . . that dark pile . . . that castle of authority . . . that outwork of prescription."[57]

The Gothic Revival style was used by nineteenth-century architects and planners, and understood by the public audience for architecture, to express a variety of meanings. Ecclesiological parish churches represented the simple piety of medieval life; the Houses of Parliament symbolized the ancient roots of English government. Affluent English Victorians would build their country houses in the Gothic style if they saw themselves as Christian English gentlemen, and in the Tudor style if simply as English gentlemen.[58] In America, on the other hand, a

56. *The Seat of Government of the United States* (Washington, D.C.: R. Farnham, 1854), pp. 115–117.

57. "Aesthetics at Washington," in *Form and Function: Remarks on Art, Design, and Architecture,* ed. Harold A. Small (Berkeley and Los Angeles: University of California Press, 1969), pp. 36–37.

58. Mark Girouard, *The Victorian Country House* (Oxford: Clarendon Press, 1971), p. 33.

villa in the Gothic style was supposed to symbolize the personality of its owner—his "originality, boldness, energy, and variety of character"—while remaining a "republican home."[59] And the Smithsonian Institution expressed the multidirectional expansionism, the independence from traditional fetters, of the American spirit. There was a justification for each of these changes rung on the Gothic vocabulary, whether in the medieval uses of the Gothic style, in the rhetorical history of the Gothic Revival, or in the appearance and design of Gothic buildings.

In a sense such interpretations need no justification. Architectural symbols, like those of verbal language, have no intrinsic meaning separate from their context and their audience. Nothing about the way a Gothic Revival parish church looks implies simple piety; that symbolism is entirely the product of historical associations. As David Watkin has pointed out in a discussion of the post-Renaissance tendency to attribute moral content to architecture, such values are fundamentally distinct from the buildings which are supposed to embody them: "If one did not know that what Pugin happened to be defending was Gothic architecture, one would certainly not guess from his principles."[60]

Although Gothic Revival architecture supported several entirely different but perfectly coherent symbolic interpretations, not all were equally persuasive. Some Gothic buildings communicated their messages more effectively than others. The Houses of Parliament, for example, was much more successful in this regard than the Smithsonian Institution—and for a major public building, an expensive national monument, this is an important success or failure.

The planners of the Smithsonian Institution refused to develop a symbolism built on ideas already latent in the public mind. Instead they tried to stand those ideas on their heads. They produced a building in a style for which the ready-made associations were highly unsuitable to the building's practical

59. Downing, *The Architecture of Country Houses,* p. 263.

60. *Morality and Architecture: The Development of a Theme in Architectural History and Theory from the Gothic Revival to the Modern Movement* (Oxford: Clarendon Press, 1977), pp. 2–3.

and symbolic functions—and pretended that those associations did not exist. Although the decision was made by a group of elected legislators, the process of negotiation essential to the development of effective public symbols was completely abrogated. Like other early nineteenth-century American reformers, Owen tried to transcend history; he wrote as though his task were simply explanation, not reeducation of people who already knew how to read the Gothic style.

The result was general failure to understand the building's symbolism, despite general approval of its appearance. Thus, the Smithsonian Institution's reception was almost the reverse of that accorded the Houses of Parliament, which was, at least initially, more successful on symbolic than on aesthetic grounds. The Houses of Parliament recombined familiar architectural elements so as to enhance and ennoble their traditional implications; the Smithsonian used the same vocabulary in a way that almost dared observers not to think of medieval castles and monasteries. Unlike their overreaching American counterparts, the English planners were well aware that the symbolism of public architecture could not be imposed. They knew that designers must work within an understanding, shared with their audience, of the conventional limits of meaning.

LISA RUDDICK

Fluid Symbols in American Modernism: William James, Gertrude Stein, George Santayana, and Wallace Stevens

A number of patterns of water symbolism emerged in the nine-teenth century from the romantics' vision of a fluxional uni-verse. Among these, one persisted in the imagination of the later century and is notable for its revival in exotic form among central figures of modernism. Although the pattern appears in versions of varying complexity, its contours may be briefly set forth.

Throughout the century there recurs a symbolism that pic-tures the human mind as a solid edifice in the midst of a fluid world. The perceived universe, it is suggested, is so vast and protean, so difficult for the intellect to master, that it is like a perplexed fluid circulating about us. If we were to spend our lives passively imbibing perceptions from the tides of the world, we would "drown"—our minds would crack apart under the influx of teeming and confused impressions.

In self-defense we form intellectual frameworks to guide us through the surrounding chaos. Among such frameworks are the categories of reason, art's inventive mappings of the world, science, even, in the view of some authors, language itself—

all, in short, of those mental fictions that help to simplify the
perplexity of creation. These conceptual structures are seen as
havens of solidity amid the experiential flood: they appear as
islands, towers, strips of land, boats. While such strongholds
provide us with rational control over our environment they
may ultimately blind us to the realities about us. Our moral and
intellectual life involves a constant choice between immersion
in the unquiet waters of the actual world, and withdrawal to
the stony edifices of our own fictions.

While this is not the single configuration of fluid and solid
symbolism in romantic literature and after, the archetype
recurs so often that it seems exceptional that it has not received more notice. It dominates, for example, the writings of
Carlyle, whose universe consists of a cosmic "Chaos-flood"
traversed by the "bridges" and "webs" of art, science, and
language. Mankind in Carlyle is born into the "Chaotic Deep,"
but of this, blinkered, he knows only what "swims thereon,"
the "habitable . . . Earth-rind" of conventional "Wisdom."[1]
Carlyle's model finds American echoes in Thoreau, Melville,
and most vividly Emerson, who pictures the mysterious universe as a great, swallowing ocean which would certainly
"drown" us if not for the "ship" of science that bears us
safely across it.[2]

In Victorian poetry the pattern falls into a configuration best
known in "The Lady of Shalott," where experience is divided
between a tower or island of fictions (a shadow-world of web
and mirror) and the tides of a more authentic existence beneath. Arnold, Clough, and, among the romantics, Byron
share with Tennyson this landlocked picture of the fictions or
faiths we live by. Although this is not the place for an exhaus-
tive survey, it might be added that in Victorian fiction the

1. See "Natural Supernaturalism" and "Circumspective," in *Sartor Resartus*, ed. Archibald MacMechan (Boston: Ginn, 1896), pp. 231, 236, and 244.

2. See "Fate": "Fate . . . is a name for facts not yet passed under the fire
of thought . . . But every jet of chaos which threatens to exterminate us is
convertible by intellect . . . Fate is unpenetrated causes. The water drowns
ship and sailor . . . But learn to swim, trim your bark, and the wave which
drowned it will be cloven." In *Five Essays on Man and Nature*, ed. Robert E.
Spiller (New York: Appleton-Century-Crofts, 1954), p. 111.

most common symbolic accompaniment for the death of illusions in a hero is an otherwise mysterious irruption of waters in his universe, sometimes immersing the protagonist himself. Instances occur in George Eliot, Austen, and abundantly in Dickens and Meredith; this pattern also receives lively expression in the twentieth century in the novels of Woolf, Henry James, and Conrad.

In the last quarter of the nineteenth century a thinker emerged who was to usher the fluid symbol into American modernism. It has not been recognized what a debt modernism owes to the figure of William James. In the 1880s and '90s James taught a psychology that grafted discoveries in the field of physiology, as well as Darwinian ideas of survival, onto the passing century's symbolism of water and land. In doing so he provided literary figures with a universe of images specially adapted to a modern view of consciousness. The purpose of this essay is to survey the symbolic worlds of James and three of his students, Gertrude Stein, George Santayana, and Wallace Stevens. As James's model of consciousness passed into the minds of these very different authors, it was silently refashioned after their own temperaments.

As students at Harvard in the eighties and nineties Stein, Santayana, and Stevens all knew James's *Principles of Psychology*.[3] The *Psychology* portrays the world outside the mind as an "infinite chaos," a "swarming *continuum*" of phenomena (p. 274)—a "flux" (p. 437). This teeming universe reaches the individual as a mass of "currents that pour in" to the brain (p. 112). Each sensation is something like "a stream of water" inundating delicate cerebral "pail[s]" (p. 767). If the individual were to accept promiscuously the flux of phenomena he would spend his life "float[ing]" in a rippling world where all "melt[ed]" before him (p. 382). In this condition he would quickly perish, for he would be unable to perform even the most rudimentary acts of self-preservation.

3. Santayana heard the *Psychology* read from the manuscript: the book was published after he had received his doctorate.

Quotations are from *The Principles of Psychology*, Works of William James, ed. Frederick Burkhardt, 3 vols. (Cambridge, Mass.: Harvard University Press, 1981).

Survival—here James reveals indirectly his Darwinian emphasis—depends upon our selecting for notice, amid the throng of phenomena, only such objects as bear upon our particular interests and anxieties. If we lost ourselves in the continuum of impressions, we would be unable to distinguish in our environment even such critical presences as food, shelter, danger, and aid. Such elements, if they are to be discerned, must actively be brought into focus while other impressions are suppressed. For James the individual may realize his interests—biological, material, and social—only by exercising a form of "selective attention" (p. 273) that admits a few chosen objects to consciousness. The remainder of the world —indeed, "most of the things before us"—"we actually *ignore*" (p. 273).

Those objects that do bear upon our own purposes and needs "we exalt to [an] exclusive status of independence and dignity." It is to these objects that "we . . . give substantive names" (p. 274). Language for James is merely a by-product of that faculty of selective attention that singles out for notice only certain objects. Moreover, language helps to stiffen these patterns of selection. "The human race as a whole largely agrees as to what it shall notice and name" (p. 277); and most of us accept passively the "stock of labels" (p. 420) furnished by our culture, letting these determine which objects we will notice. Thus "the only things which we commonly see . . . are those which have been labelled for us."[4] Language virtually predetermines perception. It is not hard to see here intimations of the later views of Sapir and Whorf; James is himself anticipated by the eighteenth-century theorist Hamann, for whom "it is . . . language that causes the . . . selections made by men from among that 'ocean of sensations' which tides, indiscriminately, through human sensibility."[5]

Hamann's word for the realm of unmediated sensation is *ocean*. James's most famous term for it is *stream*. James's "stream of consciousness" is composed in large part of the currents of sensory experience that pour into the mind at all

4. P. 420; James's italics deleted.
5. George Steiner in *After Babel* (New York: Oxford University Press, 1975), p. 77.

times. Words are a means of bringing only certain elements of this stream into focus, so that what approaches the mind as an intermingling mass is differentiated into a few distinct perceptions. "Thinking in words" helps us artificially to reduce and clarify experience by substituting "terms few and fixed" for the "terms manifold and vague" in which the stream of sensation comes to us (p. 872). "If we lost our stock of labels we should be intellectually lost in the midst of the world" (p. 420).

Observe that James has freshened the traditional symbol of the "flood" of experience by bringing it into the service of the novel question of *attention* that so occupied German and American physiologists of the period. He completes the picture by describing language, as well as the entire apparatus of selective attention, as a fortification against fluidity, a foothold in a dissolving universe. Words are solid; they "[stand] out from . . . the stream" of consciousness, supporting thought "like bridges." [6] Habits of attention "set" the mind "like plaster";[7] the man who perfects them "will stand like a tower" while all wavers about him (p. 130).

But the hardness of words, if it preserves us from chaos, has hazards of its own. There is always the danger of becoming enslaved to words, or—so runs the image—"petrified intellectually" (p. 961). For language by its very nature translates the simmering "flux" of experience into "stagnant and petrified terms" (p. 442).[8] It seems that the more a person depends on words and conceptual systems to filter his experience, the less he is able to experience objects directly. A "cloud of associates" (p. 727), having to do more with words than with things, intervenes between him and the object, and language becomes a veil separating the perceiver from the thing perceived. In fact

6. Pp. 251, 656. The second quotation here applies to "conceptual systems" in general, of which language is an example. James goes on here to compare "sensation" to "the stable rock" into which the "bridges" of conception "must plunge themselves," here substituting (somewhat fancifully) a solid image for the usual "stream" of sensation. The same use of the image of the rock appears in Stevens.

7. P. 126. James is here discussing the issue of "character" as a whole, but he includes under the heading of character "the formation of intellectual . . . habits."

8. Again, "conception" is the general issue.

the characteristic adult in James is almost incapable of absorbing a sensation without instantly burying it in words. Habitual
labels tyrannize over our sensational life, more and more as we
age. What James calls, in an important lecture, "old-fogyism"
—the enslavement to labels and stock conceptions—"is the
inevitable terminus to which life sweeps us on" (p. 754). Increasingly we call familiar objects by familiar names, and those
"objects which violate our established habits of 'apperception'
are simply not taken account of at all" (p. 754).

But the triumph of perceptual habit is never complete. The
crust of the mind never becomes so firm as to exclude altogether the unfamiliar. James counters the mentality of "old-fogyism" with that of "genius": "the faculty of perceiving in an
unhabitual way," the ability to assimilate "fresh experiences"
(p. 754). And he indicates that both genius and old-fogyism
exist in some degree in every mind. While part of us clings, in
the face of flux, to old labels, and shields itself from the confusion of sense by "thinking in words" (p. 872), another part is
always reaching after the new, the as yet unlabeled. "There is
an everlasting struggle in every mind between the tendency to
keep unchanged, and the tendency to renovate, its ideas. Our
education is a ceaseless compromise between the conservative
and the progressive factors" (p. 753).

The "progressive factor" continually subverts conception
by letting in the rush of direct, wordless experience. For ultimately it is only through absorbing the shock of the unknown
that the fabric of the mind may be realigned with fact. Our
stock of labels itself changes in the face of sensation; a "new
observation transforms or enriches the apperceiving group of
ideas." "A child," for example, "who hitherto has seen none
but four-cornered tables apperceives a round one as a table;
but by this the apperceiving mass ('table') is enriched" (p.
753). Our labels for things do not remain entirely alienated
from realities; always we are vulnerable to unfamiliar perceptions which alter our linguistic and conceptual mapping of the
world.

Language is a solid fortress in a fluxional universe. These
moments of intellectual "renovation," when old labels are
transformed by novel sensations, are for James a sort of rup-

ture or flooding of the petrified mental structure. They represent a brief disintegration of the mind as it is inundated with experiential currents that habit has suppressed. "Experience . . . *boils[s] over,* and make[s] us correct our present formulas."[9] The ability to absorb new streams of experience is the essence of the mental "plasticity" that James describes in the opening chapters of the *Psychology.* Each novel sensation is naturally perceived a "threatening violator or burster of our well-known series of concepts" (p. 754). But its admission to consciousness is essential for the "victorious assimilation of the new" (p. 754) that alone will keep our concepts themselves fresh and alive to fact.

This is the model of the mind that James passed on to a generation of modernists. Among these, Gertrude Stein is James's most faithful literary follower. It has long been evident that as a Radcliffe student in the early nineties Stein became James's intellectual "disciple."[10] The implications of this for her own writing, however, have never been entirely clear. I hope to show that her early fiction meticulously imports into narrative the Jamesian model of consciousness.

Stein's most complete essay in characterology is *The Making of Americans,* the work that she was to look back upon as her greatest achievement. In this massive and uneven novel Stein sets out to delineate the "bottom nature" of a variety of personality types. It has always seemed that some sort of clinical opposition is astir when, about one-fourth of the way through the book, Stein begins to divide her characters into two classes: "attackers" and "resisters." What precisely do these categories mean? An essential step is to recognize that they refer only incidentally to behavioral types; more profoundly they are varieties of perceptual habit.

Resisters, Stein tells us, are sluggish in their responses to external stimuli. Their minds have a "slow resisting bottom"[11]

9. William James, *Pragmatism,* Works of William James, ed. Frederick Burkhardt (Cambridge, Mass.: Harvard University Press, 1975), p. 106.

10. Richard Bridgman, *Gertrude Stein in Pieces* (New York: Oxford University Press, 1970), p. 22.

11. Gertrude Stein, *The Making of Americans* (New York: Something Else Press, 1966), p. 343. Further references to this work will appear in the text. For

that muffles entering impressions so that "there is not in them a quick and poignant reaction" (p. 343). Sometimes "a stimulation entering into the surface of the mass that is them to make an emotion does not get into it" (p. 343): numbers of sensations, it seems, are ultimately excluded from notice. It should be evident that Stein's resisting class bears filaments of connection with the Jamesian faculty of "selective attention," the mental hardness that suppresses certain parts of experience.

The critical factor in selective attention is a mass of conventional names and ideas that triumphs over the immediacy of life. In fact the typical resister of *The Making of Americans* is distanced from the world by a dust-cloud of words and stock conceptions. "There are in many of such ones . . . convictions due . . . to books they are reading, to the family tradition, to the lack of articulation of the meaning of the being in them" (p. 463). Some have a habit of "incessant talking," while others are so steeped in "thinking[,] and impersonal in feeling," that they actually lack "enough stimulation to make them keep really alive inside them" (pp. 468, 522).

James would have called these huddled conceptualizers "petrified intellectually." In Stein they are precisely "solid" and "dry" (p. 343). *The Making of Americans* is a tremendous storehouse of figurative invention; it is Stein's most extravagant exercise in symbolism. But it adds up to little more than a chaos of fancy if the stubborn logical threads that bind it are not considered. When Stein calls a person "block wood" or "bar iron" (p. 548), she has a strict meaning. The stuff of a resister's mind is such a stony mass of ideas that it repels the flow of sensation. This Jamesian echo explains a number of extraordinary passages in which the thickened textures of the resisting mind are described:

> Resisting being in [some] is . . . solid and firm and hard . . . It is not profoundly sensitive in them, it is as it is with wood[,] . . . a solid thing . . . In a true sense they have not in them individual being, they are . . . schoolmen.   (pp. 547–548)

---

the sake of conciseness I shall use throughout the terms "resisters" and "attackers" for Stein's "the resisting kind of them" and "the attacking kind of them."

This is a resisting earthy slow kind . . . The slow resisting bottom . . . in them then in some can be solid, in some frozen, in some dried and cracked, in some muddy and engulfing, in some thicker, in some thinner, slimier, drier, very dry and not so dry . . . There is not in them a quick and poignant reaction . . . [In some] the mud is dry and almost wooden, . . . or metallic. (p. 343)

Now the resisters are to be contrasted with a second class, that of "attackers." Attackers are characteristically "excited," as well as "poignant and quick [in] reaction"; "emotion in . . . them has the quickness and intensity of a sensation" (pp. 643, 343). If they are so much more alive to stimuli than resisters it is because their "substance" is—of course—more "fluid" (p. 384). Stein thinks "of attacking being not as an earthy kind of substance but as a pulpy [one,] not dust not dirt but . . . slimy, gelatinous, gluey" (p. 349). In an extreme instance an attacker may be so "completely fluid" that he is little more than "a mushy mass of . . . being with a skin holding it together from flowing away" (p. 384).

If some of this sounds fantastic, it is because Stein has chosen to treat so literally James's fluid and solid figures. In one significant respect *The Making of Americans* expands on the Jamesian model. For James the "conservative" and "progressive" factors exist in some combination in every mind. Stein agrees on this point;[12] but she feels just as strongly that the constant "compromise" of mental antipodes is played out in people's relationships with one another.

The Making of Americans, like much of Stein's early fiction, abounds in pairings of "fluid" and "solid" characters. For in Stein the best relationships are unions of opposites. The reasons for this are simple. Fluid characters are made vulnerable by their indiscriminate "courage for living," and need firmer minds "supporting" them (p. 654); a "soggy" individual requires someone less "sensitive" "to hold him . . . together," a "solid thing . . . [to] harden for him the muddy

---

12. See, for example, p. 253. This explains the admixture of some characteristics like "slimy" and "muddy" in Stein's description of the "solid" temperament.

passion in him" (pp. 74–76). And conversely, solid minds find in more volatile ones "some one very vibratingly existing to give to them enough stimulation to make them keep really alive inside them" (p. 522).

In short, Stein has allegorized James's paradigm, making human love and sexuality stand for what in James was merely the marriage of rival qualities in a single psyche. With this in mind we may briefly consider "Melanctha," Stein's finest work of fiction and her most sensitive account of the magnetism of unlike minds.

Much commentary has appeared on "Melanctha," most of it emphasizing the story's characterization, its technical innovations, and its use of the rhythms of the spoken sentence. It is my sense, however, that the plot of "Melanctha" has largely been missed. It is customary to read the story as the chronicle of a relationship "in a standoff,"[13] an account of two people who "destroy"[14] each other because of their hopelessly incompatible natures. But the story is laden with hints that there is something more intricate and benign in the bond that unites Stein's lovers.

Jeff Campbell, as we find him at the beginning of the story, is characterized as recoiling from all "new things and excitements."[15] He is in the habit of "think[ing] . . . in words" rather than "really feeling" (pp. 155, 135). In fact, he has been "thinking" and "talking" so long that "really he [knows] nothing" (pp. 124, 130, 137). He is, in other words, an unfortunate specimen of the petrified mind. Patterns of selective attention—a habit, as Stein expresses it, of "always know-[ing] . . . what you wanted" from experience (p. 117)—have blinded him to life.

But he is not so hardened as not to know where to turn for help. What the customary reading of the story misses is that

13. Bridgman, *Gertrude Stein in Pieces*, p. 53.

14. Rosalind S. Miller, *Gertrude Stein: Form and Intelligibility* (New York: Exposition Press, 1949), p. 31.

15. "Melanctha," in *Three Lives* (1909; rpt. New York: Vintage, 1936), p. 117. All further references to this work appear in the text. See also Lisa Ruddick, " 'Melanctha' and the Psychology of William James," *Modern Fiction Studies* (forthcoming, 1982).

Jeff sees in the young Melanctha a teacher who will instruct him in "new feeling" (p. 158), in "a way to know, that makes everything over" and that will bring him into contact with "real being" (pp. 138, 149). For Melanctha has the "sense for real experience" (p. 97). She is always seeking out "new things just to get excited" (p. 119). She is promiscuous—or, in Stein's phrase, a "wanderer"—in the richest sense of the term, a perfect Jamesian "mind-wander[er]" (James, p. 394) in whom selective attention never intervenes to screen out the multiple impressions of life.

As they become intimate Jeff gradually learns through Melanctha to stop thinking "in words" (p. 155). He "beg[ins] to feel a little" (p. 116); and before long he is "los[ing] all himself in a strong feeling" (p. 154). At the same time selective attention is relaxed, and his mind is filled with "new things, little pieces all different, like I always before been thinking was bad to be having" (p. 158).

Jeff is experiencing what James would call a disintegration of attention. It should hardly come as a surprise that he feels this entire process as a strange watery infusion cracking the hardened boundaries of the self. "The sodden quiet began to break up in him. He leaned far out of the window to mix it all up with him . . . Oh! Oh! Oh! and the bitter water once more rose up in him" (p. 159). At the same time, "moist," "watery" forces break out in the landscape about him (p. 195).

Jeff experiences an inundation of sense so powerful that "it almost kill[s] him" (p. 203). But he ultimately recovers his balance, and at the end of the story the insights that he has acquired in the realm of "real, deep feeling" (p. 143), where Melanctha has "ma[de] him feel her way" (p. 174), are converted into useful knowledge. He returns to "regular" life (p. 193) in the realm of convention, safety, conservatism—but with a formulation of the world that has been newly enriched through contact with immediate experience.

In James, indeed, this is the pattern that characterizes all mental growth. Old concepts dissolve with the influx of novel impressions but are rebuilt in truer form. In Jeff Campbell, as he imbibes through Melanctha the capacity for direct, "fluid" perception, the struggling polarities of the Jamesian mind are synthesized, and the result is an instance of intellectual enrichment in which mental structures are subtly altered through contact with the world of "real being" (p. 149) that exists outside the self.

James's symbolism of the mind filters into the early narratives of Stein in pristine form. We now turn to a figure whose debt to James was as great but whose reaction was more ambivalent. In the prose of George Santayana we find the fluid symbol of James put to extraordinary new uses that reflect Santayana's own intellectual biases.

Interpretations of Poetry and Religion was published in 1900, ten years after the completion of James's *Psychology*. (This was, incidentally, the volume that James himself pronounced "the perfection of rottenness.")[16] In this series of essays Santayana uses as the groundwork for a critical theory the vision of the mind that had been impressed upon him as a student of James in the 1880s. Santayana's own dynamic of land and sea is articulated in the last essay of the volume, "The Elements and Function of Poetry."

The essay opens with strong Jamesian overtones. Language, says Santayana, is commonly made to serve "utilitarian" ends.[17] "Naming" is a way of "thread[ing] our way through the labyrinth of objects which assault us" at all times (p. 259). As in James and Stein, "our work-a-day language" helps us to "make a great selection in our sensuous experience," so that "half of what we see and hear we . . . pass over as insignificant" (p. 259). This process of selection is necessary for the achievement of particular goals, but it carries unfortunate consequences. It generates a great machinery of "trite conceptions" and "prosaic associations" that works to separate us from the pungency of "immediate experience" (pp. 258, 260). We begin to "think entirely in symbols" and ignore the cha-

16. George Santayana, "Apologia Pro Mente Sua," in *The Philosophy of George Santayana,* ed. Paul Arthur Schilpp (New York: Tudor Publishing, 1940), p. 498.

17. George Santayana, *Interpretations of Poetry and Religion* (New York: Charles Scribner's Sons, 1900), p. 259. All further references to this work will appear in the text.

otic, invigorating "noise and movement of the scene" directly before us (p. 260).

We become, in James's expression, old fogies, "enslaved to . . . stock conceptions" and incapable of assimilating "fresh experiences" (James, p. 754). Recall that in James— and in Stein—this habit of mind was described in symbols denoting solidity: it was a mind "set like plaster," "petrified intellectually" (James, pp. 126, 961), "dry" and "solid" (*The Making of Americans*, p. 343). The mind, on the other hand, that refused to impose a structure on experience "float[ed]" with incoming currents (James, p. 382). Santayana contrasts these fluid and solid factors in a single, pivotal metaphor. The world as perceived unselectively is a chaotic "sea" of "sensation" (pp. 260–261). Over this our "work-a-day language," with its "prosaic associations[,] habitually carries us safe and dry"—like a "bridge" (pp. 259–260). Most of our perceptual life is conducted atop this linguistic bridge, in a realm of "convention" and "servile speech" (p. 266).

Yet, as in James, fluidity is never mastered entirely by language and perceptual habit. Our rigidified modes of perception "dominate experience only as the parallels and meridians make a checker-board of the sea. They guide our voyage without controlling the waves, which toss forever in spite of our ability to ride over them to our chosen ends" (p. 261). For all the efforts of language, part of perceptual life continues to be conducted on the tides of "chaos and unrest" (p. 261).

Into these tides the poet plunges. Recall the figure of the "genius" in James, who "perceiv[es] in an unhabitual way" (p. 754) and lives in a fluid world of unlabeled sensation. This figure finds an echo in Stein's Melanctha, a promiscuous imbiber of experience. In Santayana it is the poet who restores contact with an animate, fluid reality. While thought and language stagnate, the poet descends to the dim region of the "nameless," there to recover "the many living impressions" which convention has suppressed (p. 259).

There results an instant of immediate sensation in which the old "fictions of common perception" are "disintegrate[d]" (p. 260). The poet, in his descent to flux, dissolves the outworn, solid-grown language of thought. He "remove[s] from our

eyes" the "veil of convention," "shakes us out of our servile
speech" (p. 266). This is an analogue for the moment of "renovation" in James, when petrified modes of perception yield to
the streams of novel sensation.

Santayana's poet, like the genius of James, "return[s] to
[the] natural confusion" (p. 266) of life as it exists without
verbal preconceptions or associations. But here the divergent
emphases of James and Santayana begin to make themselves
felt. For Santayana the poet who has "plunge[d] . . . into
[the] torrent of sensation" (p. 260) has only begun his task.

Mere genius, in James's special sense of the word, is not sufficient. The poet who does no more than descend into sensational waters is for Santayana the poet of barbarism. Santayana's famous essay on "The Poetry of Barbarism," in the
same volume, crystallizes the prejudices that distinguish him
from James. The essay is leveled of course at a breed of poets like
Whitman and Browning who "delight in imbibing sensations"
for their own sake, and who wallow "in the stream of [their] own
sensibility" (p. 180). Their poetry "excites us" (p. 174) admira-
bly by showing the world in an unusual aspect and by reducing
experience to its primitive elements of keen feeling and direct
sensation. It effects precisely that dissolution of conventional
thought that is the basis of all intellectual renovation.

But "the power to stimulate" is for Santayana only "the beginning" (p. 174). "For every art looks to the building up of
something" (p. 269). Mere sensational excitement is useless—
even pernicious—unless it becomes the basis for a "total vision" of the world (p. 168). The "lava" of feeling must be
"moulded, smelted, . . . refined" by "reason" (p. 200) to
produce a new set of labels for the world—what Santayana
calls elsewhere a "relevant fiction" (p. 290).

Ultimately, "sense" must function only as "food for reason" (p. 270). Closely allied to this insistence on reason is Santayana's sense of the power of "ideals" (p. 250). The "knowledge of good as an ideal" (p. 47), wherever it takes root, draws
all sensual existence after it. Every disintegration of one conceptual framework makes possible the modeling of a lovelier
form, one that more closely approximates "eternal essences"
(p. 96) stamped in the human mind.

Here we seem to have departed altogether from the universe of William James. In his emphasis on "ideality" and "reason," Santayana shows that Christian moral orientation that always combines in him with a strain of Platonism.[18] He has adopted the Jamesian model of the mind, but he has brought it into the service of his own idea of "essences." He has as it were "suspended above the flux of natural things"—above the physical world which for the James of the *Psychology* was the only world—eternal "forms" (p. 96), toward which James's pattern of mental dissolution and reintegration is made to draw.

For Santayana the descent to fluidity is valuable only insofar as it generates a broader "ascent" (p. 270). Outworn structures of thought may be destroyed only in order that "new structures" may be built, "richer, finer, fitter to the primary tendencies of our nature" (p. 270). It is thus telling that one of the central symbols of Santayana's universe—one that has no appeal for James—is that of the edifice. "We can turn . . . to the building of our own house, knowing that . . . [the] universe . . . [may] be partially dominated by our intelligence" (p. 245). The noblest occupation of the mind is the building of "our Cosmos," that structure that embodies "our ideals" and reflects our attempt "to live rationally" (p. 250).

Santayana once remarked of James that he was unable to "build a philosophy like an edifice."[19] James had indeed an aversion to the edifices of reason, and perhaps on this ground denigrated Santayana's own "white marble mind."[20] For him the shattering of intellectual frameworks by some novel truth was a more momentous and livening occasion than the completion of such a framework. Life, for him, always began and ended with the surprise of the fluid moment and the tang of immediate fact.

Santayana has profoundly altered his master's emphasis. He distrusts the ocean of sensation, and calls not, like James, for a descent to experience but for an ascent into the splendid house

18. Newton P. Stallknecht, *George Santayana* (Minneapolis: University of Minnesota Press, 1971), p. 14.

19. Ibid., p. 92.

20. Stallknecht, *George Santayana*, p. 18.

of the imagination. Such a dramatic reversal seems unaccountable unless it is viewed in connection with the cultural heritage that Santayana himself felt separated him from his American colleagues. Santayana attributed to his own Catholic background a reverence for "fictions inspired by the moral imagination," of which he felt religion to be one.[21] Such fictions, even if untrue in a scientific sense, expressed the highest desires of the human spirit and "were better than any known or probable truth."[22] To compound this bias, the believers in Santayana's family had impressed upon him early the idea that "the whole real world" was "ashes in the mouth."[23] It is quite understandable if he felt that James and others who prized the truths of sensation were capitulating to a crude and inhospitable universe. But, most important, Santayana's Catholic temperament carried with it a strain of classicism (much as it later would in his student Eliot) that called for withdrawal to the "islands" of tradition rather than what Santayana felt was a Protestant and romantic immersion in the "fatal flux" of the individual's experience.[24]

In the years following the publication of *Interpretations of Poetry and Religion* Santayana's classicism would soften, and he would come to have a greater sense for the value of unmediated life. Indeed, his thought would come closer to that of his teacher, James—and to that of Santayana's own closest literary heir.

In the 1890s Santayana himself became James's colleague in the philosophy department at Harvard, and passed on his modified version of James's psychology to his students. Wallace Stevens was the literary figure most strongly influenced by Santayana. But while Stevens readily acknowledged a debt, here again we find the student reworking his master's materials to conform to his own views of experience. And again the change in moral perspective finds no more dramatic evidence

21. Santayana, "Apologia," in *The Philosophy of George Santayana,* p. 497.

22. Ibid.

23. Santayana, "A General Confession," in *The Philosophy of George Santayana,* p. 7.

24. Ibid., p. 11.

than shifts of emphasis in the treatment of the symbolic universe of ocean and land.

Stevens—like his predecessors—envisions the world outside the mind as an ocean. It is an "unnamed flowing," not conquered by speech.[25] Over this "world of clear water, brilliant-edged," as Stevens calls it in "The Poems of Our Climate" (*Poems,* p. 94), the mind erects a refuge of "flawed words and stubborn sounds." In the face of a raw reality that offers us nothing but "meaningless plungings of water" (*Poems,* p. 55), the individual constructs a more congenial, imagined world, built upon speech.

If the world is a "veritable ocean" (*Poems,* p. 54), this imaginative realm is a habitable strip of land. Stevens calls it in one poem "the imagined land," a land "created in [the] mind" (*Poems,* p. 102). Often it appears in Stevens as an edifice—a symbol of refuge from flux that certainly owes a debt to Santayana's "house" of the intellect.

"The Comedian as the Letter C" is one of Stevens' fullest meditations on the role of the poet in a watery universe. This narrative bears close parallels to the thought of Santayana, and—beginning as it does with an ocean voyage and ending with the building of a house—might be viewed as Stevens' reply to the poetics of *Interpretations of Poetry and Religion.* Stevens' Crispin is an echo of the figure of the poet in Santayana, who moves alternately between the edifice of words and the sea of nameless existence. At the outset of the poem he has "an eye of land": he resides in the world of mind and human artifice, of "gelatines and jupes" (p. 30). But he feels driven to immerse himself, to lose the "terrestrial" (p. 30). For in Stevens—as in James, Stein, and Santayana—mental life has a tendency to become "stale" (*Poems,* p. 112) if it remains too long out of contact with the realm of immediate fact. Periodically the mind must go to sea to recover a knowledge of actualities.

In Stevens the collapse of intellect is commonly a watery im-

25. Wallace Stevens, "The River of Rivers in Connecticut," in *Poems* (New York: Random House, 1950), p. 165. Hereafter cited as *Poems* followed by page number. "The Comedian as the Letter C," however, will be referred to by page number alone.

mersion, in which "something imagined" is "washed away"
(*Poems,* p. 151). It is precisely in order to dissolve his own
worn-out fictions that Crispin becomes a seafarer. Once he has
left land "Crispin [is] washed away by magnitude," and all
that remains is "some starker, barer self / In a starker, barer
world" (pp. 31–32). This process corresponds, of course, to
the moment of disintegration in James, Stein, and Santayana.
It is important that at the moment that "an ancient Crispin was
dissolved" at sea his powers of language begin to fail:

> What word split up in clickering syllables
> . . . . .
> Was name for this short-shanks in all that brunt?
> Could Crispin stem verboseness in the sea . . . ?
>
> (p. 31)

At the culmination of Crispin's drenching, "here [is] the veritable ding an sich," "reality" (p. 32). Crispin has descended
from words to bare fact. Further voyagings take him even
deeper into what Stevens, glancing at Santayana, calls the
world of "barbarism" (p. 34). But a turning point occurs when
Crispin unexpectedly renounces a barbarous actuality for
the construction of "A Nice Shady Home" (p. 41), an imaginative world of his own. No longer "the prickling realist" (p. 41),
Crispin moves from the waters of stark sensation to "land" (p.
41). "Every art," said Santayana, "looks to the building up of
something" ("The Elements and Function of Poetry," p. 269),
and Crispin closes by erecting for himself "a cabin who once
planned / Loquacious columns by the ructive sea" (p. 42).

Linguistically as well Crispin begins to build anew. At the
beginning of the poem he aimed to "stem verboseness in the
sea" (p. 31). But as his voyage closes, he learns again to emit
"portentous accents, syllables" (p. 45) and produces four
daughters who, in the common reading, stand as types for poetic utterance, "four blithe instruments / . . . , four voices
several" (p. 45). Like Santayana's poet he subjects experience
finally to "the method of . . . art" and "the discipline of expression" ("The Elements and Function of Poetry," p. 259).

It is not difficult, then, to see in Stevens' seafaring hero a repetition of the figure of the poet in Santayana. But somehow Crispin fails to conform to our idea of what the builder of a "Cosmos" should be. He is too small and ungraceful to have any real place in Santayana's world. Crispin comes to us as a "short-shanks," "a profitless / Philosopher, . . . / Concluding fadedly" (pp. 31, 46).

For Santayana and Stevens ultimately disagree on the possibilities for imaginative victory in a fluid universe. For Santayana the moment of "building up" marked an advance in the life of the human spirit. But for Stevens each new fiction is every bit as tentative and impermanent as the last, and—so fast does reality overtake our visions—must be abandoned the moment it is achieved. This is what makes Crispin a "profitless philosopher," a doomed illusionist trying vainly to build himself a refuge from the waves.

Consequently, Stevens undermines the vision of linear ascent that was precisely Santayana's answer to James. For Crispin it is eternally unclear whether experience is "Anabasis or slump, ascent or chute" (p. 44). All that he has learned at the end of his journey is that knowledge does not advance, however much it fluctuates. The world remains "the same insoluble lump," whether it is dressed in fictions of our own devising or "pruned to the fertile main" (p. 45).

Experience for Stevens is not a progressive advance but an ironic cycle in which man oscillates between the same impermanent mental edifices and the same unbearable ocean. It is this fact of intellectual existence that makes Stevens, like Crispin himself, a "fatalist" (p. 45)—with the qualification that both are genial fatalists, accepting the hopeless cycles of life "without grace or grumble" (p. 45).

Stevens' universe is that of Santayana gone awry, a world of perpetual "dilapidations" (*Poems*, p. 149) in which whatever "houses" the mind constructs are instantly "empt[ied]" by flux (*Poems*, p. 154). But Stevens sees this "dilapidation of dilapidations" (*Poems*, p. 149) as the stuff not of tragedy but of gentle comedy. "The sea," he says, "is a form of ridicule" (*Poems*, p. 86), dissolving our vain fictions just in time to force us to rebuild, and perpetually reminding us that there exists a reality greater than the edifices of the mind.

J. HILLIS MILLER

The Two Allegories

> We do not always proclaim loudly the most important thing we have to say. Nor do we always privately share it (vertraut er es) with those closest to us (dem Vertrautesten), our intimate friends, those who have been most devotedly ready to receive our confession.
>
> Walter Benjamin, "The Image of Proust"

> When, as is the case in the Trauerspiel, history becomes part of the setting, it does so as script (als Schrift). The word "history" stands written on the countenance (Antlitz) of nature in the characters of transience (in der Zeichenschrift der Vergängnis). The allegorical physiognomy of the nature-history (der Natur-Geschichte), which is put on the stage in the Trauerspiel, is present in reality (wirklich) in the form of the ruin. In the ruin history has physically (sinnlich) merged into the setting. And in this guise history does not assume the form of the process of an eternal life so much as that of irresistible decay (unaufhaltsamen Verfalls). Allegory thereby declares itself to be beyond beauty (jenseits von Schönheit). Allegories are, in the realm of thoughts, what ruins are in the realm of things (Allegorien sind im reiche der Gedanken was Ruinen im reiche der Dinge).
>
> Walter Benjamin, The Origin of
> German Tragic Drama.

Allegory—the word means to speak figuratively, or to speak in other terms, or to speak of other things in public, from the Greek *allegorein, allos,* other, plus *agoreuein,* to speak (in public), from *agora,* an assembly, but also the marketplace or customary place of assembly. If agoraphobia is fear of open spaces, would allegoraphobia be the fear of that form of language which speaks otherwise? The word *allegory* always implies not only the use of figures, but a making public, available to profane ears, of something which otherwise would remain secret. The something other can only be made public, visible and audible, "theatrical" in the root sense of open to seeing, by such means. "Therefore speak I to them in parables," said Jesus, "Because they seeing see not; and hearing they hear not, neither do they understand" (Matt. 13:13).

The word and the concept of allegory in English is part of a chain of related terms and concepts, including *parable, symbol, image, sign, emblem, figure, aphorism, metaphor,* and *translation.* All name ways of saying one thing with another thing, or by means of another thing, in short, ways of speaking in figure. The system of these terms is slightly different in each of our Western languages, so that they are not exactly translatable from one to another. *Parable* in German, for example, is *Gleichnis,* which also means figure or likeness, while the English word *parable* still retains the Greek nuance of throwing one thing beside another thing, as the parabolic curve is cast at a distance from the imaginary line on the imaginary cone which controls it and which is in a sense its "meaning." *Figure* in German is *Bild,* which also means picture or face, a meaning more or less lost in English, though it is present in *disfigured.* In each language, however, the law of the system of words is a shifting, ambiguous division between literal and figurative, mimetic and indirect, representational and displaced. The odd thing is that each word tends to be divided within itself and so open to employment as the right name for the linguistic procedure at either end of the spectrum. *Gleichnis* can mean either that most indirect of forms, parable, or that most photographic of copies, exact likeness. Even *allegory,* in so far as it says it otherwise in homely realism, such as is fit for profane ears, involves an expectation of mimetic verisimilitude, which seems to be its own opposite, as in *The Pilgrim's Progress*, in the parables of Jesus, or indeed in the *Divine Comedy* and in *The Faerie Queene*.

What seems specific to allegory is a larger degree of manifest incompatibility between the tenor and the vehicle than we tend to expect in symbol, where the "material" base and the "spiritual" meaning are thrown together, as the name suggests, with some implication of overlapping, consubstantiality, or participation. In allegory the one does not directly suggest the other. This means, oddly enough, that the more exoteric, the more appropriate to the marketplace, the more down to earth, homely, and realistic it is on the one hand, the more esoteric and in need of commentary it is on the other. The most important thing we have to say we do not say to our most intimate friends, but we may make it public, speak it not "loudly" but "allegorically," in the marketplace, since that is a sure way to keep it still secret. Persons who have things of this sort to say may be, willy-nilly, allegoraphiliacs.

In this tendency to keep secret in the act of making public, allegory is like parable. In the parables of Jesus the Word of God himself accommodates itself to human understanding. This means, I take it, that the most literal of words, the divine Logos himself (or itself), can only speak to man in riddling figures. These figures, as Jesus says, are, according to the cruel law of parable, certain to be misunderstood by those who seeing see not and hearing hear not, for neither do they understand. If you do not understand already or have the predisposition to understand, you will not understand. "Whosoever hath not, from him shall be taken away even that he hath" (Matt. 13:12). The parabolic expression is not perspicuous in itself. A parable veils as much as it unveils, and the parables must be interpreted by Jesus even to the disciples. "Hear ye therefore the parable of the sower," says Jesus to the disciples (Matt. 13:18), and then he proceeds to explain to them what the parable means. The meaning, of course, has to do with the efficacy of the word, that is, of parable. The parable has to do with its own efficacy. Jesus' need to explain the parable to the disciples surely presupposes that even they, to whom it is given to know the mysteries of the kingdom of Heaven (Matt. 13:11), have not been able to understand the parable as such, though this contradicts the distinction Jesus has just made between those who see and those who do not, those who are fertile ground for the Word and those who are stony ground. If even the disciples could not see and hear, how can we be expected to? It is even more disquieting to learn that some at least of the moral and theological spellings out of the meanings of the parables in the Gospels are later interpolations and probably not the record of the words of Jesus at all. He gave the parables, at least some of them, straight, without interpretation, and the later interpretations to some degree narrow, blur, or falsify the meanings the parables have in themselves.

As in parable, so in allegory, as a linguistic procedure used at any time or place, one shifting bar is the dividing line between the realistic story and the spiritual or moral meaning. What the allegory reveals at the same time it hides, since the more visible and audible it is to ordinary eyes and ears, the more accommodated it is to limited vision, and therefore the less directly representative of the secrets it would tell. Direct interpretation can only falsify the allegory, since the presupposition is that allegory is necessary as the only possible expression to those who have eyes and see not, ears and neither hear nor understand, of the mysteries in question: "Therefore speak I to them in parables."

Parallel to this bar (perhaps it is the same bar) is the perennial division, within allegory, concerning the source of the authority validating the allegorical image. This is the distinction between allegory of the poets and allegory of the theologians, as applied, for example, to the question of the authority of the *Divine Comedy*. Does a given allegory derive its authority from the imaginative power of the artist, his ability to embody his vision in a "realistic" story, or does it derive its authority from an intention coming from the other direction, for example in the decision of Christ the Word to say it otherwise, in allegorical indirectness, to his all too human auditors, or in Milton's claim to be inspired and to speak only in the name of his muse, therefore not to be himself responsible for such things in *Paradise Lost* as the way in which the war in Heaven is described as though it were an earthly combat. It is God who ac-

commodates things unseen to earthly powers of vision, not the
poet. Milton has seen no more than his readers and is a re-
porter, not a creator. As John Guillory has shown, however,
Paradise Lost turns on a profound uneasiness about this claim
for a repression of human imagination.[1]

A splendid allegory of this second bar within allegory, or bar
over a bar, is a curious footnote John Ruskin added when in-
dexing Letter Seven of *Fors Clavigera*. The letter was first
published in July 1871. The frontispiece to the number of *Fors*
containing this letter is the *Charity* from Giotto's *Allegory of
the Virtues and Vices* at Padua, surely an allegorical work if
there ever was one. A series of references to the *Charity* of
Giotto threads its way through Ruskin's work, from *Stones of
Venice*, to *Giotto and His Works in Padua*, to *Fors Clavigera*.
The questions at issue are the following: What does Giotto's
Charity hold in her hand, and is she receiving something from
God or is she giving something to God? At first, in *Stones of
Venice*, 2. 8. 82, Ruskin thinks Charity receives a purse from
God's angel. Then in *Fors* he sees the object as a heart: "His
Charity tramples upon bags of gold—has no use for them. She
gives only corn and flowers; and God's angel gives *her*, not
even these—but a Heart. Giotto is quite literal in his meaning,
as well as figurative. Your love is to give food and flowers, and
to labor for them only." This association of love with the heart
and with a reciprocal movement which goes from man's love
to God's love and returns again, back and forth in a movement
based on faith, is of course biblical. It appears, for example, in
St. Paul's words in Ephesians 3:17–18: "That Christ may
dwell in your hearts by faith; that ye, being rooted and
grounded in love, may be able to comprehend with all saints
what is the breadth, and length, and depth, and height." Then
later, in the index to *Fors*, Ruskin reverses himself again: "I
do not doubt I read the action wrong; she is giving her heart to
God, while she gives gifts to men."[2]

1. See his *Poetic Authority: Spenser, Milton, and Literary History*, Diss.
Yale University 1979.
2. See John Ruskin, *Works*, ed. E. T. Cook, and Alexander Wedderburn
(London: George Allen, 1902–1912), X, 397; XXIV, 118; XXVII, 130.

The reader will see what is at stake in Ruskin's mistake and correction of that mistake. For one thing, it is a good example of the difficulty of interpreting uninterpreted allegory. An allegory without explanation is like a picture without a legend. The objects and the actions represented may be this or they may be that. Without the explanation it is difficult to tell. The more concrete the representation the greater the difficulty. In this case the final enigma is an emblem of the question crucial to allegory. Which way does the action go across the bar separating the material realm from the spiritual? Is meaning received as a gift from Heaven or does man offer it to Heaven as the greatest gift he can give to God, the gift of imaginative love, the gift of an allegorical representation which is "quite literal . . . , as well as figurative"? Ruskin's shift corresponds, of course, to the crucial shift in his own life, his loss of Christian faith, though with many waverings. That shift, it must be understood, does not correspond to a specific historical shift from religious to secular allegory, a shift occurring once and for all, but to an enigmatic wavering within allegory itself at any time or place in the West, for example in Giotto's *Charity*. The possibility that the allegorical representation is a human fancy thrown out toward something which is so beyond human comprehension that there is no way to measure the validity of any picture of it is the permanent shadow within the theory that allegorical representation is given from the other direction and so authorized. Does Charity receive its heart from God or does it offer that heart, hold it out toward something whose existence can only be taken on faith?

Within the Christian tradition this opposition is necessarily associated with the mystery of the Incarnation, a stumbling block to the Greeks and to logical thought generally which is parallel to the question of how spiritual meaning and realistic base are associated, across the uncrossable bar of their difference, in allegory. Honoré de Balzac, in a striking formation in *Louis Lambert,* expresses the opposition between the two theories of allegory in terms of a figure drawn from the biblical formula for the Incarnation. In one case the spirit becomes flesh. In the other the flesh becomes spirit: "Aussi, peut-être un jour le sens inverse de l'Et verbum caro factum est, sera-t-il le résumé d'un nouvel évangile qui dira: Et la chair se fera le Verbe, elle deviendra la Parole de Dieu.'' (''Thus perhaps one day the inverse sense of the 'And the word was made flesh' will be the formula of a new gospel which will say: And the flesh will become the Word, it will become the Word of God'').[3] The application of this to the double intertwined theory of allegory is clear. In one case the Word precedes its incarnation in the concrete pictures of allegory. Word becomes flesh in allegory. In the other case the embodiment generates the spiritual meaning. The flesh becomes word in this other allegory, this other way of speaking otherwise.

I have elsewhere identified a modern tradition turning on this opposition and involving in one way or another references to those Virtues and Vices of Giotto at Padua.[4] The sequence goes from Ruskin to Pater to Proust to Walter Benjamin. W. B. Yeats, whose immediate roots are in Pater and in the Pre-Raphaelites, may be added as an important figure in this sequence. In *A Vision* Yeats puts Giotto in the series from phase 9 to phase 11, among those artists for whom: ''Every old tale is alive, Christendom still unbroken; painter and poet alike find new ornament for the tale, they feel the charm of everything but the more poignantly because that charm is archaistic; they smell a pot of dried roses.''[5] The sequence from Ruskin to Benjamin has behind it not only the ancient, medieval, and Renaissance tradition of allegory, but also, more immediately, the exploration of allegory in German and English romanticism, for example in Friedrich Schlegel and in Samuel Taylor Coleridge. If Benjamin's *The Origin of German Tragic Drama* was about seventeenth-century baroque *Trauerspiel*, his doctoral thesis was on Friedrich Schlegel. The special quality of this modern tradition of allegory, it must be emphasized, does not lie in its introduction of a unique concept of allegory, unheard of before, but in its particular exploration of an oscillation within the theory and practice of allegory which has al-

3. Honoré de Balzac, *La Comédie humaine* (Paris: Editions du Seuil, 1966), VII, 323, my translation.
4. See ''Walter Pater: A Partial Portrait,'' *Daedalus* CV, 1 (Winter 1976), pp. 97–113, especially pp. 109–111.
5. W. B. Yeats, *A Vision* (New York: Macmillan, 1961), p. 289.

ways been present in one way or another, in any historical
epoch. To explore in detail this modern tradition of speculation
about allegory and practice of it would require a book-length
study. I propose rather to focus on one moment in this sequence: the early work of William Butler Yeats.

As a transition to that, the second of my epigraphs from
Benjamin will serve as summarizing allegory of what is at stake
in any theory of allegory, ancient, medieval, Renaissance, romantic, or modern.

"Allegories are, in the realm of thought, what ruins are in
the realm of things"—it is a striking aphorism.[6] *Aphorism*
means etymologically, "from the horizon." An aphorism sets
boundaries. It attempts an encompassing from a distance, or it
casts a linguistic formulation toward an unknown region from
the edge of it. An aphorism always employs figure in one way
or another in this casting. Often it employs overt metaphor in
the form of a statement saying "*A* is *B*." Benjamin's aphorism
has the form of a classic proportional metaphor, *A* is to *B* as *C*
is to *D*: Allegories are to thoughts as ruins are to things, or
rather, allegories are to the realm (*Reich*) of thoughts what
ruins are to the realm of things. The figures on both sides of the
equation involve the relation of container to thing contained.
Among the totality of thoughts are included those sorts of
thoughts called allegories, just as the whole spatial layout of
things includes, among other things, ruins. The question on
both sides is what effect this particular thing has on the whole
of which it is a part.

In both cases the effect, it is clear, is devastating. Benjamin
invites the reader to think of the devastating effect of allegory
on the region of thought in terms of the devastating effect of
ruins on the region of things. The effect of ruins on things is to
introduce visible evidence of the eroding effect of time. Ruins
show that things are not permanently fixed, enduring in their
solidity and presence, or engaged in a progressive evolution

6. Walter Benjamin, *The Origin of German Tragic Drama,* trans. John Osborne (London: New Left Books, 1977), pp. 177–178; from the German
Ursprung des deutschen Trauerspiels (Frankfurt: Suhrkamp Verlag, 1969), p.
197.

toward better and better. Time rather introduces into nature a process of irresistible decay (*Vorgang unaufhaltsamen Verfalls*). This is made visible in ruins. Once the building was seemingly perdurable and new, each stone sharply cut. Now it has crumbled away. The presence of allegories in the realm of thoughts has the same effect on them. What does this mean? In what way does the presence of allegories in the realm of thought have a devastating effect on it?

Benjamin's miniature allegory of allegory gives the reader the answer in its oblique references to the Hegelian system of thought. The alternative, metaphysical or religious theory of allegory is present in these references, intertwined inextricably in the ruinous one, just as the deconstructive one is present as a shadow in the use of allegory by Dante, Spenser, or Milton, according to the general law of the in-mixing of the two allegories. Nature, history, and the allegorical work of art—the three are analogous in that two different theories of their relation to time are possible. One may be conveniently personified allegorically as "Hegelian," the other as "Benjaminian," but in each case, as an interpretation of either shows, both "Hegel" and "Benjamin" are present in one form or another of double person or double face, double mask. In one theory nature, history, and art are the process of an eternal life (*Prozess eines ewegen Lebens*). They move dialectically and harmoniously through better and better toward a goal which will be their absolute spiritualization, their vanishing or disembodiment in the fulfillment of a total meaning. In the other theory nature, history, and the work of art are inhabited by no such teleological spiritual drive. Their tendency is rather toward an irresistible decay. This decay has the effect of bringing into the open detached fragmentary bits of matter not transfigured by any totalizing idea. Nature, history, the artwork become body merely body, without soul, a dead body so to speak, as a ruined building is moving toward becoming a heap of rubble, without informing shape or wholeness, as if its ruination through time were to reveal what it has secretly been all along.

When Benjamin says "Allegory thereby declares itself to be beyond beauty" (*jenseits von Schönheit*) he does not mean

that allegories are ugly in the sense that ruins might be thought
of as unaesthetic, lacking beauty. The reference is a specific
one: to the theory of beauty in Hegel's *Ästhetik*. According to
Hegel's celebrated formula, "The beautiful therefore is defined as the sensible 'appearance' of the idea" ("Das Schöne
bestimmt sich dadurch als das sinnliche 'Scheinen' der
Idee").[7] The beautiful in Hegel's definition is inextricably associated with the view of nature, of history, and of art as the
dialectical progression toward the fulfillment of absolute spirit,
the manifestation of the "Idea" as such. The beautiful is a
stage in that process. It is the sensible manifestation or "shining" of the idea in matter, that is, "sensibly." To demonstrate
the complex intertwining of this concept of the beautiful in
Hegel with its counterpart would require an elaborated reading
of the *Ästhetik*, for example of the discussion of the sublime
and of allegory in the section on symbolic art, and an identification of the crucial distinction Hegel makes between "sign"
and "symbol." In Benjamin's formulations allegory is beyond
beauty because in it, as in the case of a natural scene with a
ruin, "history [as irresistible decay] has physically merged into
the setting." The word translated as *physically* is in Benjamin's German, *sinnlich*, a key term in Hegel's formula. In allegory, what is sensibly apparent (*sinnlich*) is not the idea, but
the absence of the idea. Allegory makes visible ruin, fragments
of matter unenlightened by any "spirit." It is therefore beyond
beauty.

The model Benjamin presents is given simultaneously in
three different analogous forms. Each stands for the others, as
its embodiment or metaphor. Each at the same time is embodied by the others. One is the presence within nature of the
signs of human history. Another is the transfiguration of a
human body into meaning by its physiognomic features, the
characters inscribed on its countenance. The third is the transfiguration of matter into signs by the act of writing. History is
in allegory, says Benjamin, written on nature in the characters
of transience. History is in the *Trauerspiel* present in nature as

---

7. G. W. F. Hegel, *Vorlesungen über die Ästhetik*, I, *Werke in zwanzig Bän-
den*, XIII (Frankfurt: Suhrkamp Verlag, 1970), 151, my translation.

script (*als Schrift*). This gives nature an "allegorical physiognomy" (*allegorische Physiognomie*), as though it were a human face or body inscribed with the signs of the person's character. In Benjamin's formulations emerges the deep necessity for allegories to take the form of personification, *prosopopoeia*, the giving of a human mask and a voice to what is dead or inanimate. The essence of allegory is the way in which this process exposes itself as an unsuccessful projection. In allegory, writing and personification reveal, bring out into the open as *Scheinen*, the eternal disjunction between the inscribed sign and its material embodiment. It is writing, the characters written on nature as features are written on a face, which devastates it. In this disjunction a disarticulation in time appears as a disarticulation in space. The spatial fragmentation of objects in the ruin and the separation of the sign from its material base stand for the differential reference across time of one sign to another sign with which it does not harmonize. This structure of incongruous allusion is characteristic of allegory as a temporal or narrative mode. The ruin alludes backward in time to the former glory of the building and so ruins that glory metaleptically in its difference from it. In allegory naked matter shines through. It shines through as the failure of the idea to transform nature or thought. In this sense allegories are, in the realm of thought, what ruins are in the realm of things.

The disjunction and necessary copresence of the two forms of allegory take special configurations in the work of W. B. Yeats. To those I now turn as an exemplification of the necessary doubleness of all allegory.

All of Yeats's poetry from one end of his career to the other is generated by an unreconciled opposition between natural image and allegorical emblem. The poetry of his first book of lyrics, *Crossways*, shows the impasse reached by the attempt to follow the way of the natural image. The impasse is not so much the paralysis of narcissism, the parrot swaying upon a tree and "Raging at his own image in the enamelled sea," as Yeats figures it in "The Indian to His Love" (ll. 4–5).[8] It is

8. W. B. Yeats, *The Variorum Edition of the Poems,* ed. Peter Allt and Russell K. Alspach (New York: Macmillan, 1977), p. 77. Hereafter *V.*

rather the discovery of the inherence within natural image of allegorical emblem. This leads in turn to the discovery of the impossibility of ever bringing them together. As soon as the pastoral harmony of self with self or self with nature is expressed in words the equivocations inherent in language pierce that harmony through and kill it. They turn the happy shepherd of the first poem in Yeats's first book of poetry into a forever unappeased quester.

The poems in Yeats's next two collections of lyrics, *The Rose* and *The Wind among the Reeds*, pursue the alternative course. They attempt to write a poetry consistently and wholeheartedly committed to supernatural emblem. As Yeats says in the preface to *Poems* (1895), the title *Crossways* was chosen because in those poems "he tried many pathways," while in *The Rose* "he has found, he believes, the only pathway whereon he can hope to see with his own eyes the Eternal Rose of Beauty and of Peace" (*V*, 845–846). This way is the reversed mirror image of the first. It reaches its dead end in the discovery of the impossibility of expunging the referentiality of natural image from even the most purified, abstract, and traditional of emblems. This can be demonstrated in the poems themselves, for example in one of the most beautiful of them, "Who Goes with Fergus," originally a lyric in *The Countess Cathleen* and then included as a separate poem in *The Rose*. William Empson, in several brilliant pages in *Seven Types of Ambiguity*,[9] convincingly puts this poem among the most radical forms of ambiguity, at the ambiguous border between the sixth type and the seventh type. The essays in *Ideas of Good and Evil*, however, are as good a place to see the impasse of the emblematic way, perhaps even a better place, since one would expect less ambiguity and more rational, self-consistent clarity in critical prose than in poetry.

The necessity to avoid the insight that language can never unequivocally coincide with itself, if Unity of Being is to be maintained, regained, or created, may explain why there is so little said about language in Yeats's earliest and perhaps most impressively consistent attempt to develop an unequivocal,

9. (New York: New Directions, 1949), pp. 187–190.

"happy" theory of poetry: *Ideas of Good and Evil* (1900). To affirm such a theory he must consistently forget that poetry is made of words and try to persuade the reader that it is made of "sounds, forms, and colours" alone. These elements are much more assimilable than words to the organic unity and self-sufficiency of natural things. An example of this forgetting is a crucial passage in "The Symbolism of Poetry":

> All sounds, all colours, all forms, either because of their preordained energies or because of long association, evoke indefinable and yet precise emotions, or, as I prefer to think, call down among us certain disembodied powers, whose footsteps over our hearts we call emotions; and when sound, and colour, and form are in a musical relation, a beautiful relation to one another, they become, as it were, one sound, one colour, one form, and evoke an emotion that is made out of their distinct evocations and yet is one emotion . . . Because an emotion does not exist, or does not become perceptible and active among us, till it has found its expression, in colour or in sound or in form, or in all of these, and because no two modulations or arrangements of these evoke the same emotion, poets and painters and musicians, and in a less degree because their effects are momentary, day and night and cloud and shadow, are continually making and unmaking mankind.[10]

This seems at first the consistent affirmation of a single doctrine about art and poetry. A somewhat more careful reading shows it to be a slippery maze of equivocations, reservations, and sentences in which one "either / or" builds on another. The passage seems to want to propose a consistent theory in which a particular sound, form, or color is the correlative of an emotion. The emotion, in turn, is the correlative of a specific supernatural power which it calls down, or embodies, or reveals. This is a familiar doctrine of symbolism, physical sign in preordained correspondence with a certain metaphysical reality. Material sign, subjective emotion, and supernatural originating power come together in the symbol.

A double doctrine of singularity is affirmed here. Each symbol is unique, different from all others. It is also single in itself.

10. W. B. Yeats, *Ideas of Good and Evil: Essays and Introductions* (London: Macmillan, 1961), pp. 156–157. Hereafter *IGE*.

The most powerful symbols, however, are combinations of many elements into a singular organic unity. As Yeats says at the end of this same essay, "You cannot give a body to something that moves beyond the senses, unless your words are as subtle, as complex, as full of mysterious life, as the body of a flower or of a woman" (*IGE*, p. 164). One of the originalities of the essays in *Ideas of Good and Evil* is the claim that a long narrative should and can have the same unity, the unity of a flower or of a woman's body, as a short lyric has. This is directed against the cult of lyric brevity in Poe or Mallarmé. It is meant to support a claim that Yeats's long works, like "The Wanderings of Oisin," also express a single complex emotion and therefore call a more powerful god among us than a simple emotional symbol would. Yeats wants to claim, in addition, that symbols, defined as the conduits through which the supernatural flows into the natural, create both the human and physical realms. Man, society, and nature, which seem so solid and self-subsistent, are made and unmade by the spiritual forces embodied in symbols.

This seems clear enough and consistent enough. Yeats's expression of this theory of symbol, however, is threaded through by reservations, waverings, and hesitations. It seems as though Yeats cannot say unequivocally what he means to say but must at the same time also say another thing. It is a crisscross or chiasmus of the situation in "The Happy Shepherd" and "The Sad Shepherd." There an emblematic theory of poetry contaminates the pastoral one. In the essays of *Ideas of Good and Evil,* on the other hand, as in the poems in *The Rose* and *The Wind among the Reeds,* a theory of the constitutive power of words contaminates the theory of their purely representative function. This contamination in part is syntactic. All Yeats's affirmations are retracted or qualified as soon as they are affirmed, often by an "either / or" which makes them waver in meaning. To say all sounds, all colors, all forms evoke precise emotions "either because of their preordained energies or because of long association" is to propose two radically different alternatives. If it is "because of their preordained energies" then some god or the inalterable nature of things has given symbols their power to generate a particular emotion. If it is because of long association, then the symbol is

manmade and arbitrary. The symbol may function "magi-
cally" now to call up the emotion, but the magic is as earth-
bound as any conditioned response.

The same vacillation is present in the opening paragraph of
the adjacent essay in *Ideas of Good and Evil,* "Symbolism in
Painting." There Yeats reports a disagreement he had with a
German symbolist painter in Paris: "He would not put even a
lily, or a rose, or a poppy into a picture to express purity, or
love, or sleep, because he thought such emblems were allegorical, and had their meaning by a traditional and not by a natural
right. I said that the rose, and the lily, and the poppy were so
married, by their colour and their odour and their use, to love
and purity and sleep, or to other symbols of love and purity
and sleep, and had been so long a part of the imagination of the
world, that a symbolist might use them to help out his meaning
without becoming an allegorist" (*IGE,* p. 147). Yeats in his answer to the German painter wavers again. To say that the rose,
the lily, and the poppy are "married" by their color and odor
to their abstract meanings is to affirm the notion of "natural
right" the German wants. To say it is by "use" makes that
marriage of object and meaning arbitrary, manmade; "traditional" and not "natural." Yeats's three nouns, "colour,"
"odour," and "use" are a heterogeneous series.

In the same way the "either / ors" throughout the first
quoted passage are incompatible alternatives, not possible
modulations within a coherent system. If symbols are merely
the correlatives of human emotions, they cannot at the same
time be the media for "disembodied powers" which we only
figuratively "call" emotions. To say emotion only exists in the
symbol for it and to say that the emotion only becomes active
and perceptible in the symbol is to say two entirely different
things. When Yeats says poets and painters and musicians are
continually making and unmaking mankind, this has two different meanings depending on whether the symbols artists make
are human performatives or vehicles of the supernatural.
Yeats's language does not choose between these two possibilities, even though he says he "prefers to think" or "thinks" he
thinks the second. To say the latter, however, is to make the
affirmation of the supernatural theory a human performative, a
matter of use, not of nature, a constitutive rather than a de-

scriptive utterance. This returns him to the first theory in the
act of affirming the second: "Solitary men in moments of contemplation receive, as I think, the creative impulse from the
lowest of the Nine Hierarchies, and so make and unmake mankind, and even the world itself, for does not 'the eye altering
alter all'?" (*IGE,* pp. 158–159). This sentence starts out affirming the supernatural theory but affirms it as an act of
"thinking." It then changes in the middle to affirm a merely
human perspectivism: things are as we see them and therefore
are made by our sight of them. This is said, however, in the
form of one of Yeats's characteristically open and unanswer-
able questions, leaving the sentence hanging in the air.

The whole passage from "The Symbolism of Poetry" has
the same tangle of the equivocations that is present in all the
poems, for example in "The Song of the Happy Shepherd"
and "The Sad Shepherd," the first two poems in *Crossways.*
The equivocations are present as a result of the fact that the
poems and the essays are both made of language, not of "symbols" which might have the objectivity and unity of living objects or of pure sensations—a flower, a woman, a sound, a
color, a form. Rather than making words or assemblages of
words into objectlike symbols, Yeats succeeds inadvertently
in demonstrating that objects used in poetry as symbols with
performative power to make and unmake mankind take on
thereby the irreducible ambiguity of words.

If the reader turns from the equivocations of the poetry to
Yeats's prose in the hope of finding there the tangled made
straight, the equivocal univocal, his hope is not fulfilled. The
equivocations of the prose match the equivocations of the poetry. They are part of a continuous web of language which is
always forced to say the opposite of what it seems to want to
say, as well as the opposite of that opposite. Yeats's work is an
admirable example of the contradictory copresence of two
forms of allegory both in allegorical poetry and in discourse
about it. If "allegories are, in the realm of thoughts, what ruins
are in the realm of things," the devastation of thought by allegory includes not only "thought" as it is crystallized in the
words of poetry but also thought in the form of an attempt to
express an unequivocal theory of allegory in critical prose.

RONALD BUSH

The "Rhythm of Metaphor": Yeats, Pound, Eliot, and the Unity of Image in Postsymbolist Poetry

If we are right in viewing lyric poetry as an
efflorescence of music in the mirror of images and
ideas, then our next question will be, "How does
music manifest itself in that mirror?"
Nietzsche, *The Birth of Tragedy*

In the summer of 1914 Ezra Pound finished "Vorticism," a landmark essay on the modern movement in the arts. The manifesto was to appear in the September *Fortnightly Review,* and Pound had great hopes for it. It so absorbed him, in fact, that he put off work on some Japanese plays he had planned to translate that summer. Then, just before "Vorticism" was set in print, he turned back to the plays and a spark flew between the projects. At the very last moment he added a long footnote to the "Vorticism" essay, a footnote which read in part: "I am often asked whether there can be a long imagiste or vorticist poem. The Japanese, who evolved the hokku, evolved also the Noh plays. In the best 'Noh' the whole play may consist of one image. I mean it is gathered about one image. Its unity consists in one image, enforced by movement and music. I see nothing

against a long vorticist poem."[1] We may regard Pound's
Cantos, which took him the rest of his life to complete, as a
long commentary on the excited question and feverish reply in
that footnote.

Nearly three-quarters of a century later the question, "Can
there be a long imagiste or vorticist poem?"—now in the
form, "How does a long postsymbolist poem work?"—still
holds a great deal of interest. What, for example, did the modernists have in mind when they stitched their poems together
with a recurrent image or symbol? The new critics assumed the
appropriateness of such organization and used it as a point of
departure for some of their most familiar practical criticism.
Thanks to their training, we instinctively sense the presence of
buried images that occasionally break the surface of poems
like *The Bridge* or *Hugh Selwyn Mauberley* and give those
poems much of their emotional pressure and coherence. And
yet the theoretical and historical underpinning of this kind of
procedure is far from clear. I know of no satisfying account of
the use of unifying images in twentieth-century poetry, nor any
history of the practice's romantic and symbolist heritage, nor
even a discussion of contemporary comment on the matter.[2]
To fill either of the first two of these gaps, of course, would
require a paper of some length. The third subject is more man-
ageable, and I wish to approach it here by invoking a series of
irrecoverable conversations that took place among Yeats,
Pound, and Eliot sometime in 1916. It should be apparent from
my reconstruction that these three poets regarded symbols as
elements of the form of their poems and understood them to be

1. From "Vorticism," *Fortnightly Review,* NS 96, no. 573 (September 1,
1914), 461–474. The essay is reprinted in Pound's *Gaudier-Brzeska.*

2. These needed historical and theoretical discussions would serve as ad-
juncts to two existing studies that treat the more general subject of postroman-
tic symbolism: Frank Kermode's *Romantic Image* (London: Routledge and
Kegan Paul, 1957) and Frank Lentricchia's *The Gaiety of Language: An Essay
on the Radical Poetics of W. B. Yeats and Wallace Stevens* (Berkeley and Los
Angeles: University of California Press, 1968). One essay that does attempt to
assess contemporary views on the question, citing mostly novelists, is Richard
Ellmann's "Two Faces of Edward," in *Golden Codgers: Biographical Specu-
lations* (New York and London: Oxford University Press, 1973), pp. 113–131,
especially pp. 123–127.

essentially related to poetic rhythm. The nature of their understanding will emerge from their own words and from a glance at the growth of *The Waste Land,* the postsymbolist sequence par excellence.

Yeats provides the starting place for any discussion of symbols in twentieth-century English poetry. In one of the first documents of the symbolist movement in England, an essay of 1900 called "The Symbolism of Poetry," Yeats writes that

> the purpose of rhythm, it has always seemed to me, is to prolong the moment of contemplation, the moment when we are both asleep and awake, which is the one moment of creation, by hushing us with an alluring monotony, while it holds us waking by variety, to keep us in that state of perhaps real trance, in which the mind liberated from the pressure of the will is unfolded in symbols. If certain sensitive persons listen persistently to the ticking of a watch, or gaze persistently on the monotonous flashing of a light, they fall into the hypnotic trance; and rhythm is but the ticking of a watch made softer, that one must needs listen, and various, that one may not be swept beyond memory or grow weary of listening; while the patterns of the artist are but the monotonous flash woven to take the eyes in a subtler enchantment.[3]

Poetry for Yeats is an expression of mood; it may involve intellectual attitudes, but it is primarily an emotional state.[4] It is thus appropriate to organize poetry around "rhythm" and symbolic "patterns," two related elements which arise together from an area of experience more profound and authentic than the conventions of the superficial self—arise, that is, from what Yeats refers to as "the mind liberated from the pressure of the will."[5] Symbols may be the agents of cognition, in

3. On the importance of "The Symbolism of Poetry" see Ellmann's "Discovering Symbolism," in *Golden Codgers,* pp. 101–112. The essay is reprinted in W. B. Yeats, *Essays and Introductions* (London: Macmillan, 1961), where this citation appears on page 159.

4. See his 1895 essay "The Moods," in *Essays and Introductions,* p. 195.

5. It is apparent that this theory of poetry appealed not only to Yeats's principles but also to his character. Like Eliot and Stevens he was an unspontaneous man who released his feelings easily only in situations where an act of concentration blocked out the inhibitions of everyday life. The exercises he describes in his *Memoirs* are characteristic and suggest the importance of dis-

which case they act as frames to make imaginative sense out of
the chaos of perception; or they may be the agents of emotional response, in which case they serve as vehicles for organizing the various impulses of different levels of the mind.[6] In
either case they allow the poet to extract human meaning from
conventionalized "waking" reality. Through symbols the truth
in the deeps of the mind "unfolds." And in this passage we can
see how Yeats—at least at an early stage of his career—imagined the unfolding: rhythmically organized flashes of a developing symbolic pattern lull the waking self almost to sleep even
as they lead the deeper self in a dance of illumination. In this
paradigm the end of a poem's illumination is a vision of the significance of a symbol which has been leading the dance from
the beginning. In Eliot's words, having experienced the poem
we "arrive where we started / And know the place for the
first time." Poems organized around this kind of controlling

---

covering images to his sense of emotional freedom: "Now too I learned a practice, a form of meditation that has perhaps been the chief intellectual influence
on my life up to perhaps my fortieth year . . . I was made to look at a coloured
geometric form and then, closing my eyes, see it again in the mind's eye. I was
then shown how to allow my reveries to drift, following the suggestion of the
symbol . . . I allowed my mind to drift from image to image, and these images
began to affect my writing, making it more sensuous and more vivid. I believed
that with the images would come at last more profound states of the soul."
(W. B. Yeats, *Memoirs,* ed. Denis Donoghue [New York: Macmillan, 1972],
pp. 27–28.)

6. In modernıst usage the first of these senses verges on the notion of myth.
Eliot, for example, writes that when the average man loses himself in one of
the archetypal figures of the music hall, he "is purged of unsatisfied desire,
transcends himself, and unconsciously lives the myth, seeing life in the light of
imagination." ("Notes on Current Letters," *Tyro,* 1, [Spring 1921], 4.) The
second, more emotionally oriented sense of symbol was always, however,
closer to the bone. Yeats's symbolic "moods" recall a passage where Eliot
speaks about his own most important symbols as representations of "the
depths of feeling into which we cannot peer": "Only a part of an author's imagery comes from his reading. It comes from the whole of his sensitive life
since early childhood. Why, for all of us, out of all that we have heard, seen,
felt in a lifetime, do certain images recur, charged with emotion, rather than
others? . . . such memories may have symbolic value, but of what we cannot
tell, for they come to represent the depths of feeling into which we cannot
peer." (*The Use of Poetry and the Use of Criticism* [London: Faber and
Faber, 1933; reprinted 1967], 148.)

symbol are, in two senses, *incantations;* they chant the pattern of a repeated symbol, and they enchant us with a vision of the symbol's significance. It is thus not surprising that at the turn of the century, along with his essay on symbolism, Yeats was writing incantatory lines like this one from "To the Rose upon the Rood of Time": "Red Rose, proud Rose, sad Rose of all my days!" or incantatory poems like this 1897 version of "Maid Quiet":

> *O'Sullivan the Red upon his Wanderings*
>
> O where is our Mother of Peace
> Nodding her purple hood?
> The winds that awakened the stars
> Are blowing through my blood.
>
> I would the pale deer had come
> From Gulleon's place of pride,
> And trampled the mountains away
> And drunk up the murmuring tide;
>
> For the winds that awakened the stars
> Are blowing through my blood,
> And our Mother of Peace has forgot me
> Under her purple hood.

Incantation, then, is one model of twentieth-century poetry. But it is a limited model, and poets began to chafe under its limitations at the end of the first decade of the century. Even in examples less emphatic than the ones just cited, by crowding out the imprint of contemporary life incantatory images tend to narrow poetry's ability to present immediate experience. As Richard Ellmann remarks while discussing a related phenomenon in Edwardian fiction, a too-insistent symbolic unity devitalizes literature; literary works become "self-conscious, almost *voulu;*" "the bird flies, but with leaden wings."[7] And since one of the axioms of modernism's developing poetic was that vision must never lose contact with the unpleasant side of

7. "Two Faces of Edward," p. 130.

experience,[8] the heyday of pure incantation was a short one.
After it was over, when poets wanted to achieve effects based
on patterns of vision and also include what Stevens abbre-
viated as "bottles, pots, shoes and grass,"[9] they had to look
for more heterogeneous and more ample forms. The search for
models for these new forms was very much at the center of
modernist poetry as it developed from around 1910 to the mid-
twenties—that is, during the period when Yeats and Pound
were remaking themselves and Eliot was learning to incorpo-
rate falling in love and reading Spinoza into a unique whole of
feeling.

In Pound's case, at least, some of the landmarks of this modernist search for new ways of handling controlling images are
identifiable. Not the least of them was mentioned in the introduction to this essay. After acquiring Ernest Fenollosa's collection of Oriental materials in 1913 Pound began to translate
and edit samples of Noh drama.[10] First in the footnote to "Vorticism" (1914) and then when his initial translations were published in "The Classical Stage of Japan" (1915),[11] he an-
nounced that studying the Noh had helped him resolve
long-standing doubts about the possibility of designing a long
postsymbolist poem.

Noh drama, composed of cycles of disconnected plays
loosely organized around a small number of symbolic stage
props, appealed to Pound for two reasons. He admired its ability to assimilate strikingly different aspects of personal experi-

8. See Wallace Stevens' remark that today's poet "still dwells in an ivory
tower, but . . . insists that life would be intolerable except for the fact that one
has, from the top, such an exceptional view of the public dump." (*Opus Post-
humous,* ed. Samuel French Morse [New York: Alfred A. Knopf, 1957],
p. 256.)

9. From "The Man on the Dump."

10. See my *The Genesis of Ezra Pound's Cantos* (Princeton: Princeton University Press, 1976), pp. 104–111.

11. *The Drama,* 5, no. 18 (May 1915), 199–247. The translations and notes
were expanded for book publication in *"Noh" or Accomplishment: A Study of
the Classical Stage of Japan by Ernest Fenollosa and Ezra Pound* (London:
Macmillan, 1916). *"Noh" or Accomplishment* was later reprinted as part of
The Translations of Ezra Pound (New York: New Directions, 1953). The notes
that follow refer to the more accessible *Translations* text.

ence, cultural history, and literary form into a "complete dia-
gram of life."[12] And he was attracted to the way it structured
its material in a manner that recalled the musical organization
of recent French poetry. Individual plays, he noticed, introduced, developed, and resolved a single dramatic image; and
the Noh sequence embodied a gradual apprehension of spiritual truth. By its musiclike development and by juxtaposing
spirit plays with secular ones, the Noh provided a continual
spiritual reference, a technique for blending secular and visionary material. Thanks to several years of work on the Noh plays
Pound developed feeling for a kind of symbolic pattern based
on the all but imperceptible ebb and flow of vision. Finally he
concluded that to accommodate more diverse material in his
own work without losing its primary focus on moments of
"sudden understanding or revelation"[13] he need only dimin-
ish, not eradicate, the insistence of recurring images. On the
strength of that conviction he intruded into the editorial apparatus of his Noh translations and declared: "The Noh has its
unity in emotion. It has what we may call Unity of
Image . . . This intensification of the Image, this manner of
construction . . . [is the] answer to a question that has several times been put to me: 'Could one do a long Imagiste
poem? . . . ' "[14] It was largely because of this enthusiasm
that the *Cantos* would present a Nohlike cycle of fragments
and display the rhythmic unfolding of certain unexplained
symbols into consciousness. And so convinced did Pound become of the relation among a poetic subject, its dominant symbol, and a related rhythmic pattern that in the same year he
completed his first volume of *Cantos* he published a "Treatise
on Harmony" that painstakingly elaborated a belief he had formulated in the early 'teens: "I believe in an 'absolute rhythm,'
a rhythm, that is, in poetry which corresponds exactly to the
emotion or shade of emotion to be expressed."[15] Years later,

12. *Translations*, p. 222.

13. *The Letters of Ezra Pound 1904–1914*, ed. D. D. Paige (New York: Harcourt, Brace and World, 1950), p. 4.

14. *Translations*, p. 237.

15. From "Credo" (1912), reprinted in *Literary Essays of Ezra Pound*, ed.
T. S. Eliot (New York: New Directions, 1968), p. 9.

in *Guide to Kulchur,* he came to call this notion the theory of the Great Bass.

The story of how Pound schooled himself on Japanese drama would be of merely passing interest had a fascination with the Noh been his alone. But as readers of Yeats know, that was not the case. When Pound received the Fenollosa papers he was serving as Yeats's secretary in the country. As things turned out Yeats collaborated on the Noh translations and subsequently wrote an introductory essay for their first book publication, *Certain Noble Plays of Japan* (1916).[16] It was then, when Pound was close friends with both Yeats and Eliot, that my hypothetical conversations must have taken place. In 1916 Pound was in the midst of his first work on the *Cantos,* and his interest in the problem of organizing a long poem was at its height. That he could not help but share his preoccupation we know from his writing on the Noh, where it permeated what should have been a detached piece of exposition. That he discussed the problem with Yeats and Eliot is apparent from the tenor of essays they each wrote late in the year. It is unlikely, to be sure, that the effect of the Noh plays themselves was as sharp on Yeats's and Eliot's poetry as it was on Pound's (though their impact on Yeats's drama was immense). But it seems beyond doubt that conversations centered around the Noh provided all three poets occasion to ponder the value of controlling images in the poetry they were preparing to write.

In the sixth section of his introduction to *Certain Noble Plays of Japan,* Yeats took note of the same kind of poetic unity that had exercised Pound, and conveyed some of the same excited sense of having come upon something precious. "I wonder," he wrote, "am I fanciful in discovering in the plays . . . a playing upon a single metaphor, as deliberate as the echoing rhythm of line in Chinese and Japanese painting[?]"[17] Then he traced the recurrence of the image of grass in one of the Noh plays (*Nishikigi*), a recurrence as intricate as the play upon horses in his own soon to be written "Nineteen

16. Also later incorporated into *"Noh" or Accomplishment.*

17. The essay is reprinted in *Essays and Introductions,* where the citation appears on pp. 233–234.

Hundred and Nineteen,'' and like that culminating in a showing forth of revealed vision. That this conjunction is more than arbitrary is suggested by the most telling of his comments, which discovers him linking the Noh to the lyrics that had previously induced him to advocate incantatory poetry. "In *Hagoromo*," he observed, "the feather mantle of the faery woman creates also its *rhythm of metaphor* . . . One half remembers a thousand Japanese paintings . . . In European poetry I remember Shelley's *continually repeated* fountain and cave, his broad stream and solitary star."[18]

In a forgotten article of 1917 Eliot payed his own homage to the Noh and the conversations it had provoked.[19] Under the title of "The Noh and the Image" he reviewed Pound's handiwork and stressed its potential impact on new composition: "Translation," he said, "is valuable by a double power of fertilizing a literature: by importing new elements which may be assimilated, and by restoring the essentials which have been forgotten in traditional literary method." What struck Eliot as essential and new about the imported goods in question was this: "Mr. Pound remarks that the plays are at their best an image, and therein consists their unity." Moreover, Eliot continued, not only are the plays unified by a recurrent image but the way that image is presented is nearly unprecedented in European drama:

> The peculiarity of the Noh is that the focus of interest, and centre of construction, is the scene *on the stage.* In reading *Hamlet,* for instance, there is a perfectly clear image of a frosty night, at the beginning; in *Macbeth* there is a clear image of the castle at nightfall where the swallows breed . . . in seeing the Noh, I imagine we have more help for our imagination. The note on "Awoi No Uye" tells us that "Awoi, her struggles, sickness, and death are represented by a red, flowered kimono, folded once lengthwise, and laid at the edge of the stage." The English stage is merely a substitute for the reality we imagine; but the red kimono is not a substitute in this sense; it is itself important. The more symbolical drama is, the more we need the actual stage. The European stage does not stimulate the imagination; the Japanese does . . .

18. Ibid., pp. 234–235 (italics mine).
19. "The Noh and the Image," *Egoist,* 4, no. 7 (August 1917), 102–103.

[The result is a method] inverse to that with which we are familiar. The phantom-psychology of Orestes and Macbeth is as good as that of Awoi; but the method of making the ghost real is different. In the former cases the ghost is given in the mind of the possessed; in the latter case the mind of the sufferer is inferred from the reality of the ghost. The ghost is enacted, the dreaming or feverish Awoi is represented by the "red kimono." In fact, it is only ghosts that are actual; the world of active passions is observed through the veil of another world.

According to this, since Shakespeare's recurrent metaphors are merely incidental to the fabric of his plays, the Noh's central images give us something lacking in even the greatest of Western dramas.[20] The images of the Noh are "*on the stage*" and are thus a figure of "the world of active passions"—the only world with which literature need be concerned—*in the same way* that character, plot, scenery, and the other elements of stylized drama are figures. Images are embodied *in* the action, as the passion of Awoi is embodied in her ghost. And in Eliot's view this reduction of all the elements of drama to one level of stylization results in a more "real," a more moving and consistent "veil" or representation of what he elsewhere calls the artist's "complex tissue of feelings and desires"[21] than anything in English drama. The images in such a representation are no longer references to another level of imaginative reality; instead they are especially intense parts of the "actual" stage world. As such they become points of concentration in the feeling dramatized by a particular play and serve as musical emphases in the emotional rhythm of that play.

One need not notice the presence of Eliot's private preoccupations here (the subject of "Awoi No Uye" is also the subject of Eliot's poetry through *Sweeney Agonistes*—the feverish rehearsal of the suffering of a young girl) to appreciate the application of this argument to his own poetry. A fusion of drama and lyric in which drama is punctuated by images that are at

20. See also Eliot's *Selected Essays* (New York: Harcourt, Brace and Company, 1932), p. 205, where this idea is amplified.
21. From "Ben Jonson," in *The Sacred Wood: Essays on Poetry and Criticism* (London: Methuen, 1920), p. 119.

once part of the action and the distillation of the feeling behind
it is something Eliot wrote about obsessively until he approxi-
mated it in *The Waste Land*.[22] His remarks on "The Noh and
the Image," however, stand out even among these writings.
They constitute the most explicit references in his critical
prose to the way images can unify a work of literature. And
they show him marking the existence of such unity in what is
unquestionably the most important of his literary models—
The Divine Comedy:[23] The Noh's "unity of image," he writes,
"is also the unity of certain cantos of Dante." Telescoping this
last remark with the growth of *The Waste Land* will illustrate, I
think, how the speculative statements we have so far considered became part of the warm-blooded history of one of the
century's greatest poems.

The third, fourth, and fifth cantos of Dante's *Purgatorio* tell
of souls rescued from the pull of sinful inclination at the last
instant of life. Though concerned with several variations—
contumacy, sloth, worldly disregard of the spirit—the cantos
revolve around the general experience of coming to a moment
when the oppressive drives of the secular world, finally spun
out into thinness and impotence, are countered by the frighten-
ingly overpowering attraction of eternity. In canto 3 Manfred
tells how in the suddenness of his violent death he intuitively
"gave . . . up weeping to him who willingly doth pardon"
and adds that the "infinite goodness" has received his soul
even though "the rain washes [his body's bones] and the wind

22. See especially the two essays he wrote on Ben Jonson in 1919: "Ben
Jonson" and "The Comedy of Humours," *Athenaeum*, 4672 (November 14,
1919), 1180–1181.
23. Eliot's 1950 remarks on "What Dante Means to Me" are well known:
"[I began reading Dante] with a prose translation beside the text. Forty years
ago I began to puzzle out the Divine Comedy in this way; and when I thought I
had grasped the meaning of a passage which especially delighted me, I committed it to memory; so that, for some years I was able to recite a large part of
one canto or another to myself, lying in bed or on a railway journey . . . I
still, after forty years, regard his poetry as the most persistent and deepest influence upon my own verse." (*To Criticize the Critic and Other Writings* [New
York: Farrar, Straus and Giroux, 1965], p. 125.)

stirs them, beyond the Realm hard by [the river] Verde.''[24] His moral: ''Man is not so lost that eternal love may not return, so long as hope retaineth aught of green [*verde*].'' Belacqua in canto 4 advises Dante that ''I delayed my healing sighs to the end,'' and suggests that Dante should yield himself up to the movement that Vergil has just told him will come to ''seem . . . so pleasant that the ascending becomes to thee easy, even as in a boat to descend with the stream.'' And in canto 5 we hear three stories of violent death and tumultuous contrition: First, Jacopo del Cassero, who tells of being overtaken in battle so that ''I ran to the marshes, and the reeds and the mire entangled me so, that I fell; and there saw I a pool growing on the ground from my veins.'' Then Buonconte da Montefeltre, who came ''pierced in the throat, flying on foot, and . . . ended my words upon the name of Mary,'' and who recounts how his body was swept to the sea: ''At Casentine's foot a stream crosses, which is named Archiano, and rises in the Apennines above the Hermitage . . . the saturated air was turned to water: the rain fell, and to the water-rills came what of it the earth endured not; and as it united into great torrents, so swiftly it rushed towards the royal stream, that naught held it back. My frozen body at its mouth the raging Archian found and swept it into the Arno, and loosed the cross on my breast, which I made of me when pain o'ercame me: it rolled me along its banks and over its bed, then covered and wrapped me with its spoils.'' Finally the waif La Pia, a young bride mysteriously murdered in the marshes of Maremma who begs of Dante ''Pray, when thou shalt return to the world, and art rested from thy long journey . . . remember me, who am La Pia: Siena made me, Maremma unmade me: 'tis known to him who, first plighting troth, had wedded me with his gem.''

The three cantos, then, are interwoven. As Francis Fergusson has observed, ''[T]he image of the down-rushing river . . . first suggested in Canto III . . . not only holds together the narratives of those who were slain before repen-

24. All Dante translations are from the 1901 Temple Classics Edition (London: J. M. Dent and Sons). This is the ''pocket edition'' Conrad Aiken said Eliot ''always had with him'' in the winter of 1921–1922. See the prefatory note to Aiken's ''An Anatomy of Melancholy,'' in *T. S. Eliot: The Man and His Work,* ed. Allen Tate (New York: Dell, 1966), p. 194.

tance . . . it also expresses the compulsions of passion and of external fate which the Pilgrim feels after all he has seen. Its stormy imagery and its headlong rhythm are resumed and intensified in Dante's outburst [in canto 6] over the condition of his native Italy."[25]

Long before Fergusson's observations, however, T. S. Eliot perceived the emotional coherence of these cantos and made them something of a private touchstone for the central experience of his life. As his letters of 1916–1922 testify, Eliot had personal knowledge of how the ways of the world can lead to a crisis of "aboulie" and a susceptibility to the pull of the absolute.[26] In 1919 he diagnosed the drain on his will as "the Boston doubt: a scepticism which . . . is not destructive, but it is dissolvent."[27] Later he would describe the modern path to faith as skepticism leading to a dark night of the soul and then illumination; the conscientious Christian thinker, according to his essay on Pascal, "proceeds by rejection and elimination," recognizes Christianity as the only valid explanation of the "world within" and ends by finding himself, as if by possession, "inexorably committed to the dogma of Incarnation."[28] Together the two experiences caused him to place the early cantos of the *Purgatorio* at the center of his study of Dante.

In his 1929 book on Dante we find him offering the Manfred, Buonconte, and La Pia segments as a few of the infrequent episodes of the *Purgatorio* that sustain the *Inferno*'s ability to "communicate before it is understood" through "clear visual images."[29] Eliot comments: "We must not stop to orient ourselves in the new astronomy of the Mount of Purgatory. We

25. *Dante's Drama of the Mind: A Modern Reading of the Purgatorio* (Princeton: Princeton University Press, 1953), pp. 19–20.

26. The letters are excerpted in Valerie Eliot's introduction to *The Waste Land: A Facsimile and Transcript of the Original Drafts Including the Annotations of Ezra Pound* (New York: Harcourt Brace Jovanovich, 1971). The word *aboulie* occurs in a letter of November 6, 1921 (*Facsimile*, p. xxii).

27. Eliot's soul-searching took the form of an analysis of one of his compatriots; see his review of *The Education of Henry Adams:* "A Sceptical Patrician," *Athenaeum*, 4647 (May 23, 1919), 361–362.

28. Eliot, *Selected Essays*, p. 360.

29. Ibid., pp. 200, 204.

must linger first with the shades of Casella and Manfred slain, and *especially* Buonconte and La Pia, those whose souls were saved from Hell only *at the last moment*."[30] And he quotes at length from the Buonconte and La Pia passages already cited. But we need not depend on Eliot's commentary for insight into the way the beginning of the *Purgatorio* affected him. In the growth of the third movement of *The Waste Land* we see the same material shaping his experience into poetry. Refashioning the first draft of "The Fire Sermon" Eliot appropriated "the unity of images of certain cantos of Dante" and transfused what had been a rough collage of dramatic fragments with a deep-seated emotional order and a corresponding narrative rhythm.

On the evidence of the manuscripts collected by Valerie Eliot in *The Waste Land: A Facsimile and Transcript of the Original Drafts,* "The Fire Sermon" was the first full movement of the poem Eliot attempted.[31] Out of the fragments he had been collecting since 1914, which he took to a Margate rest cure in 1921, Eliot chose as a starting point "London, the swarming life you kill and breed," a passage already several years old.[32] This is a programmatic statement, an announcement that at least "The Fire Sermon" would consist of a hypersensitive record of two phenomena—London's teeming crowds and the cryptograms of significance curled around them. Eliot's portraits would be the stuff of journalism, his method spiritual analysis, his manner nightmare-gothic, and his emotional subject the emptiness of lives bound upon the wheel of passion and misdirected by the values of the modern city. Beginning with this program Eliot sketched in the heart of his presentation: two extended pictures of oversexed and unhappy city girls—an upper-class dilettante named Fresca and a middle-

30. Ibid., p. 214 (italics mine).

31. See Grover Smith, "The Making of The Waste Land," *Mosaic,* 6, no. 1 (1972), 127–141; and Hugh Kenner, "The Urban Apocalypse," in *Eliot and His Time,* ed. A. Walton Litz (Princeton: Princeton University Press, 1973), pp. 23–49.

32. I cite from Eliot's typed version of a holograph version which is also included in the manuscript. See the *Facsimile,* pp. 42–43 and 35–36. Lyndall Gordon dates the holograph 1917 or 1918 in her *Eliot's Early Years* (Oxford and New York: Oxford University Press, 1977), p. 95.

class typist. In the draft Eliot gave Pound in late 1921 these two portraits were surrounded by a second nightmarish evocation of terrors hidden beneath the surface of life ("A rat crept softly through the vegetation") and several short episodes of loveless sex, starting with Mr. Eugenides' invitation to "a weekend at the Metropole" and ending with three brief tales of girls exploited near Margate, where Eliot had written and observed. Among the three was Eliot's modernized La Pia: "Highbury bore me. Richmond and Kew / Undid me." And the whole was punctuated by half-nostalgic, half-ironic soundings of the Philomela myth, a story unlike any in Eliot's London in which passion and suffering were transfigured into beauty, understanding, and peace. These almost buried suggestions of Philomela served as the wellsprings of Eliot's conclusion, which is both a *cri de coeur* and an acknowledgment of the wisdom of antiquity: to submit to passion is to be lashed to the wheel of "burning burning burning burning."

In short, the draft of "The Fire Sermon" that Eliot showed Pound in the winter of 1921 had an undeniable coherence and the rudiments of that kind of rhythmic or musical development in which "the mind liberated from the pressure of the will is unfolded in symbols." In it an undertone of horror in a group of emotionally charged vignettes grows gradually more distinct until its tenor is revealed in the dreamlike fragments of a visionary conclusion. What the draft still lacked, however, was an achieved emotional shape, the kind of organization that Eliot once called a "re-creation of word and image" that allows the full charge of a poetic symbol to arise from its context "like Anadyomene from the sea."[33] In 1921 "The Fire Sermon" needed to be reimagined and infused with such organization. And—inadvertently—Pound forced Eliot to do just that. Because of their problems with poetic idiom Pound advised that "Fresca" and "London, the swarming life" be dropped. Eliot agreed, and complied, but the cuts required some reworking. "The Fire Sermon" now needed a new opening and—to maintain the urban focus—a new London

33. Eliot, *The Use of Poetry and the Use of Criticism*, pp. 146–147.

poem. Where Eliot started and how he went about it can be deduced from one of Pound's smaller suggestions.

On both the carbon and the original typescript included in the *Facsimile,* Pound deleted the second half of the line that introduces Mr. Eugenides: "Unreal City, I have seen and see."[34] The shape of this hemistich had itself been cannibalized from a line in a rejected lyric which does not appear on the carbon, "O City, City, I have heard and hear."[35] Eliot apparently, when he drafted "The Fire Sermon" at Margate, decided to use only one city lyric and chose "London" because it was more appropriate to his emotional progression. At that point he scrapped "O City, City" and salvaged its first line for "Mr. Eugenides." The lyric appears at the end of the original typescript only because it shares its page with the holograph original of "London." But when Pound cut both "London" and the second half of "Unreal City, I have seen and see," "O City, City" again became available. That is, it would have been available had its emotional coloring not been so different from that of its hysteria-filled predecessor. Suffused with an almost irrepressible yearning for the love of men and God and for the sea, it must for a while have seemed indigestible. But only for a while. Only until Eliot realized that its yearning was not unrelated to near-despair—was in fact simply the *other side* of the tormenting restless emptiness which had always been "The Fire Sermon's" salient mood.[36]

When he realized *that* Eliot must have looked at his imitation of Dante's "La Pia" and remembered the organization of *Purgatorio 5.* (I use the word *remember,* but what I mean is an act of assimilation that takes place when a poet intuits the spirit of another poet's work so that it becomes part of his personal property—an act about which Eliot often wrote, but for which we have no name.) In that moment the unity of subject, image, and rhythm that he had remarked in Dante became his own, and the third part of *The Waste Land* assumed a shape

34. See the *Facsimile,* pp. 42–43 and pp. 30–31.

35. *Facsimile,* pp. 36–37.

36. See *Inferno 5,* where the depth of Francesca's torment comes out in her impassioned evocation of the situation of Ravenna, her hometown: it "sits on the shore, where Po descends to rest with his attendant streams."

that had potentially existed all along. In the fifth canto of the *Purgatorio* the poignancy of La Pia's words is a product of narrative preparation; the two souls whose speeches precede her own are overwhelmed by God's will, a shared fate objectified by the image of a swollen, rampaging river and by a narrative rhythm built up through two progressively more violent stories of watery death followed by a swift coda. Coming hard on the heels of the long Buonconte segment and finished almost before it has begun, La Pia's story—the coda—accretes the power of what comes before it and releases its force in a few explosively charged words. The narrative that culminates in La Pia's brief, passion-filled speech thus has the shape of a cascade, a shape which conforms to the image that mirrors it— a river cascading into the sea—and to the action it renders—a life forced into crisis and suddenly flowing into eternity. When Eliot realized in the last phase of composing "The Fire Sermon" that Dante's subject coincided with his own, this all came clear. He saw then that his concluding epiphany not only marked a heightened somberness but also a great release, a relinquishing of feverish emptiness to fire *and* to the down-flowing river and the welcoming sea.

In December 1921 or January 1922 Eliot finished "The Fire Sermon" as we know it. On the verso of the first of the "Fresca" pages he drafted a watery prelude, in which a speaker yearns on the banks of the Thames for a kind of love that Spenser once sublimely envisioned. Then he made minor changes throughout, eliminating the repetition of Philomela, giving "O City, City" prominence, and shaping an organization of image and narrative that underscored the hammer-stroke brevity and force of the Thames maidens sequence. It is this emotional organization that makes "The Fire Sermon" great poetry, and it was how to achieve this organization—not some vague "power . . . to suggest new verbal formulations"[37]—that Eliot learned from Dante. Ezra Pound once phrased the principle behind the lesson in these words: "[N]either prose nor drama can attain poetic intensity save by

37. Graham Hough's words. See "Dante and Eliot," *Critical Quarterly*, 16, no. 4 (Winter 1974), 295.

construction, almost by scenario; by so arranging the circumstance that some perfectly simple speech, perception, dogmatic statement appears in abnormal vigour."[38] What he might have added is that poetry, through what Yeats called "the rhythm of metaphor," can charge its utterances with more intensity than either prose or drama. Such is the shaping power of the controlling image.

38. From "Henry James" (1918), in Pound, *Literary Essays,* p. 324.

Contributors

MURRAY KRIEGER
  Department of English
  University of California, Irvine and Los Angeles

SAMUEL R. LEVIN
  Hunter College and The Graduate Center
  The City University of New York

MARTIN IRVINE
  Department of English
  Harvard University

JON WHITMAN
  Department of English
  University of Virginia

STEPHEN A. BARNEY
  Department of English
  University of California, Irvine

MARGUERITTE S. MURPHY
  Department of Comparative Literature
  Harvard University

HOLLY WALLACE BOUCHER
  Department of Comparative Literature
  Brown University

PATRIZIA GRIMALDI
  Department of Comparative Literature
  Harvard University

MAUREEN QUILLIGAN
  Department of English
  Yale University

MILLA B. RIGGIO
  Department of English
  Trinity College (Hartford)

JOHN L. KLAUSE
  Department of English
  Harvard University

PRUDENCE L. STEINER
  Department of English
  Harvard University

JAMES ENGELL
  Department of English
  Harvard University

JOHN A. HODGSON
  Department of English
  University of Georgia
PETER ALLAN DALE
  Department of English
  University of California, Davis
HARRIET RITVO
  Department of Humanities
  Massachusetts Institute of Technology
LISA RUDDICK
  Humanities Collegiate Division
  University of Chicago
J. HILLIS MILLER
  Department of English and Comparative Literature
  Yale University
RONALD BUSH
  Department of English
  Harvard University